The Professional Practice Problem Solver

Do-It-Yourself Strategies That Really Work

Laura Sachs

Prentice-Hall, Inc.
Englewood Cliffs, New Jersey

Prentice-Hall International (UK) Limited, *London*
Prentice-Hall of Australia Pty. Limited, *Sydney*
Prentice-Hall Canada, Inc., *Toronto*
Prentice-Hall Hispanoamericana, S.A., *Mexico*
Prentice-Hall of India Private Limited, *New Delhi*
Prentice-Hall of Japan, Inc., *Tokyo*
Simon & Schuster Asia Pte. Ltd., *Singapore*
Editora Prentice-Hall do Brasil, Ltda., *Rio de Janeiro*

© 1991 *by*
PRENTICE-HALL
Englewood Cliffs, NJ 07632

10   9   8   7   6   5   4   3   2   1

The information provided in this book is for general information only, and is not intended as specific legal advice. Readers are urged to contact their local attorneys for advice on specific legal practice management problems.

Library of Congress Cataloging-in-Publication Data
Sachs, Laura.
    The professional practice problem solver : do-it-yourself
strategies that really work / Laura Sachs.
    Includes bibliographical references and index.
    ISBN 0-13-719956-2
    1. Medicine—Practice.   2. Office management.   I. Title.
R728.S24   1991
610'.68—dc20   91-18256
                                            CIP

ISBN 0-13-719956-2

PRENTICE HALL
BUSINESS & PROFESSIONAL DIVISION
A Simon & Schuster Company
Englewood Cliffs, New Jersey 07632

Printed in the United States of America

This book is lovingly dedicated to my parents.

DAVID AND JANICE KIRSCHENBAUM

Acknowledgments

The list would be too long to name everyone who helped in some way with this book. However, those who provided special knowledge, encouragement, inspiration, ideas, and/or assistance include: Bob Crawford, Hammer Sletson, Sera Duff, Catherine Frazar, Bob Levoy, Joanna Chai, Holly Tucker, Dr. Richard Hubler, Olivia Lane, Jean Nowland, Dr. Vincent Flowers, Rick Pereira, Harriett Stein, Fran Goldstein, Dr. Louis Sportelli, American Health Consultants, Jim Davis, Attorney William Isele, Tom Coleman, Abby Obenchain, Donald Lowery, Dr. Charles Wilson, Tom O'Brien, Jim McCarthy, Gates Whiteley, Paul Goldman, Layton Stewart, Tim Smyth, Larry Wintersteen, Gary Clinton, Alison Brahe, Bob Proebstle, Richard Shuck, Denis Brissette, Jeff Goldstein, Barada Associates, Karen Moawad, MD Connections, Dr. Ted Halatin, Bruce Lowy, Dr. Richard Kattouf, Barbara Stennes, Janet Houser Carter, Attorney Rita Risser, Dr. Norman Fine, Dr. Jerry Mittleman, Attorney William O. Morris, Dr. Clifford Tym, Dr. John Kelly, Karen Hurst, Dr. Steven Hill, Dr. Ronald Howard, Dr. Woody Oakes, Dr. Arlen Lackey, Dr. Ward Gravel, Dr. Mel Moss, Kathy Harrison, Dr. Michael Goldstein, Jan Fenson, Dr. George Beckwith, Dr. Craig Callen, David Cottle, Dr. Barry Litwin, Mary Carter, Naomi Tapper, Evelyn Stein, Ellen Coleman, Rick Biehl, Karen Zupko, James Unland, Jack Coker, Dr. Nancy Chiswick, Dr. Neil Gailmard, Dr. Gary Jacobsen, Dr. Curtis Roy, Dr. Burt Press, Dr. Allen Schneider, Dr. Jon Clark Pensyl, Dr. Linn Mast, Dr. Charles Rohrbeck, Dr. Gus Roumani, Dr. Phil Alberts, Dr. Mitchell Rabkin, Dr. Harvey Knoernschild, J.F. Jelenko & Co., Larry Schwartz, Pearl Sax, Ron Bilsky, Fred Dahl, Linda Sudimack, Ronald Cohen, Sharon Black, Cathy Jameson, Dede Goldman, Dr. Jack Runninger, and the many private practice professionals and their staffs who shared their experiences and ideas so freely.

There are many sources of good material on this subject, which may have contributed to my background and knowledge over the years. I apologize to any publications or individuals not mentioned who may have contributed to this book.

To my husband, Bob Sachs, thank you for all your love, encouragement, understanding, and hard work. You have been my rock, sounding board, personal cheering squad, playmate, partner, confidante, and best friend for fifteen years. If I had it to do all over again, I would not change a thing.

Next, to my daughter, Meredith Nicole Sachs, I wish to express my gratitude for the constant love and warmth I received, even when I spent hour upon hour behind my closed office door to get on with the writing—an abstraction one could hardly expect a four-year-old to understand, but you did. You demonstrated more patience and understanding throughout this effort than anyone could reasonably expect. You are by far and away my best effort in life, and have brought more joy to me and to your father than you will ever know. We love you.

And finally, to my parents, David and Janice Kirschenbaum, I wish to offer a million thanks for your constant love and support. In particular, I'd like to thank you for your innumerable sacrifices over the years, the piano lessons, dance lessons, swimming lessons, orthodonture, birthday parties, Tiger, driving me to the ends of the earth, saying no, saying yes, my college tuition, the Pinto, making me stand up straight, nursing me through mono, taking me to Expo '67, and giving me my brother Stephen. Let the record show that it all paid off.

About the Author

Laura Sachs is the author of the highly-acclaimed book, *Do-It-Yourself Marketing for the Professional Practice* (Prentice-Hall, 1986). In this landmark text, Ms. Sachs unfolds her step-by-step, how-to-do-it marketing program that she has developed through her study and work with private practice professionals nationwide.

Ms. Sachs has served as editor of *Physician Manager* and *Practice Owner's Advisor* monthly newsletters. Formerly, she served as Executive Editor of American Health Consultants' *Update* monthly newsletters for eye care professionals and dentists. In addition, Ms. Sachs has contributed numerous practice management and marketing articles to such publications as *Review of Optometry, Physicians Financial News, The Internist, MedStart, The American Chiropractic Association Journal, Patient Pleasers, Optometric Management, Optometric Economics, Dental Images, PVS Advantage, Doctor's Tax Report, The Doctor's Office,* and *HMI Update* for optometrists.

Laura Sachs is the president of Laura Sachs Consultations, a Clifton, Virginia-based marketing and management firm that specializes in working with private practice professionals. Through this, she has worked extensively with doctors across the country to develop custom marketing plans and marketing tools, such as logos, brochures, patient newsletters, and advertisements, and to address practice management problems.

Ms. Sachs is a popular public speaker for professional groups, and serves on the faculty of the Northern Virginia Community College continuing education division. She has presented a variety of practice management and marketing courses for numerous organizations, including Optifair (New York, Midwest, and West), the Center for Continuing Medical Education, The American Chiropractic Association, the North Central States Optometric Council, the Ohio Dental Association, the Dental Group Management Association, the Nebraska Optometric Association, the Indiana Optometric Association, Hartman Dental Laboratories, Pacific University College of Optometry, Penn State University, the Indiana Podiatric Medical Association, Eyequest, the British Columbia Optometric Society, the North Carolina State Optometric Council, and DPI Dental Laboratories of Mount Vernon.

The former Laura Kirschenbaum, Ms. Sachs graduated with honors from Rutgers College, is a member of *Phi Beta Kappa,* and was chosen as an Outstanding Young Woman of America for 1985. She makes her home in the Washington, D.C. suburbs with her husband Robert Sachs (a mathematics professor at George Mason University), and their daughter, Meredith.

Also by Laura Sachs:

Do-It-Yourself Marketing for the Professional Practice

Preface

In this book, you'll find solutions to an overwhelming number of practice management problems. As you read, you may be struck by the amount of time and effort needed to follow the advice I give, and how complicated and hard it is to run a successful professional office. You may wonder why you have to worry about so much, simply to practice your profession.

Every practice management mistake will cost you dearly, not only in terms of money, office morale, and patient dissatisfaction, but also in your own happiness. A practice plagued with problems will slow you down, cut your production, and take the fun out of your work. If the problems are serious enough, they can cause patients to leave you, discourage referrals, and even land you in court. Practice management problems will reach deep into your pockets, but also into your heart.

Putting the extra effort into your practice is a good investment, not only in your financial future, but in your patients, the people you employ, and in yourself. A successful practice is most definitely a lot of work. But the doctors I've worked with over the last ten years tell me that when push comes to shove, they'd travel the same path again if they had the choice. I assume that by reading this book, you agree.

I wish you much success in your practice, and hope this book helps to free you up so you can concentrate on doing what you do best—providing quality professional care for your patients. That, to my mind, is what a successful practice management and this book are all about.

Laura Sachs

Clifton, Virginia

What This Book Will Do For You

"What's your biggest practice management problem?"

When Laura Sachs asks this question at her seminars, she hears it all. Problems rear their ugly heads in all areas—staff management, appointment scheduling, record keeping, patient retention, recall, collections, insurance claims processing, professional liability, patient confidentiality, financial arrangements—the list goes on and on.

The Professional Practice Problem Solver contains Laura Sachs's very best solutions to these and other nagging problems in literally all areas of professional practice. It provides practical, step-by-step answers, without fluff or theory, and all the complete, how-to-do-it instructions you'll need to make serious improvements in your practice. In addition, this book is supported with field-tested examples, sample dialogues, action checklists, and well over 200 "Tips" separated from the text, all based upon what has worked and not worked for others in your situation.

The solutions offered in this book are presented in a 1-2-3 fashion for your easy use, making it possible to see immediate results, starting today. These solutions work regardless of the size of your practice, your profession, or your focus. And, Laura Sachs has tailored the material to fit exactly with your needs and resources, no matter where you practice, your specialization, or your experience managing others.

The Professional Practice Problem Solver offers an impressive array of special features that will help you manage your practice to its full potential. Most notably, it:

• **Presents scores of practical ideas that have worked for others.** The Table of Contents or the Chapter-by-Chapter Summary of Practice Management Problems and Solutions (page 589) should whet any practitioner's appetite for the extensive menu of practice management techniques that follow. In all, literally hundreds of great ideas are given.

• **Provides all the how-to-do-it, step-by-step instruction you need to take any technique from theory to reality.** Laura Sachs has overflowed this book her popular "this is how you do it" instruction you need, but that you won't find in other management books. It cuts through the theory and gets right to the heart of what you'll need to know—whether it is about handling a subpoena of records, avoiding credit card fraud, reigning in professional courtesy, joining a third-party prepaid plan, automating your records, improving your personal productivity, or collecting the money that's due you. When you're done reading this book, you'll have no doubt about what to do or how to do it.

• **Gives numerous examples and samples.** When you're about to implement a new management strategy, it is invaluable to see successful examples and illustrations of how you might do it. Laura Sachs has laced this book with scores of successful applications, sample letters, dialogues, tables, and checklists. In addition, Appendix 2–1 provides fifty questions your receptionist should be able to answer, with specific answers.

• **Alerts you to potential problems and errors.** This book will save you a great deal of time, money, and aggravation by pointing out the mistakes others have made in their practice management efforts. Use this book to put Laura Sachs' expertise and the experiences of others to work for you.

• **Helps you take stock of your current situation.** Every practitioner needs a clear, accurate assessment of his or her practice management needs and problems to develop a successful strategy. This book will help you assess your current practice and its shortcomings. Through clear exposition, and a number of self-evaluation exercises, Laura Sachs teaches you how to evaluate your situation, build upon your strengths, and tackle your weaknesses.

• **Uses no-nonsense, down-to-earth, concise style.** Much of the instruction in this book has been boiled down to easy-to-follow checklists. Laura Sachs purposely uses simple, clean, everyday language and writes in her signature "newsletter" style. You won't waste time or effort trying to decipher garbled instructions or convoluted ideas.

• **Organizes the material in logical, easy-to-follow sequence for quick reference.** Each short chapter unfolds logically, and is supported with many descriptive subheadings. As well, Appendix 1 offers 26 time-saving checklists to help you address some of the most perplexing practice management problems.

The Professional Practice Problem Solver will be an invaluable aid to any practitioner in any profession—and to any office manager in a professional practice. It takes the mystery out of a complex, often bewildering subject, and can guide you to a more productive, trouble-free practice. Take the time now to skim the Table of Contents, and become familiar with the many problems addressed in this book. Then, refer to these pages throughout your career as you encounter problems, or seek specific strategies to improve.

In your hands, you have one of the best reference guides and time-saving tools you will ever find. Use *The Professional Practice Problem Solver* again and again, to help you develop a successful, productive, and satisfying professional practice.

Contents

PART 3: MANAGING THE MONEY COMING INTO YOUR PRACTICE

PART 4: KEEPING TIGHT GRIPS ON THE MONEY YOU SPEND

PART 7: MANAGING PROBLEM AND SPECIAL-NEED PATIENTS

PART 8: MANAGING YOUR PHYSICAL PLANT

PART 9: PERSONAL SKILLS DEVELOPMENT FOR BETTER PRACTICE MANAGEMENT

APPENDIX 1: A–Z TREASURY OF QUICK-REFERENCE PRACTICE MANAGEMENT CHECKLISTS

APPENDIX 2: GLOSSARIES OF USEFUL PRACTICE MANAGMENT TERMS AND PROBLEMS

P·A·R·T   1

Laying the Foundation for a Problem-Free Practice

Evaluating Your Practice
with a Quarterly Analysis

S everal simple practice management calculations will enable you to pin-point and measure your practice's weaknesses and strengths. It is gen-erally a good idea to conduct a practice management analysis every three months. In this way, you can compare your results with previous quarters, to measure the progress or decline of your practice.

Once you know with certainty what your management problems are, and how severe they are, you can take steps to correct them. The first step is in identifying and measuring them, with the quarterly analysis.

GATHER ALL THE NECESSARY RAW INFORMATION

What you'll need to complete your quarterly analysis:

1.   Total the number of appointments you completed in the last three months. Count them all, including emergencies and consultations.

2.   Total the number of hours you worked in the last three months. If you don't know the exact number, estimate by multiplying your average working hours per day times the number of days worked. Be realistic, and count only the days you saw patients.

3.   Total your production and collections by month for the last three months.

4.   Count the number of new patients who came into your practice in the last three months, including new emergency patients.

5.   Total your accounts receivable on the last day of the three-month period.

6.   Total the number of staff incentive bonuses reached for each of the last three months, and the total dollars earned in incentive bonuses.

7.   Total the number of patients who broke an appointment without 24-hour notice, and who arrived more than 10 minutes late for an appointment.

8.   Total the number of inactive patients you contacted in the last three months. Total how many made an appointment, how many left the practice, and their reasons.

9.   Total the number of delinquent account calls you made during the last three months, and the number of dollars collected on these accounts.

10.   Total your overhead dollar amounts and calculate their percentages of practice gross for each of the last three months. Break overhead into categories, such as salaries, supplies, lab costs, rent, etc.

COMPARE YOUR RAW INFORMATION WITH PREVIOUS QUARTERS

Some of this information will be useful to you with no further calculation. For example, it is helpful to know whether the number of broken appointments in your practice is on the rise or decline. It might also help to know whether you paid more or less to your staff for incentive bonuses, so you can measure the effectiveness of your bonus programs. And it can be very useful to know whether you're contacting fewer or more inactive patients, and with what results.

However, some of these raw figures will *not* be useful in and of themselves. They need further manipulation, as you'll see below. Once you've done these calcuations, compare your findings with previous quarters, to spot and measure declines, increases, and trends in your practice.

HOW MUCH DID YOU EARN PER APPOINTMENT, ON AVERAGE?

To begin, divide your total production in dollars by the total number of appointments. This will give you your average gross income per appointment.

If this figure is noticeably lower than the previous quarter, or if it is showing steady decline over time, you may not be scheduling enough into each appointment, or you may be scheduling frequent, short, nonproductive appointments, and only a few more productive ones. Your goal, clearly, will be to make each appointment more productive.

HOW MUCH DID YOU EARN PER HOUR, ON AVERAGE?

Now divide your total production by the total number of hours you worked. A low or declining hourly rate may indicate that you're wasting time or not planning appointments well. It may also mean that your fees need updating.

ARE YOU COLLECTING WHAT YOU EARN?

Next, divide the total dollars you collected by the total dollars you produced. The result is your collections ratio. Rule of thumb: In general, a collections ratio below 95 percent, two quarters in a row, indicates a collections or insurance handling problem.

HOW MANY NEW PATIENTS DID YOU SEE?

Compare the total number of new patients you've seen in the last three months with previous quarters. Then, total your production in dollars for new patients only. You may have to dig for this information, but it will be worth it.

Low or declining figures may indicate that you're not attracting an adequate number of new patients. Or perhaps you're not attracting the kinds of patients you'd most like to have in your practice.

HOW OLD ARE YOUR ACCOUNTS RECEIVABLE?

Next, break your accounts receivable for each month into four age brackets:

a. Current (those that are under 30 days old).
b. Those billed 30–59 days ago.
c. Those billed 60–89 days ago, and,
d. Those billed over 90 days ago.

Prepare a report of the *percentage* that each age bracket bears to the total outstanding receivable. This age ratio report will enable you to spot potential financial trouble.

Example: Suppose you have $100,000 of open receivables, and $60,000 were billed recently (under 30 days old). The age factor would be "60% current." If another $20,000 were billed the month before (30–59 days old), the age factor would be "20% at 30–59," and so on. Thus your management report on the subject would look like this:

Date: September 1, 199-
Total outstanding: $100,000

Current	$60,000	60%
30–59	$20,000	20%
60–89	$10,000	10%
Over 90	$10,000	10%

If, for example, the same report next quarter shows that the percentage in the "Over 90" column has increased substantially, it's a warning to examine your collection performance more carefully. Conventional wisdom tells us that the older an account becomes, the harder it will be to collect. Many collections experts warn that accounts over 120 days old are next to impossible to collect yourself, and should be written off or turned over to a collections agency or small claims court for further action.

HOW LARGE IS YOUR TOTAL
ACCOUNTS RECEIVABLE?

Next, divide your total accounts receivable by one month's total charges. Check this accounts receivable ratio quarterly. Rule of thumb: Your receivables at any given time should never amount to more than three times your monthly charges.

Example: If you bill $25,000 per month, accounts receivable should never exceed $75,000.

IS YOUR TOTAL OVERHEAD PERCENTAGE
ON THE RISE?

There are two possible causes of an increased overhead percentage. Either you're producing less. Or, you're spending more. It's essential that you determine the cause of any increase you observe.

A runaway overhead often indicates inefficiencies, waste, and poor cost control. Compare your quarterly percentages per category—salaries, rent, lab costs, etc., to help you locate the precise problem.

WHAT'S YOUR BATTING AVERAGE
WITH NEW PATIENTS?

Reconstruct a list of new patients you saw over a three-month period three years ago. Then, check to see how many of these patients are still active. Do you have a "revolving door" practice where a tremendous number of new patients come but don't stay? A low percentage of new active patients generally indicates a problem in a practice that provides routine ongoing care to patients (such as a dental or optometric practice).

COMPUTER SOFTWARE CAN SPEED YOUR QUARTERLY ANALYSIS

These calculations are simple enough to do manually. However, a manual anaylsis does take a fair amount of time. And, since the information must be reconstructed from several sources, there's great opportunity for error.

An appropriate computer program can help you shorten the time it takes to do your analysis, and also eliminate a lot of the human error. Therefore, bring this list of practice management calculations with you when shopping for new software. Be sure any program you're considering can total the raw information you need. Ask your sales rep to demonstrate the program's ability to calculate the monthly and quarterly averages for you.

C · H · A · P · T · E · R   1-2

Going It Alone or Joining a Team: What's the Best Practice Arrangement for You?

Are you best suited to solo or group practice? Would you be most satisfied in a same- or multi-specialty group? A large group, or a small one?

There is no one practice arrangement that suits everyone. Your choice will depend upon a number of factors, including your personality, finances, desire to maintain control of the practice, and how comfortable you are at taking risks.

As we explore the most common practice options, note which arrangements seem to be the most and least appealing to you. And, take a few minutes to answer the self-assessment checklist at the end of this chapter. It is designed to help you assess quickly and accurately which type of practice arrangement best suits your lifestyle, personality, and goals.

SOLO PRACTICE—THE POSITIVE SIDE

Practicing solo means maximum independence and freedom to run the office as you choose, unrestricted by a partner or bureaucracy. Decisions are not impeded by committee meetings, politics, or conflicting opinions. You decide whether to buy new equipment, implement new procedures, associate with prepaid programs, move, open a satellite office, hire, promote, or fire a staff member, or redecorate the reception area.

In solo practice, you select and train every staff member to reflect your own practice style. You have a smaller staff than does a typical group practice, allowing you to spend more time getting to know each employee and developing personal relationships. Many solo doctors cite this as a great advantage, since rapport influences staff motivation and management.

Building a good relationship with patients is often easier in solo practice. With only one doctor's patients to deal with, your staff is more likely to remember patients by name and develop relationships with them. This personal touch is invaluable in promoting patient loyalty and generating referrals.

In solo practice, there is no internal competition between doctors for extra privilege, space, status, or personnel. Fewer diversions of this type mean you can give more undiluted attention to your patients. Productivity often increases when the entire office operation is geared to the practice style and preferences of only one doctor.

By practicing solo, you're not responsible for a partner's actions, and you'll never be involved in partnership dispute or dissolution. Your reputation will not be linked to that of another doctor in the practice.

One more advantage of solo practice is that some patients prefer it. Perhaps as a result of sweeping technological growth over the last several decades, many people now want more personalized service. There will always be those patients who will be attracted to the solo doctor, believing that a smaller practice is best able to provide individualized, highly personal attention.

SOLO PRACTICE—THE NEGATIVE SIDE

Despite these many advantages, there are some drawbacks to solo practice. One of the most obvious is isolation. Solo doctors can't easily turn to colleagues for consultation or support. They sometimes find it difficult to secure coverage for times when they're out of the office. They alone must deal with the daily problems of running the practice, the tough patients, the problems with staff.

Tip: For a partial solution to the isolation problem, see "How the Solo Doctor Can Combat Isolation," page 508.

Economics is another concern for the solo doctor. You may be unable to buy supplies and equipment in large volume to obtain the best cost advantages, or to afford the same amount of equipment as a group practice. You might have to form alliances with other doctors to purchase supplies, and share lab equipment and office space with them, to keep your costs under control and to ensure that your patients will have the best possible care.

Facilities are another economic factor. You will need to buy or rent your own office, equipment, furniture, and supplies. That means securing financial backing on your own, and taking all the risks yourself. In solo practice, space and equipment may lie dormant for a long time, especially in the early years. Since you will be paying staff salaries yourself, you alone must find ways to keep your employees productively busy, since there won't be other doctors to generate work for them and share costs.

As a solo doctor, you may not have the same time or money that a group practice has to develop practice-building programs. It may be more difficult to develop name recognition in your community. In addition, you are responsible for developing your own referral base, without aid of other doctors.

For these reasons, many solo doctors have more difficulty getting the practice up and running in the early years. They don't have immediate access to the patients, physical facilities, staff, or the referral base that a group doctor might have in an established group practice.

GROUP PRACTICE—THE POSITIVE SIDE

The advantages of solo practice are reversed in group practice. The isolation so many doctors feel in solo practice is certainly not a problem in most groups. One or more other doctors are right there for consultation. You can rely on others to share administrative and management responsibilities and decisions.

All doctors in a group share the financial burdens and risks of being in practice and, thereby, gain certain advantages. Group practices can generally purchase in larger volume, and enjoy better per-unit costs. Staff is often shared between two or more doctors, and equipment and office space rarely go unused. This makes overhead less of a concern, and new purchases easier to justify.

Group doctors generally have more funds and time for practice-building activities. They often find it easier to achieve a presence in the community. In addition, groups usually have more avenues for referrals.

Doctors frequently join groups because the hours can be more regular. Many doctors need to work fewer, more predictable hours because of family and other responsibilites. A group practice may allow them the flexibility they need.

Group practices can be appealing for other reasons as well. They offer greater opportunities to teach or conduct research. In addition, the group doctor generally has greater access to practice management assistance, malpractice and legal help, consistent caseloads, competitive and predictable compensation, continuing education programs—even personal financial and tax-planning help. And, in some groups, especially larger ones, doctors have the option of spending more time on favorite types of patient care and professional activities.

GROUP PRACTICE—THE NEGATIVES

A good "match" among doctors is the foundation of a successful group. Careful screening and a sound written agreement can greatly improve the chances that a group will be successful.

Even when the group is compatible, there can be problems. There must be some flexibility and compromise to permit the group to run efficiently. Consequently, group doctors may not have the control they'd like. In addition, practice decisions often take more time and patience, since two or more group members must agree.

In a busy, larger group, the doctors may find it hard to get to know all of the staff well. Similarly, the staff may have a difficult time keeping track of patients, since they will be seeing so many each day. Therefore, patients may feel they are not getting the same individualized attention they might receive in a smaller office.

As a group doctor, your reputation will be linked to the group's reputation, and that of the other doctors. Under the usual group arrangements, you can be legally responsible for the actions of the other doctors. This brings about obvious risks.

If you are thinking about practicing in a group, consider how large a group you'd like. Would you prefer working with relatively young doctors? Senior doctors? A combination? Would you be more comfortable in an egalitarian structure? Or would you prefer a hierarchy of responsibility?

Tip: For more information on partnerships, see "Partnerships: Why They Fail, How to Make Yours a Success," pages 15–20.

SAME-SPECIALTY VS. MULTISPECIALTY GROUPS

Same-specialty groups offer maximum coverage when you're out of the office, and they give you an opportunity to work side by side with members of your specialty. Some of your fellow doctors may have had much more experience with certain types of cases. They may be able to offer information from continuing education programs, professional contacts, or their own study. In some same-specialty groups, you may also have an opportunity for subspecialization. And, in same-specialty groups, it may be more economically feasible to purchase expensive, highly specialized equipment, since it will be used more frequently.

A multi-specialty group offers a wide range of patient services. As a result, you can make and receive referrals within the practice, and, depending upon the mix of the group, you may be able to see a broader range of patients. If your interests should change over time, a multi-specialty group offers opportunities to explore other areas of your profession. And some doctors enjoy the multi-specialty structure because it allows them to draw clearer lines of responsibility, with less overlap than the same-specialty group practice arrangement.

SELF-ASSESSMENT CHECKLIST:
WHICH PRACTICE ARRANGEMENT SUITS YOU BEST?

Answer each of the questions below in one of the following ways:

A. Strongly agree
B. Agree
C. Disagree
D. Strongly disagree

PART 1
1. I enjoy committee work.
2. I'd prefer to practice without having to worry about every last management problem all by myself.
3. I'd feel comfortable knowing that a colleague was readily available to consult on difficult cases.
4. I can't afford to (or prefer not to) take big financial risks.
5. I greatly dislike having to spend time looking for ways to attract new patients into the practice.
6. Being on call frequently is much too disruptive.
7. I like to bounce my ideas off of other people.
8. I enjoy persuading others to adopt my point of view. However, I don't mind compromising when I have to.

PART 2
1. I'm comfortable taking and living with financial risk.
2. I want absolute control over my work environment.
3. I've found that my perceptions are different from most people's.
4. I intend to live in one town or city for a long time.
5. I hate compromising.
6. I think that having too many people involved in a project can lead to problems. ("Too many cooks spoil the broth.")
7. I'd rather make my own mistakes than do something I don't agree with.
8. I'd rather do the work myself than serve on a committee.

To determine your score, give yourself:

• 4 points for every Strongly Agree.
• 3 points for every Agree.
• 2 points for every Disagree.
• 1 point for every Strongly Disagree.

Total your score for Part 1. If you scored 25 more more, your attitudes suggest that a group practice may suit you well. If you scored below 15, group practice may not be for you.

Now total your response for Part 2. If you scored 25 or more, solo practice appeals to you greatly. Scores below 15 suggest you would be happier in another practice arrangement.

Tip: If scores for both Part 1 and Part 2 were inconclusive, you may be happy in either solo or group practice.

C·H·A·P·T·E·R   1-3

Partnerships: Why They Fail, How to Make Yours a Success

S ooner or later, all partnerhsips will either end or change substantially. Most of them can come to that point happily, if the partners plan and work for success. Below we will explore the most frequent reasons partnerships fail, and the steps you can take to make yours succeed.

Tip: If you are not in a partnership at this time, this chapter may help you decide whether a partnership arrangement is for you. Also, see "Going It Alone or Joining a Team: What's the Best Practice Arrangement for You?," pages 9–14.

A WRITTEN AGREEMENT: THE FOUNDATION OF A SUCCESSFUL PARTNERSHIP

Many group practitioners today are operating without a written partnership agreement, or with one that is lacking in vital information. Such situations are dangerous. Partners without firm agreements are likely to disagree when the unexpected happens, for instance, when a partner becomes disabled, dies, retires, conveys his/her interest in the partnership to another person, attempts to dispose of specific partnership property through his/her will—the list could go on and on.

When disagreement among partners can't be resolved, loss of patients, declining practice income, and legal action often follow. Many practices don't survive under these trying circumstances.

A thorough, carefully written agreement is the foundation upon which to build a successful partnership. While no partnership agreement can anticipate every possible circumstance or change, a good one *can* cover those problem areas that frequently arise, and provide guidelines for handling the unexpected ones.

THE FIVE TOPICS THAT A PARTNERSHIP AGREEMENT MUST COVER

A partnership agreement is a legal contract that describes the partners' understanding and decisions regarding their business relationship. Those decisions can most often be divided into five categories:

1.   *The usual matters:* These include the name of the partners and the partnership, the partnership's purpose and goals, the length of the partnership and the date it began, and the duties of the partners.

2.   *The partners and their relationship:* This often includes:

a.   Things partners can't do. *Examples:* Borrow money in the partnership's name. Subject partnership property to a lien because of a personal debt or borrowing. Agree to a judgment for the other side in a law suit.

b.   Guidelines for partnership decision-making, including the way votes are distributed among partners, the percentage of votes required to make a major partnership decision, and who can or must sign contracts: *Examples:* Each partner's voting power might be assigned in proportion to his/her interest in the partnership's capital. Or, all partnership decisions might be made by the unanimous decision of all partners. Or, one partner might be designated as the "managing partner"—he or she might be permitted to make day-to-day management decisions (as defined by the agreement) without the consent or prior knowledge of the other partners.

c.   Each partner's authority to borrow money. You may have heard of cases in which one partner secretly withdraws money from the partnership bank account for personal purposes. This usually results in legal action and partnership break-ups.

Tip: Spell out your decisions about borrowing privileges in your written agreement, even if none of the partners anticipates the need to borrow money at the time the agreement is written.

d.   The partnership's liability to the public. A legal action brought against one partner subjects all partners to unlimited liability for their colleague's performance. In cases where a suit is brought against a partner, all other partners may suffer equally because of their liability. A large suit can easily break up a partnership and eat up the partnership's assets.

Tip: The written agreement should include this information to ensure that all partners recognize and acknowledge their liability.

e.   A partner's legal rights against the partnership.

f.   Limitations on absences and outside activities of the partners. Disagreements about hours, vacation, sick leave, professional time, educational time, disability procedure, moonlighting, etc., can lead to partnership break-up.

3. *Financial considerations:* The agreement should outline each partner's contributions to the partnership (including contributions of cash, property, patients of record, and services). It should also describe the partnership's decisions about profits and losses, ownership of property, and check-signing privileges. As well, it should describe how compensation is to be based. (On production, collections, or some combination? What percentage should each partner get, and for how long? What are the provisions for retirement and disability?) Finally, it should review all relevant tax and accounting matters. (This might include a definition of the fiscal year, each partner's right to inspect the partnership books of account, or special banking arrangements.)

4. *Disputes:* The agreement should provide for what happens in the event of serious disagreement among partners. Examples: Professional arbitration or mediation. Arbitration by a trusted friend or designated group of colleagues. Partnership counseling.

5. *Expansion, change, or termination of the partnership: Examples:* Death. Retirement. Disability. Termination or expulsion of a partner. Addition of a new partner(s) or of limited partners. Buy-out agreements. Valuation methods. Control of the business name in the case of a break up. Non-competition agreements. Transfer of a partner's interest in the partnership.

FIVE REASONS PARTNERSHIPS SPLIT UP AND HOW TO PREVENT IT

Lack of a thorough agreement is a leading cause of partnership failure, but it is not the only one. Here are five more reasons partnerships break up, and what you can do to prevent them:

1. *Lack of personal compatibility:* Partners who have radically different beliefs, goals, styles, and work habits can sometimes serve as complements to each other. Most often they just drive each other crazy.

Tip: Good friends don't always make good partners. Talk honestly with prospective partners, even those you think you know well. Share your aspirations, habits, and pet peeves. Recognize and admit when personality differences are so sharp that they'll hurt your chances for success.

If you're involved in a partnership where personalities clash, seek compromises through discussion, and if necessary, through arbitration or partnership counseling (discussed at length below). However, you may reach a point when you have no choice but to terminate the partnership, especially if the partnership relationship is detrimental to the practice.

2. *Lack of communication among partners:* When the partners stop talking to one other about practice and financial matters, conflicts tend to arise and don't become resolved.

Tip: Hold regular meetings with your partners—as well as periodic partnership retreats. Discuss goals, progress, problems, strengths, and weaknesses. Use these sessions as opportunities to reshape policies, and define which types of decisions and other information need and need not be shared with the partners. Include new guidelines in your written agreement.

Example: You might decide that all new purchasing decisions of over $_____ must be discussed with and agreed upon by all partners. Or, you may agree that all practice marketing campaigns, including advertising, must be approved by unanimous decision of all partners.

3. *Lack of a prepartnership analysis:* Practitioners must assess their true potential before entering into a partnership. In particular, they should ask:

a.   Can the existing patient load and potential new patients sustain the partnership? (Sometimes a solo practitioner will have overly optimistic expectations of patient load growth. When a partner is added and the growth doesn't come as expected, both practitioners lose income.)

Tip: Carefully assess your practice and potential patient pool. Find out through market research whether your community has enough potential patients to sustain a vigorous partnership.

b.   Does the physical plant provide sufficient room for a partnership practice? (The solo practitioner may feel that he/she has plenty of room for expansion. However, when one or more partners are added, small facilities can quickly become too crowded.)

Tip: Objectively assess present levels of staffing and available office space. Can these sustain a partnership? Plan for expansion, relocating, and hiring new staff if necessary.

4. *Spouses and other relatives:* One very common reason for partnership break-ups is that the spouse of one partner, who was hired in the practice, is not able to get along with the other partners, and vice versa. In a typical situation, the spouse will bring home stories to her husband about activities of partners that she feels her husband should know about.

Tip: Discuss hiring of spouses with your partners and reach an agreement. If you do hire your spouse, try to remain as objective as possible. Allow your partners the opportunity to talk with you about your spouse's job performance—honestly, privately, and without fear. For more information on this subject, see "Working with Your Spouse, Children, and Other Close Relatives," pages 341–347.

5.   *Perceived inequality among equal partners:* In an equal partnership (50–50, 25–25–25–25, etc.), all the partners should feel that each one of them brings something equally valuable to the practice. Hard feelings and eventual break-ups occur when one or more partners feels that another partner isn't pulling his weight.

Tip: Identify the specific contributions a potential partner has to offer the practice. Ask: Are these contributions as valuable as *my* contributions (and those of the other partners)? Contributions extend far beyond the obvious ones of cash and property. They include professional excellence, reputation in the community, existing patient load, and number of hours the person is willing to devote to the practice.

Tip: Equal partners should contribute *equally,* but not always *identically.* For example, an established doctor who is planning to cut back on his/her hours may make an equal partner of a person who does not have a reputation in the community, but who is willing to work more hours.

PARTNERSHIP COUNSELING: A NEW TECHNIQUE FOR PREVENTING AND SOLVING PROBLEMS

Most of the strategies and techniques for successful partnerships in this chapter require advance planning and anticipation of problems. Partnership counseling, a relatively new concept, is one of the few alternatives for partnerships that are already in trouble. It is also an excellent way to improve upon a good partnership or to keep a successful one healthy.

Partnership counseling provides a forum for information sharing, constructive criticism, and open communication between partners so that each can better understand each partner's function in the practice. It is a process by which partners evaluate each other's performance and development, and explore problems, expectations, new techniques in management and delivery of services, compensation, and goals.

In many counseling processes, a professional counselor serves as a mediator. He/she meets with each partner alone. Later, all the partners meet with the counselor as a group to iron out a plan for settling disputes and solving problems. In some cases, no professional counselor is used. (One of the partners serves as the counselor.)

Either way, it is helpful to understand how a counselor prepares, conducts, and follows up the partnership counseling process. Here's what generally happens:

1.   Prior to the first session, the counselor identifies what the partners expect to cover and what they're trying to accomplish through counseling.

2.   He then gathers all pertinent background information. For example, he may review self-evaluation worksheets, individual partner's goals, examples of correspondence between partners, and the partnership's written agreement.

3.   Next, he meets with each partner individually to find out what he/she wants to talk about or clear up. In these sessions, he listens, takes notes, and generally asks open-ended questions. (For example, he might ask, "How do you want to spend your time?" or "What frustrates you most about the office?")

4.   When needed, the counselor may hold a follow-up session with each partner, to give him time to reflect.

5.   After all individiual sessions are completed, the counselor will summarize, in writing, the results. In so doing, he may find it helpful to consult with persons not in counseling, such as members of the staff and patients.

6.   Finally, the counselor meets with all the partners together. He will discuss the results of the first sessions, specific problems he's identified, how he feels the group should proceed.

7.   Serving as the group's mediator, he will lead the partners to agree on detailed, concrete plans for solving identified problems. He may push the group to establish a schedule for changes, and methods of evaluating results.

8.   As a last step, the counselor will document the results of each session and the group's plan. And, he will usually follow up by meeting with the partners again after they've had a chance to put their plans into effect.

FOR MORE INFORMATION

Successful partnerships require hard work and planning. A thorough, written partnership agreement is the basis for a good partnership relationship. Other techniques that contribute to successful partnerships include regular meetings among partners, a pre-partnership analysis to determine the practice's potential, honest discussion among partners about working habits, goals, hiring of spouses, etc., and partnership counseling.

For more information on deciding whether a partnership is right for you, see "Going It Alone or Joinging a Team: What's the Best Practice Arrangement for You?," pages 9–14.

How to Evaluate and Get the Most out of Your Team of Advisors

T he team of outside professionals you engage to advise you form your personal "cabinet," and can often make or break your career success and satisfaction. While your accountant, financial planner, attorney, practice management consultant, insurance representative, and banker each provide different services, your relationship with them will have many things in common. In this chapter, we explore specific strategies for evaluating each advisor's contributions, and maximizing his or her effectiveness.

TEN WAYS TO GET MORE FROM ALL ADVISORS

1. Remember that it is *your* practice and livelihood that are at stake. Consider your advisors' suggestions, but take responsibility, too. Don't rely on an advisor to make decisions for you or to set goals for your practice or your life. Insist that advisors consult you before taking action on your behalf.

2. Be prepared for meetings with your advisors. You can usually save your advisors' time (and consequently, some of their fees) by doing your homework, preparing notes, and bringing all necessary supporting materials with you to your meetings.

3. Alert your advisors to any matters and information you feel might be significant, even if you are not sure. Let your advisors tell *you* whether the information is relevant or not.

4. Ask your advisors to estimate the cost of their services before you engage them or begin a project. (If dealing with a hierarchical firm, learn the billing rates for each partner/associate/paraprofessional who will do work for you.) Ask for timely bills as well. While a billing delay may seem like an advantage to you, it generally is not. As time passes, you tend to forget whether you authorized certain work, or whether you actually had the number of

phone calls and meetings listed. This makes it near impossible to catch or argue about billing errors.

5.   Ask who specifically within the advisor's firm will handle each aspect of your projects. Insist that your advisor gain your approval before a new partner/associate/paraprofessional is assigned to you. As well, ask that your bills be itemized not only by project, but also by who worked on it and for how long.

6.   Let your advisors know to expect your scrutiny. (If they do, they won't mind your periodic quizzing.)

7.   Be honest with your advisors. Don't withhold information or materials they might need.

8.   If you engage advisors to handle matters for a group practice, tell them which doctor is the primary contact, and whom to contact if that individual is not available.

9.   Get a second opinion if your advisors' recommendations don't seem right (or if the stakes are particularly high).

10.   If you are unhappy with something an advisor has done or not done, tell him what's bothering you and set up a meeting to discuss it. If you don't get satisfaction, you may decide to discharge the advisor and/or file a grievance with his professional society. In any case, immediately retain another advisor, so you have continuous professional service.

HOW TO EVALUATE AN ADVISOR'S PERFORMANCE

These questions will help you evaluate any member of your team:

1.   Does my advisor know my profession? Is he sensitive to my unique needs? Does he have other clients in private practice who have needs and goals similar to mine?

2.   Does my advisor know enough about the types of problems he is trying to solve? Can he keep pace with my changing needs?

3.   Is my advisor as interested in my practice now as he was at our first meeting?

4.   Am I comfortable calling my advisor to ask a question? Does he seem prepared when I ask him questions he should be able to answer?

5.   Does my advisor get annoyed when I call to ask him about the status of pending projects (assuming that you don't nag him by calling every half hour)?

6.   Does my advisor charge more than other advisors in my area? If so, is he giving superior service?

7. Am I surprised when I get my advisor's bill? (You shouldn't be.)

8. Does my advisor present and express himself well? Does he inspire confidence?

9. Do I trust my advisor? Are we personally compatible? Do my advisor and I listen to each other's points of view? Can we work together harmoniously? Is he genuinely interested in learning about the details of my practice? Is his advice clear and specific? (The best advisors offer concrete, practical advice, not abstruse theories.) Is communication with my advisor a two-way street?

10. Would I recommend my advisor to a colleague?

NINE WAYS TO EVALUATE YOUR ACCOUNTANT/FINANCIAL PLANNER

Some doctors engage an accountant to handle all financial matters, while others use the services of both an accountant and a financial planner. Whichever advisor(s) you employ, tell those who direct your practice finances that you don't want them only to prepare profit and loss statements and file the necessary tax forms. You should also expect your financial advisor to steer you to every legitimate deduction, bring new ideas to you, make recommendations about cutting overhead and increasing collections, and forecast where you are headed financially.

You can help matters enormously if you take some time to familiarize yourself generally with the tax laws. That way, you'll have at least some knowledge of your liabilities and opportunities. Then, to evaluate your accountant/financial planner, ask:

1. Does he inform me of new and revised tax laws, and explain their impact on my practice and personal finances?

2. Would I feel confident asking my advisor about employee retirement programs? Estate planning? Inventory valuation? Reporting rules? Inheritance and gift taxes? Incorporation? Benefit packages? Inflation or recession management?

3. Is my advisor particularly well versed in tax shelters, professional corporations, estate and retirement planning, and other specifics that affect me?

4. Is my advisor aggressive about saving tax dollars? Does he take all legitimate deductions and recommend new tax-deferred methods, ideas, and products?

5. Does my advisor forecast where I am headed and use the past as a guide? For instance, does he project what I will owe in income taxes by Sep-

tember or October of each year? Does he recommend increasing my estimated tax payments as needed?

6.   Does he work well with my other advisors to coordinate special projects? For instance, if you're incorporated, did he make the necessary arrangements with your attorney? If you've expanded your office, did he contact your insurance representative to tell him that your office contents policy should be increased? (Or at least, did he advise you to do this?)

7.   Does he review my investment portfolio and retirement plan, and make recommendations for maximum asset earning capabilities?

8.   Does my advisor review my present and future needs of life, disability, and business casualty insurance? Does he make useful recommendations in this area?

9.   Is my tax advisor as aggressive as I am? For instance, is he willing to take an ambiguous deduction on my tax return? (If *you* are highly aggressive, this is generally preferable to an accountant who shies away from deductions that could be disallowed. However, if you're the type of investor or tax payer who wishes to err on the side of safety, such an advisor might be a poor match for you.)

Tip: Before engaging an investment manager, ask some additional tough questions, such as:

• What has been your performance each quarter for the last eight years?

• What is your average annual rate of return?

• What has been your compounded rate of return? (Compare each quarter to the Standard & Poor's 500 Stock Index. Contrast Up and Down cycles with both the Standard & Poor's 500 Stock Index and mutual fund results.)

• What is the value of the assets you manage?

• Are the people currently managing the portfolios in your firm the same individuals who were responsible for prior years' performance? If not, what is the performance history of those persons added to your firm?

• What are your custodial arrangements for client accounts?

HOW TO MAKE WORKING WITH YOUR ATTORNEY EASIER AND LESS EXPENSIVE

There are many things you can do to make working with your attorney easier and more affordable. For openers, you should request that all the important or complicated advice your attorney gives you be documented in a written report, so that you avoid misunderstandings and have time to study the recommendations. You also should learn the kinds of documents you must deal with in handling your legal affairs, to avoid lengthy, needless discussions of why you need this paper and that. Furthermore, you might:

1.   Review every document, filing, or correspondence between your attorney and any other party in which your business is discussed.

2.   Ask to see your files from time to time to check up on your attorney's diligence, and to make sure you've been kept informed of all matters.

3.   Try to save your attorney's time. (Attorneys are generally paid for their time, unless a contingency fee is used.) In particular, avoid handing your attorney an unsorted box or bag of papers to "go through and take what you need." Instead, organize materials, separating them by relevance to the project the attorney is working on (most important, least important) or by type (memos, documents, reports). Also remember that the meter is ticking whenever you talk to your attorney, whether in person or on the phone. Therefore, outline your phone calls in advance. Be prepared, brief, and come to the the point right away.

4.   Learn to evaluate your attorney critically, yet fairly. Ask:

a.   Is my attorney a generalist? Is he well versed in malpractice prevention and litigation? Labor law? Tax and estate planning? Professional corporations? Retirement plans? (These are generally the areas beyond the day-to-day legal questions where you're apt to need his expertise.)

b.   Does my attorney know when to refer me to other attorneys who specialize, such as labor, malpractice, civil litigation, estate planning, or tax attorneys?

c.   Does my attorney handle matters promptly? You don't want your attorney to hold up important decisions or dawdle on documents, especially if you'll be unprotected and vulnerable until such documents are completed and signed.

d.   Does my attorney give me an itemized bill?

e.   Does my attorney limit consultation time with additional partners? (You might insist on prior approval for consultation lasting more than x hours. Otherwise, you may find that your expensive attorney is actually having to consult the real expert in the firm, and at your expense.)

f.   Does my attorney charge a reasonable minimum fee for short phone calls? (Don't expect free calls, but also don't accept an attorney's attempts to charge you a high quarter-hour minimum for every two-minute phone conversation.)

g. Does my attorney notify me if he must do large amounts of photocopying on my behalf? (You can arrange for copying to be done either at your own office, or at a facility with reasonable rates. Law firms often charge high per-page fees for photocopying.)

h. Does my attorney charge me reasonable expenses for work done on my behalf? (You can request that your attorney live as you do when on business trips for you, for example, by travelling coach class if you travel coach, or staying in a regular hotel room, rather than a luxurious suite.)

TIPS FOR GETTING THE MOST FROM YOUR PRACTICE MANAGEMENT CONSULTANT

You might seek a practice management consultant's help on an ongoing basis, to institute a program of continual practice enhancement and growth. However, most doctors engage such a consultant when they see a developing problem, or the need for major evaluation of the practice's management systems. In these cases, it is prudent *not* to wait until a problem has become critical or out of control.

Before calling in a consultant, try to define the specific practice management problems and goals for which you are seeking assistance. Ask your staff for their input, since they may be closer to some of the problems than you are. (Hold a staff meeting, meet one-on-one, or have staff members define problems in writing.)

Objectively evaluate whether you have the commitment you'll need to make changes, both in yourself and in your staff. If you are reluctant or averse to making changes as the result of the consultant's recommendations, you probably won't change, and the consultation will be of limited value.

Some of the goals you might reasonably expect from a practice management consultant (depending upon your needs and circumstances) include:

• Achievement of a measurable goal. In many cases, you can enjoy a complete return on the consultant's fee within a few months of the consultation. (If your goal wasn't to increase profits, you should reach some other measurable goal, such as reducing your hours or turnover, or increasing recall or case acceptance.)

• A more cohesive staff.

• Greater satisfaction with your practice. Less personal stress and frustration.

• Increased referrals and improved patient flow.

• Improved quality of patient services.

To evaluate the performance of a practice management consultant, ask:

1.   Does my consultant contact me after a consultation, to monitor my progress? Does she suggest follow-up meetings and advanced consultations as they are needed?

2.   Does my consultant offer an impartial viewpoint, uninfluenced by internal loyalties and traditions that exist in my practice?

3.   Does my consultant use the experiences of other practices' mistakes and successes to make recommendations for me?

4.   Does my consultant have realistic objectives and time frames about changes for my practice? Does she guide me and my staff through the change process in a way that minimizes resistance and obstacles?

5.   Does my consultant teach me and my staff to master new systems so we are able to handle them without his continual help?

Tip: To determine whether a management consultant can be of benefit to your practice, see "Can a Management Consultant Help You?," page 515.

HOW TO GET THE MOST FROM YOUR INSURANCE AGENTS OR BROKERS

Most doctors begin insurance planning by discussing their overall insurance needs with their accountant/financial planner. Then, they explain their needs to their insurance representative.

You can usually help things along with an insurance advisor if you ask him to prepare a list of alternatives that he feels best meet your insurance needs. Then, in preparation for these proposals, review the insurance company's brochures to familiarize yourself with the various types of policies your advisor may suggest.

Tip: When you pay your insurance representative, you are paying the insurance company. Therefore, be certain to get and keep a receipt that indicates that the insurance firm is contracting to provide the specific policy and is crediting the premium to be paid to the agent. A detailed receipt is your proof of your coverage until your policy arrives.

To evaluate your insurance representative, ask: Does my insurance representative look out for my best interest? Or, is he out to sell me something? Does he disappear once he's sold me a policy, to resurface only when it's time to renew? Or, does he inform me of changes that could effect me? Does he call periodically to see if I need to update my policies?

WHAT TO LOOK FOR FROM YOUR BANKER

Many doctors mistakenly rationalize a purchase or improvement simply because the bank is willing to finance it. If you have sound financial reasons for seeking a loan, the single most important move you can make to assure that the funds will be there when you need them is establishing a solid relationship with a banker over a period of years. For more information on loan acquisitions, see "Getting the Loan You Need, When You Need It," pages 35–37.

To evaluate your banker, ask:

1.   Did my banker explain clearly what information he was looking for when I applied for a loan?

2.   Is my banker available for general consultation? Does he (or will he) help me arrange purchases of banker's acceptances, treasury bills, commercial paper, and the like?

For more information on this subject, see, "Making Better Use of Your Bank's Many Services," Appendix 1-T, page 551.

C · H · A · P · T · E · R   1-5

Negotiating a Favorable Office Lease

If you decide to lease office space, there are several terms that you will want to negotiate with your landlord, above and beyond the simple monthly rental fee. The following information should be helpful.

FIRST, KNOW THAT YOU HAVE
THE RIGHT TO NEGOTIATE

Most (if not all) landlords will hand you a pre-printed lease, tell you that it's the standard contract, and ask you to sign it. They like to do that for good reason: Most leases are written to favor the landlord.

Be aware that you do have the right to review the lease the landlord offers, and suggest modifications as you see fit. Don't let the landlord bully or rush you into signing a lease simply because it is standard, and especially if you haven't had time to review it.

15 ITEMS WORTH NEGOTIATING

Of course, your attorney will be helpful in deciding which lease items are most worth negotiating, and what terms will be best for you. However, you might begin your discussion by considering these 15 common lease items:

1.   If you are leasing an office in a new building (or one being remodeled or customized), make sure you know the quality of the building materials, carpet, etc. being used. Ask to see a finished suite, or other examples of the same contractor's work. If you wish, you can usually specify higher quality materials in all or part of your office, as long as you are willing to pay the difference.

Tip: If you opt for this approach, negotiate hard for a break on the rent. Should you terminate the rental agreement down the road, you will be leaving the landlord with these leasehold improvements, which may be worth quite a bit to him.

2.   If you're renting space by the square foot, make certain that your lease defines square footage. Then make sure that you and your landlord are using the same definition:

- *net* square footage means only the area your office occupies.

- *gross* square footage includes public hallways, elevators, public bathrooms, stairways, and the thickness of walls.

3.   Which services are included in your rent? For example, who is liable for janitorial service, maintenance, and repairs? How often is routine maintenance (such as painting) to be done? At whose expense? Can you arrange separate energy metering for your office space?

4.   Did your landlord write an escalator clause into your lease? Such a clause allows landlords to pass on their rising costs to you. If you must be subject to an escalator clause, make sure it reflects your landlord's *actual* costs, and not, for example, the Consumer Price Index.

Tips: Always avoid retroactive escalator clauses. And, make sure the lease provides for *decreases* in utility costs, and has a cap on how high costs may rise during the rental period.

5.   If the lease includes a clause requiring you to pay legal fees if the landlord takes you to court, make sure you are liable for the costs only if the landlord *wins*.

6.   Does the lease allow you to sublet your office space? If this is important to you, or may be in the future, insist on a sublet clause to provide the flexibility you need.

For more information on subleasing office space, see, "Caveats and Guidelines for Subleasing Office Space," below.

7.   Does the lease accurately describe the present condition of the office? If it doesn't, you could be charged later for damages that existed when you moved in. Insist on a documented inspection of the premises before you move in.

8.   Are there any restrictions on your use of stairways, elevators, parking lots, and other common areas? Do you have the right to post signs directing patients to your office? If so, are there any limitations on these?

9.   Is there a security deposit required? If so, what happens to the interest on that deposit?

10.   If the space is in a downtown office building, or similar structure, and you wish to have evening or Saturday hours, will the building be open then? If so, are standard services (such as security and utilities) cut back? How much would you have to pay to obtain these services during these hours?

11. If the space is in a shopping center:

• Do you have to make any agreement to pay a percentage of your "sales" in addition to a fixed amount of rent? For more information on this subject, see "Know the Kind of Rent You Must Pay," below.

• Will you be required to be open whenever the retail stores are open (normally 10:00 a.m. to 9:00 p.m.)? Can you be open at other times (such as very early in the morning)?

• Can you add a clause to your lease that prohibits certain types of businesses (such as massage parlors, X-rated bookstores, etc.) from operating near you?

• Do you have the right to approve or veto all remodeling changes, to make sure that they don't make your location less desirable?

12. If in a shared space (such as a shopping center or office building), must you join a tenant's association, and participate in cooperative advertising? In other words, could you be required to put your name up in neon lights, or participate in a sidewalk sale, if you didn't want to?

13. Which local zoning ordinances might restrict your operation? For instance, could the ordinances prevent you from adding a parking lot, or displaying a certain type of sign?

14. In the event of your death, what will happen to your lease? If possible, insert a clause into your lease giving your estate the option of cancelling your lease *without penalty* in the event of your death.

For more information on this and related subjects, see "Preparing Your Practice for Your Death," pages 275–278.

15. In all other circumstances, what are the terms and penalties for you cancelling your lease? Will the landlord be able to cancel the lease, and if so, how? What will happen to you if the landlord chooses to sell the building?

KNOW THE KIND OF RENT YOU MUST PAY

Rents are generally measured by the annual cost per square foot of the space. But there are at least five common ways to calculate rent, every one of which uses square footage as the basis for comparisons. They are:

• *Gross leases.* These require you to pay a flat monthly amount. The landlord is responsible for all expenses of operating the building, including taxes, repairs, and insurance. Many landlords now charge tenants separately for heat and electricty, which were once part of most gross rents.

• *Net leases.* The tenant must pay for some or all of the real estate taxes on the property, in addition to the base rent.

• *Net-net leases.* The tenant must pay the base rent, taxes, plus the insurance on the space he or she occupies.

• *Net-net-net* (also called *"triple net"*) *leases.* All costs of operating the building, including repairs and maintenance, are passed on to the tenant.

• *Percentage leases.* The tenant pays a fixed rate, plus a percentage of gross income. This is a popular rental arrangement in multiple-tenant shopping centers.

CAVEATS AND GUIDELINES FOR SUBLEASING OFFICE SPACE

An increasing number of practitioners are now subleasing underused office space to another doctor, often for one or two days per week. Subleasing may be a worthwhile way to spread overhead costs over more practitioners. But take care before entering (or allowing) such an agreement.

If you're the tenant, and decide to sublease your space, first check your lease to see if you'll run into any problems with your landlord. Establish a written contract with the subleasing doctor, stating firm hours, rent, and maintenance terms. Make it clear who is responsible for damage caused by the subleasing doctor, how specifically the office is to be maintained and cleaned, what equipment and space the doctor can and can't use, who is responsible for repairing and servicing equipment, etc. Put a time limit on the subleasing agreement, and provide a mechanism for terminating it sooner.

Tip: If you are the landlord of your building, consider how the sublease might affect you. You or current tenants may have special interest in certain professions and specialties being practiced or not being practiced in your building. If you wish to restrict subleasing, be sure your lease agreement is adequate.

CASE STUDY: GENERAL DENTIST SUBLEASES TO SPECIALIST

A general dentist practicing in a small town in Georgia reports an interesting sublease agreement. In this case, the periodontist who practiced nearest to this doctor was 30 miles away—far enough to deter many patients from seeking care. As a result, the general dentist decided to recruit a periodontist from a city 40 miles away to occupy his office *on his day off.*

The periodontist sees primarily the general dentist's patients, but is also getting an increasing number of outside referrals. According to the general dentist, this arrangement has provided many benefits:

1.   Higher acceptance of periodontal cases. All referred patients at least make an inital consult/exam appointment with the periodontist.

2.   Convenience for patients.

3.   More efficient use of office space.

4.   Reliable emergency coverage for the general dentist's day off.

5.   Better communication with the specialist about overall treatment. (No x-rays need to be sent out of the office.)

6.   Additional avenue to attract new patients to the practice, who are referred by the periodontist.

7. $1,000–$2,500 estimated profit per month.

As for costs, the general dentist reports that this arrangement required $400–$500 in set-up costs (for forms, surgical instruments, etc.), and costs about $200 per month for the periodontist's supplies. The periodontist pays for the assistant, and the general dentist pays for the receptionist, who would be working anyway.

The general dentist reports, "Very little additional overhead is incurred." Of course, a similar office-sharing arrangement might be made with any needed specialist.

Getting the Loan You Need, When You Need It

There may be several times in you career when you need to secure a loan for your practice. Obviously, when you open your doors for the first time, you need financing. But you may also need a loan to improve, renovate, or enlarge your existing office, to move to new quarters, buy new equipment, or to open a satellite office. Getting the exact amount of money you need for reasonable terms when you need it should not be a problem, *if* you follow certain guidelines.

SIXTEEN ERRORS TO AVOID WHEN ASKING FOR A LOAN

Banks have become more defensive about loans in recent years, hit by record numbers of unpaid loans. Therefore, when approaching a bank (or any lender) for a loan, be sure to avoid these common mistakes:

1. *Waiting until your need becomes desperate.*

2. *Approaching a bank you don't deal with normally:* Your chances will improve tremendously if you walk in as a valued customer, not a stranger.

3. *No appointment:* Making an appointment with a loan officer is the mark of a good planner.

4. *No knowledge of the bank:* Look at the bank's brochures to learn:

• The size of the bank.

• The number of branches.

• The services offered.

5. *No savvy:* You shouldn't have to ask the meaning of "line of credit," "commitment fee," or other common financial phrases.

6. *No perspective:* Look at your situation from the bank's angle. Bank-

ers need to know the loan will increase the value of your practice, not make *your* life better.

7.   *No documentation:* Your rough estimates of costs won't suffice. Get quotes and invoices from suppliers, contractors, etc.

8.   *Incomplete data:* Pull your practice's profit-and-loss statements for the past 3–5 years. Bring personal financial papers, too, including income tax returns.

9.   *Sketchy or unrealistic plans:* Draw up a careful, realistic scenario, with concrete figures you can explain and support.

10.   *Asking for the wrong amount:* Don't ask for a suspicious sum, greatly more or less than you actually need, figuring the difference will give you bargaining power. It won't, but *will* make the banker question your judgment. However, it may make sense to offer very generous estimates of costs, in case actual expenses end up being higher than estimates.

Tip: Here is advice from a Las Vegas practitioner who learned this lesson the hard way:

> "We recently needed financing to move our offices. I asked the bank for the *exact* amount I thought we needed. But I should have asked to borrow more. Banks don't always want to take 100% of the risk, and your actual costs may be higher than you anticipated. Furthermore, I didn't realize that we didn't *have* to use all the money—that it could be set aside in a savings or CD account or paid back early. I asked for the exact amount, the bank cut back 10%, and actual costs were higher than expected. Now, I have to do some juggling, as well as postpone new equipment purchases that I'd planned. From this experience, I'd advise you to ask for for about 30% more than you think you'll need. You can always not use the loan balance."

11.   *Mismatched purpose and loan.* Don't seek long-term money to finance a short-term asset.

12.   *Focusing on future promises.* Far more impressive to a banker are present strengths.

13.   *Overvaluing/overselling collateral.* Don't inflate figures.

14.   *Insufficient information about the practice.* Begin your loan proposal with a paragraph or two on your practice's history and development, special features, capabilities, and philosophy, as well as your training, specialization, etc.

15.   *Illegible materials.* Neatness counts more than you may realize.

16. *Coming across as a big spender.* Don't boast of living lavishly or display showy or gaudy objects of wealth.

DON'T GET SWINDLED WHEN BORROWING FROM AN UNKNOWN LENDER

Con artists are plentiful, and the astute doctor will want to take several steps before borrowing large sums from an unfamiliar lender:

1. Use the services of a reputable attorney or accountant, who is familiar with the lender in question.

2. Get a good reading of a lender's reputation. Check your local sources, such as the Better Business Bureau, consumer protection agencies, and law enforcement offices.

3. Ask the lender for a client or reference list. Contact several, to gather their opinions about the lender.

4. Disregard unaudited financial statements. They are often little more than glowing public relations devices.

5. Submit all loan contracts to your own bank, for a third-party opinion, and to see if they can match the offer.

6. Transfer funds by check, preferably certified. Never hand over cash.

7. Demand that all refundable fees be placed in an escrow account, held by an independent agent.

8. Remember that although lenders from foreign countries and small islands may offer attractive incentives, banking regulations in those places may not be as strict as they are in the United States. This can increase the potential for fraud.

9. Ask for an itemized account of all extra fees and expenses.

10. If you have suspicions of fraud, contact law enforcement officials immediately. Fast action is often needed to thwart illegal deals.

For more information on protecting yourself against scams, see, "Are You a Sitting Duck for Con Artists," pages 209–211.

C·H·A·P·T·E·R   1-7

Special Problems When You're Your Own Landlord

M ost doctors who rent office space dream of owning their own buildings. And for many, office ownership is the ideal way to practice, since it provides the greatest amount of flexibility, control, and often, a worthwhile investment.

Keep in mind, however, that the majority of doctors who own their own buildings find that doing so has its drawbacks, usually many more than were originally anticipated. With ownership comes new responsibilities, and of course, many potential problems.

HOW TO DECIDE WHETHER TO RENT OR BUY YOUR OFFICE SPACE

Answering these questions will help you decide whether now is the time to buy office space, or whether you'd be better off continuing to rent:

1.   Why are you now renting your office? Is it to remain as flexible and mobile as possible? Do you anticipate relocating soon or needing to expand or reduce the size of your office? If so, renting may be the best option, particularly if you negotiate a short-term lease.

2.   Which is cheaper, buying or renting? Conduct a 10-year projection analysis for both, including the tax consequences. If rental-per-square-foot costs are greater than ownership costs, it usually makes economic sense to own your office, particularly when you consider the appreciation potential.

3.   Can space you rent accommodate your practice's needs? Do you find that you have unique office design needs that would require an unusual floorplan or amenities that are not possible in the usual kinds of rental space? If so, building from scratch may be the only way to get the unique office space you want.

4.   Can rental space grow with your practice? If you intend to expand, will you have to move? If so, can you rent the quantity and quality of space you will need?

Tip: When forward-thinking doctors build, they plan for extra square footage. They may choose to lease or not develop the surplus until it is needed.

5.   How liquid is the office market in your area? Office resale values may be unstable, and will vary depending upon your location, amenities, marketplace, and current interest rates. If you buy, what would be your chances of selling in a timely manner, and at a reasonable price down the road?

6.   Would you rather be in an office building, or in a one-unit, single detached office? Owning space in an office condominium means you depend on all of the building's owners to control expenses, and often, make decisions, which opens up many potential problems. (More on condos, below.)

7.   Will you be able to secure the financing you need? (For more information on this subject, see "Getting the Loan You Need, When You Need It," pages 35–37.)

Tip: If renting seems to be your best option for the foreseeable future, see "Negotiating a Favorable Office Lease," pages 29–33.

TAKING OVER A PRACTICE, OR BUILDING FROM SCRATCH

If you have decided that office ownership is for you, your next step is to decide whether to take over an existing practice, or to build from scratch. When assuming another doctor's practice, you're usually buying most of the following:

• A known and proven location for a medical/dental/other professional office.

• A telephone number and phone book listing.

• Often, some used clinical and business equipment, office furniture, and supplies.

• Billing and filing systems.

You may also have an opportunity to purchase the office building (or the right to take over the lease), or the chance to keep some of the office staff. And of course, you can also buy implied access to existing patients and referrals. (You don't technically buy patient records, since the release of medical records is protected by law.)

Tip: It is usually best *not* to buy accounts receivable from the selling doctor, since this money may be hard to collect.

The advantages of taking over an existing practice are obvious. A portion of the practice's patients may want to continue their care with you, giving you a strong patient base. Much or all of your equipment and furnishings are there and ready to use. If you can retain a good staff, you won't need to recruit and train employees. A complete management system, including record keeping, appointment scheduling, collections, billing, filing, and inventory control will already be in place.

There are, however, some potential drawbacks. You will be practicing in an office designed by someone else, with equipment that you may not want to use, or that may be outdated (or in disrepair). Practice management systems may be poor and need updating/revamping, especially if the practice was not run efficiently.

Building your own practice from scratch can be highly satisfying, since you will be choosing everything yourself and starting with a clean slate. However, much of your effort will be directed towards locating a suitable space, designing it, shopping for it, and living through the construction process. This should not be underestimated.

BUILDING YOUR OFFICE: TYPICAL MISTAKES AND HOW TO AVOID THEM

There are unfortunately many pitfalls awaiting doctors who build their own facilities from scratch. The most common:

1. *Underestimating costs.*

2. *Attempting to cut costs by buying residential land, in hopes of changing zoning to commercial:* Residential land is often not re-zonable, and may not be well-located for a professional office.

3. *Overemphasizing bottom line per-square-foot costs:* A building with the lowest per-square-foot costs may not be the cheapest, most efficient, or best. Well-designed spaces may cost more per square foot, but you'll need less of it, and get better use out of it.

4. *Not getting financing commitment early:* Finances should be well in place before construction begins.

5. *Building too small:* Many doctors omit needed storage and expansion space, in an effort to save money. This is short-sighted thinking. Good office plans generally include a certain amount of unfinished space for future

development (often an additional 30 percent), plus the capacity to add on later.

6. *Choosing a building and lot that are unsuitable for expansion:* The most versatile single-unit building sites allow for either horizontal or vertical construction, or both.

7. *Choosing equipment at the last minute:* It makes much more sense to select equipment and design rooms around it, rather than designing the rooms and making last-minute alterations to accommodate the equipment.

8. *Not working with medical/dental design specialists:* General builders don't always know about the unique needs of a professional practice. For instance, sound control is crucial in most practices, and requires special attention. And, many builders will suggest putting plumbing in adjacent examining rooms on a common wall, to save money. However, as a result, the arrangement of equipment in the two rooms is reversed, requiring the doctor to switch back and forth, working on the left side of the patient in one room, and on the right side in the other. (This may seem to make sense. But in the long run, it is considered poor design, since cloning exam rooms has been shown to increase doctor efficiency.)

Tip: For additional strategies for increasing doctor efficiency, see "85 Ways to Save Time and Increase Your Personal Productivity," pages 483–488.

IS A CONDO YOUR BEST OPTION?

The high cost of building and owning office space has caused many doctors to look at one of the newest alternatives for professional office space— office condominiums. Condos are attractive to doctors for many of the same reasons that residential condos have become so popular. Owners enjoy the benefits of property ownership, but share maintenance costs and responsibilities. In some areas, prime locations are hard to come by, and some of the choicest office buildings have been converted to condos.

Some tips before you jump into the condo market:

1. Find out if the developer retains a majority of the condo association votes. In such arrangements, you and your co-owners could end up paying excessive management fees or suffer mismanagement, and have little or no recourse.

2. What restrictions would be placed on you (signs, construction, etc.)? Are there restrictions on the types of offices that can be run in your building? Will the building be strictly professional, or will other types of busi-

nesses be allowed? (In other words, can an X-rated book store open up next to you?)

3.   What regular maintenance will be done, and what will be your maintenance fee? What will happen when maintenance beyond the usual is needed? (Will there be a contingency fund established for major repairs? If so, how?)

4.   Who owns and maintains the common areas (lobby, parking lot, garage, lounge, etc.)?

IMPROVEMENT OR REPAIR? THE IRS DEFINITELY SEES A DIFFERENCE

It's essential to understand the difference between "improvements" and "repairs" on property you own (or lease), because they're in different tax categories. Improvements are generally deductible over a period of several years. But repairs are usually fully deductible in the year they're completed. This could be an important consideration when you plan to make some changes in your office, especially if you don't need more deductions right now, but might in the future.

The line between improvement and repair is sometimes thin. The basic difference: Repairs keep property in efficient operating condition without adding to its value or utility, as is the case with improvements. Interesting: Cost is *not* a determining factor.

Some examples of repairs and improvements:

Repair:	Improvement:
Filling in a driveway's potholes.	Resurfacing the driveway.
Patching a leaky roof.	Recovering the roof.
Reinforcing a sagging floor.	Replacing or recovering a floor.
Repainting your reception area.	Wallpapering a previously painted reception area.

Tip: There's one exception that allows tenants to deduct the expense for an improvement immediately (which ordinarily would have to be depreciated or amortized). That's when you renovate because of contractual obligations.

For instance, your lease (or condo agreement) may provide that you must replace (not patch) worn-out property. If the carpeting wears out when you're three years into a five-year lease, you may deduct its cost in the year it's installed, rather than write it off over the usual number of years.

30 Questions to Ask Before Joining a Third-Party Prepaid Plan

T hird-party prepaid plans, if chosen with care, can increase cash flow and patient volume, and fill empty appointment time, all with little or no financial risk. Third-party patients can also help build a fee-for-service practice. (If a doctor sees more patients in total, it's logical that he'll generate more referrals—both prepaid and fee-for-service.) And, prepaid plan champions say that member-patients never put off needed care because they can't afford it.

However, while prepayment plans dangle these enticing carrots, dangers do exist. If the doctor does not evaluate and choose a plan well, and makes a poor decision, his involvement might mean that he ends up losing, not gaining income.

One of the most obvious potential dangers is that doctors might sign up for a prepaid plan that has inadequate reimbursement, just so they can keep busy. But a more common problem is that the doctor might join without clearly understanding his obligations and the plan's expectations.

For these reasons, it is best to have an attorney review any plan's contract before signing, to uncover hidden or ambiguous requirements. As well, it is wise to talk to other doctors already enrolled in the program to seek their candid reactions. Below are 25 questions you should ask before taking the leap with any prepaid plan. While this list is not all-inclusive, it does offer a firm base upon which to develop further questions. Again, your attorney is your best advisor in this area.

25 QUESTIONS TO ASK ABOUT THE PLAN

1.   Specifically how and when will I be reimbursed? Monthly? By submission of claims forms? Will the patient pay a small laboratory or "visit" charge?

Tip: Most plans emphasize fast payment. However, you may get the impression that you'll receive your money within 30 days, when you won't. Study the contract language carefully. Note whether it says something like, "All approved claims will be paid within 30 days." Such a statement is *not* a contractual commitment to *approve* the claim within 30 days. In fact, if that's all the contract said, there would be *no* time limit on approval. For guaranteed fast payment, look for contracts that state flatly that all claims filed by the doctor will be paid within *x* days of *receipt* and that if they aren't, the doctor is paid interest.

2.   Will I have the last word in treatment planning and delivery of services? Or, does the plan's medical/dental/other consultant have final say in this area? Who mediates disputes, if they arise?

3.   Will patients have freedom of choice? Will they be able to see another doctor, if they so choose? Do group members voluntarily choose whether to participate in the plan?

4.   Will I be required to take any and all plan patients who come to me?

5.   How many plan patients can I expect to see each month?

6.   What percentage of eligible plan members usually seek treatment? What types of treatment do they usually seek?

7.   What groups have actually signed contracts with the plan? At this moment, how many patients are in the plan? What are the patient growth projections?

8.   What are the plan's costs, other than health care costs? On a percentage basis, how much goes to expenses such as salaries, supplies, marketing, and overhead?

9.   Are all benefits and exclusions clearly outlined for patients in writing? Precisely what literature do plan members receive when they join/enroll?

10.   What are the terms of specialty care?

11.   Does the plan engage in any practices that might place me in either ethical or legal jeopardy? Do the plan's promotional activities comply with my national professional association's and my state and local societies' code of ethics?

Tip: Some contracts ask you to pay a percentage of the gross receipts from services rendered to plan participants. This request is a potential violation of a professional code prohibiting payment of rebates or referral fees.

12.   Does the plan mandate:

a.   Office hours?

b.   Vacation schedules?

    c.   Patient waiting times?

    d.   Record keeping techniques?

    e.   Any other practice management systems?

13.   How many doctors now participate? May I have a list?

14.   What are the projections for doctor participants?

15.   How are doctor participants selected?

16.   How long does the agreement last? (Most contracts are for one year and are renewable. However, some bind you for as long as two years after terminating membership, if you continue to treat plan enrollees.)

17.   How will reimbursement adjustments be made in the future, to cover the doctor's increasing costs? Will a cost-of-living index be used? If so, which one? Will there be periodic automatic adjustments? Or will some other means of determining increases be used?

18.   Is the plan "held harmless" against any liability or claim that arises out of the services you provide for group members?

Tip: Get your attorney's advice. Most malpractice insurance policies exclude or limit coverage for liability assumed under a contract if you are not covered for it *without* the contract. As well, broadly-worded provisions may create responsibility for you *beyond* your own acts or omissions.

19.   Is this an exclusive agreeement? May I contract with other prepaid plans, if I so choose? (Some contracts discourage you from participating in another plan.)

20.   May I advertise directly to patients enrolled in the plan? (Some contracts prohibit this.)

21.   Am I free to establish my own plan after I terminate my membership? (Some plans prohibit this.)

22.   Exactly who is organizing the program? Will the plan's administrators be accessible to me? What is the organizer's experience and reputation?

23.   What are the means and reasons for terminating a doctor from the plan? Precisely how would a doctor terminate the contract, if he or she chooses to?

24.   How long are patients obliged to stay in the plan? (For instance, do they make a one-year commitment? Longer?)

25.   Must all the doctors in a group practice participate in the plan? Or, can an agreement be made on individual basis with each doctor? If so, are there any restrictions on the non-participant doctors remaining in the group? (For instance, are they free to participate in competing plans?)

FIVE SOUL-SEARCHING QUESTIONS
TO ASK YOURSELF

1.   How many more patients do I honestly want? How many do I need? Is the prepaid plan my best way to get them?

2.   How many of my patients of record will be eligible for discounted fees because they are members of the subscriber group? How much revenue do I stand to lose from these patients? How does that figure compare with the revenue I expect to gain from treating new patients from that group?

3.   How will I explain my acceptance of reduced fees to my patients of record who are non-subscribers, if they ask?

4.   What will my recourse be if my participation in a prepaid plan does not improve my practice? What will happen if I participate in a plan now and wish to get out of it in a few years? Will I alienate (and lose) my plan patients?

5.   Will I eventually resent taking a reduced fee for plan patients? Is there any chance that I might view them (and treat them) differently from my fee-for-service patients?

FOUR WAYS TO INTEGRATE PREPAID PATIENTS INTO
A FEE-FOR-SERVICE PRACTICE

If you join a prepaid plan, you will need to find out if each new patient is a prepaid plan participant, or if he is fee-for-service. Later, you will need to identify each patient as one or the other in your records. However, in making this necessary distinction, it is extremely important *not* to make either type of patient feel that he is receiving a different quality of professional care than the other.

When current and potential patients call your office to make an appointment, ask a queston, etc., instruct your receptionist to answer their most pressing clinical and related questions fully, before asking what kind of insurance they have. Otherwise, patients may incorrectly assume that your quality of treatment and/or appointment availability will depend upon whether or not they participate in a prepaid plan.

Once you have tactfully learned that a patient is a prepaid plan participant, you will need to identify him as such in your records. Four simple suggestions:

1.   *Charts and folders:* For patient charts, you might use different color folders to represent different prepaid groups, and a single color to identify all fee-for-service patients. (You might then apply color-coded stickers to the

folders to represent the patient's doctor preference in a group practice, or other information. For more color-coding records management tips, see "All About Color-Coding," page 424–425.)

2. *Daily log sheet:* You might divide your pegboard system into two sections—one for prepaid patients, and one for fee-for-service patients. Then, you can subdivide each section into the various areas of your service. (For example, a dentist might create sections for operative, endodontic, and hygiene patients.) Why: This tracking system will enable you to determine the percentage of practice revenue that comes from prepaid and from fee-for-service patients, as well as which types of services are most frequently required by each group. This breakdown is useful when negotiating or contemplating future prepaid contracts (and also helps you make informed inventory, personnel, and planning decisions).

3. *Appointment book:* Note all the usual information in your appointment book (the patient's full name, phone number, type and length of appointment, when lab case is due, etc.). As well, note the classification of patient (fee-for-service or prepaid plan). Also note the balance due for treatment with fee-for-service patients, as well as prepaid plan surcharges.

4. *Billing:* One of the most attractive aspects of prepaid plans is that there is no billing for patient members. Thus, to keep matters simple, you will need to require that all prepaid patients pay any surcharges to you at the time of their appointments. (If treatment occurs over several appointments and the surcharge is greater than a nominal sum, you may need to allow some patients to pay half the surcharge on the first appointment, and the remainder upon completion of your services.)

C·H·A·P·T·E·R 1-9

Switching Over to a Computer, Without Tears

O nce your sparkling new office computer is unpacked, wired, and ready to go, you're going to be eager to put it to good use. However, the initial data entry necessary to convert your practice to a computer system may well be the biggest headache any doctor faces with computerization.

Organization and forethought are the keys to taming this gargantuan task. Much as you might like to, you CAN'T take disorganized records, input them all as is into a computer, and expect anything intelligible to come from it. Painful as it may be, you have no choice but to go through your files, one by one, and remove the garbage.

As a next step, it helps to organize yourself mentally. Ask, "Exactly what am I trying to accomplish with this computer?" Then, categorize your data based upon your answer. For example, did you buy your computer to:

- Track the success of various marketing efforts?
- Improve recall?
- Simplify financial matters?
- Generate new practice management reports?

Establishing concrete goals of this kind, and then deciding how to break down the information, is the *single* most important step you can take before tackling data entry.

CONSISTENCY AMONG DATA ENTRIES A MUST

Data entry will also go incredibly smoother if you begin by preparing a few "glossary" lists. These lists specify precisely how you're going to code every piece of information you use in your practice.

Example: You will probably need to prepare a glossary of your most common insurance carriers. To do so, simply list the name and address of each carrier, along with the abbreviation/code you assign it. That way, you'll always use the same code when referring to that carrier, ensuring consistency.

Additional glossaries you might find useful include:

1.   Common patient health alerts. (For example: Diabetes, High Blood Pressure, Pregnant, Heart Disease, etc.)

2.   Primary care physicians who treat your patient.

3.   Area employers offering health insurance.

4.   Clinical procedure codes/abbreviations.

5.   Practice management abbreviations specific to your office. (*Example:* NSF = Not Sufficient Funds. NP = New Patient.)

THE BEST WAY TO ACCOMPLISH DATA ENTRY

A common mistake many doctors make is trying to enter data on a piecemeal basis, on top of their usual daily schedules. Your staff needs time to do this job right. During the conversion, it is usually best to close the office for a week, or at the very least, to work a reduced schedule.

Most doctors resist the idea of closing their offices. However, it's better to get data entry done at once, so you can get your data entered correctly and quickly. Until your computer has *all* the information, you can't reap its benefits.

Tip: Closing your office does cost an additional 10% above the cost of the computer, on average. Many doctors fail to add this expense into the initial cost estimate of their systems. However, it's a smart investment, and well worth it to do the job right.

15 ADDITIONAL DATA ENTRY TIPS

Usually, the front desk people are best qualified to do the actual data entry. They know the practice best. However, before they begin the task, review this list of do's and don'ts:

1.   Do protect your practice in case of a computer "crash." Back up at least once a day (more often, if possible). Make printed hard copies of all codes and lists.

2. Don't have patients complete your data entry forms. What seems like a helpful tool only complicates matters. Some active patients won't fill in your form correctly or completely. Plus, it's just one more piece of paper. You'll probably still have to look in the file, the ledger, or even in the recall record to complete the data entry.

3. Don't hire a consultant who hasn't computerized a professional practice. Knowledge of both computers and the business of your profession is essential to entering data for your office.

4. Don't try to enter patients as they come in for appointments. This is messy, ends up taking more time in the long run, and can be disruptive to your schedule.

5. If your office will be open during the data entry effort, do designate a private room in your office as your temporary "computer room." Move all of your terminals into this space during this time period, to keep problems away from the front desk where patients are aware of them.

6. Do assign a "runner" to each data entry person. The runner will retrieve and refile patient records, and gather all other missing information, so the data entry person is most efficient. It's quite inefficient and tedious to have your data entry person stop and run around your office looking for the spelling of a street name, a zip code, or recall history.

7. Don't hire a temporary employee or someone from your computer company to enter your data. Your own staff knows your practice better than anyone else, and this is more important than previous knowledge of the computer system. Also, your staff will gain experience with the system through data entry, and will probably be more conscientious than non-employees (since they will have to live with sloppiness and errors).

8. Do handwrite the patient's account number on his file and ledger. This is especially helpful during your first three or four weeks of computerization.

9. Don't enter wrong information. This may sound silly, but it's a common mistake. *Example:* If you are aware that a patient has moved, but don't have his new address, leave a blank, asterisk, or another consistent symbol in that field. That way, when the patient comes in, you'll see that you don't have the address, and you can ask him for it.

10. Do make sure everyone in your office knows your plans for every piece of data. For example, each staff member should be aware that you intend to generate a list of people who live in a specific zip code area for a demographic study. Knowing this plan for the information from the start makes your data entry people more diligent about using correct codes.

11.   Do have the absolute minimum amount of time between finishing your data entry and "going live." Once you're "live," all work which was formerly paperwork is done at the terminal, such as name or address changes. If you let time elapse once data is entered, the information in the computer quickly becomes outdated.

12.   Do contact references provided by your computer company of doctors and other small businesses using your system before you begin data entry. Ask them how they'd handle data entry if they had it to do all over again, and for other advice.

13.   Do enter a special code for red flag patients (for example, no-shows, non-compliant, or those who've been turned over to a collection agency). You'll want to know at a glance that these patients have caused you problems, in case you have future contact with them.

14.   Do check everything you've entered by printing out a copy of each file and enlisting all employees to check it for errors. (It's sometimes easier to see mistakes on the printed page than on the terminal screen.)

15.   Do enter initial data for the accounts receivable during a weekend, if possible, when everything is up-to-date.

Note: Special thanks are due to Linda Sudimack, president of Practice and Computer Management for the Professions, Warren, OH, who contributed much of the material in this chapter.

For more information, see, "Checklist for Overcoming Staff Computer Anxiety," Appendix 1-H, page 527.

Naming Your Practice

There's probably no subject more emotional and less open to rational analysis than a name. It requires great imagination to picture what a person or a practice would seem like if his or its name were changed. All the possible new names appear strange, irrelevant, and arbitrary, because until they're used, they're simply exercises in imagination (or lack or it).

Consider your own name. Can you imagine being called anything else? However, many women who marry take their husband's name without appearing to suffer major inconvenience or trauma. Those of you who've been through the exercise of naming children will recall how difficult it is to make the choice in the first place. Yet, once the choice is made, how rapidly a name gains momentum, weight, and credibility. Whatever name is chosen seems to suit each child perfectly, and in retrospect, usually appears to have been the only reasonable decision.

Shouldn't the same thing happen when you name your practice? Provided that you make your choice on clear criteria, pick a name that's appropriate, and promote it with enthusiasm, the name *will* fit the practice and seem relevant.

YOUR NAME OR AN UMBRELLA NAME?

Many doctors use their own names as the names of their practices. This is the best course in many cases. Yet, even doctors in solo practice may have good reason to name the practice in another way.

There are obvious advantages to using an "umbrella" name for a practice. Most importantly, it allows for changes in associates and partners over the years without confusing the patients. An umbrella name is also very useful when a practice is sold, since the name is not linked heavily with the original owner. And, depending upon the actual words used, an umbrella name can sometimes convey a particular image or attract a certain type of patient better than the doctor's name would.

CATEGORIES OF NAMES

To begin, let's consider the six general categories of names you might have for your practice:

1.   *Name of individual(s):* The practice name is the same as the doctor's.

2.   *Descriptive name:* These usually describe the practice's activities and often have some geographical qualifications. American Motors is this type of name, as is Cheyenne Mountain Dental Center, Family Dental Center, The Smile Center, and Dental West (these names are in actual use.)

Tip: This category has some potential disadvantages. The main one is that what starts out by being an accurate description can quickly become outdated. For example, what happens to the OB-GYN Clinic of Manhattan when it moves to Hoboken, NJ, or when Family Chiropractic Center wants to attract more single people? As you'll see further on, the best names are those that don't date or limit themselves.

3.   *Abbreviated names:* Familiar corporate versions are PanAm and Conoco. There's something to be said for abbreviated names—they're short, easy to use, and can be empowered with some kind of relevance. Yet, they're not as restrictive as some fully descriptive names.

4.   *Initials:* Initial names generally need much heavier promotion than other names in order to break through the barrier or anonymity which they themselves create. The trouble with initials is not only that they start anonymous, but they also quite often stay that way.

5.   *Abstract names:* These are usually coined in the way that Eastman invented *Kodak,* which he thought sounded like the click of a camera shutter.

6.   *Analogous names:* These draw an analogy between the company and a specific object or quality. For example, *Quaker Foods* is analogous to integrity and solid worth. *Sunlight Detergent* implies bright, shining, and sparkling. *The Dentist's Tree,* a name in actual use, implies tradition, strength, stability, and natural beauty, as well as a clever play on words.

10 CRITERIA FOR CHOOSING A NAME

1.   It should be easy—not confusing to the ear or eye. (Usually, that means it should be short, simple, and clear.)

2.   It should be easy to pronounce, preferably in any language.

3. It should have no disagreeable associations whatsoever, again, in any language. *Example:* A doctor whose last name is Payne might have to name his practice carefully, or else he'll end up with The Payne Center, which has obvious bad connotations.

4. It should be suitable for use if your practice expands or shifts geographically, or in its range of services.

5. It should be unique and easily distinguished from other practices (and businesses) in your town.

6. It should not date itself. Be careful not to tie into current events, styles, or fads too closely.

7. It should, if possible, relate to your profession or practice activities.

8. It should be something with which a powerful visual style can be associated—colors, symbols, typefaces, or images.

9. It should have charisma—what marketing experts call "sex appeal"—to lend professional charm to your practice.

10. It should fit consistently with your professional image and appeal to the types of patients you serve (and would like to serve).

Tip: Names can be borrowed from other areas. Take *Avon,* for example. It can be cosmetics, a river, a jet engine, and a rubber company. Nobody confuses them because the contexts in which they operate are so different. Similarly, Lincoln can be a president, a car, or a city, depending on the visual and verbal context.

Tip: Many regulations control what a practice name can or can't include. For example, you can't name your practice *The Best Optometric Practice of Springfield,* because such a name claims superiority. Check with your professional society before using any new name. As well, consult your attorney for information about searching, trademarking and protecting a fictitious business name.

P·A·R·T   2

Basic Practice Management Systems That Prevent Costly Mistakes

C · H · A · P · T · E · R   2-1

Taking Control of Your Appointment Book

An ill-handled appointment book can throw an entire day into chaos, wasting time and money, and creating stress. However, managing an appointment book is not a difficult task, *if* it is done consistently and correctly. The key is to take control of your schedule, not to allow your schedule to take control of you.

WHAT INFORMATION SHOULD BE INCLUDED?

Whatever type of appointment book or computer program you use to schedule appointments, it should be easy to read, showing the entire week at a glance. There must be adequate space to record the patient's full name (so he isn't confused with another patient), daytime and home telephone numbers, length of appointment, the services to be rendered, and a variety of symbols (described below).

The time breakdown of your day will depend upon the nature of your practice. However, each hour is usually divided into four 15-minute segments or six 10-minute segments. Be sure your appointment book is broken down to the smallest increments of time that you need—even if that is as little as 5 minutes.

In a tight reception area, storage of the appointment book can be a problem. Since the book itself is so large, smaller offices sometimes use a shelf-like drawer under the reception desk to accommodate it. That way, the drawer can be pulled out when the book is needed, but conveniently tucked away when not in use.

ONE PERSON IN CONTROL

It is essential that only one member of your staff control the appointment book for each doctor and make all the appointments. She will ensure that doctor flow and transition between patients is smooth, and that jam-ups don't occur. Other staff members should know how to manage the appointment book, but should do so only in case of an emergency. All patients, even staff members and the doctor's friends and relatives, should schedule their appointments with the person who controls the appointment book.

USING THE TREATMENT/SERVICE PLAN

Only the doctor can predict how much time will be required for each visit in the course of a patient's treatment/services. For this reason, he should indicate this information on the patient's treatment/service plan, which will be a guide for scheduling future appointments. This written plan should state the services to be rendered, the time necessary for each appointment, and the required lapse between appointments (for laboratory fabrication, test results, healing, etc.).

Without a written treatment/service plan, the appointment secretary has only verbal instructions from the doctor. This can lead to confusion, misunderstandings, or forgotten instructions. With the plan, you have everything you need to know clearly outlined in advance so you can make well-planned appointments.

SCHEDULING EMERGENCIES

In a practice that routinely handles emergencies, it is a good idea to set aside a period of time each day to handle emergency patients. Many offices find that 15 to 30 minutes is ample emergency time and like to schedule it just before lunch. If you find that emergency patients mostly call on certain days (Fridays and Mondays are most common), set aside more emergency time on those days.

Tip: Your goal is to leave ample time to see the usual number of emergency patients without interrupting your schedule. To do this, track your emergency appointments over several weeks or months, to identify patterns.

Learn to screen patients for true emergencies and how to say "no" to others. Train your receptionist to ask specific questions to determine the patient's status. *Examples:* She might ask, "Is there discomfort, bleeding, or swelling?" . . . "What is it that you'd like the doctor to do for you?" . . . "How long has it been like this?" Of course, your receptionist should never deny a patient access to you if she is in any doubt about whether it is an emergency, or if the situation appears to be an *urgency*. (In such a case, the patient does not have a true emergency, but is extremely upset and believes he does.)

When you appoint a patient during emergency time, make sure he knows that the time is for relief of discomfort, concern, or urgent problems only, and that another appointment may be necessary for follow-up and more extensive treatment/services. For example, "The doctor's schedule is completely filled with patients and treatment today. However, he does have a few minutes at 11:30 this morning to see you and try to relieve your discomfort."

When the patient comes in, do whatever is necessary at that time, and schedule another appointment to do what can be delayed. Avoid procedures that can be rescheduled and that will throw your appointment schedule off kilter.

Tip: The more times a new emergency patient sees you, the more comfortable he becomes, and the more likely he will be to continue to see you and refer others. By limiting the procedures you do right away to only those that are essential, you will have to see the emergency patient several times, and in so doing, strengthen your relationship with him. Completing treatment/ services for a new emergency patient at only one appointment may actually *thwart* your chances of ever seeing him again.

Tip: As a practice builder, keep your fee for the emergency appointment low. Encourage emergency patients you've never seen before to return to you for a complete new patient examination, or for additional treatment.

Inform the patient of your maximum fee for the emergency appointment, and that payment is expected at the time of the appointment. For example, when making the appointment, your receptionist might say, "The fee for an emergency visit will not exceed $_____ , without prior discussion with the doctor, and is expected at the time of the visit."

Finally, here's an offbeat idea from a Midwest practitioner. When you squeeze an emergency patient into your busy schedule, especially on the weekend, it's nearly impossible to charge enough to cover your costs. So why try? A general practitioner may be able to turn the time given to the patient into something much more valuable than a simple fee:

1.   Say, "My fee for today is that I need to see six of your friends in the next 90 days."

2.   Give the patient six of your business cards.

Even if you get only one referral, this practitioner reports, the practice building benefits of this strategy greatly outweigh the loss of a small fee. And the patient will think you're the *greatest* for not charging him for the emergency visit.

LIMIT ADVANCE APPOINTMENT SCHEDULING

Despite popular belief, it is not always best to be fully booked months and months ahead. Doing so can make your schedule inflexible and lead to problems.

For one thing, if your practice routinely submits insurance predeterminations, limiting advance scheduling to only a few weeks into the future will enable you to accept insurance patients as predetermination is received. This is important in maintaining a smooth flow of paperwork and insurance payments. For another, limits on advance scheduling allow flexibility in the schedules of the doctor and staff. With the limits, the doctor is free to take vacation or attend a seminar, without waiting several months until time becomes available.

When setting up an appointment book in a new practice, there is no problem limiting your scheduling and using a call list (explained below). However, if you are in an established practice that's booked months ahead, you can still take control of your appointment schedule:

1. Remove the names of patients for whom no services have been started. Call each one and explain your new method of scheduling no more than a few weeks in advance. Put these patients on a call list in the order that they'd been appointed.

2. Next, remove all but the first appointment of patients under treatment/services. When these patients come in for their next appointment, explain your new system. Stress that there will be no break in their treatment/services.

Example: Your appointment secretary might say, "It is not possible for me to give you a definite appointment at this time, because the doctor schedules only three weeks into the future so he can complete treatment promptly for patients actively under treatment. I should be able to contact you in a few days to set up a definite appointment. Once I call you there won't be any further delay in your appointment. When do you prefer your appointment, in the morning, or afternoon?"

Once the patient has been told of your policy, use projected appointments for them (explained below).

USING A "SHORT-NOTICE" CALL LIST

A short notice call list is a list of patients who may come for appointments on very short notice. Such a list is easy to compile and will prove useful for filling the schedule at the last minute when changes occur unexpectedly.

Tips:

1. When you appoint patients, ask them whether they'd like to come in earlier if a schedule change occurs.

2. Keep a list of those patients who'd like to be called on short notice. As well, you may have some names on this list of patients who have broken several appointments (and to whom you do not wish to schedule another appointment.) And, you may need to put some patients on this list if your appointment book is filled too far ahead.

3. On your list, record the phone number where each person can be reached, what days of the week and time of day would be most convenient, and approximately how long it will take them to get to your office.

4. Ideally, there should be a smooth flow of patients from the call list to the appointment schedule. Take the names in order except when the next name on the list is not available during the newly opened time. In that case, the appointment should go to the next name on your list.

5. Obviously, you can't put a patient on your call list who has an emergency or urgency, or for some other reason needs to see you at a certain time. Don't use the list if you believe a delay will hurt your relationship with the patient or your quality of care. As well, don't put first-time patients on your call list. Making them wait for a first appointment may encourage them to go elsewhere, since they have no relationship with you yet and may be anxious to receive professional care.

6. Monitor your call list. If you use it often, explore ways to expand your practice. For example, you might add extra staff or an office manager to take over more administrative duties. Or, you might hire an associate or paraprofessional to help handle your case load, or invite a new partner to join you.

USING PROJECTED APPOINTMENTS

Projected appointments help free up a fully-booked appointment schedule, and are most useful for patients under regular treatment/services. In essence, your appointment secretary would actually book and tell the patient about only one or two appointments at a time, and enter later appointments in the book on a tentative, or "projected" basis.

Example: If Ms. Green has a confirmed appointment for Thursday, July 22, your secretary can project one for her on Tuesday, August 3. That way, if it turns out that Mr. White requires an appointment at the time already projected for Ms. Green, your secretary can switch her projected appointment, and she'll never even know about it. As the time approaches for Ms. Green's next appointment, have your secretary confirm it with her and project the next one.

DOCTOR'S STUDY TIME AND PREFERENCES

One of the keys to controlling the appointment book is that the doctor make clear what he wants from it. Before you schedule any appointments, block out time in the appointment book for the doctor's study time. Every doctor needs this time in the office to read, prepare treatment plans, do research, and gather materials for thorough case presentations. If the doctor takes the case work home, he is taking away personal time and trying to do important work at the end of a long, busy day. It is usually more efficient and productive to use office time for these tasks.

Another important aspect to consider is the doctor's preferences for performing various procedures. Each of us has peak times that would be best for the most difficult or challenging patients and procedures. Most doctors like to avoid appointments that may cause excessive strain late in the day when everyone is understandably tired. Thus, each doctor should review a list of the most common services and procedures he provides, and note what time of day is preferred for each one.

As well, the doctor should decide how he'd like the rhythm of his day to be scheduled. For example, he may like the morning to be sectioned into only a few longer appointments, and the afternoon into many shorter ones. Or, he may want a mix throughout the day.

Finally, the doctor should page through the appointment book several months in advance and mark out those days which he expects to be out of the office for meetings, vacations, and holidays, as well as staff meetings and retreats.

AVOIDING HOLES IN THE APPOINTMENT SCHEDULE

To avoid "air holes," schedule appointments from noon backwards in the morning, and from noon forwards in the afternoon. That way, you'll fill late morning and early afternoon appointments first, gradually filling the earlier and later spaces.

In this way, if the entire morning doesn't fill, the doctor can come in later, or use the time productively for a staff meeting or project. An idle half hour trapped in the middle of appointments is more apt to be wasted.

USING SYMBOLS IN THE APPOINTMENT BOOK

Symbols enable you to keep your appointment book or computer record neat, orderly, and easy to read. With them, you can record a great deal of information about each patient in minimal space. While it doesn't matter which symbols you use, it is important that they are used consistently so they'll be interpreted the same way by all team members.

To help you get started, here are some commonly used appointment book symbols:

• A "T" after the patient's name indicates a tentative (projected) appointment which the patient is not aware of.

• A "T" is turned into an inverted triangle after the patient is informed of the appointment.

• A dollar sign ($) means that you must make financial arrangements or an overdue account at the appointment.

• An emergency patient's name is written in red pencil.

• A new patient examination is written in blue pencil.

• All other appointments are written in black pencil.

• An arrow below the patient's name shows the length of the appointment.

• A "C" means the patient has confirmed the appointment.

• An "L" means a laboratory fabrication or test result is due. A circled "L" means it has arrived.

• NP stands for New Patient.

• A red dot before a name means the patient is a poor payer. This person should be advised of the charge before treatment begins.

PROTECTING YOUR APPOINTMENT BOOK

When a Midwest dentist's office was destroyed by fire, he was fortunate to have planned ahead and fireproofed his clinical records. As well, the computer billing service had taken steps to ensure that billing and financial data weren't lost. However, the appointment book was destroyed, causing chaos for several weeks.

Tip: Place your appointment book or computer file in a fireproof vault every night.

Once you've used up your appointment book, don't discard it. It may be valuable evidence down the road in the event that you're sued for malpractice.

C·H·A·P·T·E·R 2-2

Advanced Methods for Staying on Schedule

A productive day that goes according to schedule doesn't just happen, but must be carefully orchestrated. Of course, good appointment planning (pages 61–67) and firm policies for dealing with no-shows, broken appointments, and late patients (pages 75–82) are the essentials. But there are many other things you can do to ensure that you stay on schedule.

AVOIDING UNNECESSARY INTERRUPTIONS

The telephone is the greatest interruption and time-waster in most practices. Taking calls during appointments not only can throw off your schedule, but it can make the patient you're treating feel inconvenienced and resentful.

The best way to avoid being interrupted by phone calls (yet still receive necessary calls) is to develop a priority list for screening calls, and to train your telephone receptionist to use it carefully. To do this, prepare the following three lists:

1. *"Put through immediately":* Make this list as short as possible. Your spouse, children, parents, and colleagues might go on this list. However, train your receptionist to ask these individuals if it is absolutely necessary that you be interrupted when they call.

Emergencies and urgencies should go on this list, as you define them. Prepare a list of questions your receptionist should ask to help identify emergencies. (For specific procedures, see, "Scheduling Emergencies," pages 62–63.)

2. *"Take message for doctor to call back":* This list should include all other callers who require your attention.

3. *"Receptionist (or other staff) to handle":* Routine matters about appointment scheduling, billing, financial arrangements, etc. should be handled by members of your staff.

Establish telephone call-back periods in your schedule, perhaps one in the morning and one in the afternoon. Have your receptionist take messages and tell callers that you will call them back during that period (or that someone else will call them back with an answer to their question, if it is a simple one.) Then, try your best not to pick up the telephone at any other time, except for emergencies.

Tip: Make it an ironclad policy that you will not speak to sales representatives during patient hours. If one calls or appears without a scheduled appointment, insist that he come at a more convenient time.

Obviously, in order for your call-back period to go smoothly, it is important that your receptionist take complete, accurate messages for you, including each caller's name, phone number, and questions or concern. When appropriate, she should pull the patient's chart, lab results, etc., in preparation for your calling back.

WHEN YOU ARE LATE: HOW TO SHOW PATIENTS THAT YOU RESPECT THEIR TIME

No matter how well organized you are, schedule delays occur from time to time. It's *how* you handle them that makes the difference to patients. If you show patients you respect their time, chances are they will reciprocate by understanding when you're behind schedule. And, they will continue to show up on time for their appointments. (If you keep patients waiting, they may decide to retaliate by keeping *you* waiting.)

Try the following strategies the next time you're running unavoidably late:

1. Have your assistant apologize and give patients frequent updates on what's happening. If you're really backed up, call patients while they're still at home or work to warn them about the delay. Don't ever fabricate stories or blame made-up emergencies. However, offer reasonable and accurate explanations if they will help.

2. Suggest that patients use their waiting time to run errands, or offer to reschedule appointments.

Tip: Practices located in shopping centers sometimes have electronic beepers on hand to lend to patients who are waiting for an appointment (or waiting to pick up someone else who has an appointment, such as a child). That way, they can run an errand in the shopping center and be "beeped" a few minutes before the doctor is ready to see them.

3. Personally apologize for the delay when *you* finally see the patient.

It can be very annoying for the patient to wait and have it go unnoticed and unappreciated by you.

4.   When patients have waited a very long time or have to reschedule, follow up with a note of apology. If you've really goofed, send a small gift with your note—flowers, a gift certificate, or a magazine subscription.

Tip: When you've fallen behind without an emergency, take a hard look at your scheduling system. Occasional bad days are one thing, but a pattern of them means you aren't allowing enough time per patient, or you're wasting time.

MAKE PATIENTS VALUE THEIR APPOINTMENTS

You can prevent many problems with schedule changes and last-minute cancellations if you help your patients *appreciate* the fact that they're getting convenient appointments. Here's how:

1.   When a patient says, "Can we do this on Thursday, my day off," don't just say "sure" right away. Instead,

2.   Try answering him by asking, "Would you *like* us to do it on Thursday, your day off?"

That way, you'll get a verbal *commitment* from the patient. After he says "yes," you can appoint him, emphasizing that he *wanted* the appointment.

Tip: When scheduling appointments, ask every patient for his preferences. *Example:* "Which is better for you, morning or afternoon?" or "Which would be better, Tuesday at 11:00 or Friday at 3:30?" After the patient states his preference, appoint him, and say, "Very good. We like to be sure patients get appointments at the times they want most."

HOW TO HANDLE THE PATIENT WHO *ALWAYS* THROWS OFF YOUR SCHEDULE

Over time, you may find that despite all your efforts, certain patients are apt to throw a wrench into your schedule. If so, you must take steps to limit these patients' opportunities:

1.   Don't be afraid to tell a talkative patient that you have another patient waiting, after you've answered all of his questions. If you know you have trouble cutting off a particular patient, instruct your business assistant to interrupt you and call you away from him. Arrange a secret signal for such an interruption.

2.   Identify patients who routinely request last-minute rest room stops before appointments. Have your assistant call these patients aside a few minutes before you're ready and say, "The doctor is very busy today and we're working extra hard to keep on schedule. If you need to make a phone call or perhaps use the rest room, we'd appreciate it if you'd do so before your appointment begins." Be sure your assistant uses tact and doesn't let other patients overhear this conversation.

3.   Avoid having patients ask to use the rest room during the appointment. Have your assistant notify every patient who's scheduled for more than one hour of treatment that a lengthy appointment is planned. Have her suggest that they get a drink of water, make a phone call, use the rest room, etc., before treatment begins.

4.   If a valued patient is routinely late for appointments, do everything possible to get him to come in on time. When all else fails, a central Pennsylvania doctor suggests that you tell him his appointment is earlier than it actually is. That way, when he arrives late, he'll actually be on time, he says. (For more information, see the last tip on page 80.)

Tip: Don't appoint traditionally late patients first thing in the morning. If they're late, you may have trouble getting your entire day back on track.

GETTING TO THE ROOT OF YOUR TIME
MANAGEMENT PROBLEMS

Sometimes, the problems doctors have staying on schedule are not caused by patients or the appointment book, but by other things (including bad habits). These need to be identified and eliminated:

1.   Streamline your physical plant work to make it work efficiently. Take a critical look at your exam room and private office. Are they set up so you can find things you need easily and quickly, with a minimum of steps and fuss?

Tip: It saves time and effort to clone your same-purpose examination rooms. You can be most efficient if equipment and supplies are always in the same place in every room.

2.   Are you delegating everything you might? For example, do you make your own financial arrangements with patients? Schedule appointments? Open and sort the mail? These are tasks that can and should be done by a member of your staff.

3.   Do you have problems managing your time wisely? Do you procrastinate or have trouble getting everything done? (For more information on time

management, see, "85 Ways to Save Time and Increase Your Personal Productivity," pages 483–488.

4.   Does a member of your staff waste your time with unnecessary interruptions? Establish availability hours, and insist that non-emergency staff matters be discussed then.

How to Keep Last-Minute Cancellations, No-Shows, and Chronically Late Patients from Crippling Your Practice

Patients who repeatedly miss their appointments or arrive late can cost your practice thousands of dollars every year. In addition, the chronically late or absent patient can ruin your office appointment schedule, if you let him, causing you and your staff to be rushed, stressed—or idle. For these reasons, every practice needs to enforce a strict policy about no-shows, cancellations, and late patients.

WHO'S RUNNING YOUR APPOINTMENT SCHEDULE?

Right now, how do you handle patients who cancel appointments, show up late, or don't show at all? In fact, DO you have an actual policy for each of these cases? Or do your *patients* control your appointment book? Specifically:

1. What, if anything, do you do to encourage appointment breakers to be more cooperative?

2. Why do your patients break their appointments? Do you try to find out and do something about it?

3. Do you give patients compelling reasons to keep their appointments? Do they know you care whether they show up on time?

4. Do you issue a firm yet sensitive response to the patient the first time he misses an appointment or arrives late?

5. How do you handle patients who *repeatedly* miss appointments or arrive late? Where, if anywhere, do you draw the line with chronic offenders?

6. Do you allow late patients to ruin your appointment schedule for the rest of your patients?

NINE REASONS PATIENTS MISS APPOINTMENTS AND HOW TO PREVENT THEM

There are logical reasons patients miss appointments or show up late. Do you take a preventative approach by uncovering the real reasons, and working against them? Or, like many practices, do you *encourage* poor attendance by aggravating patients' fears, pet peeves, and anxieties?

Each patient is different, but most are driven by the same things. In general, patients miss appointments or arrive late because:

1.   *They are afraid.* Some practices are particularly prone to a fearful patient response. Horror stories, past bad experiences, and human nature all play a natural role in fear. Are you now doing all you can to minimize patients' fears?

For example, do you tell patients what to expect in advance of their appointments? Do you avoid clinical or frightening words whenever possible? Does your decor put patients at ease? (For more fear control techniques, see "Dealing with the Anxious or Fearful Patient," pages 359–365.)

2.   *They owe you money.* Patients behind on their payments may not show up because they're embarrassed about the debt. Or, they may simply fear your criticism. Do you make fair, firm financial arrangements patients can live up to? (For more suggestions on making financial arrangements, see "Making Firm but Fair Financial Arrangements with Patients," pages 113–119.)

3.   *They don't appreciate the need for the appointment.* "See you in six months," is not much of a motivator to keep an appointment, especially when the patient is feeling fine in six months and is busy or short on cash. Do your patients understand and appreciate the importance of your routine exams? Follow-up care? Regular treatment?

Well-organized case presentations, support literature, and the right words from your staff can all help your patients appreciate the value of your services. This, in turn, will motivate them to keep their appointments.

4.   *They aren't seen on time.* Patients routinely kept waiting may feel that it's only fair to keep *you* waiting. Or they may reason that by arriving late, they won't have to wait as they usually do.

5.   *They committed to the appointment too far in advance.* Do you know what you're doing 17 weeks from this Thursday at 2:45? Probably not. And probably, your patients don't either. That's why it makes sense to keep your appointment book open, so you're not fully booked months ahead. In a very-busy practice, this can be accomplished only through radical change—a new associate, expanding hours, etc.

6. *They're short on cash.* In a cash-only practice, patients who don't have the cash the day of the appointment may not show up. That's why it makes sense to offer a choice of payment plans and methods. For more information on this subject, see, "Making Firm but Fair Financial Arrangements with Patients," pages 113–119.

7. *They couldn't schedule a convenient time for the appointment.* Evening, weekend, and after-school hours are usually in high demand. It makes sense to reserve prime times like these for patients who absolutely can't make it at any other time. For example, if you can't accommodate all the children in your practice during after-school hours, you might reserve that time for students with poor grades, so they don't have to miss classroom time.

Tip: To help patients schedule convenient appointments, try offering them a *choice. Example:* "Which would be better, Tuesday at 10:15 or Thursday at 3:30?" Or, "Which would be more convenient, morning or afternoon?"

If many patients complain of scheduling inconveniences, re-think your workday. Many practices now open very early in the morning, to accommodate working patients before they have to be at work.

8. *They didn't know how much notice you need to cancel an appointment.* Most offices will need 24–48 hours to fill an empty appointment slot. Decide how much notice you need, and publicize it with a sign, in your practice brochure and verbally, when patients make appointments.

9. *Patients feel you don't care if they keep appointments or show up on time.* This can happen when a patient arrives late, and no one seems to notice. He may get the message that since no one cared, it's OK to be late next time. Or, maybe he won't bother to show up at all.

Do you reinforce patients who arrive on time? Do you consciously publicize the importance of keeping appointments in your practice brochure, newsletter, signs, and when you meet the new patient at the first appointment?

HOW TO HANDLE FIRST-TIME OFFENDERS

Anyone could have a legitimate, forgivable reason to miss or be late for one appointment. We are human, after all, and we will make mistakes, or have to deal with circumstances beyond our control. For this reason, most practices go relatively easy on first-time offenders. However, you should never let an absence or tardiness go completely unnoticed.

Below, missed appointments are divided into three categories. Each first-time offender should be handled differently:

1. *Cancelled appointments:* A cancellation occurs when the patient calls and gives your appointment secretary adequate notice of changing the appointment. Most practices need 24–48 hours to schedule another patient for the open appointment.

When a patient calls to cancel within the specified time, your receptionist should thank him for giving adequate notice. Then, reschedule the appointment by saying, "Let me reschedule the appointment for you now."

Tip: Don't ask, "May I reschedule the appointment?" or "Would you like to reschedule the appointment now?" That gives the patient an easy way to refuse.

2. *Broken appointments:* A patient breaks an appointment when he calls to tell you he's not going to make it, but *not* in adequate time. The first time this happens, have your receptionist ask for a reason. Then respond according to what the patient says.

Example: If a highly valued patient says he's tied up at work, you might simply say "It happens," and let it go at that. If he says his car won't start, offer to pick him up or send him a cab. Or if he calls to say he's sick, say you're sorry, and send him a get-well card.

These are strong but appropriate responses that give the message that the patient is important to you. Receiving a get-well card or a free ride would make the patient feel wonderful if he's telling the truth, and deservedly guilty if he's lying to you. And that might make him think twice about lying next time.

For firmer action with the first-time offender, say something along these lines: "This time we can reschedule the appointment for you without charge. We'd normally like ____hours notice so we can give your appointment to another patient who is waiting to see the doctor." Afterwards, your assistant would alter the patient's ledger card and monthly statement to say:

For reserved time (date), no charge this time.

3. *No-Shows:* A no-show is a patient who neither calls ahead nor shows up. Call the no-show within *five minutes* of the appointed time to find out why he failed to show up. Waiting longer accomplishes nothing, and may give the patient the impression that you didn't notice his absence right away, or care about it.

Again, your response will depend upon what you learn. For example, suppose the patient says he never intended to show up, and didn't bother to let you know. In such a case, let the patient know firmly thay such behavior can't be tolerated. Tell him you need 24–48 hour notice, and why. If you reach him early enough and it makes sense, ask him to come to your office immediately so you can do at least part of what you'd planned to do during the appointment.

For added impact, you might tell the thoughtless no-show that you can reschedule without charge this time. Then note the incident on the patient's ledger card and statement. You might add that because he didn't give you enough notice, the time couldn't be used for other patients who were waiting for an appointment with the doctor.

Now suppose you come across a well-meaning no-show who simply goofed or was a victim of circumstance. This patient just plain forgot, even though he's never done so before. Or, maybe he didn't show up because of personal tragedy, like an automobile accident. Or let's suppose the patient's car broke down on the way to your office, or he was stuck in traffic or a snowstorm, and not near a phone. In all of these cases, it's wise to go easy.

Be understanding when the patient goofs. Express your concern when something happens to prevent him from keeping the appointment. Forgive him. Be enthusiastic about rescheduling the appointment. And of course, send a condolence or get well wish to the bereaved or recovering patient.

If you can't reach the no-show by phone, send him a letter within a day along these lines:

Dear Mrs. Patient:

You were scheduled for an appointment on *(date)* which you did not keep. We have been unable to reach you by phone, and are beginning to become quite concerned about you.

We want to be sure that you are all right, and of course, we'd like to complete your examination/treatment as soon as possible. Will you please call us today?

4. *Late appointments:* Your receptionist should acknowledge at once that the patient is late for his appointment. *Example:* "I'm sorry you were delayed today. Dr. Patterson expected to complete X, Y, and Z for you this morning, but since you were late, he may not have time to do everything he'd planned."

Your next step will depend upon how late the patient is and what you'd planned to do. In some cases, you'll have time to do a portion of what you'd planned. In others, you won't have time to see the patient at all. When that happens, schedule another appointment. And, as in the above examples, note on the patient's ledger card and statement that you're not charging for the missed appointment.

Important: It is a poor practice to throw off your entire appointment schedule, and see on-time patients late, to accommodate the late patient. Except in the case of an emergency, it is best to reschedule the late patient, and keep the rest of your day intact.

Tip: Some practices schedule appointments with teenagers who come on their own, without a parent. If such a patient is late or misses an appointment, call his parents at once, to find out if he's all right. These days, anything can happen to a kid, and your quick response can be a big help. If the child simply forgot, reinforce the value of the appointment. Then mail a reminder slip for the next appointment *to the parents.* If the child misses another appointment, ask that the parent to accompany him on the next visit.

THE REPEAT OFFENDER

The patient who repeatedly misses or is late for appointments requires firmer action. Ask your appointment secretary to notify you the second and subsequent times a patient cancels, breaks, doesn't show, or is late for an appointment.

Only *you* can decide how many offenses you'll allow before taking firm action. Many practices use a "three strikes and you're out" policy, allowing three offenses without consequences. Some allow only two strikes, others four or five. The number of strikes is not as important as the "out." At some point, there must be consequences.

Firmer action will ultimately be unavoidable and necessary. When you've exhausted all other possibilities, you may need to have your appointment secretary say something like this to the chronic offender:

> Your schedule doesn't seem to allow you to be on time (keep scheduled appointment). Please give us a call when your schedule does allow it and we'll make an appointment then.

You can then put the patient on your short-notice call list. If he insists he'll be on time or keep his appointments from now on, you may decide to let him make one more appointment. If so, tell the patient that *he* must call *you* by noon on the day before the appointment to confirm or you'll give the appointment to someone else. As always, promises such as this one require follow through.

Tip: One Pennsylvania dental practice employs the three-strikes-and-your-out policy, but reports one glaring exception—a highly valued patient who is *always* a half hour late. Rather than getting tough, they've worked around the problem by telling this patient her appointments are half an hour earlier than they actually are. That way, she arrives on time, even though she thinks she's half an hour late.

HARD TACTICS FOR THE CHRONIC OFFENDER

Some practices charge the chronic offender for broken appointments. However, such action, while seemingly fair, is usually best avoided.

For one thing, a nominal charge won't compensate you for the missed appointment. A small fee is usually little deterrent, and may backfire. The patient may justify not showing up, claiming it was worth the charge, and that now you're even.

Second, missed appointment fees are usually very hard to collect. The expense and effort involved in collection letters, calls, or a collection agency is usually worth much more than the small sum.

Finally, patients may be angered by the missed appointment charge and retaliate. For example, they may not pay their bills. Or, they may bring a retaliatory lawsuit against you, claiming to be dissatisfied with your care.

If you do charge for missed appointments, give patients ample warning that you'll do so, and administer the charge only when the patient leaves you no alternative. As well, levy this charge uniformly, without fail, or a discrimination suit could be brought against you. (The patient could argue that the charge is discriminatory if other patients guilty of the same offense are *not* charged.)

DISMISSING THE CHRONIC OFFENDER

When all else fails, you may have no choice but to dismiss the chronic offender. There are only so many times you can allow a patient to make an appointment and not show. Ultimately, you've got to put your foot down.

Dismissal of a patient must be done formally and legally. Basically, there are two scenarios:

1. *If you never saw the patient:* Your assistant may tell him simply that no further appointments will be scheduled for him in your office. Interesting: One Midwest doctor reports that a troubled teenager in his practice was scheduling appointments for a fictional patient, who of course never showed. While this is unusual, you may encounter a real new patient who for one reason or another, never quite makes it into your office, despite several attempts.

2. *If you **have** seen the patient:* Dismissal should be done via a letter from you sent by certified mail, return receipt requested. This letter should

be drawn up or reviewed by your attorney, especially in cases where the patient was in the midst of active treatment, or was known to have a condition warranting treatment. Proof of the missed appointments and your efforts to see the patient will be valuable evidence that you didn't abandon him. Therefore, note all missed appointments, log all phone calls, and keep copies of letters to patients regarding broken, no-show or late appointments.

HOW TO DOCUMENT MISSED APPOINTMENTS

Many practices use a pre-printed form like this one to record missed, broken, cancelled, and late appointments:

Name: _____   Date: _____   Form   # _____

_____ No-Show. Missed the appointment without notice.
_____ Broken appointment. Called _____ hours ahead.
_____ Cancelled appointment.
_____ Late for appointment by _____ minutes.
_____ Rescheduled for _____ .
_____ Did not reschedule.
Who contacted the patient?_____
How:_____
When:_____
What happened?_____

To make this system run smoothly:

1.   Print the form on colored paper so it will stand out in the patient's file.

2.   Staple to the form a copy of any correspondence related to the missed appointment that you send the patient.

3.   Within each patient's file, number the forms starting with *1* in the upper right-hand corner. That way, you'll know at a glance whether it's the patient's first, fifth, or tenth offense.

C·H·A·P·T·E·R   2-4

Setting Up and Maintaining a Recall System that Works

Do you recall your patients at regular intervals for periodic examinations? Dental, optometric, gynecology, and many other practices that depend on recall find that a high recall success rate is important not only for the patient's sake, but also for the practice's referral rate.

Active patients seen regularly in a recall-based practice are most likely to be satisfied with that practice. And, in turn, it is satisfied, active patients who are most apt to refer *new* patients.

Tip: According to one consultant's study of dental practices, it takes an average of eight active recall patients to generate one new patient through referral each year. That means that a dental practice with 2,000 patients of record and a 70% recall success rate can expect 175 new patients per year through patient referrals. If such a practice can increase its recall success rate by only 10%, it can expect 25 *additional* new patients per year!

If patients don't come in for their regular periodic recall exams, something is probably wrong, either with the patient's satisfaction or circumstances, or more likely, with the practice's recall communication process. Below, we explore practical suggestions for increasing your recall success rate without twisting patients' arms (or making your staff miserable).

MOTIVATING PATIENTS TO
KEEP RECALL APPOINTMENTS

Patient motivation is the key to increasing recall effectiveness. When the office is busy and you've got a dozen other things to do, it may be tempting to tell patients simply that they're due to return in x months for a "check-up" or some such thing, and leave it at that. However, patients will rarely be motivated for recall if you use such a casual approach. *Motivate* patients to schedule and keep regular appointments in the following ways:

1.   When you tell the patient that he is due for a recall appointment, indicate a specific *reason* for that appointment. If at all possible, refer to an aspect of the patient's treatment or services.

Example: Here's the kind of motivational script a dental assistant might use when calling a patient to schedule her recall appointment:

> Hello, Mrs. Campbell. This is Stephanie Tucker from Family Dental Center. Dr. McNamara asked me to call you today to schedule an appointment. As he recommended when he saw you in February, you will want to see him this month so you can have your teeth cleaned and your mouth examined. He also plans to check the margin on your crown during your appointment.

Additional motivational reasons a dental assistant might suggest that the patient is due for recall:

- Check the result of periodontal treatment.
- Check the progress of fissures or beginning decay.
- Observe the tissue condition under full dentures.
- Watch teeth which are particularly susceptible to decay.
- Examine the partial denture abutments.
- Check amalgam or inlay margins.
- Check fixed bridges.
- Observe how the patient is doing with the prescribed home care regimen.
- Check occlusion or restorations.
- Review cosmetic dentistry options.

Tip: Many practices develop a checklist of common reasons for recall, like those above. If you're shopping for a computer, look for one that allows you to assign a reason each patient should return for recall, preferably with a code number or letter. With these reasons coded into your system, you'll be able to generate personalized recall notices quickly and easily.

2.   The language you use when discussing recall with patients often influences how they feel about it and their level of motivation. Be sure that you don't actually use the word *recall* with patients. It has a negative connotation. (People often think of defective merchandise being "recalled" by a man-

ufacturer.) More positive terminology: periodic examination, re-examination, re-evaluation, regular appointment, follow-up appointment, regular or follow-up visit, continuous care.

3.   Also consider some of the other words and phrases that can enhance (or destroy) patient motivation during discussions of recall. For example, you'll be much more motivational if:

Your Assistant Says:	Instead of:
"You'll *want* to see the doctor."	"You'll *have* to see the doctor."
"The doctor asked me to call you today to schedule an appointment."	"You're due for an appointment." Or, "It's time for your check-up."

4.   Patients who are *prepared* or *conditioned* for recall in advance are more likely to make and keep recall appointments. Before the patient leaves your office, be sure to tell him when and how you'll be contacting him to schedule his recall appointment. Explain that you'll call him (or drop him a note) when he'll want to see the doctor again, and once again, *why* he'll want the recall appointment.

5.   Tell patients the *month* they're going to be called (or written to) for recall, not just the number of months. For example, say, "You'll want to see us again *in February,*" not "You'll want to see us again in *six months.*" Linking recall to the name of a month is a mnemonic device that motivates better recall. It gives the patient a verbal cue that will remind him when it's time for his recall appointment.

6.   Take this idea a step further. If possible, link the recall appointment to a specific, easy-to-remember *date* or *event.* For example: "You'll want to see us again . . .

   —in mid-February, right after Valentine's Day."
   —in June, right after school lets out."
   —in November, sometime around Thanksgiving."

Tying recall to these kinds of occasions will make it easy for the patient to remember when he needs to see you. This will prepare him better for your recall reminder notice or call. In some cases, the date or event will jog the patient's memory and motivate him to call *you* to schedule his appointment.

7.   When you call the patient to schedule his recall appointment, do not ask him whether he'd *like* to make an appointment. That gives him the chance to say *no.* Motivate him to recall by phrasing it as a *choice* of appointments.

Example: Your assistant might say:

> . . . and you will want to see the doctor this month so you can have *x*, *y*, and *z* examined. Would you prefer an appointment in the morning or the afternoon?
>
> or
>
> . . . Dr. Edmonson will be able to see you next Tuesday, the 23rd, at 9:45 in the morning, or on Thursday, the 25th, at 2:00 in the afternoon. Which appointment is more convenient?

Tip: Place recall calls at times when you're most likely to find the patient in and receptive. Many practices find that the best times to call patients are 4:30–5:30 in the afternoon, in the early evening after the dinner hour, and on Saturday. However, be sure to respect each patient's particular wishes. (For example, some may ask you not to call them at work, others may work at night and prefer not to be called in the morning, etc.)

8. Publicize your recall program. For example, you might write about the value of recall appointments in your practice brochure and patient newsletter. Or, you might introduce recall and its importance at your get-acquainted meeting with new patients. Through your publicity efforts, describe what you do at the typical recall appointment. Explain how serious problems can be detected and caught early at recall exams, even ones that patients themselves may not be aware of.

9. Keep recall fees relatively competitive. Besides fees for the initial exam and emergenices, your recall fee is most likely to be discussed by patients and compared with friends' doctors' fees.

Tip: If your recall fee is reasonable, patients will often assume that *all* of your fees are reasonable, and be less likely to compare or challenge them. For more information on this subject, see "Basic Guidelines for Structuring Your Fees," pages 107–108.

MOTIVATING STAFF TO INCREASE YOUR RECALL SUCCESS RATE

Many practices establish recall incentives for the staff, especially for the assistant who calls patients to schedule recall appointments. Typically, the assistant is paid a small cash bonus for each patient who makes a recall appointment (beyond an established goal).

Tip: While it can be a good strategy to give your staff an incentive to improve your recall rate, don't make the incentive too high. When large sums are at stake, staff may be tempted to put undue pressure on patients to make recall appointments.

NINE WAYS TO MAKE YOUR RECALL NOTICES
MORE EFFECTIVE

Are you dissatisfied with the success of your mail recall efforts? If so, take a look at the letter or postcard you're sending to patients. Is it as motivational as it can possibly be? Some tips that may increase your response:

1. Sign the letter. A signature makes it seem much more personal and motivational than a note sent anonymously, even if it is obviously a form letter.

Tip: The doctor's signature usually pulls the best response. However, in many cases, an assistant's signature will do just as well, and will save the doctor's time.

2. Attribute the idea of the notice to the doctor.
Example: Your assistant might write:

Dr. Langston asked me to send you this note . . . .

3. Remind the patient that he already knows that he needs the appointment:

As Dr. Langston recommended to you at your last appointment, you'll want to see him this month to . . . .

4. Write an explanation for the appointment. If you use a standard recall notecard, you might want to print a blank line or two so you can write in the reason for each patient.

5. Enclose an informative brochure or pamphlet concerning some aspect of your treatment or services. A brochure that describes the dangers of neglecting a problem, or of an attractive and potentially beneficial service, for example, could provide good motivation for a patient to call and make an appointment.

6. Tell the patient to call a specific person in your practice directly, giving her name and phone number or extension. This sometimes motivates a better response than a vague invitation to "Call our office to schedule an appointment."

7. Jazz up the appearance of your recall notecards so they'll be more easily spotted and remembered.
Example: You might send extra-large cards in a bright color. Or, you might put reminders on small pressure-sensitive labels that patients can stick on their calendars.

8. If possible, ask patients to address their own cards during their last appointments. (They'll be more apt to notice a card that's addressed in their

own handwriting. This, in turn, may help them remember that you've already discussed the need for this appointment.)

9.   Make the recall notice itself valuable.

Example: Let the recall card serve as an entry blank in a contest drawing. Patients who bring the card to their appointments can drop it in a fishbowl and be eligible for a prize. Then draw one card (or several) each month to establish the winner(s). Publicize the contest, winners, and prizes on your office bulletin board and in your patient newsletter.

Tip: Along similar lines, you might explain on the card that the patient may present it at his appointment and automatically receive a free gift. These can be pens, refrigerator magnets, pocket calendars, or other similar inexpensive items.

DILIGENT FOLLOW-UP IS ESSENTIAL

The patient may not be able to schedule his recall appointment when your assistant calls him. He may have to consult his calendar, secretary, or spouse to see when he's free for an appointment. If so, it's important not to leave things so *he* will get back to you. If you do, the patient will have little motivation to call you back in a hurry.

Tip: Motivate patients to get the appointment scheduled as soon as possible. Have your assistant review the importance of the appointment, and what you are planning to do. Instruct your assistant to agree on a time when *she* will call *the patient* again to schedule the appointment.

If your written recall notice asks the patient to call you to schedule an appointment, be sure he calls for the appointment promptly. Otherwise, your recall assistant should follow up and call him. A tickler file will help.

Tip: A recall reminder notice loses its motivational value if a long time elapses between the notice and an attmept to schedule the appointment.

If a patient objects to scheduling a recall appointment, have your assistant try to find out the reason and turn around objections. For example, if the patient says he doesn't have the money right then, she might outline your financial options. If the patient says he's doing fine and doesn't need a checkup, she might review the clinical reasons for recall, stressing hidden dangers.

Tip: If a patient has switched doctors or still objects for other reasons, follow up personally with a letter or call, to try to rectify any misunderstanding. For more information on this subject, see, "Bringing the Inactive Patient Back to the Fold," pages 367–370.

MANUAL CARD METHOD SIMPLIFIES
RECALL RECORDS

A computerized practice will have a program available for tracking recall appointments. However, if you're not fully automated, here's an excellent manual system for organizing your recall records:

1.   Design a 3 × 5-inch recall card to be used for each of your patients who is to be recalled. On this card, leave room for the patient's name and phone number, particular reasons for recall (if they exist), and the date he's to be recalled. Also leave spaces to record the results of the contact:

_____ Set appointment for: _____*(Date and time)*_____.
_____ Call again: _____*(Date and time)*_____.

2.   *Never* allow yourself or your staff to place these cards in the patients' record. They'll have absolutely no value to your recall efforts there.

3.   When treatment is completed, complete a card for the patient. On it, note what should be checked at the next recall and the approximate month (and date) for that appointment.

Tip: Also note (in pencil) the month of the next recall on the patients' folder. That way, even if the patient returns before the next scheduled recall, you'll know where to find his card in your recall file. Thus, you can make necessary adjustments on it.

4.   Keep recall cards in a file tray with twelve-month divisions. File the completed cards alphabetically behind the month in which the patient is due to be called to make his recall appointment.

5.   During the last ten days of each month, remove cards for patients to be called the next month. Have your assistant determine the number of working days in that month and divide the recall cards evenly among them.

Tip: The task will be much more manageable if she plans to call roughly the same number of patients each day.

6.   After she calls the patient, have her write the appointment date and time on the card and in the appointment book. Then, she can place the card behind the confirmed date in another file with divisions numbered one through 31.   Hold the card there until the recall appointment.

Tip: If your assistant can't make an appointment when she calls, she should record the reason and refile the card under the date she's going to call him again. If the patient refuses to make a recall appointment, she should note the reason on the card, and give it to you so you can follow up personally.

C · H · A · P · T · E · R   2-5

How to Tame the Telephone "Beast"

Your office telephone can be one of the biggest abusers of your time and energy, if it is not properly handled. In addition, a poorly mangaged telephone can alienate patients and colleagues, and lead to other more serious management problems.

Like the vast majority of practice management problems, the key to good telephone management is in managing the telephone, rather than allowing it to manage you.

SEVEN NEVER-FAIL STRATEGIES FOR SAVING TIME ON THE PHONE

1.   Cut calls short when you've finished. Some graceful yet effective end remarks:

Have I answered all your questions?

I have to go now. Is there anything else we need to cover?

Just one more thing before we hang up.

2.   Set the stage for short calls at the onset:

I want to give this the attention it deserves. Let me call you back tonight.

I have three quick questions for you.

Nice to hear from you. What can I do for you today?

3.   Set times each day when you're available to non-emergency non-urgency patients—and more importantly, when you're not.

4.   Anticipate calls, and call first, at the time that's best for *you*.

5.   Think before you dial the phone. Ask, "Is calling the most time-effective method of accomplishing this task?" Plan what you'll say, using a written outline.

6.   Don't mix business with pleasure calls. If a colleague starts to socialize to extreme, just say, "I'd love to talk but I'm swamped at the moment. How about lunch next week?"

7.   Log your phone calls to get an accurate assessment of your own telephone habits and time wasters.

TIPS FOR WINNING AT "TELEPHONE TAG"

If the party you call is out:

1.   Leave a detailed message of the subject of the call and the specific information you're looking for.

Exception: Never reveal sensitive or confidential information about a patient.

2.   Note the time when you'll definitely be available.

3.   Or, make a phone appointment—a definite time for a later phone call.

When you don't want the other party to call you back:

1.   Ask for a specific time when he'll be available, so you can try again. Try setting up a phone appointment.

2.   Find out if the person can be paged.

3.   Ask the secretary to relay the information or an answer you need to your secretary, keeping the bosses out of it. Or, see if someone else can help you.

FOLLOW PROPER TELEPHONE ETIQUETTE WHEN PLACING CALLS

Your practice's image is very dependent upon your staff's telephone manners when they place calls on your behalf. Some tips:

1.   Always be ready to talk when you place the call. It's discourteous to call and ask the person on the other end to hold. Have ready all the background information you need.

Tip: Choose a time and place to make your call where interruptions are unlikely.

2. Identify yourself and your practice immediately.

3. Briefly state the purpose of your call.

4. Ask: "Do you have a few minutes for us to discuss (named subject)?" If the person you're calling says he can't talk, believe him, and arrange a more convenient time to call back.

5. Choose the time of your call with the person's convenience and preferences in mind. Respect patients' wishes if they ask you not to call them at work, or during the dinner hour.

6. If you wish to speak to a patient and he's not available when you call, leave a brief message with the person who answered the phone. However, do not reveal personal and potentially confidential information about the patient, or the nature of your call. When dealing with sensitive matters, simply state your name, the practice's name, and the phone number where you may be reached.

Tip: Sometimes, indicating that the person you're leaving a message for is your patient can be considered a breach of confidence. For example, a patient may not wish others to know that he is seeking the services of a psychiatrist, psychologist, plastic surgeon, etc. When dealing with highly sensitive matters, these practices should generally omit the practice name and their profession in their messages.

HOW TO DEAL WITH A BUSY SIGNAL PROBLEM

If your patients tell you that your lines are often busy, begin by assessing the extent of your busy signal problem. When only a few callers complain of the problem, realize that many others may not feel comfortable speaking up. Thus, it's generally a good idea to conduct an annual busy signal study. Call your telephone company for more information on this.

If a busy signal problem does exist, regular additional lines are one option. However, depending upon the extent and nature of your problem, you might also consider:

• Motivating patients to call your office during your non-peak hours by listing them on statements, appointment cards, and recall notices. For example, "For fastest service, call our office after ____a.m."

• Limiting your outgoing calls as much as possible to non-peak hours. Or, install a separate line for your outgoing calls.

• Installing a separate line for billing and insurance matters. List this number on your statements, business cards, and in your practice brochure.

• Installing a separate local-call-only outgoing line for office visitors to use. This can be placed on the wall of your reception area.

• Installing a separate line for incoming calls from other professionals and laboratories.

DON'T OFFEND CALLERS WHEN TAKING MESSAGES

Your receptionist should follow these fine points of telephone message etiquette:

1.   Don't let callers believe you don't have their telephone numbers. You always want your receptionist and answering service to get the phone number of the caller. However, instruct them not to say, "Does he/she have your number?" It hurts a friend's or an established patient's ego to think that you don't recognize them, or that you might not have their numbers.

Better: Tell your receptionist/service to ask for the phone number, noting that it makes it easier to return the call when you have the number with the message.

2.   Tell your receptionist not to promise a call-back by you if you can't deliver. There will, of course, be some messages your receptionist will know you want to return personally, and soon. In those cases, she can go ahead and tell the caller that you will do so, and when. However, in all other instances, she should *not* tell the caller that *you* will call back. (Perhaps you can answer the question and have the receptionist make the call for you. Or, you may need more information from the caller.)

Better: In those cases, your receptionist should say simply that she will be sure you receive the message. If the caller requires an answer, she can promise that *she* will call back (and when) with the answer, or at least to inform him of the progress on his request.

WHEN AND HOW TO USE THE HOLD BUTTON

Of course, you and your staff should avoid putting any caller on hold. However, sometimes you just won't have any choice. Some tips when you must put someone on hold:

1.   *Give the caller a choice.* Ask if he'd prefer to hold or be called back. If the caller will hold, tell him what's going to happen. *Example:* "I'll have that information for you in a few moments." Or, "I'll transfer your call to Joan. She'll be with you in a few moments."

2.   *Don't leave the caller on hold too long.* According to one study, most people will hold for 40 seconds—no more. Another finding: If you return to

callers within 20 seconds, less than 1% will have hung up. Therefore, get back to the caller within 20 seconds to let him know you haven't forgotten him. If you need more time before you can give him the information he needs, tell him so and ask *again* if he prefers to hold or be called back.

3.   *When you return to the caller, smile, use his name, and thank him for his patience.*

Tip: Don't be put on hold yourself for long periods. Either refuse to be put on hold and call back later, or set a limit on how many minutes you'll wait. Keep paperwork handy so you won't just waste time doodling or staring into space.

TIPS FOR TELEPHONE EQUIPMENT
AND ACCESSORIES

1.   Get a telephone directory for all major cities in your geographic area.

2.   If you (or your receptionist) spend a great deal of time on the phone, buy and use a quality headset. That way, your hands will be free to do other tasks while you're talking.

3.   Use a speed-dialer, to dial automatically your most frequently called numbers.

4.   Use an automatic last-number re-dial whenever you get a busy signal.

5.   Avoid using speaker phones and cellular phones when you may need to discuss sensitive/confidential information.

HOW WELL DO YOU MANAGE YOUR PHONE?

You're not using your phone well when you:

1.   Make and return calls throughout the day, instead of in batches at specific times of the day.

2.   Don't have your non-emergency calls held when you're with a patient.

3.   Don't delegate the task of making calls that are delegable.

4.   Fail to set a time for a call-back when the person you're trying to reach isn't available.

5.   Don't ask whether the person answering the phone can help you when the person you tried to reach is unavailable.

6.   Don't have notes and other necessary papers ready when you make a call.

7.   Allow yourself to be put on hold often, or for long periods.

HOW WELL DOES YOUR RECEPTIONIST HANDLE YOUR PHONE?

Here's a little quiz to see if your receptionist's telephone technique is up to par. Her goal should be to improve until you can answer *yes* to every question. Does she:

1.   Answer the phone with a smile? (Actually smiling into the phone can create a "smiling" telephone personality.)

2.   Answer within three rings?

3.   Have a pencil and paper ready to take notes? Keep all necessary references such as charts, records, a calendar, and the appointment book handy?

4.   Start with a sincere "Good Morning" (afternoon, evening)?

5.   Identify your office?

6.   Identify herself?

7.   Ask the caller's name only after she's answered his first questions? (Otherwise, he may think the answer varies depending upon who asks the questions.) Once she knows the caller's name, does she address him by it at least once during the conversation?

8.   Speak directly into the mouthpiece? (The phone should be held about one inch from and directly in front of the lips. It should not be held under the chin as some people do.)

9.   Give the caller her full attention? (Does she put other tasks aside while she's on the phone?)

10.   Control the conversation courteously by saying "please" and "thank you" when appropriate?

11.   Thank the person for calling?

12.   Speak slowly, clearly, and distinctly? Keep her voice pitch low, calm, and even? Keep her volume moderate?

13.   Communicate a positive and professional image of your practice? ("Aahs" and "uuhs," "yups" and "nopes," do *not* communicate the right image. Neither does eating, drinking, or chewing gum while speaking on the phone.)

14.   Provide an adequate reason if the doctor or a member of the staff can't come to the phone right away?

15.   Screen callers properly to reduce unneccesary transfers and interruptions of the doctor's schedule?

16.   Tell the caller when his call will be returned and by whom?

17.   Have a thorough knowledge of your practice?

18.   Transfer calls only when necessary, and then to the correct people in your practice?

19.   Use the hold button sparingly? Ask the caller if he prefers to hold or to be called back? Get back to the caller on hold quickly— ideally within 20 seconds?

20.   Take complete telephone messages? Note any follow-up action that needs to be taken as a result of the call? (For example, she might note that she needs to send written materials to the caller, call back with needed information, or write a follow-up letter to review the points that were made during the call.)

Tip: If the calling patient expresses dissatisfaction or confusion (no matter how trivial it may seem), follow-up measures are *always* necesasry. In addition to any action the receptionist, the doctor, or any member of the staff will take, your receptionist should be extra sure to note the time, date, purpose, and recipient of the call (and the action that followed it). This documentation could become extremely valuable later, especially if the patient decides to take legal action. For more information on this subject, see "How to Respond to Patients Who Complain," pages 371–374.

21.   Make sure that the caller has obtained all the information he requested before concluding the call? (She might ask, "Was there anything else, Mrs. Blakely?")

22.   Take complete messages (including phonetic spellings of difficult names, phone numbers, the question or concern that needs to be addressed, etc.)?

23.   Transfer calls to you that are emergencies, or from individuals on your list of calls to be put through right away? Take messages for all other callers, or transfer them to someone else?

24.   Wait for the caller to hang up first?

25.   Return the receiver gently to the cradle at the end of the call or transfer?

Tip: For further telephone information for your receptionist, see "50 Questions Your Receptionist Should Be Able to Answer," pages 569–579.

C · H · A · P · T · E · R   2-6

Covering Your Phones When You're Not There

Your phone coverage when you're not in your office is extremely important, especially in the case of a patient emergency or urgency. Clear, complete, and accurate messages for you, and calm, professional assistance for your patients are a must. Obviously, this is not an area where any doctor can afford to have mistakes.

Most doctors will opt for an answering service to cover their phones. Unfortunately, some services are understaffed and/or poorly trained. Thus, most of us need to be somewhat selective when choosing a service. Then, we must supervise the service carefully, and ensure that it is providing a high quality of service to our callers.

HOW TO FIND A FIRST-RATE ANSWERING SERVICE

1. Choose a service other doctors use and recommend. With their permission, call the service when they're not there to see how you're handled, and whether your messages get through quickly and accurately.
Tip: Leave a relatively complicated message, such as one with difficult words and spellings.

2. Once you've narrowed your choices to one or two services, pay a visit to each one—without an appointment, if possible. That will give you a first-hand look at the operators in action.

As you observe, try to see if they are pleasant and polite. Do they allow the phones to ring more than three times before answering them? Do they try to be helpful to callers? Are they courteous if they must put a caller on hold to pick up another incoming call?
Tip: Remember that the operator(s) appearance is not important to the caller. If the operator's clothes or other physical attributes throw you, close your eyes and *listen* to him or her at work.

3.   Explain to the owner or supervisor exactly how you want your calls to be handled. Is the service going to be able to accommodate all of your requests?

4.   Ask the supervisor to show you how messages are stored. (Usually, each client has a folder or computer file for incoming messages.) Find out how often the folder is reviewed to be sure messages are picked up. Will the service call to relay urgent messages? How do they handle an emergency if a patient must reach you (or a colleague covering for you)?

5.   Request the names of several additional professionals who use the service. If you're still in doubt, contact these doctors to see whether or not they're satisfied with the quality of the service they're receiving.

10 TIPS FOR GETTING A FIRST RATE JOB
FROM YOUR SERVICE

After you engage a service, there are many things you can do to ensure that you receive first-rate services:

1.   Tell the supervisor exactly what the operator should say in order to personalize the response.

Tip: Don't let the service answer your phone by reciting your telephone number, "Doctor's office," or "Dr. Goldman's office." Better: Have the answering service identify itself as such. For example: "Dr. Goldman's answering service. May I help you?" Patients should know when they're talking to an answering service. That way they're spared having to reveal more information than necessary to the operator.

2.   Be sure to let the service know whenever the office will be empty, so the operator will pick up calls quickly.

3.   Try to visit the service regularly. Often, you can motivate your operators to go the extra mile for your callers once they get to know and like you.

Tip: When appropriate, give your operator(s) small gifts such as flowers, take her to lunch, and/or write a letter of commendation to her supervisor for a job well done. And, remember your operator(s) at Christmas. Being nice to your operator(s) will be well worthwhile.

4.   Do not allow the answering service to make appointments. However, *do* have them tell callers what your office hours are, or when you're expected back.

5.   Set aside regular times for calling the service to get your messages.

6.   Let the service know how a colleague who's covering for you during an absence can be reached at all times.

7.   Call the service occasionally when you're out of the office. Have friends and family members do this randomly, too.

GUIDELINES FOR USING AN ANSWERING MACHINE

Most doctors will prefer to use an answering service, not a machine, to cover their phones. After all, when patients call a doctor's office, even after hours, they expect a person to answer. They may have a serious and personal medical problem, and need immediate comforting, as well as information. An answering machine can't provide that all-important human touch.

If no answering service is available to you, you may have no choice but to use a machine. If so, strive to create messages that use the same principles your receptionist should be following when she answers the phone in person—be friendly, efficient, and professional. Here are some additional tips to help you create the most effective answering machine message you possibly can:

1.   If you already have an answering machine, listen to its sound quality very critically. If you were a patient, would you feel good about leaving a message in response to it?

2.   If possible, make the voice on the tape your own. Even if the patient only wants to make or change an appointment, your own voice can be very reassuring, and will create the impression that you'll receive important messages.

3.   Set the answering machine to pick up incoming calls no later than the fourth ring—preferably after the second. If you set the machine to wait any longer, callers may become impatient, and hang up.

4.   Start with a positive, upbeat greeting. "Hello. This is Dr. Vincent Montgomery" will do fine.

5.   Thank the caller for calling.

6.   Tell the caller that he's reached an answering machine, and why. You may want to change your messages to suit the occasion. For example: "Our office is closed now" or "Estelle Davidson, our receptionist, is away from the phone for a short time."

7.   State the telephone number patients can call in case of an emergency. Then, repeat this number, so your patients won't have to call back to jot down the number.

8.   Encourage callers to leave a message for non-emergency matters: "Please leave your name, the time, your phone number, and a short message at the sound of the tone."

9.   Tell callers, "We will return your call as soon as we can," or, better yet, *when* you will return calls. By using "we" instead of "I," you won't be promising that you personally will call back.

10.   Allow callers at least 60 seconds to leave their messages. It can be very frustrating for a caller to be cut off before he's been able to finish.

Tip: A "voice-activated" answering machine is your best bet. This feature allows the caller to leave as long a message as he likes, since it will keep recording as long as he keeps talking.

P·A·R·T   3

Managing the Money Coming into Your Practice

C · H · A · P · T · E · R   3-1

Setting, Raising, and Presenting Fees

Fees are an interesting subject for most doctors, and for good reason. Deciding what is a fair fee for a particular service, both to the doctor and the patient, is often quite difficult. And, making the fee schedule acceptable to patients can be even harder.

THE EIGHT BIGGEST MISTAKES DOCTORS MAKE WHEN DISCUSSING FEES

Even the most reasonable or low fees can seem outrageous to the patient if they are presented poorly. See if you find yourself doing any of the following:

1. *Discussing fees midway through the exam.* Imagine what would be going through the patient's mind during your exam. Depending upon his condition, he may be very frightened or angry. He may be trying very hard to deny the fact that anything is wrong with him, and that he needs your treatment. Or, he may be feeling absolutely fine, and see no need for preventative care that you recommend.

His mind racing, he asks you for the fee. If you tell him then, with no preparation or explanation (in other words, without any benefit of a full case presentation), he is quite likely to shut his mind to the whole idea.

Therefore, the next time one of your patients asks you about fees too soon, you might suggest:

> Let's talk about fees later. Right now I'm too busy concentrating on your health.

Assure the patient that afterwards, you'll have plenty of time to discuss your recommendations in depth, and your fees, preferably in your private office.

2. *Apologizing about fees.* Don't say, "This fee may seem high to you, but . . . ," or anything similar that will plant the idea that you have high fees. Fair fees need no apology.

3. *Making a habit of asking about patients' finances.* That should become your concern only when a patient seems anxious about costs or if he tells you outwardly that he has a problem. Until that happens, assume the patient is prepared to pay the normal fee.

4. *Being vague or evasive about a fee range.* Don't say only that your usual fee ranges from $225–$450. Also explain it:

> The higher fee applies only if you require more than regular care, or if x happens.

5. *Being vague about what a fee covers.* A patient who knows what to expect, and what he's getting for his money, is less likely to complain later that your fee is too high. Therefore, at the end of the appointment, have your business assistant explain:

> The total for today is $_____ , and that includes A, B, C, D, and E.

Tip: Along similar lines, it is essential to give patients fully itemized statements, so they know what they're being asked to pay for. A sure way to raise eyebrows is to state:

> For professional services $350

6. *Discussing fees with the wrong person.* Many patients don't handle their own finances. And often a patient will want you to discuss your recommendations and fees with someone else—spouse, child, parent—so that person can help make a decision. Therefore, a great question to ask is:

> Would you like to know about the expenses now? Or is there someone else you'd like to have here with you when we discuss that?

7. *Making assumptions.* Don't judge a patient's financial status by outward appearances and ask, "You'll probably need some time to pay this, right?" Many patients will be embarrassed with that assumption, even if it is correct. And if a patient is prepared to pay cash, that kind of question may plant the idea of delaying payment unnecessarily.

8. *Getting involved in the nitty-gritty of financial arrangements.* Once a patient accepts your treatment recommendations and fee, and needs a financial arrangement, leave the details to your business assistant. Tell the patient:

> My financial secretary, Sally, will be right with you to make the financial arrangement. Anything you and she agree upon will be fine with me.

Then leave. Let your assistant iron out the payment schedule and terms. For more information on making financial arrangements with patients, see, "Making Firm but Fair Financial Arrangements with Patients," pages 113–119.

BASIC GUIDELINES FOR STRUCTURING YOUR FEES

In most practices, it is smart to keep your fees low and competitive for the following four types of procedures: new patient examinations, common/regular procedures, emergencies, and urgencies. Let's look at each of these separately.

1. *New patient examination:* A very thorough examination and low fee will impress new patients. If you do *more* than is usually expected at a first exam, and charge *less* than is expected, the new patient will perceive great value, and will be drawn to your practice.

In addition, low exam fees will set the stage for getting better case acceptance. If the patient thinks you're giving great value on your initial exam (and on your recall exams), he'll be less apt to shop around when you recommend higher-fee services to him.

2. *Very common and regular procedures:* In the case of a general dentist, fees for routine procedures such as diagnostic casts and x-rays, periodic examinations (recall), cleanings, and fluoride treatments would be best left very low and competitive, because they are done regularly. Patients will be likely to compare fees for these common procedures with fees of their friends' dentists. *Example:*

My dentist charged me $54 for a cleaning. You mean your dentist charged you only $27?

3. *Emergencies:* When a new patient comes to you with an emergency, he may be sizing you up to see if he wants a further relationship with you. He will base that decision in part on whether he likes the fee you charged him for the emergency visit. Therefore, it generally makes good sense to keep the fee for the emergency visit low. For more information on this subject, see "Scheduling Emergencies," pages 62–63.

4. *Urgencies:* The patient with an urgency is one who has a concern that he wants checked out that is not an emergency (no serious discomfort or alarming symptoms). When the urgency patient stops in for you to have a look at his problem, it may be wise to keep your fee for that visit very low, or perhaps to charge no fee at all. If you then recommend treatment at a later appointment, even treatment with some pretty substantial fees, the patient

will be more likely to accept. He will be willing to believe that all your fees must be reasonable, because you were so reasonable about his urgency visit.

FOUR KEY FACTORS TO CONSIDER BEFORE RAISING YOUR FEES

Before raising your fees, you will want to consider many factors, in particular, your:

1. *Productivity:* If present production is coming from high volume (many patients, short/low-fee appointments), you may wish to explore ways to expand your services or concentrate more on larger cases. Doing so may eliminate the need for fee increases.

2. *Community:* Every time you increase fees, you risk that some patients will feel you've become too expensive for them. Try to allow fee increases to become accepted as the norm in your area before you consider another increase.

3. *Costs:* The last time you increased fees, did your costs increase as well? What was your *net* increase? If you are dissatisfied with your bottom-line figures, you may need to explore ways to increase your production and efficiency (making better use your auxiliary staff, cutting down on waste, streamlining your inventory system), instead of or in addition to fee increases.

4. *Economy:* Will an increase keep you current with the economy? Or will it enable you to surpass it?

Don't confuse fee increases that keep you in line with inflation with fee increases that bring you greater profits. If you raise fees only to keep up with the inflation rate, you're not actually increasing net profits, but rather, maintaining your present profit level. (This distinction is akin to that between a pay raise for merit, and a pay raise for cost-of-living adjustment. Be sure you know what your fee increase is going to accomplish in your bottom line.)

Tip: In a depressed and declining marketplace, you may not be able to increase fees enough to keep up with the national economy. In such an environment, alternative methods will be essential if you're to maintain or boost practice income.

HOW TO EXPLAIN FEE INCREASES TO PATIENTS

Below are three excellent guidelines about fee increases:

1. *Don't be apologetic.* When asked, acknowledge the increase directly:

Yes, the fees have increased.

2. *Tie rising costs to the fee increase.* Remind the patient that the cost of groceries, cars, travel, housing, etc. have all increased to keep pace with inflation. Then explain:

> In optometry (chiropractic, osteopathy, veterinary medicine, etc.), it's necessary to increase fees, too.

3. Explain that you had to increase your fees for the patient's benefit:

> I had the option of using cheaper materials of less quality, but I refuse to compromise. I want only the best for my patients, and so I had to raise my fees.

RESPONDING TO "HEY THAT'S A LOT OF MONEY!"

One common reaction to a fee increase or fees in general is, "Hey, that's a lot of money!" If you're hit with that kind of remark, your best strategy may be to agree with the patient: "Yes, it's a substantial investment in your health." It's crucial that you use the word *investment* here, rather than *expensive, costly,* or other potentially negative words. Then ask: "What do you mean it's a lot of money?" The patient's answer will tell you which way to go. For example:

1. If he says, "I mean I don't have that much money saved up," indicating a financial problem, discuss the various methods of financial arrangement available, the possibility of doing the treatment in phases (if that exists), etc.

2. If the patient says, "I mean I can't see spending that much on this," indicating that he doesn't *value* the services you proposed, say, "An investment in health is one of the best investments you can ever make." Then help the patient see the value of the services by explaining how long it will last, what will happen if it isn't done, etc. You might preface this part of the discussion by asking, "Which aspects of the treatment do not hold value for you now?"

Tip: Realize that an objection to your fees may be the patient's way of making other, more urgent objections. If you feel that you've answered the questions about fees, but the patient still has other objections, ask:

> Is money the only thing stopping you from going ahead with my recommendations?

Then, address the patient's real objections (fear, a desire for a second opinion, etc.).

MORE TIPS ABOUT RAISING FEES

1.   Try to compare your fees with those of other practitioners in your area. Set fees that reflect your professional image and setting. For example, if you practice in a low-income, low-status part of town, you'll probably want to keep your fees toward the low end. However, if you practice in a high-income, high-status part of town, chances are your patients will tolerate—or even expect—higher fees.

2.   Patients tend to tolerate slight frequent fee increases better than sudden sharp ones. Therefore, it is good practice to review all fees every four to six months. That way you can raise them slowly and gradually.

3.   List no-charge services on your statements, to remind patients of all the things you *don't* bill them for (and that other practitioners might).

4.   Don't charge for missed appointments. Patients usually feel such charges are not justified, and may do harm to your image in revenge. For positive, effective ways to handle no-shows, see, "How to Keep Last-Minute Cancellations, No-Shows, and Chronically Late Patients from Crippling Your Practice," pages 75–82.

5.   If you're tempted to charge patients $29.99 for a particular service, think again. According to one business school study, patients may equate those 99-cent fees with low quality. Conversely, they are likely to equate high quality with a doctor who charges whole dollar amounts.

6.   According to another study, patients may be more apt to question round-figured fees than less-round ones. In view of this, you might consider revising your fees using figures like $165, $530, and $3,300 instead of rounder numbers (like $150, $500, and $3,000).

Tip: According to the study, higher un-round fees received less resistance than lower round ones. (That is, $104, $108, and $115 all received fewer complaints than a flat $100.)

7.   Would you consider lowering your fees because a patient asks you to? Even though your intentions might be of the very best kind, accepting lower fees can be damaging:

a.   It may make the patient feel that your fees were too high in the first place. He may wonder if he could have negotiated an even better deal.

b.   It may communicate to the patient that you have no other use for your time and are desperate for his "business." This may undermine the patient's confidence in your abilities.

c.   The patient may wonder if he's getting cut-rate services.

d.   It establishes a dangerous precedent.

e.   Other patients may become justifiably angry, if they learn about it.

Tip: If you want to provide your services to a patient who has great difficulty paying for them, you may be best off waiving your fee entirely, or perhaps charging only what is necessary to recover your material and lab costs. That way, you can regard your services as a charitable contribution to your community.

In all other cases, explore with the patient your various methods of payment. Also, discuss the option of undergoing treatment in phases, if that is possible. Always explain the disadvantages of the less-expensive alternatives, and justify your initial recommendations. Many patients will then decide that the extra expense is indeed worthwhile, and give up the notion of your lowering your fee.

C · H · A · P · T · E · R   3-2

Making Firm but Fair Financial Arrangements with Patients

E stablishing an organized approach to financial arrangements is a must for good patient relations and a high collections rate. Patients are ultimately the ones to choose methods of payments, make financial commitments, and agree to dates to make payments. By helping them recognize their options and obligations, you may expect that they will follow through as agreed.

The business assistant is the person best able to complete financial arrangements with patients for several reasons. First, she is also the person who carries out the collection routine. It is therefore useful for her to have first-hand knowledge of the patient's financial commitment. Second, patients often feel that discussing money matters with the doctor lowers his image as a professional. In their eyes, the business assistant is the appropriate person to be discussing finances. And third, by taking care of financial arrangements, the business assistant frees the doctor so he can concentrate on providing the best possible professional services for his patients.

There are several steps to making effective financial arrangements with patients. Have your business assistant study them carefully, and rehearse her part. Once she begins to discuss financial arrangements with a patient, she should be able to do so with complete confidence. *She* should always be the one controlling the situation, and not allow a patient's questions or manner throw her. With your help, your business assistant should be able to anticipate various problems and be ready to handle them.

SIX REASONS FINANCIAL ARRANGEMENTS MAKE SENSE

Many doctors are tempted to run a cash-only practice. However, financial arrangements are usually in everyone's best interest, for the following reasons:

1.   Many of your patients may have reached the borrowing limit on their credit cards, even though they can still afford to make additional payments to you or a health care credit plan.

2.   Your patients want to be in your good graces financially. When they owe you large sums of money that are past due, many become embarrassed and will avoid you. When you allow fair regular payments over a period of time, you remove the stigma of unpaid debt, and so, your relationship improves.

3.   Your patients will be unlikely to recommend you to their friends if they have made no arrangements to pay and are distressed by their debt. Thus, you may lose valuable referrals.

4.   Patients tend to think of their debt in terms of the current installment, rather than the whole sum. They prefer thinking they owe $40 per month rather than a total of $400. Often, a manageable monthly installment will be the only way they can proceed with your recommended services.

5.   Your patients deserve the best professional care available, and they want it. You'll enable them to have elective procedures, and enjoy your own ability to provide it, if you offer them a way to pay for it over a period of time.

6.   Financial arrangements discourage patients from breaking appointments. On a "pay-as-you-go" basis, the patient will often break an appointment if he doesn't have the money in his pocket that day to pay for it.

Tip: Some practices find it beneficial to publicize the availability of financial arrangements. In addition to mentioning it in their practice brochure, ads, and newsletter, some post a sign in the reception area that says, "Ask us about our payment policies."

FACILITATING YOUR ASSISTANT'S JOB IN MAKING FINANCIAL ARRANGEMENTS

Your assistant should *memorize* the payment methods available to your patients. Basic ones used by many practices include:

a.   Payment in full in advance—often with a discount.

b.   Credit cards or a health care credit plan.

c.   Monthly payment plan (with a large initial payment).

d.   Three equal payments—prior to services, halfway through, and upon completion.

   e.   Half now, and half at a later agreed date.

   f.   Unequal monthly payments, issued as work progresses.

Tip: Your assistant should also become familiar with all financial arrangements papers you use in your office.

Set the stage. The doctor should complete his full case presentation in his private office, and get the patient to agree to go ahead with the recommended professional services. He should introduce the fee and the subject of payment to the patient, but only in general terms. The doctor's introduction should also include his assistant's role in making financial arrangements. He should make clear that this person is acting on his behalf, with a statement along these lines:

> Mrs. Dawson, I'm certainly happy to hear that you're going to go ahead with the treatment I've recommended. I'm going to have my business assistant, Cathy Tucker, come in and speak with you. She'll discuss any financial arrangements necessary. Any arrangements that you and she agree upon will be more than satisfactory with me. I'll be looking forward to seeing you on your first appointment. Cathy will be with you in a few moments.

Tip: For more information on gaining the patient's acceptance, and on conducting the case conference, see, "Getting Patients to Accept Your Clinical Recommendations," pages 449–457.

Meet briefly with your assistant. With the patient primed for the financial arrangement, the doctor is free to leave his office and acquaint his assistant with the case. He should tell her how much time he will need for the first few appointments, and the total fee for the services the patient has accepted.

Tip: Put this information in writing, so your assistant will have it to refer to and quote when meeting with the patient.

The assistant should then gather together all the materials she will need for making financial arrangements:

   1.   Notes about the fee and the amount of time needed for the first appointments.

   2.   A list of the payment methods available to patients.

   3.   Several appointment cards.

   4.   The appointment book.

   5.   A notepad and pen.

6.   Financial arrangement papers used in your office.

Have your assistant meet with the patient. Once fully prepared, your assistant should enter the office where the patient is waiting, and sit in the chair the doctor just vacated. Her first remarks should show that her main concern is the same as the doctor's—the patient's well-being and providing quality professional services. It is often very helpful if your assistant says something like this:

> Mrs. Dawson, I'm happy to hear that you are going to go ahead with the treatment Dr. Nicholson recommended. So that we can get some time reserved for you in the appointment book, I'd first of all like to get some appointments scheduled for you. Dr. Nicholson indicates that on your first appointment he'll need approximately 45 minutes of your time. Which is more convenient for you, mornings or afternoons?

Then, your assistant should make one or two appointments in the appointment book, completing an appointment card for each appointment. These should be laid to one side.

Have your assistant open the topic of finances. With the appointments made, your assistant should broach the subject of financial arrangements. *Example:* She might say:

> Mrs. Dawson, did Dr. Nicholson discuss with you the various methods we have available here in the office for taking care of your fee?

If the patient says, "Yes, he told me I could spread it over several months," or something of this nature, your assistant can immediately establish a payment schedule. However, if the patient says she's not sure what to do, your assistant should describe once again each of the payment methods already mentioned by the doctor.

Tip: A visual aid often improves patient understanding. Your assistant might write down each method of payment as she describes it. Or, she might use a pre-printed list, and check the methods off one at a time.

Suggest sources of financing. If a patient decides he wants to have the services the doctor recommended, but doesn't know where to get the money for the fee, your assistant might suggest the following sources:

1.   Savings account, Christmas club, or other bank accounts.
2.   Loans: Banks, credit cards, life insurance policies.

3. Finance companies, including health care credit plans.
4. Relatives and friends.
5. Insurance policies.
6. Credit unions.
7. Payroll advance.

PREPARING INFORMATION FOR THE PATIENT'S SPOUSE

If the patient says he must consult his spouse or some other person before making a financial arrangement decision, your assistant might give him a note indicating the total fee and the various payment methods. Then, the financial arrangement can be completed at a follow-up visit.

Tip: While your assistant should do her best to nail down the financial arrangement at this time, she should never exert undue pressure on a patient to choose a method of payment. If during the financial arrangement discussion the patient has wavered about whether to proceed with the doctor's recommended services, it is usually best for the doctor to return to to the patient at once to address these nagging questions or doubts.

COMPLETING THE NECESSARY PAPERS

Once a patient has agreed on a method of payment, your assistant should have him complete all the appropriate forms. Many practices design their own forms for this purpose, stating the total amount of the fee, and the dates and amounts of each payment. A truth-in-lending form may be needed for certain types of financial arrangements, typically when:

• Any type of delinquency or service fee is charged.

• There are four or more payments.

• The amount of an installment is changed.

Your attorney or accountant can advise you about the use of such a form, and other legal obligations.

Once your assistant has prepared the necessary forms, your assistant should have the patient read them, and ask for questions. If the patient has none, she might say:

Mrs. Dawson, Dr. Nicholson's name appears here and your name goes here.

Tip: Your assistant should *avoid* such phrasing as, "Sign at the bottom," or "Put your name on the dotted line," which might make the patient feel that he's signing his life away.

Tip: Keep in mind that it is essential to monitor your financial arrangements. Therefore, it makes sense to create a tickler file and never put active financial arrangements in with the patient's chart (or it might never be seen again). The file should have 31 dividers (one for each day of the month). The written financial arrangements should be kept in it under the date the next payment is due. That file should be checked daily, and always be at your business assistant's fingertips. (Move the financial arrangement to the patient's file after the final payment has been received.)

CONCLUDING THE FINANCIAL ARRANGEMENT MEETING

To conclude the financial arrangements, your assistant might smile and say:

> Mrs. Dawson, here is a copy of our agreement that you have signed. Here also are your two appointment cards. Dr. Nicholson and I look forward to seeing you on your first appointment. Thank you.

Then, she should stand up, escort the patient out to the reception area, and say goodbye.

REINFORCING THE FINANCIAL ARRANGEMENT

A well-written letter can strengthen and reinforce your financial arrangements, and reduce misunderstandings. A good letter also demonstrates to the patient that there is an efficient business procedure in operation. This will make him take his obligation more seriously.

To be most effective, letters about financial arrangements should be initiated promptly and regularly. Make it a habit to mail letters immediately, or at the same time each week, for occasions such as these:

- To acknowledge signing of a financial arrangement.
- To follow-up on collections.
- To acknowledge the final payment.

Tip: Put some thought into developing prototype form letters. They can do wonders for patient relations.

FINANCIAL ARRANGEMENTS AND DISCRIMINATION

Keeping your credit policies legal means you must be familiar with a number of laws. In particular, doctors offering financial arrangements must be careful not to discriminate, or leave themselves open to such an accusation.

You can legally refuse to grant any credit at all, as long as you apply the cash-only requirement fairly and equally to *all* patients. The Equal Credit Opportunity Act of 1975 forbids discrimination in granting credit on the basis of race, color, sex, religion, or national origin. The law also forbids discrimination due to age or marital status. It provides that creditors, in deciding whether to extend credit, can't refuse to consider the following as income:

1. Reliable public assistance.
2. Regular part-time or retirement income.
3. Regular alimony or child support payments.

Your attorney can advise you further in this matter.

COUPON BOOKS: AN ATTRACTIVE PAYMENT OPTION

Coupon books have been used successfully by orthodontists for years. However, many other doctors might consider using them for larger, higher-fee cases.

Coupon books are useful when extensive procedures will be paid in regular monthly installments. They save you time and money, both for bill preparation and postage costs. Many patients like coupons because they offer a systematized approach for making payments, with immediate receipts.

Stationery supply firms offer pre-assembled coupon books with 12, 24, or 36 pages. They provide a page to send with the remittance and a stub for the patient's personal record. Once a total treatment fee has been established and a portion paid initially, the remaining fee is divided into equal monthly payments.

You can give or mail a coupon payment packet to each patient who chooses the coupon method. Fill out each coupon in the book with the amount of payment due and the date. As well, include a supply of pre-addressed return envelopes, and a cover letter reviewing the agreement.

Tip: Although coupon books simplify matters tremendously, continue to keep records and be sure that monthly payments are made.

How Not to Let "Professional Courtesy" Get Out of Hand

P rofessional courtesy —free or discounted professional services to special individuals—can easily get out of hand, especially if you find yourself providing it unfairly, unhappily, or too often. However, abolishing professional courtesy from your practice entirely, while an easy-to-implement policy, would not necessarily be in your best interest.

Professional courtesy is a fantastic goodwill builder. And, as we all know, it is customary in many places, and can lead to valuable referrals and important contacts in your professional community. Moreover, professional courtesy, when reciprocated by other doctors, can lead to substantial savings for you and your family.

For these reasons, most doctors extend professional courtesy privileges to some individuals, at least to some extent. The problem is in deciding:

• Who should benefit from professional courtesy, and who shouldn't? How can you establish limits without offending?

• What is a reasonable (and unreasonable) amount of courtesy (discount) to offer?

• How can you gracefully turn down requests for the courtesy from people who shouldn't receive it?

Obviously, a few simple decisions are necessary to help you establish a fair and consistent policy.

DECIDING WHO GETS WHAT

While each doctor may want to establish somewhat different professional courtesy limits, the following is a list of typical courtesies provided in professional practices:

1.   The doctor's immediate family (defined as parents, in-laws, grandparents, spouse, and children) receive all professional services and materials at no charge whatsoever.

2.   The doctor's extended family (defined as all other relatives, such as siblings, nieces and nephews, aunts and uncles, etc.) receive professional services at 20% of the usual fee, plus the cost of materials.

3.   The doctor's special friends (limited to six or eight persons total per year) receive professional services at the discounted fee of 20% off the total billing.

4.   The doctor's clergyman receives all professional services and materials at no charge whatsoever.

5.   Other clergymen receive professional services at the discounted fee of 20% off the total billing.

6.   All practice personnel receive all professional services and materials at no charge whatsoever.

Tip: Many offices do charge staff a portion of their usual fee, as well as the cost of materials. However, free professional services can lure top job applicants, especially in dental, chiropractic, optometric, family medical, and OB-GYN practices.

7.   The staff's immediate family (defined as spouse and children only) receives routine examinations without charge. All other professional services and materials are charged at 20% off the total billing.

8.   The doctor's personal physicians, optometrist, chiropractor, dentist, etc. receive a 20% discount off the total billing. These doctors' family members receive no discount, nor do other health care professionals (as a general rule). However, special consideration is usually given to certain professionals, and is determined on an individual basis.

ESTABLISHING FAIR EXPECTATIONS FOR
PROFESSIONAL COURTESY

Professional courtesy should be a plus for your practice, not a minus. Courtesies offered grudgingly or unfairly can sometimes do more harm than good. Therefore, some clear expectations are in order:

1.   When you extend professional courtesy to other professionals, be sure you are doing so out of respect. Do not assume that they will reciprocate with free or discounted services, unless you have a clearly stated barter agreement.

2.   Patients receiving a professional courtesy are entitled to the same level of care that you would provide for a "full-fee" patient. Don't economize. However, it is reasonable and usually wise to schedule courtesy patients' appointments during non-peak office time.

Tip: When providing routine, non-emergency professional courtesy services for your staff, it usually makes sense to do so when you have an unexpected opening in your schedule, due to a last-minute cancellation or broken appointment.

SAYING "NO" GRACEFULLY

Occasionally, a long-term patient, distant relative, or some other acquaintance may ask for unreasonable courtesies (or financial arrangements) for themselves or members of their families. Saying "no," while justified, can be awkward for you, especially since you don't want to seem greedy, or offend or alienate anyone you care about or who could help you build your practice.

Of course, you must look at every request for professional courtesy individually. In a few rare instances, it may be best to give in, either by bending or changing your policy. However, these cases are few and far between.

When responding to the vast majority of these requests, going against a fair, well-thought-out professional courtesy policy is poor practice management. You may resent it, and the individual may take unfair advantage of you. Obviously, giving away your services indiscriminately will eventually take its toll on your practice profit and loss statement. But most importantly, providing the courtesy to one individual who doesn't deserve it, and not to another of equal relation, is unfair—and potentially damaging to your practice's goodwill. Imagine what would happen if a colleague found out that you were charging him for your services, but not charging another colleague of equal relationship.

Ultimately, it is best to draw the line somewhere, and then stick to your guns. When you've got to say no, it is usually best to refuse to discuss money with the individual yourself. Instead, try sidestepping the issue with a simple statement such as,

Joan takes responsibility for all billing arrangements, according to clearly outlined policies. She simply won't let me get involved.

Then, warn your financial secretary of what's coming, and your stance. Make sure she's well-versed in your practice policy about professional courtesy (using a written policy as a guideline, if possible).

This way, all individuals are treated equally and receive identical explanations from the same person. Delegating authority about courtesies and payment arrangements also makes your financial secretary's job easier. (For more information on making fair financial arrangements, see, "Making Firm but Fair Financial Arrangements with Patients," pages 113–119.)

But most importantly, having someone else handle money matters and say "no" for you enables you to stay out of the discussion, and concentrate your time and efforts elsewhere. It makes the refusal seem less personal to the inquirer, and usually, easier to accept than if it had come from you.

25 Ways to Improve Insurance Claims Processing

I nsurance claims processing takes a substantial amount of time and diligence. It is a task many assistants dread, especially if they have experienced first-hand the extra paperwork, repetition of entries, red tape, and payment delays that often accompany the process.

Fortunately, claims processing can be streamlined (and problems avoided) if you keep on top of things and have a well-organized system. Below are 25 specific, field-tested tips for improving insurance claims processing in your office.

25 WAYS TO IMPROVE INSURANCE CLAIMS PROCESSING

1. Learn what each area insurance plan covers.
Tip: Patients are often mistaken about the extent of their coverage, so don't rely on them to give you accurate information. Instead, have your assistant contact the personnel/insurance department of each insured group and ask for booklets that describe eligibility, payments, deductibles, and exclusions.

2. Prepare an information sheet for each company that states:

a. The insurance company's name.

b. The group's name.

c. Mailing address, phone number.

d. Contact person, phone number/extension.

e. Deductible (per calendar or fiscal year—with dates), amounts per person and family.

f. Whether preventive/well care is deductible.

g. Maximum coverage per year (and whether calendar or fiscal).

h.   Do they accept a standard insurance claim form? (You'll want to co-operate with the company on the use of superbills and computerized billing. Delays and expenses may result when unprocessed forms are returned or when the company must transpose all the information onto its preferred forms.)

i.   Do they *require* preauthorization/predetermination, and if so, by phone or in writing? What's the typical waiting period?

j.   Other limitations/coverages.

Tip: Keep these sheets in a ring binder in alphabetical order according to group name. Don't rely on information received over the phone regarding benefit allowance or eligibility. (Get this information in writing.)

3.   If carriers don't supply you with envelopes or mailing labels, pre-address your own. (The task can be delegated to your business assistant or even a temporary employee.)

Tip: To speed the pre-addressing task, have a rubber stamp or gummed labels printed with each carrier's name and address.

4.   Tactfully learn whether every new patient has insurance.

Tip: Don't ask this question of a new patient until you've established rapport, scheduled the first appointment, gotten his name, address, and phone number, given him directions to your office, etc. When ending the call, your receptionist might say, "By the way, Mr. Hadley, do you have health insurance?"

5.   When the new patient registers, collect the information you'll need for insurance claims processing.

Tip: If he forgot anything, politely ask that you receive the information as soon as possible. Stress the benefit to the patient—quick and efficient claims processing.

6.   Have new patients complete their section of their group's form. Make 10 or so copies of the form, and file the copies in the patient's chart. That way, you can fill one out each time a patient completes a visit, and have it ready for his or her signature.

7.   When the patient signs any of your forms, make sure his or her name is also clearly printed or typed. (When processing claims later, it may be difficult to determine whose claim it is if the patient has poor handwriting.)

8.   See if your carrier will accept "Signature on File." If not, explore other ways to eliminate the need for getting the patient's signature on every form.

Tip: Some carriers allow you to use self-adhesive labels that resemble the signature boxes on the insurance forms. When the insured patient visits your office, you'd ask him to sign a set of stickers. Then, you'd keep these on file, and use them in the signature boxes on the carrier's claim/ predetermination forms.

9.   If processing an insurance claim for a patient who can't sign his or her name:

a.   Have him sign the form with an "X" in the appropriate places. Then, print the patient's name next to it.

b.   Have two witnesses sign the form. The Social Security Administration says anyone can be a legal witness—an assistant, the patient's relative, a friend, or even another patient—as long as each witness writes his or her name and address next to the patient's mark.

c.   Attach a note to the insurance form explaining the situation, and listing the witnesses.

10.   Complete and mail required pre-determination forms as soon as possible after the examination. That same day is best.

Tip: If the patient agrees to go ahead with the treatment whether or not he receives authorization from the insurance company, schedule his first appointment. If he wishes to wait for authorization, tell him that you're mailing in the request, and that you'll call to schedule an appointment once you receive a reply from the insurer.

11.   Call the patient at once when you receive authorization. Tell him about any portion of the fee not covered by insurance. If he was waiting for authorization, schedule the first appointment for the soonest possible date.

12.   Review the treatment schedule. Be sure that lengthy services planned for the patient will be completed in as few appointments as is practical. (The sooner treatment is completed, the sooner you can submit a claim, and the sooner you'll receive the insurer's portion of your fee.) Look for opportunities to divide claims to boost cash flow. (See if you're going to perform involved treatment that can logically be broken down into two or more steps. If so, don't wait until you complete the entire case before you submit a claim.)

13.   Try to submit a claim at the end of each step when you refer the patient to a specialist for part of the treatment. There's usually no reason to let the paperwork stack up while waiting for the specialist to complete his or her services.

14.   Keep up with insurance claims daily. A smooth flow of paperwork is the best way to have a consistently efficient insurance claims program.

15.   Copy every form you send to an insurer, and keep these separate from the patient's clinical file. If the insurer requires diagnostic films or similar items, keep duplicates of these, too. Write the date it was sent in large numbers on the top of your copy.

16.   Establish a good system for tracking insurance paperwork. For example, you might set up a folder for each month of the year. You'd then file a copy of each claim in the month of the last service for the form. Within the folder, file claims either by date or alphabetically. (The larger the office, the easier it is to file claims alphabetically.) When you receive payment, you'd look at the date of service and pull the form from the folder. Then, you'd mark it paid and file it in an alphabetical file. Keep it for one year, then throw it away. What's left in your month file would be claims that haven't been paid. With these in hand, following up by telephone will be relatively easy. (This same tracking system can also be used for predeterminations.)

Tip: Another method for tracking insurance paperwork is to use an insurance tickler file. Simply, you'd indicate on a calendar the date by which you expect to get a response from the insurer. Then, check your calendar daily to verify that you've heard from the insurer as you anticipated. (Unpaid claims could be stored alphabetically in a common file.)

17.   Follow up. Call if the insurer sits on any of the paperwork you submit—predetermination or claim.

Tip: It often helps to develop one regular contact person at each insurance company with whom you can check on the status of your paperwork.

18.   Whenever an insurance consultant denies benefits or offers "alternative benefits" that you feel are wrong, call him or her right away and present your side. Many consultants will choose not to fight. If lodging a complaint in writing, don't be bitter or offensive. Include only factual information about treatment planned and events or circumstances leading to your complaint.

Tip: According to a Los Angeles court ruling, doctors will be held liable if, against their professional judgment, they comply without protest with limits imposed by third-party payers. Thus, if you believe that a patient should receive certain types of care or treatment not covered by his or her plan, you must make your recommendation anyway or be held liable for injury that results.

Tip: It sometimes helps to remind the patient that predetermination or preauthorization does *not* indicate that the doctor's diagnosis and recommendations were correct. It indicates only that the carrier will cover the proposed treatment under the patient's plan.

19.   Appoint one member of your staff an in-house "Insurance Claims Reviewer." Generally, the best person for this post is an experienced clinical assistant, who already has a solid foundation in clinical terminology and treatment and may even be familiar with the case. Your staff reviewer would:

a.   Review all charts and narratives for accuracy.

 b. Check all x-rays and other diagnostic aides to make sure they clearly show the problem and are clean and properly labeled and mounted.

 c. Make sure insurance companies receive all of the information they need, even if it means resubmitting claims or asking a patient to return to the office for another test.

 d. Double check to see that all necessary information has been given, including signatures and procedure codes.

 Tip: Always be sure to use the patient's correct first name. Delays often occur when different forms of the patient's name are used, such as Robert, Bob, Bobby, Rob, or Robby.

 e. Offer a narrative explanation for any claims that may raise the carrier's eyebrows. (For example, higher-than-usual fees.)

 20. If a patient is confused or dissatisfied with the extent of his coverage, remind him that the program is a contract between him, his employer, and the insurance company. Patients don't always appreciate that you are *not* a party to the contract.

 Tip: The insured patient should understand his financial liability. Therefore, when your assistant discusses financial options with an insured patient, she should tell him that even though your office will assist him in filing the claim, responsibility for payment is his. (As well, you may wish to provide a printed notice to this effect.) You may need to remind patients that insurance plans are designed to *help* them pay for care, not necessarily pay the entire cost for them.

 21. When the patient has dual insurance coverage, send the claim form to both carriers. (Patients who have dual coverage are often able to receive 100% coverage when the benefits of both plans are coordinated.) Indicate the name and address of both carriers on each form, and explain the situation briefly.

 Tip: For dependent children, the father's plan is usually primary, and the mother's secondary. However, there are exceptions to this rule as a result of various divorce and adoption situations.

 22. Note the difference between *preauthorization* and *predetermination:*

 a. Preauthorization is the guarantee of a company that the authorized amount will be paid provided treatment is completed within the period of eligibility marked on the claim form.

 b. Predetermination is a calculation of the dollar amount payable if the person is eligible for the benefits when the treatment was performed. There is usually no guarantee of payment by the company for any specific period of time. At the time of treatment, eligibility must be checked by your office.

23.   Create a form to simplify your insurance communications with patients. *For example:*

Patient's Name: _____

Date: _____   From: _____

_____

_____ Please sign and return this form so we can file your claim for you.

_____ Your insurance covered all but the amount shown on this statement. Please use the enclosed envelope to mail your payment to us.

_____ Your insurance does *not* cover the services listed on this statement.

_____ If you have insurance coverage, please send us a completed claim form.

---

24.   If an insurer says it never received a given claim form, which sometimes happens, try to remain calm. Arguing in such situations usually does little good. If it's a predetermination or preauthorization form, send another. If it's a claim, send another form accompanied by a photocopy of the approved predetermination form.

25.   Remember that health insurance generally benefits patients and the practice. Because of insurance, many people can obtain needed health care with less out-of-pocket costs. This encourages them to seek care that they might otherwise feel that they couldn't afford. Insurance also improves the practice's cash flow and helps the doctor raise his case acceptance rate.

Tip: By remembering that insurance is generally a plus, claims processing will seem more worthwhile and positive.

FOR MORE INFORMATION

Your assistant will find it very helpful to memorize relevant insurance information, including common terms and their definitions. For a list of these, see "Common Insurance Terms and Their Definitions," Appendix 2-2, pages 581–584. When computer shopping, see "Insurance Musts for Your Office Computer," Appendix 1-I, page 529.

C·H·A·P·T·E·R 3-5

How to Avoid Getting Burned When You Accept Checks

Your patients' personal checks will generally be good, and you'll have no difficulty depositing them. However, every now and then you may encounter a problem check.

Usually, the difficulty stems from an oversight by the patient— he didn't complete the check properly, or didn't have sufficient funds in the account. These honest errors are easy to catch and rectify. On the other hand, there will be those patients who write meaningless check after check, to get you "off their backs," never with the intention of paying.

Take a few simple precautions the next time a patient presents you with a check, to reduce the chance of problems.

WHAT YOU NEED TO KNOW ABOUT THE CHECK-PAYING PATIENT

These days, almost every supermarket in the country obtains credit information on its customers before cashing the first check. Shouldn't you take the same precautions?

Have the new patient complete a pre-printed form with the following information on it, and file it in his record:

- Name(s) on checking account and bank.
- Place of employment and phone number.
- Home address and phone number.
- Driver's license number and state. Make sure the photo on the license is of the patient. Compare the address on the license with that on the check. And, see if the license has expired. Interesting: More than 60% of all forged checks are cashed on an expired license.

- Social security number.

- Credit card company and number, if you are legally able to ask for this. Ask the patient for a credit card from a local department store, unique to your city. Forgers are unlikely to have these—most use phony major credit cards as identification. As well, the major card companies are unlikely to provide you with information about their customers, while local stores may.

- Birth date and sex. *Tip:* Compare the birth date the patient tells you to the one listed on his driver's license.

- Patient's signature indicating that all of this information is correct and complete.

While the patient is writing out his check, your assistant can review his form and verify that the information has not changed. An up-to-date form is your best defense against a patient who tries to skip or pass a bad check.

Tip: If you prefer to write identifying information on the check itself, do so on the *front*, not on back. Most checks are marked with bank cancellations that can make information on the back illegible. You'll lose your prosecuting information on the back of the check when this happens.

SIX IRON-CLAD NEVERS ABOUT CHECKS

When your patient pays with a check in your office, your assistant should adhere to six nevers:

1. Never cash a personal check.

2. Never accept a check for more than the amount due and hand out cash in change. A problem could emerge even with an honest, well-intentioned patient.
Example: One doctor's elderly patient, who'd been paying a $500 fee by installments, wrote numerous checks for larger amounts. He died still owing the doctor $300. The attorney for the estate wrote, "We hold cancelled checks in the amount of $400. Please send us a corrected bill for $100." The doctor's kindness cost him $200.

3. Never accept a check that's made out to someone else and endorsed over to you—even if the payee is the patient. If the check bounces, you may have a real mess on your hands.

4. Never accept a postdated check. The bank will not honor it before the date shown on the check, and the lag may buy the patient the time he needs to skip on you.

5.   Never accept antedated checks. Banks will often return checks that are more than six months old.

6.   Never accept a check written in pencil or erasable pen. While such a check is negotiable, it is easily altered.

CORRECT PROCEDURE FOR ACCEPTING A CHECK

Once your assistant verifies that you have up-to-date identifying information about the patient, he should next take a good look at the check itself:

1.   Inspect the check for completeness. Does it contain the correct written and figure amounts, date, and signature?

2.   Does the sum expressed in figures differ from the amount written out in words? If such an error is not corrected, the bank will pay the amount written out in *words*.

Example: If a patient owes you $1,000, and his check says "$1,000" and "One hundred dollars," you'd receive $100.

3.   Do not try to alter anything on the face of a check yourself. Ask the patient to make the change, and initial it.

WHAT TO DO IF YOU NOTICE AN ERROR LATER

Occasionally an error on a check will go unnoticed until you're ready to deposit it. For instance, the patient may misspell your name, or write "Dr. Stanley" when he should have written "Dr. Livingston." When that happens, the correct procedure is to endorse the check exactly as written and then add your proper endorsement beneath it.

Tip: If your name is long, unusual, or difficult to spell, you may have a lot of these errors on your checks. If so, make up a self-inking rubber stamp with your name on it, and leave it at your checkout counter. Patients can then stamp the appropriate spaces on their checks. This not only eliminates errors, but also saves time and effort.

If you notice that the patient has neglected to sign the check, a common oversight, you might ask your bank if it will allow you to deposit the check with a guarantee that you'll take it back if protested. If they'll allow it, simply write "over" on the line where the signature should appear. Then on the back of the check, type "Lack of Signature—Guaranteed," and your practice's name, address, and telephone number. If the missing signature is an honest oversight, the patient won't protest. However, if the omission was a deliberate stalling tactic, the patient will know that you mean business.

EXAMINE THE PAPER THE CHECK IS PRINTED ON

There are several ways to detect a phony check, and the paper is the best place to start. Your assistant should look for the following if you have any reason at all to be suspicious:

1.　A legitimate check will have a perforated edge on at least one side. Phony checks are usually smooth all around. Why: Con artists use paper cutters to separate counterfeit checks after printing because perforating equipment is generally bulky and expensive. Exception: Some government-issued IBM-type card checks are not perforated. To verify authenticity, look for a diagonal cut in the upper left corner.

2.　See if the check is magnetic. On good checks, the routing numbers and other information are printed with magnetic ink, which doesn't glare, shine, or reflect light.

Tip: Look at one of your personal checks and you'll see that it doesn't reflect light when you tilt it. However, con artists generally don't print with magnetic ink, because it's relatively rare.

3.　Try to smear the ink. Good checks are printed on safety paper with non-smear, permanent ink. If a bank or traveler's check has been copied on a color copying machine, it will smear with a little pressure from your thumb.

ROUTING CODE CAN HELP YOU SPOT A BAD CHECK

If your suspicions continue, look next at the routing code—usually the first two bracketed numbers in the bottom left corner. These represent the Federal Reserve Banking district where the check was issued. There are only 12 such districts in the United States. Thus, the first two numbers in brackets can never be higher than 12 for any commercial bank.

Exceptions: Routing numbers may start with the digits 2 and 3 on drafts issued by savings and loan institutions and mutual savings banks. Government checks show the routing number 0000-0051.

Make certain that the Federal Reserve code numbers match the area of the bank where the check was drawn. *Example:* If you see that a check was drawn in New York and that its routing number is 09, you'll know immediately that the check is bad. The routing code for New York is 02. Keep a copy of this list of codes in your business office. (*Note:* Some states are divided over more than one district.)

01:　Massachusetts, Maine, New Hampshire, Connecticut, Vermont, Rhode Island

02: New York, New Jersey, Connecticut

03: Pennsylvania, Delaware, New Jersey

04: Ohio, Pennsylvania, Kentucky, West Virginia

05: Virginia, Maryland, North Carolina, Washington D.C., South Carolina, West Virginia

06: Georgia, Alabama, Florida, Tennessee, Louisiana, Mississippi

07: Illinois, Michigan, Indiana, Iowa, Wisconsin

08: Missouri, Arkansas, Kentucky, Tennessee, Indiana, Illinois, Mississippi

09: Minnesota, Montana, North Dakota, South Dakota, Wisconsin, Michigan

10: Missouri, Colorado, Oklahoma, Nebraska, Iowa, Wyoming, Kansas, New Mexico

11: Texas, Arizona, New Mexico, Louisiana, Oklahoma

12: California, Oregon, Washington, Utah, Hawaii, Alaska, Idaho, Nevada, Arizona

WHY YOU SHOULD DEPOSIT CHECKS PROMPTLY

Depositing checks promptly reduces the chances of problems, for four reasons:

1. It improves cash flow.

2. It ensures that you'll spot errors and bad checks quickly. The sooner you identify problems, the sooner you can act, and the more likely you are to collect the money you're due.

3. It means you get paid promptly if the patient dies. A patient's checks will be honored for only ten days after his death. After that, they are returned and become part of the obligation of his estate, which can delay payment considerably.

4. Checks are good for a "reasonable" length of time, according to the Uniform Commercial Code. Usually, this is interpreted as 30 days after the check is dated and seven days after it's endorsed. Banks are not required to cash a check that's more than six months old.

HOW TO HANDLE NSF CHECKS

You may sometimes have a check returned for "not sufficient funds." When this happens, your business assistant should call the responsible person at once to explain what has happened, pause, and wait for a response.

Unless the patient has suffered a personal catastrophe, tell him that you are redepositing the check that day and that he should make sure that there are sufficient funds in the account. Afterwards, document and summarize the conversation on the patient's ledger card.

Tip: If you'll charge patients a penalty fee for redepositing NSF checks, (this is usually a flat fee, such as $5, $10, or $20), publicize this policy with a sign in your office.

If the check is returned for a second time, it is time to make an entry in your financial record. If you're using a pegboard bookkeeping system, enter the amount of the check under your "payment" column and circle it to show that it is to be treated as opposite from an actual payment. Increase the patient's previous balance by the amount of the check. When adding the total of payments for the day, be sure your bookkeeper treats the NSF check as a minus quantity.

THE CORRECT PROCEDURE FOR ACCEPTING
TRAVELLERS CHECKS

First, look for federal code number 8000 printed in brackets at the bottom of the check. This indicates that the check is authentic. A series of four additional numbers can be found after the 8000 code.

If the validating second signature has already been filled in, don't accept the check. Ask the patient to countersign the check in front of a representative of your practice, and make it payable to you. Compare the two signatures on the check. They should be the same.

Finally, don't accept a signed travellers check if it is out of your sight— even for a few seconds. *Example:* If the check falls to the floor, and the patient stoops to pick it up, your assistant should ask him to sign it again on the back. A clever con artist could use the distraction to substitute a carefully forged check.

WHAT TO DO IF YOU THINK A CHECK IS LOST

If a patient tells you "the check is in the mail," and several days have passed, you'll probably assume either that he's lying, or that the check is lost somewhere. To be tactful, you may be tempted to suggest that the patient put a stop-payment order on the "lost" check. Don't do it—that is, unless you're prepared to pay the typical $15 charge for a stop-payment order.

Under federal law, if debtors stop payment on their checks at your request, they can deduct the cost of the stop-payment order from the amount they owe you. However, if the debtors decide to stop payment, they cannot deduct the $15 fee from the payment.

Ask the patient with the "lost" check to send you another one. Assure him that if his lost check does arrive at your office after his accounts have been paid, you'll be sure to notify him immediately and return the duplicate check. Document your conversation with the debtor on his ledger card. That way, you'll have a record of who made the stop-payment suggestion and of the debtor's promises.

C·H·A·P·T·E·R   3-6

How to Avoid Credit Card Fraud

E ach year, credit card fraud climbs to a new all-time high. The latest estimate puts the amount lost in fraudulent transactions at a whopping $6 billion annually.

Perhaps you don't think that a professional practice would be a likely target of such a crime. However, chances are excellent that your office already loses a considerable amount of money annually because of fraudulent transactions. Many of these may be hidden in your statements under headings like "bank charges," "credits," and "bad debt," and therefore, they may be very hard to recognize. Nonetheless, chargebacks to your account can easily add up to thousands of dollars every year you're in practice.

According to credit card consultants Larry Schwartz and Pearl Sax,* who can be credited with much of the material in this chapter, "It is now easier, safer, and more profitable to steal with a credit card than with a gun." The chance of a credit card criminal ever being apprehended or brought to trial "is less than 1 in 100," Schwartz and Sax say. At the same time, they add, there is an incredible amount of money to be made with fraudulent credit card transactions. Thus, the crime seductively combines minimal risk and potentially great profits—what they call a "simply irresistible" lure for some.

Fortunately, Schwartz and Sax say that your practice can prevent most fraudulent transactions if you do four things:

1. Use a standard procedure for checking the validity of the cards patients present to you.

2. Prevent your own employees from stealing credit card numbers and using them themselves—or selling them.

*Larry Schwartz and Pearl Sax are the founders and directors of the Fraud & Theft Information Bureau, a publishing and consulting organization that specializes in credit card fraud control and loss prevention for businesses and banks. Their manual, *Credit Card & Check Fraud: A Stop-Loss Manual,* is an excellent source of more information on this subject. Order it from The Fraud & Theft Information Bureau, 217 N. Seacrest Blvd., Box 400, Boynton Beach, FL 33425, 407-737-7500.

3. See that your account is credited properly.

4. Be more aggressive about reversing chargebacks.

THE THREE MOST COMMON TYPES OF CREDIT CARD FRAUD

Before we can protect ourselves against credit card fraud, we must learn to anticipate how the criminal is likely to operate. There are three likely scenarios:

1. The criminal uses a stolen credit card or card number. He makes large purchases until the credit limit is reached, then concentrates on under-$50 purchases until the card is reported lost or stolen.

2. The criminal manufactures a credit card from scratch, using a stolen number and any name. Some frauds make counterfeit cards from genuine card blanks, stolen from bank warehouses.

3. The criminal alters a lost, stolen or expired card. He will pound flat the raised number on the front and re-emboss a new, stolen number in its place. Thus, the phony card can be processed with an imprinter. He may also change the magnetic stripe on the back of the card, so it can be processed at a computer terminal.

THE 11-STEP PROCEDURE FOR PROCESSING A CREDIT CARD TRANSACTION

Your best defense against credit card fraud is a standard procedure for handling every single transaction. Therefore, it is essential to train your business assistant on this important subject.

Unfortunately, most assistants fall short in this area. According to Schwartz and Sax, 98% of all credit card training they observe pertains to writing up the charges and other similar tasks, while only 2% pertains to fraud control. "Yet fraud prevention training is easy to do, and can pay off handsomely," they urge, suggesting the following procedure:

1. Verify that the patient who presents you with a credit card has already submitted at least two other forms of identification, preferably a driver's license and another credit card from a local department store. The best procedure: Complete a pre-printed credit history form for each patient, on which you list his name, address, phone number, driver's license number and state, social security number, other credit card numbers, birth date and sex, and signature. Keep this form in the patient's file and verify the information

before each transaction. (This procedure is described more fully under "What You Need to Know About the Check-Paying Patient," on page 131.)

2. Make an imprint of the patient's card on a sales draft, and have the patient sign it. That signature will be extremely important evidence if it is indeed a case of fraud.

3. Take a good look at the name on the card and at the patient. Are there any apparant discrepencies? *Example:* Is a 13-year-old patient trying to pay you with a card that says "Dr. Morris Johnson"?

4. Take the signed sales draft and the card to an area *away* from the patient's sight and hearing. You will need privacy and quiet to check the card's validity.

5. Once away from the patient, compare the signature on the sales draft with that on the card. It should be the same. Check the card's expiration date, and see if it is on the restricted card "hot" list. Also, look at the card itself. Does it seem genuine? Specifically, check the edges of the card—counterfeits are sometimes ragged. Look at the embossing carefully, to see if it has been altered. And check the magnetic stripe on the back. Is it in the correct place? Has a new stripe been pasted over the original?

6. Call for authorization for every single transaction, regardless of the amount.

7. Look for signs that betray a fraudulent cardholder. Often, those trying to perpetrate a fraud keep the card in their pockets, not in their wallets. Also, be suspicious if the cardholder seems uneasy, is looking around to see if others are watching him, or if he is trying to dissuade or distract you from getting proper authorization for the transaction.

8. If you are even minimally suspicious about a transaction, consult *The BIN Member Directory of All Visa & Mastercard Issuing Banks,* available from the Fraud & Theft Information Bureau, cited at the beginning of this chapter. This annual publication lists all the banks in the world that issue VISA and MasterCards. It will enable you to tell whether the numbers on the card correspond to the proper numbers for the issuing bank. And, it will provide the phone number of every bank, so you can call to verify a suspicious cardholder's name and address.

9. Do not accept a card from anyone but the cardholder. In the case of the 13-year old card user described earlier, the most prudent course would be to refuse to accept the card at all. But if you feel you must, call the issuing bank, using the BIN directory described above to confirm that his name and address are the same as the name and address that appear on the bank's computer. This will verify that he is indeed the authorized user of the card. Common fraud: A patient may try to use a card belonging to a family member,

without his permission or knowledge. A divorced or separated spouse, or a child is the typical culprit in these cases. Interesting: Some frauds have tried to use cards belonging to a deceased family member.

10.   Once you get authorization, note it on the sales draft and return to the patient to complete the transaction.

11.   Return the card to the patient, and give him his copy of the sales draft. Tear up credit card charge slip carbons in front of the patient. Or, offer them to the patient.

Tip: You can request carbonless slips from the bank, which will be cleaner, easier, and safer to use. However, you should know that some people have allergic reactions to them.

WHAT TO DO IF IT IS FRAUD

Credit card companies suggest that *if possible,* you should hold the fraudulent card and sales draft. They will typically pay you a reward if you send them the bad card, cut up.

However, once you have spotted a fraud, it is absolutely essential that you don't do anything to endanger the people in your office. If the cardholder is potentially dangerous, refuse to accept the card, and return it to him. Tell him simply that there seems to be some problem with the card, and ask him to pay in another way. Then report the attempted fraud after the patient leaves.

WHEN ARE YOU LIABLE FOR A FRAUDULENT TRANSACTION?

Companies vary on their policies about your liability in accepting a fraudulent transaction. Most will hold you liable if:

1.   You fail to authorize transactions over the floor limit.

2.   You don't catch a card on the restricted card list.

3.   You don't see that the card has expired.

4.   You fail to notice a discrepancy between the name on the card and the signature on the sales draft.

5.   You fail to authorize a card being used by someone it *obviously* doesn't belong to (such as a child).

MAKE "NO CARD-NO TRANSACTION" YOUR IRON-CLAD POLICY

What would you do if a patient in your office told you he forgot to bring his credit card with him, but that he knows the number and expiration date by heart? What would you do if a patient called and asked to settle his account with you over the phone, with a credit card?

Perhaps you'd be tempted to trust the patient and *write* the card number on the sales draft in these cases. However, you put yourself in great risk whenever you accept a verbal credit card transaction. Protect yourself by getting an imprint or computerized magnetic reading of a tangible credit card every time.

Once you take the patient's word for it and write the numbers on the sales draft, you are liable for the transaction, even if you called for and received authorization. Therefore, although it may be an inconvenience for the patient who has forgotten his card or who calls, ask him to pay another way, or to come to to your office with the card in hand to complete the transaction.

HOW TO KEEP YOUR STAFF HONEST

It is unlikely that a trusted member of your staff will steal credit card numbers or make multiple imprints. However, it is possible, and it does happen. Fortunately, there are several things you can do to prevent internal credit card fraud:

1. Keep your credit card imprinter, restricted card list, BIN directory, and other materials secure and out of sight when not in use. These can be quite valuable to a fraud. Lock them in a cabinet or desk when your office is closed.

2. Establish a negative file of the names and addresses of known credit card thieves or people who have tried to use a card unauthorized. Then place the names and addresses of all of your employees in this negative file. Doing so prevents them from sending credits to themselves.

3. Carefully screen all new employees, especially those who will be handling credit card transactions. Check several references carefully.

4. Use sequentially numbered sales drafts, and instruct your business assistant to keep all used sales drafts in order, even voided ones. Then, do an occasional spot check to see that all drafts are accounted for.

5. Treat completed sales drafts and carbons as though they are cash, not scrap paper. Keep them in a secure location, and limit access only to those employees with need. Watch new employees carefully.

WHAT YOU NEED TO KNOW ABOUT
REVERSING CHARGEBACKS

There are 65 different kinds of chargebacks that banks levy against merchants (including some against mail order companies and retailers). For this reason, it is imperative that you check into all chargebacks, and seek explanations for those you don't understand.

Should you encounter a chargeback you don't agree with, take the appropriate steps to reverse it. You will need complete documentation to build your case—your copy of the completed sales draft, proof of authorization, etc. With this, redeposit the transaction, and explain your position. Keep copies of all correspondence and document all phone calls pertaining to your case.

HOW TO PROTECT YOUR OWN CREDIT CARD

Nearly all doctors use credit cards to pay some bills, especially when they buy gasoline for a practice-owned car, or travel for continuing education or other practice business. Some find it convenient to establish a separate corporate credit card, to be used specifically on such occasions for practice-related expenses. If so:

1. Limit the use of corporate credit cards to those individuals you can truly trust.

2. Do *not* have a card made that bears the name of the practice only. Rather, have each authorized user's name imprinted on his or her card.

3. Don't permit your card or card number to be used by anyone who is not an authorized user.

4. Review the procedures for protecting your own credit card, listed under "Reduce the Risk of Unauthorized Use of Your Credit Cards," on pages 216–217.

C·H·A·P·T·E·R   3-7

How to Protect the Cash in Your Office

Many practices will find that they receive a lot of their payments in cash, especially those that offer incentives for cash payments at the time services are rendered. Cash is without doubt the easiest form of payment to steal. It is also extremely easy to make mistakes with cash. Therefore, you'll want to institute several procedures for protecting the cash in your office.

THE SUPPLIES YOU'LL NEED FOR HANDLING CASH

Before you can begin to accept cash from patients, you'll need several supplies:

1. Every office needs two cash boxes or drawers. One, labeled "Payments," will serve as your office cash register. In this, store the cash that you receive from patients, and the change you will give them. Choose a relatively large box for this task, with separate compartments for each type of bill and coin. The other, smaller box, should store your office's petty cash fund. Label it "Petty Cash."

Tip: Each box should be made of strong metal, and have a sturdy lock and a handle. Choose boxes in obviously different colors, to help you distinguish between them.

Tip: You may prefer to have lockable cash drawers installed in your business office.

2. Get a supply of containers in which to place the deposits you'll be taking to the bank. These are usually plastic money holders or canvas bags, or you can use simple heavy-grade envelopes. Be sure you also have rubber bands or paper clips to hold bills together, and a supply of small coin envelopes to keep the change secure. Also get some coin wrappers for pennies, nickels, dimes, and quarters.

3. Ask your bank for a supply of deposit slips. That way you can get the deposit completely ready in the privacy of your office. Doing so not only

saves time, but also avoids mistakes and theft that can occur when you're trying to recount cash in a crowded bank.

4.   Be prepared to make change for patients. Establish a set distribution of change that you will need in your cash drawer at the start of each day. Then tape this distribution list on the inside lid of your "Payments" cash box. Make it your business assistant's responsibility to replenish the drawer every morning, and to account for the change in your financial records. As well, your assistant should learn to anticipate and head off change problems during the course of the day.

SAFETY TIPS

Your best course is to keep as little cash in your office as you possibly can. Therefore, get in the habit of making frequent bank deposits. In so doing, be careful that you don't establish a predictable pattern for bank trips. An astute robber will come to recognize it. To protect both your cash and your staff, vary the time of day for your deposits, and have different members of your staff go to the bank for you. Conceal the deposit bag or envelope in a briefcase, purse, or other container.

Keep your cash boxes in the most secure place possible. A small office safe is an excellent idea. But if this is not practical, keep your cash boxes in a locked cabinet or drawer when not in use, and limit access to the keys.

THE CORRECT PROCEDURE FOR ACCEPTING
A CASH PAYMENT

Have your business assistant narrate what he is doing as he takes cash and makes change for patients.

Example:

Thank you. That is forty dollars—(counting the money) ten, twenty, thirty, thirty-five, forty. Your change is seven dollars— [counting the change] that is five, six, and seven.

The narration helps eliminate mistakes and also prevents the patient from claiming that he gave your assistant more cash than he actually did. A standard con: "I gave you a twenty, not a ten."

For the same reason, your business assistant should not put the cash the patient gives him into the cash box or drawer until the entire transaction is completed. Instead, he should put the patient's payment to one side and make the change. That way, if the patient says, "I gave you a twenty, not a ten," your assistant can pick up the bills the patient actually gave him and recount them. (If they're already in the box or drawer, this is impossible.)

KEEP A TIGHT GRIP ON YOUR PETTY CASH ACCOUNT

It makes good sense to pay for as many business transactions as possible by check. Properly used, checks provide a record of how much you paid, when you paid it, to whom it was paid, and what you paid it for.

However, it's not possible to pay for everything by check. You need cash to pay for postage-due mail, charges on packages, parking and tolls, small office supplies needed in an emergency, and other miscellaneous items. In short, you need a petty cash fund.

Your business assistant or office manager should have access to and be solely responsible for your petty cash fund. Every expense should be documented. This not only prevents theft, but also is important documentary evidence for the IRS, to show you're handling even small sums in a business-like manner. Remember, the amounts drawn from petty cash are usually small. But they may add up to a substantial figure by the end of the year. To set up a trouble-free fund:

1. Draw petty cash from the "Petty Cash" box only. Never take petty cash from your "Payments" box.

2. Decide the amount of cash you'll need in a week and make out a check for that amount. Stock your "Petty Cash" box with the cash, broken into small bills and change. Tape a list of the amount and breakdown on the inside lid of your "Petty Cash" box.

3. When your business assistant makes any payment from petty cash, no matter how small, he should make out a receipt such as the following, and put in in the cash box:

Receipt: Petty Cash Fund
Date: _____
Time: _____
Amount: _____
For: _____
Paid to: _____
Receipt Attached?   yes   no
By: _____

Instruct your assistant to obtain and staple a receipt to this whenever he can possibly get one. (A postal employee or store clerk will always give you one. Only in the case of a tip, parking meter, or similar expense will he be unable to get a receipt.)

Be sure your assistant then records the transaction on the day sheet or in your computer record, and lists the amount paid, as well as the item purchased or reason for the expense.

3.   Don't use stray scraps of paper as receipts. Supply your business assistant with a book of consecutively numbered receipt forms. (These may be bought at office supply stores, or you can make your own.) File the receipts in your "Petty Cash" box.

4.   At the end of each day, your business assistant should balance the petty cash account. The cash left over and the totaled receipts should equal the amount listed on the inside lid of the box.

5.   Have your assistant replenish the account as needed.

6.   Periodically review the receipts, so you can see where your petty cash is going, and identify and eliminate waste. On the one hand, don't be so restrictive that your assistants are required to get your advance approval for every dime they need to spend. That's a poor use of your time and a waste of their ability. But on the other hand, don't allow your staff to spend unnecessarily or wrecklessly out of this fund.

If you don't understand or agree with an expense, investigate it, and establish a new policy. If cash routinely disappears from the fund with no record, make a serious change. If you suspect that someone has tampered with the lock on the box, get a box that's more secure, or change the lock on the cabinet where it's kept. If you suspect that the person with the key has dipped into the till, gather indisputable evidence, and take the appropriate steps.

HOW TO TELL IF A BILL IS COUNTERFEIT

Counterfeit currency is more common than you may think. Since a patient may unknowingly try to pass a counterfeit bill onto you, it's a good idea to know what to look for. Have a genuine dollar bill in front of you as you review the following chart:

If you suspect that a bill is counterfeit, don't accept it from the patient. And, don't try to pass it yourself. Surrender it to the police or the nearest regional office of the U.S. Secret Service. (Check Information for a listing.) Unfortunately, the government won't refund money you hand over. However, it is tax deductible.

In a Genuine Bill:	In a Counterfeit:
Red and blue fibers are embedded in the paper.	Red and blue lines may be drawn on the surface.
The sawtooth points on the circumference of the treasury seal should be even, clear, and sharp.	The sawtooth points are often uneven or broken off.
The portrait should appear three-dimensional and life-like. Hairlines should be distinct.	The portrait may appear flat and unreal. Hairlines may be blurred.
The background of the portrait should be of medium tone.	The background of the portrait is often dark.
The crisscrossing lines on the border of the bill should be clear, distinct, and unbroken.	The crisscrossing lines on the border of the bill usually appear blurry.

C·H·A·P·T·E·R 3-8

Collecting the Money That's Due You: Preventing Unnecessary Collection Problems

W ouldn't it be fantastic if you could collect every dollar you ever produced? Fair as this seemingly modest goal may appear, a 100% collections rate is probably *not* in your best interest, at least not in the long-run.

Many doctors are surprised to learn that the most successful collection systems typically collect 95–98% of the practice's production—no more. If your collections average is 94% or less, your collection system probably could stand a little improvement, and, odds are, you already know that. However, if you're averaging 99–100%, chances are good that your financial arrangements, while preventing collections problems, are too rigid.

Tip: An overly strict collection system can thwart long-term practice growth. Cash-on-the-spot-only collection systems can encourage patients to postpone or cancel needed services, or to go to another practice where the credit "grass" is greener.

Of course, every practice should try to eliminate as many *unnecessary* collections problems as it possibly can. However, some collection problems are indeed necessary (or at least unavoidable) when a practice offers its patients a variety of flexible financial options. The trick is to prevent the unnecessary problems, and then, to handle the few unavoidable ones as professionally, promptly, and painlessly as possible.

Tip: For more information on calculating your collections ratio, see, "Are You Collecting What You Earn," and "How Old Are Your Accounts Receivable," pages 5–6.

COLLECTING PAYMENT AT THE APPOINTMENT

Clearly, every dollar you collect at the appointment is one less that you will need to collect later. It stands to reason, then, that the place to begin beefing up collection efforts is at the conclusion of the appointment.

Unfortunately, this is an area where business assistants are poorly trained. It often seems easier in the heat of the moment simply to bill the patient (or to ask him to pay half-heartedly), especially when other demands are pressing on the assistant's time and attention. However, a few simple tricks will improve your in-office collection rate without taxing anyone or making them feel uncomfortable.

Obviously, the thing to do is to ask. When asking for payment, however, avoid questions that require a *yes* or *no* answer. For example, "Do you want to take care of this today,?" requires a yes or no. If the patient says *no,* it's very hard to pursue it further without seeming pushy. Similarly, if your assistant says, "The fee for today is $_____ ," she's inviting the patient to say, "Okay, send me a bill," which again puts her in an awkward position.

The most tactful way to ask for payment is to stay in control by giving the patient a choice. How:

> The total for today is $_____ . Would you like to take care of that with cash, check, or credit card?

Tip: If a patient who has a financial arrangement or a past due balance forgets to bring his checkbook to the office when payment is due, have your business assistant give him a pre-addressed envelope and say,

> Here's an envelope for you to mail your check in when you get home. Let's see, today is Wednesday. I'll look for your check in Friday's mail.

This strategy might be used with *any* patient who claims that he'd pay if only he had his checkbook with him.

PREPARING THE PATIENT TO PAY
AT THE APPOINTMENT

There may be some occasions when cash should be expected at the end of the appointment. For instance, a new patient might always be expected to take care of his account right away. After all, as a new patient, he's a stranger and you know virtually nothing about him. (It may be too soon to accept "charge it" from a stranger.) Other occasions that might require cash payments include emergency patients, single service appointments, or even recall appointments.

If you wait to inform a new patient of your fee and cash payment policy until the end of the first appointment, you will have set the stage for a problem. Your assistant should welcome the new patient into the practice properly and try to reduce the chances of collection problems and bad feelings.

Thus, the patient should be prepared for the cash payment, perhaps with a statement along these lines:

> Dr. O'Neal's new patient examination consists of a complete medical history, a thorough examination, and all necessary x-rays. The fee for this examination will not exceed $55 without prior discussion with the doctor (that's in case something out of the ordinary happens) and the fee is expected at the time of the visit.

USING INCENTIVES TO INCREASE IN-OFFICE COLLECTIONS

Discounts on daily fees (typically 3–5%) can be most effective in practices that are having collection problems and whose image does not stress high cost, high prestige services. However, if you already collect 95–97% of your accounts the day services are rendered, or if the majority of your accounts are paid within 30 days, discounts for daily fees will probably lower your profits, and should be avoided.

If this is not your situation and you decide to offer the discount, hang a tasteful plaque in the business office that says,

> We extend a __% bookkeeping adjustment for payment on the day that services are rendered.

When the patient is brought to the business office at the end of his appointment, your assistant might say:

> The fee for today's services is $_____ . Are you aware that we can make a __% bookkeeping adjustment if you take care of your account with cash or a check today?

Some things to consider before instituting a discount:

1. The potential benefits of the discount are:
a. Reduced billing costs.

b.   Improved cash flow.

c.   Fewer collections problems.

d.   Practice building.

2.   The potential disadvantages of the discount are:

a.   Patients may fear that the doctor may be giving them less attention because they are paying less.

b.   It is very easy to overspend when you get payment in advance. Thus, most of us need to learn to budget.

c.   Discounts for patients with insurance is a gray area with possible legal and ethical considerations. (Check with your local and state societies for more information.)

d.   Doctors who currently enjoy good collection results could lose income by instituting a discount policy.

3.   Do not extend a discount to a patient who pays with a bank card. Your practice will already pay the bank card fee, which ranges from 3 to 7%.

4.   You can stop a discount policy at any time or limit it to accounts over certain amounts. However, while your policy is in effect, you must offer the same discount to everyone. For instance, if you say the discount applies to a patient who pays for extended services in full on the first appointment, you can't then give a discount for later payments, unless you revise your policy.

5.   You may offer a discount for certain occasions and groups, such as back-to-school check-ups or senior citizens. However, be cautious when instituting these discounts. Some individuals may qualify for two or more of them.

6.   Initiate a bookkeeping system to track discounts. (For example, you can use your pegboard's right-hand extension columns for this purpose.) Review all the adjustments monthly or quarterly, to evaluate your results.

Tip: Cash discounts are not the only way to spur in-office collections. A Deltona, Fla. doctor gives a pen to each patient who pays at the appointment. The 60-cent pens reinforce payments at the appointment, and also serve as a low-key practice building tool. (They're imprinted with the practice's name and address.) A Midwest practitioner tries something along similar lines by giving every patient who pays at the appointment a first-class postage stamp. He explains that the payment saves his mailing a statement. The least he can do is give patients the postage they're saving him, he says.

Tip: You may wonder whether a negative incentive might induce patients to pay. For example, adding a finance charge on bills unpaid after 30 days may seem like a good idea. However, while finance charges are generally not considered to be unethical or illegal, some of your patients are bound to resent them. Check with your professional society and your attorney before instituting a finance charge. Where interest is frowned upon, some business owners charge a "rebilling" charge.

Tip: If you're offering either a discount or a finance charge, include this information on all bills, statements, contracts, and insurance forms. This will eliminate misunderstandings, or make the inevitable ones easier to resolve.

STAFF INCENTIVE CAN BOOST IN-OFFICE COLLECTIONS

In addition to (or instead of) giving your *patients* a good reason to pay at the appointment, it sometimes helps to provide an incentive for your *business assistant.* However, be warned that a very high bonus incentive puts a great deal of pressure on the assistant to succeed, and may in turn tempt her to strong-arm patients into paying. Of course, you'll want your incentive to encourage your assistant to do her best. But you don't want it to be so attractive that it makes her use too much force.

The most effective incentive program of this type is thus a relatively mild one, where your assistant receives a small reward for improving her in-office collections ratio. Begin by tracking what she's now able collect, by studying the last several months. Then, establish a new goal, and help her prepare and practice dialogue that will gently encourage in-office collections. A small bonus for improvement, perhaps for a short period such as one month, can be most effective.

Example: If you learn that in a typical month only 60 of your patients currently pay at the appointment, you might pay your assistant 50 cents for every patient beyond those 60 who pays at the appointment in the coming month. Continue to monitor carefully what your assistant actually says to patients, to ensure that she's not putting too much pressure on them.

Tip: Most in-office collection ratios and bonuses are based purely on the dollars collected—how much money was collected, divided by total charges. While this is certainly a worthwhile tracking method, the *amounts* of money involved can throw the analysis off and not measure accurately how successful your business assistant is in receiving payments. An easy method for evaluating your receptionist's ability to collect from patients at the time of service: Do a patient count. If your business assistant made ten attempts to collect money from patients and was successful only three times, *that's* important to know, not only the actual dollars she collected. To be fair, count partial payments, since they show that your assistant tried and got something.

GATHERING USEFUL INFORMATION ABOUT
PATIENTS WHO OWE

If you've tried to collect at the appointment but failed, your next line of defense is to make sure you have adequate information about the patients you'll be billing. That way, if one later skips out on you, or if you turn the account over to a collection agency, you will greatly increase your chances of ever collecting the money that you're owed.

Most collection agencies can trace skippers if you supply them with the following information:

1.   Social Security number.

2.   Date of birth. This is very important because there could be 150 people called Mary Carter in a given state. A birthdate helps to identify the one who owes you money.

3.   Employer's phone number. Many skippers leave the state. However, when they do, they often contact former employers for W-2 forms. Thus, many collection agencies check with an employer around tax time, when the former employee is most likely to contact him.

4.   Driver's license number. When a person files for a new driver's license in another state, a collection agency may be able to trace him through a master file.

5.   Name, address, and phone numbers of the person's nearest relative and two close friends.

6.   Names of all family members.

7.   The spouse's employer.

8.   Schools attended by the patient's children. (Schools will be asked to transfer records when the patient moves.)

9.   The patient's legal name, including middle name and maiden (or other previous) name.

10.   Names and addresses of parents (on both sides, if patient is married.)

11.   A street address if the patient fills in an address with a post office box.

12.   The patient's previous address.

13.   When the patient asks for credit terms, get a loan history and the names and addresses of banks where the patient holds accounts. Also ask for a major bank credit card and the name and address of the bank where the account is maintained.

Tip: Keep this information current for every patient in your practice, and you'll be more likely to find skippers. To simplify this task, you might prepare a form for gathering this information, keep it in the patient's file, and periodically ask him if any of the information has changed.

ADDITIONAL TECHNIQUES THAT PREVENT COLLECTIONS PROBLEMS

1.   Print "Address Correction Requested" on the left-hand side of all envelopes you send to patients. When the letter is forwarded, you will be notified of the address by the post office and charged a small fee.

2.   Learn to spot likely credit risks. For example, the following traits sometimes suggest a potential problem:

a.   A questionable employment background.

b.   No telephone.

c.   Frequent change of address.

d.   Residence in a motel or rooming house.

e.   Frequent change of doctors.

Tip: The Federal Trade Commission (FTC) requires you to be consistent and specific in your reasons for denial of credit, to prevent discrimination and other unfairness. Some legitimate reasons could be: incomplete credit application, insufficient credit references, temporary or irregular employment, temporary residence, inadequate collatoral, delinquent credit obligations, garnishment, repossession, and bankruptcy.

3.   If you live in a relatively small city or town (population smaller than 1.5 million), become familiar with the city directory published by R.L. Polk & Co. (Polk publishes more than 5,000 of these books.) The directory contains the names of persons 18 years or older in a particular city or town. Householders are listed by street address, along with their occupations and business addresses. The names of spouses and other family members or roomers at the same address are also listed. In addition, the directory lists residents by phone numbers in numerical order, as well as local businesses (their owners, officers, products, and services).

Most public libraries and chambers of commerce have a Polk directory for their area. If you can't find the book locally, you can buy the appropriate volume directly from the sales department of R.L. Polk & Co., Detroit, Mich.

Collecting the Money That's Due You: Establishing a Firm but Fair Collection Program

Y our best collection program will keep accounts receivable to a minimum, but not refuse care to those who can't pay immediately. It's important to prepare a standard schedule of billing statements, collection calls, letters, and final collection tactics, so you're sure your staff is handling your collections promptly and fairly.

Tip: Your collection program should be routinely enforced in usual situations. However, keep it flexible and show compassion for patients who can't pay because of legitimate hardship. As well, be sure your collection program tries to find out WHY a patient is not paying you, especially before taking further and harsher action against him. He may be dissatisfied with or confused about your services, and if so, a strong collection letter or the efforts of a collection agency might prompt him to take retaliatory action in the form of a costly lawsuit.

BEGIN BY SENDING A CLEAR, PROFESSIONAL, TIMELY STATEMENT

The best statement to send patients will be one that clearly itemizes all of the services and goods for which he is being charged, and that spurs prompt payment.

To begin, consider how much time should elapse between the time you render services and the time you mail your first bill. Obviously, your best course will be to bill the patient promptly, so he's aware of his obligation as soon as possible.

Your business assistant should enter charges for services daily on patient financial records and bill all unpaid balances monthly. Therefore, the maximum time between rendering services and billing is *one month*. Obviously, the sooner you can send your statements, the sooner you'll receive your payments, and the fewer collection problems you'll have.

Tip: If the patient is insured, it's good practice to send a bill promptly anyway, even if the service is fully covered. Enclose a notice with the bill that reminds the patient that you have filed the insurance claim, and of any portion of the bill not covered under his policy. Most offices wait until the normal end-of-the-month billing time to bill patients for copayments after the insurance has paid. However, to improve cash flow, you might have your business assistant send the patient a copy of his statement as soon as she posts the insurance payment. Then, send the patient a second statement if he has not paid the copayment by your regular billing time. Keep track of the account as you normally do from then on.

Do your monthly statements have a due date on them? They should! Patients want to know what is expected of them. And, every other bill they receive has a due date. Why shouldn't yours?

For added impact, try listing the specific date payment is due, not the number of days. For example, say "Due: November 30," *not* "Payment Due in 30 Days." That way, there is little confusion about the actual due date. And, the date on the statement may become a mnemonic device that may jog the patient's memory.

WILL RETURN ENVELOPES IMPROVE
YOUR COLLECTIONS?

The questions persist: Will including return envelopes with monthly billing statements speed payments and reduce accounts receivable? Will a postage-paid envelope achieve an even better response? Unfortunately, the experts don't agree on this issue. There's only one reliable way to tell how well envelopes work: Try using them in your own practice with your own patients.

Tip: If you have balances forward on 25% or more of the bills you send out, it pays to run a test. Try sending return envelopes with a reasonable sample (at least 10%) of statements per month for two months. Choose the sample randomly, or if that adds a lot of work, pull a string of statements in the middle of the alphabet. Track your results and figure them against the cost of the envelopes. (Most practices use simple 6¾" commercial white wove business reply envelopes, preprinted with the billing address.)

SAMPLE COLLECTION PROGRAM FOR A
PROFESSIONAL PRACTICE

Here is a collection program that is typical of those used in professional practices:

1.   Age your accounts each month into current, 30, 60, and 90 days and over categories. If possible, show the age of the account on your statements. (This has become very practical on computer-generated statements.) Aging accounts lets the patient know that you're handling your accounts in a professional, orderly, and businesslike manner, that his acccount is overdue, and that you know it.

Tip: For more information on this subject, see, "How Old Are Your Accounts Receivable?," pages 5–6.

2.   Simply rebill 30-day accounts, with timely and professional-looking statements. Try adding some color to your envelope, since it will be more likely to get the patient's attention and action.

3.   Rebill 60-day accounts and add to the statement a message that explains that the account is overdue, and requests payment.

Tip: It may be most expedient to place a past-due sticker or rubber-stamped message on a collection notice. However, these messages may indicate to the patient that he is nothing special, and unfortunately, that you handle a lot of overdue accounts. Clearly, this is not the message you want him to get. Therefore, your collection assistant might take the extra minute to handwrite personal notes on statements. Consider how effective a signed, handwritten note such as this might be:

> Please call me if you have any questions or would like help arranging payment of this overdue account. It's now been 60 days.

After reading this note, the patient will feel that he's special, and that the overdue account means something to you. If the account is not paid within a reasonable time, the signed note also gives your assistant a logical opening for her follow-up phone call.

4.   If after 60 days the patient shows some indication of regular payment, however small, avoid any drastic collection tactics. The most your business assistant might do is send a short note thanking the patient for his last payment, and requesting that the next payment be x dollars so that the account can be processed properly. In the note, she should invite the patient to call her if there is any problem. If the patient calls with a problem, she should ask him to come to the office to discuss the matter, work out an acceptable financial arrangement, etc.

5.   Patients who show no sign of paying after 60 days need a firmer course of action. Usually, a phone call is the place to begin. However, there are certain pitfalls you must avoid as you try to collect the money that's due you. For more information on this, see "What You Can't Do to Collect Overdue Accounts," page 164.

6.   On the 75th day, your business assistant might call the patient again. After greeting the patient and identifying herself, she should explain the purpose of the call. For example:

> Good Morning, Mr. Haney. This is Alice Crandall. I'm calling about your account with Dr. Stern. The account is 75 days past due.

She should then pause and wait for a reply. The patient often responds by agreeing to pay. In this case, your assistant should say:

> Fine, Mr Haney. Let's see, today is Monday. That means I'll expect your check in the mail this Wednesday.

If the patient explains that he is unable to pay, your assistant should arrange for the patient to come to the office, discuss the matter, and establish a definite financial arrangement.

7.   On the 90th day, rebill the patient and include a note or letter. Like collection calls, collection notices (whether purchased from a professional forms company or written yourself) should be firm and to the point.

8.   On the 100th day, your assistant should call again. As always, she should be courteous and firm.

9.   On the 120th day, rebill the patient and include another collection note or letter. This time, spell out the consequences of not meeting the payment deadline.

Tip: Consistency is important. You must follow through on whatever consequences you mention. For example, if you say that the account will be turned over to a collection agency by a certain date, you must do so.

10.   On the 130th day, your assistant should make the final call to the patient. She should review the consequences of not meeting the payment deadline that were explained in the last letter. She should give the patient one more opportunity to pay, within five days. And, she should tell the patient that this is your office's last attempt to collect the money before following through on the consequences.

11.   If you haven't received payment on the 135th day, take the action specified in the final notice, letter, or call.

COLLECTION AGENCIES ADVISE HARSHER TACTICS

A basic rule of thumb in collections is that the older the account becomes, the harder it becomes to collect. Most experts believe that accounts older than 120 days that have had good in-house efforts should either be written off or turned over to an outside professional for further collection efforts. After four months and repeated efforts, they suggest, its unlikely that most practices can get the delinquent patient to pay.

The collection program outlined above, while typical in many practices, is considered weak by some collection agencies. According to one Silver Spring, Md. collection firm, doctors should consider the account delinquent at 60 days and give the patient final notice of two weeks. Then, if you don't receive payment by the 74th day, you should turn the account over to an agency or collection attorney, it says.

A Columbus, Ohio senior collection consultant advises turning the account over to an agency on the *61st day*. Although this is a hard-nosed and unconventional approach, she concedes, it's cost-effective in the long run to have collections handled by professionals outside the practice.

When establishing your own collection program, it is important to consider not only the best way to make sure you collect the money you're owed, but also, your patient relations. Only you can decide how strict your program should be, at what point, if any, you turn the account over to someone else, who that person should be, and what he or she should do (and not do).

WRITE OFF AND REMOVE ACCOUNTS RECEIVABLE ON SCHEDULE

Do you routinely remove stale, delinquent accounts from your active files and reduce your receivable figures accordingly? These procedures have several advantages:

1. Removing account cards cuts the number of items your assistant must handle in the collection process. This makes the job more manageable.

2. You need a realistic evaluation of what your present accounts receivables are really worth.

At the conclusion of your collection program, instruct your staff to reduce the active ledger tray and make the corresponding bookkeeping write-offs.

WHAT YOU CAN'T DO TO COLLECT
OVERDUE ACCOUNTS

You may contact debtors in person, by mail, phone, or telegram. However, there are several things you can't do, and which might bring legal action against you:

1.   Don't call the debtor before 8 a.m. or after 9 p.m., unless you can prove extenuating circumstances or have the debtor's or a court's permission to call at other times.

2.   Don't harass, oppress, or abuse the debtor. That means you can't call him or her without identifying yourself, approach the debtor at odd times or in inappropriate places (like a funeral or his daughter's wedding), or use obscene or profane language.

3.   Don't threaten the debtor, his property, or his reputation, either physically or otherwise. Even holding the debtor's arm or simply saying, "I'll get you for this" can leave you open to accusations of assault or extortion.

Tip: You can't publish a list of debtors.

4.   Don't lie or misrepresent yourself, for instance, as a lawyer, a government agent, or a credit bureau employee (if you're not). Likewise, you can't tell the debtor that ordinary documents are legal papers that he or she must obey by law, or imply that the debtor has committed a crime and say he'll be arrested if he doesn't pay. You can't threaten to seize, garnish, attack, or sell property or wages unless you'll actually do so and it is legal.

5.   Don't invade the debtor's right to privacy. This includes sending collection notices to the debtor on postcards or mailing notices in envelopes printed with words or symbols denoting "collection," or discussing the debt with the debtor's friends, employers, co-workers, or anyone (except the debtor, a collection agency, or a lawyer) without the debtor's or a court's permission. For more information on protecting the patient's right to privacy, see, "The Problems of Guarding Patient Confidentiality," pages 261–265.

6.   Don't say or write anything slanderous or libelous about the debtor.

7.   Don't try to collect any amount greater than the debt, unless allowed by law.

8.   Don't deposit a postdated check before the date on the check.

9.   Don't make the debtor accept your collect calls or pay for your telegrams.

Tip: A debtor can stop you from contacting him. For example, he may write to the collection agency you've engaged and tell them he insists on no further contact. Once they receive such a letter, they can't contact the debtor again, except to say there will be no further contact. The collector is allowed to notify the debtor that some specific action will be taken (such as a lawsuit), but only if you intend to take that action.

FOR MORE INFORMATION

For more information on collection calls and letters, see, "Making Effective Collection Calls," pages 167–170, and, "Writing Effective Collection Letters," pages 171–177.

For more information on working with collection agencies, collections attorneys, small claims court, and other hard-line collection tactics, see "Innovative Collection Strategies for Dealing with the Hard Cases," pages 179–184.

Collecting the Money That's Due You: Making Effective Collection Calls

F requent, courteous, yet firm communication from your office is the only way you'll be able to collect overdue accouts, or to uncover problems. The telephone will without question be your strongest collection tool, and is far more effective than collection letters alone. The key to success is in having a well-trained, thoroughly-prepared collections assistant do your calls for you at the appropriate times.

BASIC RULES FOR ALL TYPES OF COLLECTION EFFORTS

Whether you contact the patient by phone, mail, in person, or by telegram, the following basic rules apply:

1. Be firm, but never nasty. The old adage is true—you'll attract more flies with honey than with vinegar.

2. Choose staff members to make collection calls and send collection letters who are not opposed to doing so. These tasks require diligence, a strong, businesslike manner, and a positive attitude. Staff members who handle collections can't be squeamish when it comes to talking about money, nor should they find the task distressing.

3. Get proper training for assistants who'll be making collection calls and sending collection letters. They can learn about collections from you and books, but also look for worthwhile programs at community colleges, business schools, and technical schools. Also available are some excellent collections seminars put on by publications, associations, or even the telephone company.

Tip: There is no substitute for practice. Role-playing both the role of the collections assistant and the delinquent patient can be the most effective form of staff training.

4.   Hold monthly billing review meetings with staff members who will be handling collection calls and letters. Review the billing for that month, unbilled work in progress, and old accounts. These meetings will encourage the people responsible for billing and collections to perform uniformly and within your practice's policies. They'll ultimately improve your collections since you'll have a chance to revise your procedures to suit your needs. Moreover, delinquent accounts become harder and harder to collect as they age. With a monthly meeting, you'll be able to catch slip-ups and do something before the account becomes too old.

PREPARING TO MAKE A COLLECTION CALL

Before picking up the phone to make a collection call, your assistant's preparation is very important. In fact, thorough preparation is every bit as important as the manner of the caller's presentation and the words she uses. Before dialing, your caller should gather all pertinent information about the account and check to see:

1.   If the patient offered any complaints about the practice, services, or fee.

2.   Whether the billing was correct.

3.   Whether partial payment was made.

4.   Whether the statement was itemized clearly so the patient could understand it.

5.   Whether insurance is involved.

6.   Whether this is the first time the patient's account is overdue, or if it is a continuing pattern.

7.   Whether the patient has signed a financial arrangement. If so, what is it?

8.   The total amount due.

9.   The number of days it is overdue.

10.   All previous collection statements, calls, and letters, their dates and outcomes.

11.   How to pronounce the patient's name and his title preference: Mr./Mrs./Miss/Ms./Dr./Other.

Tip: Your assistant should also take time out to put herself in the right mindset before she calls. The best attitude for collection calls: One that is friendly and sympathetic to the patient's problems, but firm about settling the account promptly.

11 TIPS FOR BETTER COLLECTION CALLS

1. *Speak to the patient* and only to the patient about the debt, unless he instructs you to speak to someone else. Don't leave a phone message about the debt. (Of course, you can leave your name and phone number.)

2. *Be pleasant but firm.* Keep your objective in mind—to obtain your payment, and to keep the patient.

3. *Make all calls in a private room* where you can keep the discussion confidential. Take steps to avoid interruptions.

4. *Come right to the point.* Don't disguise the reason for your call behind extensive opening chit-chat. A courteous, simple greeting, such as "Good morning" is best followed by a succinct statement of your call's purpose.

Tip: Ideally, collection calls should last no more than three minutes. Otherwise, you may lose the patient's attention. According to one banking consultant, the longer the conversation, the less likely the debtor will pay.

5. *Check and update all the facts before you call.* (See "Preparing to Make a Collection Call," page 168.) It's embarrassing and potentially damaging to tell a patient his account is overdue when his check came in yesterday's mail.

6. *Let the patient do most of the talking.* Ask: "Is there some problem with your bill?" and remain silent. Then, seek details by asking follow-up questions. If the patient says that he has "temporary cash-flow problems," ask him to define "temporary." However, avoid lengthy and detailed discussions about the patient's financial woes.

7. *Ask for partial payment now and schedule installments, if the patient can't pay the whole bill.* This is far better than a promise of payment "as soon as possible." If payments are to be extended over a period of time, have the patient sign a written financial agreement that outlines the payment schedule. (Set up a firm payment schedule with the patient, even if he won't agree to give you partial payment when you call.)

Tip: Resist settling for partial payment if you believe it's still possible the patient will pay in full. Compromise only when there's no other way to collect.

8. *Avoid potentially offensive language.* Terms such as "debtor," "you are delinquent," "you are in arrears by two months," or "the delinquency of this account," may offend your debtors and make them resist paying their bills. A nice way to put it: "past due." This phrase is understandable, yet gentle.

9. *Tailor your approach to each debtor.* For instance, one person might be most likely to pay if you appeal to his sense of fairness, while another might

respond better if you stress that you'll turn the account over to a collection agency. Choosing the best approach will depend on what you know about the debtor, as well as the age of the account and previous collection attempts.

10. *Try timing collection calls to the patient's pay day.* Typically, good times to call are on the first and 15th days of the month. That's when most people get paid, so that's when they may be most likely to take care of an overdue account.

11. *Send a copy by certified mail, return receipt requested,* if a patient repeatedly claims he hasn't received a bill. It's futile to argue this point with patients. Without a return receipt, it's simply your word against theirs.

Collecting the Money That's Due You: Writing Effective Collection Letters

A one-to-one telephone conversation is probably the most effective collection method. However, there are some patients who are either unreachable, or who find it easy to make verbal promises by phone but never follow up with payment. A written appeal in the form of a collection letter may be a better way to get your message across to those patients. Letters also serve as excellent documentation of your collection efforts, which can be helpful should you later decide to take legal action.

The best collection letters are usually those that are built around an appeal. They induce debtors to pay because they hit some responsive chord. The letter's appeal may be to one or more of these five causes of human behavior:

1. A feeling of pride.
2. Self-interest.
3. A sense of fairness.
4. Goodwill toward others.
5. Fear.

One standard collection letter will probably not work in all cases, since different people are motivated by different things. For this reason, a variety of prototype collection letters is offered in this chapter for your use.

Tip: Always note the date payment was due and the number of days past due at the top of each letter.

SAMPLE COLLECTION LETTER TO A FIRST-TIME OFFENDER

Dear [Name of Patient]:

We couldn't help holding in high esteem the standards which you had for prompt payment of your account in the past. We want you to know that we've appreciated this.

At present, however, your account is past due in the amount of $_____ , and we are reminding you of it knowing that you would not generally permit it to remain unpaid for this long.

May we have your check covering the amount stated? We are counting on your continued cooperation.

SAMPLE COLLECTION LETTER FOR A MATURE ACCOUNT

Dear [Name of Patient]:

We are urged to make collection of your outstanding balance of $_____ .

Under our usual procedure, this matter would have been referred to a collection agency for adjustment before this time. However, we do not believe that such action will ever be necessary on your account and we believe that you have withheld payment through some misunderstanding or through some inability to make payment.

When you receive this letter, we'd appreciate it if you'd investigate this matter. If there is any question about it, please call our business assistant, Doris, right away so we can make any investigation or adjustment which may be necessary on our part.

We are confident that we'll either receive your check or hear from you soon.

SAMPLE COLLECTION LETTER APPEALING TO THE PATIENT'S SELF-INTEREST

Dear [Name of Patient]:

We have several times called to your attention your unpaid balance of $_____ . Why have we heard nothing from you?

In simple language, we are disappointed. We have provided our services for you, and felt warranted in placing confidence in you to pay us promptly. You have not done your share to uphold our confidence.

It is unnecessary to point out that only by meeting obligations justly can an individual maintain his/her credit standing. Most people today can't afford to endanger their credit records by withholding promised payment as you have done.

We hope, therefore, that you'll restore our original confidence with a prompt payment. Put your check in the mail today, and let's close this chapter and start anew with a clean slate.

SAMPLE COLLECTION LETTER REGARDING COLLECTION AGENCY

Dear [Name of Patient]:

May we make a suggestion for your benefit?

At our next meeting with our collection agency, it will be necessary to report your name among those patients who have been owing payment for a considerable length of time.

We thought you'd like an opportunity to prevent our having to submit your name by paying the $_____ which you now owe us. Unless satisfactory arrangements are made by (date), your name will be reported.

We hope you'll act promptly to clear up your account with us. That will be the much better thing for everyone in the long run.

SAMPLE COLLECTION LETTER APPEALING TO A SENSE OF FAIRNESS

Dear [Name of Patient]:

We confidently expected payment on your outstanding balance of $_____ as a response to our last letter.

Frankly, we were disappointed, for we can't believe that you'd intentionally impose upon us. And that is what it really amounts to, for by not paying promptly, you do impose upon us the difficulties that go along with carrying an account longer than we had agreed to do.

We're still confident that we can count on you to be fair and just with us in this matter.

SAMPLE COLLECTION LETTER APPEALING TO FAIRNESS, ONLY STRONGER

Dear [Name of Patient]:

Your attention has been called to your statement of (date) for the amount of $_____ , but we've had no acknowledgment to our letters. This statement is now more than two months past due and frankly, we think it ought to be paid without further delay.

You'll remember that last summer your account fell into confusion through lack of attention on your part. After writing to you several times, the account was straightened out and we hoped that no more difficulty would be experienced with your account. We think it is hardly fair for you to inconvenience us again by withholding payment.

We ask you to consider the inconvenience to us when you do not make payments as promised. We hope you'll put your check in the mail today and put an end to this problem.

SAMPLE COLLECTION LETTER STRESSING GOODWILL

Dear [Name of Patient]:

We've enjoyed serving you over the past three years, and hope that we may continue to do so in the years to come.

As you know, we've still not received your check for $_____ . We wonder if there is something troubling you about our service or if there's something else holding up your payment. If so, please call us so we can work it out together.

If not, we assume that you'll put your check in the mail today to show us your continued support. Please, won't you let us hear from you, one way or the other?

SAMPLE COLLECTION LETTER SUGGESTING AN OVERSIGHT

Dear [Name of Patient]:

Your check for $_____ has not yet been received. We assume that the delay is the result of an oversight.

Although in itself the amount is small, when multiplied by the number of accounts we have that are similar to yours, small oversights become tremendously important. We are quite confident that our patients will realize the hardship that is worked upon us when we are forced to bring the matter to their attention.

If you will, therefore, please let us have your check covering the amount promptly, we'll consider it an accommodation to us.

SAMPLE COLLECTION LETTER APPEALING TO FEAR

Dear [Name of Patient]:

Despite the fact that we've sent you numerous letters and called you several times regarding your past due bill of $_____ , we've heard nothing from you and are at a loss to understand the situation. We feel that we've waited long and patiently, and now urgently request your immediate attention.

We have no desire to embarrass or trouble you, but it is necessary that this account be settled at once and that you make satisfactory arrangements to do so without delay. If we do not receive your check by (date), we will turn this matter over to our collection agency.

SAMPLE COLLECTION LETTER APPEALING TO FEAR, ONLY STRONGER

Dear [Name of Patient]:

We wrote to you on (dates) stating that a balance of $_____ is well past due on your account. Copies of these letters are enclosed for your information.

Each of our many letters and subsequent phone calls was meant to provide you with an opportunity to make settlement with us and avoid our having to take further action. We're afraid that your failure to work with us is leaving us with no choice.

If we don't hear from you in five days, our collection agency will receive the account. We urge you for the last time to take care of your balance now to avoid this unpleasant action.

SAMPLE COLLECTION LETTER OFFERING CHOICES

Dear [Name of Patient]:

Because your account is long past due, we'd normally turn it over to a collection agency. However, we'd prefer dealing directly with you. Please read and check one of the three options below and return to us.

_____ 1. I'd prefer to settle this account. Please find payment in full.

_____ 2. I'd prefer to make monthly payments of $_____ until the balance is cleared up. I understand that no interest will be charged for this delayed payment schedule. Note: Minimal acceptable monthly payments are the larger of:

   a. 10% of the balance each month, or

   b. $25 each month.

   Failure to make monthly payment by the due date will result in other collection efforts.

_____ 3. I'd prefer that you assign this account to an agency for collection.

Signed: _____

SAMPLE COLLECTION LETTERS: VERY SHORT

Some experts suggest that a good collection letter is short, ideally no more than six sentences. Thus, here is a sampling of super-short, effective letters for you to use:

1.   Perhaps we should be thanking you for your payment, since it may have crossed this letter in the mail. However, if you have not mailed your payment of $_____ , may we look for your check in the next few days?

2.   Your check for $_____ has not yet been received. We assume that this is an oversight. If you will, therefore, please let us have your check covering the amount promptly, we'll consider it an accommodation to us.

3.   We have not yet received your check for $_____ . We wonder if there is something troubling you about our service or if there is something else holding up your payment. If so, please call us so we can work it out together. If not, we assume that you'll put your check in the mail today to show us your continued support.

4.   We have received neither a response from you nor payment on your past-due account, despite our numerous reminders. We must have your payment at once or we will have to take further steps to collect the $_____ you owe us.

5.   We have called to your attention several times the unpaid balance of $_____ , and have heard nothing from you. If you do not contact us within the next five days, our collection agency will receive the account. We urge you for the last time to take care of your balance now to avoid this unpleasant action.

OVERDUE "CHECK" STATEMENTS—SURE TO BE OPENED AND READ

Do you suspect that some of your delinquent patients are ignoring your statements, without ever opening them?

If so, you might buy special overdue statement forms that look like checks. These are mailed in the same kind of double-window envelopes that are used for mailing checks. The practice name and address show through one window. The other window shows the patient's name and address on what appears to be a check.

Few people ever fail to open an envelope that seems to contain a check. This trick should at least ensure that patients are opening and reading your collection notices.

DEVELOPING A SEQUENCE OF COLLECTION LETTERS

Collection letters should become increasingly stronger as the account matures. One traditional system for writing collection letters is known as RRAD, for *r*eminder, *r*equest, *a*ppeal, and *d*emand:

1. *Reminder:* The sequence begins with a polite reminder letter that is usually sent soon after the account is overdue. This first letter is as friendly as possible and implies that the patient must have simply overlooked the due date on the statement.

2. *Request:* A firmer "request for payment" letter follows the reminder letter. It begins by expressing concern for the past-due balance and asks for prompt payment.

3. *Appeal:* If the request for payment fails, strive for an explanation of why the payment is late, appealing to the patient's pride, good credit reputation, and fear. At this point, you might recommend that partial payment could restore faith.

4. *Demand:* A final demand letter should point out to the patient the seriousness of the delinquency and the unpleasantries that are likely to ensue if payment continues to be neglected.

Tip: As a follow-up to the demand letter, the practice might consider sending a final notice that the account will be placed for collection if payment is not made by a certain date.

Tip: Phone calls to the patient are extremely important throughout this sequence. If possible, call the debtor before sending each type of letter. And, do not send letters of this type if the patient makes any kind of regular payment, no matter how small.

Collecting the Money That's Due You: Innovative Collection Strategies for Dealing with the Hard Cases

W hen your in-office collection program has run it's full course and failed, you have the choice of writing off the bad debt, or taking further action. In this chapter, we explore the usual further actions, as well as some unusual last-ditch collection strategies.

TURNING THE ACCOUNT OVER TO A THIRD PARTY

Typically, when a business finds that it can't collect using the usual in-office collections program, it turns the account over to a third-party for further action. There are three general options for turning the account over to someone else, specifically:

1. *A collection attorney:* Many collection attorneys handle accounts for one-third of the fee, and work on a retainer.

2. *A percentage-system collection agency:* Most such agencies charge 28 to 50% of the fee collected, and do not charge at all for any work they've done on accounts that remain unpaid.

3. *A flat-fee collection agency:* Such agencies charge a relatively small flat dollar amount for every account they handle for you, whether they collect the money or not.

GUIDELINES FOR CHOOSING A COLLECTION AGENCY

1.   Seek an agency with a high standard of ethics and an attitude toward debtors that's compatible with yours. Visit firms to assess them. If your state oversees collection agencies, be sure the one you choose is licensed.

2.   Ask for and check references.

3.   Make sure the agency provides at least these services:

a.   A two-letter or two-call attempt to collect before the agency confronts the patients in person.

b.   A guarantee that the agency will tell you exactly how collections are made, including the dialogue and letters used with debtors. Also, a guarantee that no lawsuit be filed or threatened against a patient without your approval.

c.   Progress reports on your accounts, presented quarterly or at another interval.

d.   Assurance that the agency will return your account within a reasonable time if it can't collect on them.

4.   Be suspicious of any agency promising to make most deadbeats honor their bills. The collection rate for doctor-assigned accounts is typically 20%.

5.   Read every word of your contract before signing.

TIPS FOR WORKING WITH YOUR COLLECTION AGENCY

1.   Try your best to collect the account on your own. Usually, collection agencies are used as a last resort, such as when:

a.   The patient promises and fails to pay on at least two consecutive dates.

b.   You've tried numerous times to reach the patient by phone and letter but have gotten no response.

c.   You haven't received a payment for quite a while (usually 120 days, but some practices take this step earlier, such as the 90th, 75th, or even 61st day).

d.   The patient expresses unwillingness to pay but has not complained about any services for which he's being charged.

2.   Before you call a collection agency, make sure:

a.   You've made and documented several collection attempts.

b.   The patient is not dissatisfied with your services.

c.   The patient is not undergoing temporary financial hardship or a personal tragedy, such as a death in the family.

d.   The outstanding balance due is substantial and worth the possible consequences (loss of the patient and his referrals, hard feelings, etc.).

e.   You've tried to get the patient to make regular payments, even small ones.

f.   You've warned the patient that by not paying, he risks your turning the account over to an agency for collection.

3.   Collection agencies usually ask for a breakdown of a delinquent patient's fees and financial record. When providing this information, be sure that you don't supply confidential clinical information along with it.

Tip: The best approach is to provide the agency with the fee breakdown it needs, but to identify entries as "professional services" or "laboratory tests." Don't give sensitive specifics about the patient's care or condition, such as "surgery," "pregnancy test," "psychologicial analysis," or "dentures."

TIPS FOR SUING TO COLLECT OVERDUE ACCOUNTS

Small Claims Courts hear legal actions that involve comparatively small sums. They are noted for their simple, fast, and inexpensive procedures, and are sometimes used by doctors as a final collection tactic. (Larger-fee and some other types of cases must be pursued in other courts.)

Of course, it does not make sense to take legal action against a patient without first weighing these benefits against the potential consequences of a court case. For example, ask yourself whether the case is worth your time and energy. How will your other patients react to your taking this action against one or your patients, even when you're justified? And perhaps most importantly, will your action risk a malpractice countersuit? (Patients sometimes refuse to pay their bills because they are dissatisfied with their treatment. In such cases, the patient may feel provoked by a lawsuit, and counter with a malpractice suit.)

If you do decide to go ahead with the lawsuit, call your attorney or the clerk of the nearest court to learn whether Small Claims Court is the appropriate place, or, if not, where and how you need to proceed. Then, follow these steps to prepare and strengthen your case:

1.   Before you end your in-office collection program, ask delinquent patients to sign a letter stating that they owe you money and listing the amount. This step is extremely important because it is an admission of debt, which can be invaluable (sometimes deciding) evidence for your case.

2.   Proceed with the legal action only after extensive and recorded efforts to collect the overdue bill.

3.   Have your papers in order so you can refer to them easily in court.

4.   Dress appropriately—professional, but without conspicuous displays of personal wealth. Remain courteous no matter what provocation you

face. Keep your voice calm, and don't interrupt or speak directly to your opponent.

5.   When representing yourself in Small Claims Court, don't try to act like a lawyer by using technical legal terms or formal cross-examining techniques that you've seen in movies. Small claims cases are down to earth. Simply tell your story.

6.   Answer the judge's questions truthfully, but never volunteer information that might weaken your case.

7.   Take your assistant responsible for collections with you to court, to support your case.

GIFT COLLECTION STRATEGY BUILDS GOODWILL

Most collection efforts do little to build goodwill among patients. Here's an unusual practice builder/last-ditch collection effort that will make patients think you're terrific and pay their delinquent accounts at the same time.

Write a polite collection letter to all patients whose payments are overdue. In it, remind them of the amount they owe and how late it is (the standard wording is fine). Then, add a final paragraph to tell the patient that you're enclosing some small gift in the envelope. Some affordable, easy-to-mail ideas for such gifts:

- Balloons for children.
- Pens.
- Bookmarks.
- Articles on a relevant health topic.
- Paperback books on nutrition, stress management, or another relevant health topic.
- Informative brochures or pamphlets.
- Pocket calendars.
- Refrigerator magnets.

Tip: Explain that you want the patient to have the gift because he may find it useful or interesting. Do *not* suggest that it is a motivator for him to pay his bill. He'll get the point without your having to be explicit.

When the patient gets the gift, he may feel a little bit embarrassed for making you wait for your payment. A little well-timed guilt won't hurt him, may make him pay his bill at once, and may prevent him from being delinquent about payments in the future.

AMNESTY LETTER WORKS WITH
OVERDUE ACCOUNTS

A Merrimack, NH doctor reports superb results from a rather unusual technique for handling long-overdue accounts. He calls it the "amnesty letter," which he sends to patients after normal in-office collection techniques have failed.

What it says:

Dear [Name of Patient]:

For some reason beyond your control, we realized you are unable to pay your bill in our office. I want you to know that as of now, your balance has been reduced to zero.

We appreciate any relative and friends you have referred to us. We want you to know that you are welcome to return to our office for care on a cash basis.

We look forward to seeing you.

According to the doctor, "This way we can concentrate on providing excellent care to those who appreciate it, and not spend hours and energy trying to collect from the small percentage who aren't likely to pay anyway." He adds, "For those who we do not want to see again, we change the second paragraph to ask where they'd like their records sent."

Tip: This technique must of course be used judiciously, and applied consistently. It might be best used with delinquent patients who:

- Have relatively small debts.
- Are potentially rich referral sources.
- Are long-term valued patients undergoing financial hardship.

WHAT TO DO IF A PATIENT FILES FOR BANKRUPTCY

1. Stop all collection efforts immediately when you receive an official notice of bankruptcy filing. Notify your collection agency, if you've turned over the account for collection.

2. Prepare and file a "proof of claim" with the bankruptcy court. This simple form is available from the court (or possibly your attorney). Complete the form carefully and promptly. (It is your claim to share in the distribution of whatever assets the court determines available.)

3.   If the bankrupt patient returns to your office for further care, you may have to provide it. If so, put him or her on a cash basis for all future services.

P · A · R · T
4

Keeping Tight Grips on the Money You Spend

Making Better Purchasing and Ordering Decisions

Running out of a needed supply is a bothersome but almost always preventable, problem. A clearly-outlined procedure for ordering and purchasing materials, coupled with a foolproof inventory system (pages 193–197) will help avoid confusion, mistakes, and wasted time.

PAST RECORDS WILL HELP YOU MAKE INFORMED DECISIONS

Purchasing begins before you place an order, when you first decide what to buy. Your own records can provide important basic information about materials you need. For example:

1. Past records reveal which items are used most frequently.

2. Inventory or stock records keep you informed of the need to reorder in time to allow for delivery. They also indicate whether past orders were correct, too large, or too small.

3. If you're buying items to give to patients (such as informational brochures and giveaways), your records can show which items patients prefer and which special features, sizes, colors, or styles are most popular.

HOW TO CHOOSE THE BEST VENDORS

Most practices need multiple suppliers in different fields. How to choose the best ones:

1. *Establish a list of preferred vendors.* Locate possible suppliers for everything you need. (You can find them through professional journals, meetings, exhibit halls, catalogues, direct mail advertisements, sales representatives, and telephone directories.)

Tip: Ask your colleagues to recommend good suppliers, and to share their experiences with sales reps and products. Investigate each company's claims for product quality and on-time deliveries.

2. *Compare vendors within each category.* Narrow your choices.

Tip: It may be tough to choose between vendors if one has better prices and another has better variety of stock or more reliable deliveries. When this happens, establish a point scale. Decide which qualities are most important and how many points you'll assign when a quality is superior, good, fair, poor, or unacceptable.

Example: A key area for your ranking may be *deliveries.* When a vendor consistently delivers on the date, time, and terms promised, give it the maximum number of points for delivery. Assign fewer points for keeping the promised date but leaving the time uncertain. Assign a zero or minus points for sporadic or consistent delays. Assign extra points for emergency deliveries. Eliminate vendors that have unacceptable deliveries.

Tip: It's not usually worth the risk to buy from an inexpensive but unreliable supplier. You'll probably realize more of a savings in the long run to buy from a more expensive company that delivers products on time and in good condition.

3. *Decide whether to deal with a few or many vendors in each category.* Some guidelines:

If You Use Only a Few Vendors:	If You Use Many Vendors:
1. You usually get more personal attention. Vendors are often more helpful if they know they have most of your business.	1. You can usually take advantage of the best prices and promotional materials offered at any given time.
2. Larger orders sometimes produce better discounts and simplify credit procedures.	2. Competing sales presentations help keep you in touch with the latest in products and services. And, you have a back-up if one vendor can't deliver on time or is out of stock.
3. Dealing with only one vendor leaves you vulnerable if it fails to deliver or suffers a disaster.	3. Dealing with many vendors usually incurs more paperwork and follow-up. And, you can lose discounts that depend on the size of an order.

SIX TIPS FOR AVOIDING PROBLEMS WITH VENDORS

1. *Don't play games.* Be frank about your needs and problems. Don't misquote one vendor's price to another. If you have budget restrictions and can get what you need cheaper from someone else, discuss it openly. The vendor may give you a better price or some useful advice.

Tip: Don't create emergencies for supplies when none really exists. Your supplier won't take you seriously if you cry wolf and make every order a "rush." Be honest, and give your supplier ample time to process your orders. That way, he'll be more apt to accommodate you when a real emergency occurs.

2. *Be tactful,* if you must reject goods or complain. Don't cancel or return merchandise unless the vendor hasn't upheld his part of the contract. Don't stop a check unless your reasons are compelling. (See "How and When to Stop a Check," page 215.)

3. *Respect the vendor's integrity.* Believe your sales rep is honest unless he gives you good reason to think he's not.

4. *Don't put a vendor on the spot.* Never repeat confidential information a vendor shares with you. Don't ask to see a competitor's order.

5. *Don't try to trick a vendor.* For example, don't ask for a low per-unit price quote on a large order and then try to get that price for a small order.

6. *Pay your bills on time.*

HEAD OFF PROBLEMS WITH GOOD PURCHASING RECORDS

Accurate records are useful when placing future orders. Maintaining such records means more work but can result in a better purchasing system. Which records are most helpful:

1. A log book keeps track of orders placed in chronological order. Each entry should include the date, a short description, quantity, price, and the vendor's name.

2. An open order file allows you to review exactly what's expected and when. It should include full information on each order, a detailed description, quantity, price, terms, billing directions, special packing or shipping instructions, and pertinent correspondence or contracts.

3. A closed order file preserves information on already-completed purchases for future reference. It usually includes detailed information on large-ticket items only. For other items, a dollar history may be sufficient.

4. Vendor files enable you to check on one vendor without having to wade through a mass of materials. It is usually divided into separate units for each vendor and includes the vendor's name, address, phone number, sales rep's name and telephone extension, records of all previous orders and terms, your findings on the quality and reliability of products/services, reactions of staff or patients who've used the products, special benefits, and perhaps products to avoid.

5.   Category files provide records of purchases by item or type. Such a file will make it easier to keep track of how much of each item is used and at what rate, seasonal differences, and price changes.

HOW TO FOLLOW UP ON ORDERS

1.   Have one person in the practice be in charge of all follow-up activities after orders are placed.

2.   Check to see that orders are delivered on the date promised. If so, verify that the orders are correct. When they arrive, compare the contents of each order with the items recorded on the order form.

3.   If the order is correct, make sure that invoices are paid on time. Make payments promptly and accurately so you can take advantage of available discount terms.

4.   If the order is incorrect, damaged, or unacceptable, contact the vendor at once. Usually the first course of action is to call the sales rep directly, explain the problem, and agree on a solution (with times, dates, and terms for re-delivery). In most cases, the outcome of this phone conversation is reviewed in a memo.

Some vendors have a return form for incorrect orders. If you complete such a form, include the date of return, a description of the items being returned, the reason, price, and whether the transaction is a refund, credit, or exchange. Prepare two copies of the form, and keep one in your files. Follow up on the re-delivery date.

STEP-BY-STEP CHECKLIST FOR BETTER PURCHASING

Step 1: Centralize control. Tell your staff that all purchases must go through your practice "purchasing coordinator." Develop an internal "requisition form," either circulated through the office, or kept in one central location. Leave space on the form for full descriptions, item numbers, quantities, units of measure, colors, and unit prices.

Tip: On your requisition form (or on a separate form attached to it), preprint the names and numbers of items you need to order most often. This preprinted "shopping list" will help you remember the basics when you place orders.

Step 2: Use a written standardized procedure. Keep the paperwork simple, but use the same procedure for all purchases.

Step 3: Involve your purchasing coordinator in all phases of purchasing. For example, route all correspondence with suppliers through him or her.

Step 4: Use competitive bidding whenever possible. Have your purchasing coordinator obtain three bids for all purchases over $1,000.

Tip: Shop the mailings before placing an order. Is something you need on sale?

Step 5: Require the doctor's approval for all purchases over $500.

Step 6: Lease (don't buy) equipment whenever possible for short-term projects.

Step 7: Create inventory control policies to avoid duplicate and unnecessary purchases. (See "Controlling Waste with a Foolproof Inventory System," pages 193–197.)

Step 8: Keep needed items in plentiful stock. Procedure should insure against running out. On high-volume, high-value items, order a one- or two-month supply at a time and take advantage of quantity pricing. On low-volume and/or low-value items, order as much as a year's supply.

Example: If your practice uses a dozen rolls of scotch tape a year, order them all at once. It doesn't represent much of an investment and doesn't take up much room, so why bother reordering and chance running out?

Tip: When possible, order items in standard packs. This will usually save you money and reduce the chance of damage during shipping.

Tip: Especially if your office is small, consider making occasional basic office-supply buying runs to local discount department stores. Office supply companies often charge considerably more for what's often the identical product.

Step 9: Have your purchasing coordinator inspect all deliveries on arrival, check all goods carefully, and keep your purchasing records.

Step 10: Be sure your purchasing coordinator is honest and well-organized.

C · H · A · P · T · E · R   4-2

Controlling Waste with a Foolproof Inventory System

C ontrolling the inventory in your practice is essential if you're to have what you need on hand when you need it, and at the same time, not buy too much. A good inventory system, however, is much more than simply counting what's on a storage shelf and buying needed supplies at special prices.

ELIMINATING SQUABBLES BY PUTTING ONE PERSON IN CHARGE

The biggest mistake a practice can make in inventory control is to leave responsibility for the inventory to the entire staff. Two problems usually occur as a result: Duplicate supplies are ordered. And, needed supplies are not. The most reliable system for inventory control is to place responsibility for the inventory into the hands of *one* detail-conscious business assistant. This staff member is designated as the practice's "inventory control clerk" or "purchasing coordinator." (See "Step-by-Step Checklist for Better Purchasing," Step 1, page 190.)

The inventory control clerk has a variety of duties. Among these, she generally:

1. Checks all treatment/examination rooms daily to see that they're equipped with the appropriate number and kind of supplies. (If not, she sees that this is done by the clinical assistant or nurse.)

2. Maintains a supply inventory record (with log forms for recording supply usage) in one orderly location. Such a record should allow for easy identification of shortages and excess inventory.

3. Makes sure the supply storage area is secure. If need be, she may limit access to supplies by locking them up, to deter or reduce pilferage. (See "Preventing Theft of Small Office Supplies," pages 331–332.)

4. Checks the supply inventory regularly. Does needed comparison shopping and orders the correct quantity of supplies before they're needed. Keeps purchasing records up-to-date.

5. Unpacks and examines supplies for quality and quantity.

6. Returns excess inventory to suppliers for credit.

7. Returns damaged or wrong items for credit or replacement.

8. Shelves supplies in the correct place. Makes appropriate records of all items that have been checked and received.

9. Initials and dates all correct invoices. Gives these to the practice's financial secretary, bookkeeper, or business manager for monthly payment.

15 TIPS FOR BETTER INVENTORY SUPPLY MANAGEMENT

1. Inventory all the items you use in your practice.
Tip: The best way to do this is to compile two lists. The first list should include all technical or clinical supplies. The other should include all business, stationery, cleaning, and miscellaneous supplies. Arrange each list in alphabetical order according to product name.

2. Next to each item on each list, record the minimum inventory that should be maintained. For example, "Number 2 Pencils—25." In general, aim to maintain at least a three-week supply of each item, unless it is perishable sooner. Revise and update the list as needed.
Tip: When possible, rubber band a "please reorder" slip (with the item number, vendor, and description) around the amount of stock that you consider your reorder point. That way, the person who takes any of that "reserve" stock can give the reorder slip to your inventory supply clerk.
Tip: In addition to quantities, also establish ordering lead times. Check past orders and invoices to determine how long it has taken in the past to get each item. *Example:* Everyday office supplies are usually available in 24–48 hours. Mail order supplies may take 10 days.

3. Once these inventory lists are completed, make copies of them. Place one copy in your office manual, and another where your supplies are kept. The door to the supply room or closet is generally a good place to post this list.

4. In the supply area, store similar or related items near one another. For example, your stationery and business supply inventory should be set up so staples and staplers, pens and pencils, and envelopes and letterhead are near one another.
Tip: A Bemidji, Minn. optometric practice suggests color coding the

supply room. "We painted each section of shelving in our supply room a different color," explains the practice's office manager. "We then set up a notebook index which we keep there. All supplies are listed in alphabetical order, and next to each item, we indicate the color of the shelf on which it can be found. This makes locating the needed supply quick and easy, even for staff members who are in a rush or who aren't familiar with the inventory system," she says.

5.   Keep the supplies you use most frequently on the storage shelves that are the most accessible—those from eye level to waist level in height. Store items used less frequently out of the way, on the highest and lowest shelves.

6.   When you place items on a storage shelf, tag the front of the shelf with a strip of plastic or a tape label approximately two inches long. On that tag, write the name of the item and immediately to the right of it, a number. This number should be the minimum amount of that supply that can be in stock, taken from the inventory lists you created. (See tips #1 and #2 above.) When that number is reached, you'll know it's time to reorder.

7.   Don't store supplies off the premises if you can avoid it. Supplies kept out of the building are hard to manage and easy to forget.

8.   Follow the "first-in-first-out" (FIFO) strategy for inventory control. Use supplies in the order they were purchased and replace stock from the back. That way you'll use the oldest items first.

9.   Pitch inventory stock items that are obsolete or that have aged beyond their useful life.

10.   Keep the supply inventory in the office to what you really need for regular use and emergencies. Don't order so much that you have an excessive inventory on hand. Most suppliers make deliveries often. Rely on them to store items until you need them.

11.   Simplify inventory tasks by setting aside different inventory areas. A good system: Establish *three* inventory areas, of which only two would be tracked:

a.   The first area to be inventoried would be the *bulk* supply area. Here you'd store supplies that are too large or bulky to be placed on limited storage shelves. These might be large boxes of towels, napkins, tissues, disposable dressing gowns, etc.

b.   A second area for tracking would be for *reserve* inventory— items that are kept on the storage shelves in complete packages. Try to maintain a three-week supply of each item in this inventory.

c.   Finally, the third area is the treatment or examination room for storage of *ready* inventory. Don't track these supplies. Once a package is taken from the reserve inventory and opened, take it off inventory. That way you'll never keep track of half a box or a quarter of a bottle. In the best inventory systems, it's either a complete package or it's nothing at all.

12.　Study your inventory log records periodically to learn how frequently certain items are replaced. Look for differences in seasonal use of supplies. The more you know about your practice's supply use habits, the better you'll be able to anticipate inventory needs. And, studying your log book can help you pinpoint supply waste or theft.

13.　If the supply area is locked, establish and publicize the hours when your inventory control clerk is available to fill supply requests. Otherwise, the doctor and staff will find it necessary to make supply requests as they come up, which will waste time and cut efficiency.

14.　If more than one person in the office is allowed access to the supply area, establish these rules:

a.　Whoever removes an item from a shelf must record the information in the log book or form.

b.　He or she must check to be sure that the items remaining on the shelf equal or exceed the number that is on the shelf's tag.

c.　If the inventory is getting too near the minimum number, that person should notify the inventory control clerk so she'll be able to reorder while there's still plenty of time.

15.　Keep your inventory control system, log sheets, and other forms as simple as possible. The simpler your system, the more likely you'll be to stay on top of it.

HOW TO SET LIMITS ON YOUR INVENTORY CONTROL CLERK

While you don't want to be involved in every small purchase of supplies for your practice, you must establish some limits for your inventory supply clerk.

To begin, you might insist that she get your approval for any single order over a set dollar amount, such as $500. You might also want to establish maximum reorder quantities. These would be the maximum quantities of each product your inventory control clerk can order at one time without your approval.

To establish these limits, first determine your rate of use. For example, it's a waste of time to reorder such items as paper clips every week. On the other hand, you will want to establish some guidelines so you don't get stuck with a lifetime supply of jumbo gem clips.

Next, consider the item's shelf life and storage needs. You can't afford to waste money by purchasing large quantities of perishable products, only to pitch half of them. You also don't want to face the problem of finding a dry storage area for unwieldy quantities of delicate or bulky items, like paper goods. Some products must be stored at specific temperatures, others in the dark. Your available storage space will help you establish reasonable limits.

Finally, consider the total investment involved. Establish a weekly or monthly budget for buying supplies beyond which your approval is needed. You don't want to tie up too much cash by purchasing excessive amounts of supplies, even if they are offered at a good discount.

C·H·A·P·T·E·R 4-3

Making Major Equipment Purchases on Your Own Terms

Buying equipment is usually stressful. It can be very hard to know that you're making the right decision, getting the right price, and dealing with the right vendor. And, because of the enormous costs involved, and the importance of the equipment to your productivity and satisfaction in practice, making mistakes can be very scary and serious.

Many doctors underestimate the strength of their bargaining position as a buyer or lessee of office equipment. The manufacturers, vendors, and their sales representatives do not hold all the cards, although they may want you to think that they do. In this chapter, you'll learn how to play your own cards well. The key is in remembering that you have the biggest ace of all up your sleeve—you can take your business elsewhere to get a better price or terms.

To decide whether to buy or lease equipment, see Appendix 1-M, "Checklist for Determining Whether to Lease or Buy Equipment," page 537.

SIZING UP THE SALES REP

The sales rep you encounter will almost always be a jovial, intelligent, ambitious, well-heeled individual who serves as a link between your practice and the equipment manufacturer or vendor. He or she is usually very friendly, and will often appreciate the difficulties, concerns, and constraints you face being in practice. Often, the sales rep will be the type of person you'd love to meet at a party or sit next to at a meeting. He or she usually is very personable, has an amusing story to tell, and thinks yours are very funny.

Of course, the sales rep is not always a true friend, nor should he be. In the final result, he or she will be judged according to how much you spend. Learn to control your feelings about the rep or he may quickly control you and the entire environment for selling you equipment.

Once you allow personal feelings to come into play, you may find it very hard to say *no* to a rep you consider a friend. In such a case, you may feel compelled to buy your friend's products, simply because of your relationship with him. Maintaining at least some distance from the rep may strengthen your bargaining position and help you make better decisions. When push comes to shove, friendship should not come into the negotiations, unless it can benefit you.

SEVEN WAYS TO CONTROL THE REP, VENDOR, OR MANUFACTURER

A knowlegable sales rep can be a great source of information and a big help in making good decisions. Certainly, ask him to explain how his equipment works, its strengths and shortcomings, and make recommendations. However, also seek information and input from other, less partial sources:

1. Do not ask the sales rep to define your method of practice, preferences, or equipment needs for you. You, after all, are the person who runs your practice. Who but you should be best able to tell you how you like to practice and what your own equipment problems and inadequacies are?

If you need guidance, ask your staff to help you determine your equipment needs and usage patterns. Your employees may be the ones who will use the office equipment you're thinking of buying (especially photocopiers, word processors, telephone systems, and other basic office machines). They will know better than anyone how much photocopying you need to do, how many times per day they need to transfer a telephone call, etc.

2. Do not ask the sales rep to define your deadline requirements. Again, you and your staff are in the best position to know when you need your new equipment.

3. Do not ask the sales rep to define your budget or to tell you whether you should purchase or lease the equipment. He is usually not be the best person to advise you about your practice's finances or tax planning strategies. Decide all of this ahead of time with your accountant/financial planner, who will stand nothing to gain no matter what you decide.

4. Do not ask the sales rep to teach you everything you know about the types of equipment that can satisfy your needs or about his competitors. Do your homework. Read, ask your colleagues about their equipment, visit the exhibit hall at professional meetings, ask questions, or if need be, hire a consultant to help you learn about the types of equipment available. If you leave your total education to the sales rep, he will very likely teach you that your needs will be best served by his manufacturer's equipment. And, he is apt to tell you why his product line far outranks anything produced by the

competition. Even though he may be right, confirm what he says with an impartial source.

5. Do insist on internal discipline when you ask others in your practice to help you decide on a purchase (a partner, office manager, business assistant, etc.). Some sales reps try to use the "divide and conquer" technique when working with a group, trying to get some of you on his side. Discipline means that all members of your purchase committee agree that the final, ultimate decision rests with one individual, and that everyone else is a consultant who will contribute opinions and research.

Tip: Always, one of the doctors should make the final decision on big ticket, major purchases for the practice. While there are some things you can delegate to employees, this isn't one of them.

6. Do realize that the sales rep usually lacks the authority to make changes in the written service contract and that his verbal promises may not hold. Make the rep give you the name of the individual at his company who does have the authority to alter a contract. That is the only person with whom you will want to negotiate your contract.

To get to Mr./Ms. Big, be prepared to reject the rep's excuses, such as, "We never make contract changes" or "There is no such person." Take charge and play it straight with the rep. For example, "You want my sale. We need a few changes in our contract. Isn't it in everyone's best interest to get that name for us?"

7. Do be persistent about contacting Mr. Big. You may find that he's not in when you call or that he never returns your calls. In that case, try calling Mr. Big person-to-person. An official sounding telephone operator is a fantastic aid in tracking down an incommunicado Mr. Big, and the service is free if you don't reach him.

If Mr. Big's secretary reports that he's just left the office, break in with this rehearsed line: "This is a matter Mr. Big can handle rather easily, but if he's unavailable, would you kindly transfer this call to Mr. Bigger?" Instruct the operator to make the call person-to-person to Mr. Bigger, whose name, by the way, you should have gotten in advance by doing your homework.

This tactic puts Mr. Big's secretary in a bind. She'll not want to waste Mr. Bigger's time with a routine matter Mr. Big should have handled and was trying to evade. Chances are very good that Mr. Big will make a miraculous reappearance at the office. ("Mr. Big has just returned to his desk" or "I think I may be able to catch him before he leaves the building.")

At this point, the secretary may promise that Mr. Big is still out but will get back to you. If this happens, give her some more pressure: "I will be at my office only until 4:30. I need to hear from Mr. Big today or I will have to take the matter up with Mr. Bigger first thing tomorrow morning." Then follow through.

DUMB IS SMART, AND OTHER TACTICS FOR GETTING THE BEST PRICE

Of course, no one usually likes to be considered dumb. Yet the illusion of dumbness, or, rather, not showing how smart you are, can be a powerful negotiating tool. A shrewd negotiator asks for lots of explanations. The more a sales rep has to explain, the more points get raised. And, with more information on the negotiating table, you'll have more opportunities for negotiation and less chance of something passing by too quickly.

More good negotiating strategies:

1. Time is control, so slow down the negotiation. Don't agree too quickly. Take time to "mull it over" and tell the rep you'll get back to him. If you don't like what you're hearing, get up to leave (or if you're in your office, escort the sales rep to your door). The threat of walking or ending the negotations usually helps break down barriers.

2. Point out the equipment's shortcomings or flaws. For example, "How many words per second does it print? That's a little slow for our needs." However, don't overdo it and knock the equipment entirely, or the rep will see right through you or become defensive.

3. Try never to give away anything without getting something in return. For example, "You mean I'll have to wait six weeks before I get it? What will I do? It will cost me a bundle to rent one in the meantime. How can you help me out of this bind?"

4. Sometimes you'll make a counteroffer to the asking price, and go through several rounds of bidding. When you must increase your bid, make it as small an increment as you can.

5. When all else fails, it never hurts to pause and ask, "Is that your best price?"

6. When the rep finally consents to lowering the price, don't smile or gloat. Move on to negotiating the terms.

NEGOTIATING THE TERMS: LOOKING OUT FOR NUMBER ONE

The typical equipment vendor's standard contract is usually weighed very heavily in his favor and gives you very little. However, you can and should change the contract to give you the protection you need.

Below are some of the most important contractual changes you can make when buying high-priced office equipment. There's probably no manufacturer or vendor who'll agree to let you make all of them. Therefore, decide which are most important to you and give them your best effort.

Tip: You'll probably make your rep defensive if you throw away his standard contract and substitute one of your own. Therefore, use the standard contract, but have your attorney incorporate your changes in a separate addendum entitled, "Revisions."

1.   Most standard contracts lock you into a specific delivery date. Amend that so you can change the delivery date without penalty. This will protect you in case you need to make a last-minute change due to fire, flood, injury, etc.

2.   The vendor's contract is a sales contract, and will probably not guarantee that the equipment will perform certain functions or that it will live up to specified standards. Change your contract so it includes the manufacturer's advertisements, promotional materials, and operations manuals. Without these, you'll have a tough time proving that the equipment didn't do what you were promised it would.

3.   Many contracts ask you to agree that the vendor or manufacturer will send your equipment free on board (FOB). That means that once the vendor gives the equipment to a carrier such as UPS or the post office, he has no more responsibility for its condition. If something happens to the equipment while it is in transit, it is up to you to make a claim against the carrier, and you'll still have to pay the vendor. Amend your contract so risk of loss or damage to the equipment remains with the vendor or manufacturer until it is delivered in your office and you have accepted it.

4.   Most contracts will assume that the day the equipment is delivered to your office is automatically the day you accepted it. Be careful here because the date of acceptance is the start of your warranty period. Amend your contract so that you'll not pay for the equipment until you've formally accepted it. Also state that you'll accept the equipment only after you've tested it to see that it works satisfactorily, for a predetermined period of time. Finally, stipulate that the acceptance date will not occur until the vendor has completed whatever employee training he has promised.

5.   Amend the contract so it defines the training you and your staff will receive from the manufacturer or vendor. Change it so the vendor will award to each of you a certificate or letter that says you've been properly trained and that you can now operate the equipment so it will perform effectively the functions indicated in the operations manual. Without this protection, the vendor can later blame problems with the equipment on the operator, who he'll claim wasn't properly trained or proficient.

6.   A standard contract will define the warranty period, but it won't protect you if the equipment is down most of the time. Change the contract so it extends the warranty period by the number of days the equipment is down.

Example: If you have a 90-day warranty and your equipment is down for 30 of those days, your warranty should be extended to 120 days from the day you accepted the equipment.

7.   Most vendor's contracts don't provide for the vendor to install the necessary cables and wires that you'll need to make the equipment function properly. Amend this so all installation requirements are the vendor's responsibility. That way, he can't later blame malfunctions on faulty wiring or inadequate cables.

C·H·A·P·T·E·R 4-4

10 Tips to Help You Buy the Right Computer

S hopping for an office computer is an important task, and simultaneously, a confusing one. The stakes are obviously very great, since a computer is expensive and one of the most important practice management tools you will ever buy. At the same time, you will be faced with virtually unlimited choices, as the number of vendors and options increase.

Carefully preparing before venturing forward into the computer market is, of course, essential to making the right choice. Below are ten important points to consider before beginning your search.

10 TIPS TO HELP YOU BUY THE RIGHT COMPUTER

1. *Don't buy backwards.* Many people buy computer systems and then ask how to apply them to their needs. It makes much more sense to assess very carefully the current and future needs of your practice first. Then, find software that meets or exceeds those defined needs.

2. *Do have reasonable expectations.* A computer can't save a failing practice, help you do things you don't already understand, or make subjective decisions for you. It is only as good as the input information it is fed. If that information is inaccurate or incomplete, the results will be inaccurate and incomplete as well. A computer will not eliminate the need for accurate record-keeping, nor will it, in most cases, allow you to reduce your current number of employees. Instead, a computer will provide new, faster, and often better ways of doing things.

3. *Do estimate all costs.* Hidden costs may include those for insurance, consultants, installation, maintenance, finance charges, legal fees, down time, new furniture and lighting, and lost production (when closing the office for initial data entry). For more information on this subject, see, "The Best Way to Accomplish Data Entry," page 52.

4. *Do make an informed, intelligent decision.* Don't let emotions, sales pressure, time constraints, or status influence your computer buying decisions.

5. *Don't buy blind.* Do be personally involved in choosing the system. You probably should delegate some of the shopping and research task to someone else. However, do roll up your sleeves for the final decision. Test drive the exact model and configuration you intend to buy.

6. *Do consider the software first.* You can buy the most expensive hardware on the market. But if the software is poor, you will have only added extra work, stress, and frustration to your practice.

7. *Do choose user-friendly software.* Avoid systems that require significant memorization or those that are so complex that they are never completely mastered. Keep in mind that several of your employees will learn to operate your computer throughout its lifetime, perhaps due to job duties, turnover, or shifting responsibilities. This makes simplicity and ease of operation extremely desirable.

8. *Don't be distracted by gimmicky special features.* If the basic software is not first rate, don't buy it.

9. *Don't rely on vendors' advice alone.* A vendor's livelihood depends upon how many computers he sells. And, his knowledge of computers is often limited to what he learned in his company's sales training course. In particular, beware of the following common vendor promises:

If the vendor says:	You should remember that:
1. A computer will enable you to make more personalized contact with patients.	1. Manual record-keeping and a good quality memory typewriter might do just as well.
2. A computer has the capability of custom programs.	2. It takes a long time to develop good software. Don't assume any program exists or will exist until you've actually seen it work.
3. This system will expand to meet your future needs.	3. Adding to your system may slow response time. Insist on a guaranteed response of 30 seconds or less. Sometimes, that's possible only by expanding disk memory.
4. You won't need special wiring or furniture.	4. Current surges and power failures are still serious problems. For more information on this subject, see, "Gearing Up Physically for Office Automation," pages 437–442.

If the vendor says:	You should remember that:
5. This computer will increase your practice by —%.	5. While a computer can speed things up, it can't do anything you couldn't do without it.
6. You can have your forms printed any way you want.	6. Items must conform to at least some spacing requirements and restrictions.
7. Just call anytime if anything goes wrong.	7. Only certain servicing hours may be available.

10.   *Do not choose a computer on the basis of price alone.* Computers in a given price range can have very different capabilities and features. Also, consider the computer's service, maintenance, compatibility, expandability, and reputation. Look for systems that can be upgraded by adding (rather than replacing) equipment.

FOR ADDITIONAL INFORMATION

For more information on office automation, see:

- "Switching Over to a Computer, Without Tears," pages 51–54.
- "Gearing Up Physically for Office Automation," pages 437–442.
- "Housekeeping Tips that Prevent Costly Computer Problems," pages 443–446.
- "Insurance Musts for Your Office Computer: A Checklist," Appendix 1-I, page 529.

C·H·A·P·T·E·R   4-5

Are You a Sitting Duck for Con Artists?

"I am the recent victim of a scam to which other members should be alerted." So wrote a Westport, CT dentist to *The American Dental Association News*. The doctor went on to explain how a magazine subscription service sent dunning notices to him for non-payment of a bill. Yet, he had no recollection of ever dealing with that company.

Nonetheless, he finally paid the bill, assuming someone in the office had authorized the subscription. Later, he received a renewal bill, but this time he was certain he did not authorize the renewal. "There is no way I will pay this bill," he wrote. "I now realize that it was a mistake to pay the other bill."

Another doctor's story is no better: "Bill" called the doctor, claiming to represent his athletic club. He told the doctor he was publishing the annual athletic club roster and directory, and asked him to take a $100 box listing in the "Professionals" section. Profits would go toward the athletic equipment fund, Bill said.

The doctor agreed to pay for the listing, and Bill explained that due to a "tight deadline," he needed the check right away. He asked the doctor to make the check payable to "Ace Publishing" and sent his "daughter" to the office to pick it up. Weeks passed, and the doctor became curious about the status of the directory, so he called the athletic club. You guessed it: The club didn't publish any sort of roster and directory, and knew nothing of Bill and his daughter, the ad, or the doctor's check. Of course, Bill and his daughter were no where to be found.

WHY DOCTORS ARE GOOD TARGETS FOR SCAMS

Unfortunately, scams like those described above are more commonplace than most of us realize. Doctors are wonderful targets for such scams for several reasons:

1.   Doctors are generally honest, trusting, good-hearted people. They're likely to assume others are honest, too.

2.   Doctors are extremely busy. They rarely have time to investigate such propositions or references. They are likely to buy on impulse, without asking too many questions or checking credentials.

3.   Doctors spend a great deal of money to operate their practices. Others in the practice are usually authorized to make small purchases. Thus, doctors are not likely to be suspicious of unfamiliar $50, $100, or $150 expenses, as long as they appear to be reasonable.

THE FIVE BEST WAYS TO PROTECT YOURSELF

Of course, we need not be paranoid and suspect that everyone is out there to con us. However, there are some sensible, simple steps every doctor can take to make himself and his practice more "scam-proof." Here are the five best:

1.   Don't assume that you can spot crooks just by looking at them. Typical con artists won't approach you with a cheap suit and a fast-talking line, as they do in the movies. Successful con artists will probably resemble you a great deal. They are very often well-groomed, well-heeled, articulate individuals, who are very likeable.

Also, don't assume that all con artists are men. Women, too, operate or play a part in scams, as do some children.

And, keep in mind that you may never even have the opportunity to meet the con artist behind the scam. The sly crook might hire honest, hardworking souls to do his dirty work for him, and in so doing, con them as well.

2.   If you sign up for a magazine subscription from a salesperson you don't know, you're running a double risk. You may not get the publication you ordered. Or, you may not get anything at all.

Tip: Send a check directly to the publisher of the magazine you want. Or, use a reputable subscription service.

3.   If someone approaches you in the office and requests a donation to a church or charity, ask for the name and address of the organization and say you will mail a check later.

Tip: Post a sign in your office stating, "Absolutely no soliciting or selling permitted in this office."

4.   If a sales rep tries to sell you something over the phone, and you're interested, explain that you never buy anything over the phone, but that you'll be glad to talk to the individual in person. Then ask the salesperson to drop by, with the proper credentials. If it's a scam, the con artist will know you're wise to con outfits, and probably won't waste any more time with you.

5.   If you're billed for an item you don't remember ordering, investigate it. If you find that no one in your office authorized the purchase, have your business assistant write to the company and explain the situation. Then, return the merchandise or cancel the subscription.

SCAM PATIENT CONS DENTIST OUT OF $900

In an interesting case, a well-meaning dentist lost $900 to a clever con artist in poor dental health, who was posing as a new patient. After carefully examining the con man, the dentist made his diagnosis, and presented his recommendations for extensive restorative dental treatment. The patient readily accepted the doctor's treatment plan and recommendations, scheduled his first appointment, and wrote out a check that day for $900, which was to serve as a deposit. The balance of the fee was to be paid after completion of treatment.

Two days later, the patient returned to the office to report that he was being transferred suddenly to another city, and unfortunately, would not be able to proceed with the doctor's recommended dental treatment, as planned. He asked for a refund of his $900 deposit. The trusting dentist advised his business assistant to write him a refund check for $900, on the spot. The patient took it, and left.

Two days later, the patient's original check came back to the practice as a bad, NSF check. By this time, the dentist was unable to track down the patient, who had skipped town. To this day, he has not recovered his $900.

Tip: A patient may have a legitimate reason to ask you to refund payment or a deposit he has made for treatment. However, you *must* slow things down, to protect yourself from possible fraud. Wait until you are certain that the patient's payment has cleared the bank before you give him the refund.

FOR MORE INFORMATION

For more information on protecting yourself from common scams used against doctors, refer to:

1.   "How to Avoid Getting Burned When You Accept Checks from Patients," pages 131–137.

2.   "How to Avoid Credit Card Fraud," pages 139–144.

3.   "How to Protect the Cash in Your Office," pages 145–149.

4.   "Preventing Employee Theft," pages 327–333.

C·H·A·P·T·E·R   4-6

Avoiding Problems When Paying Your Bills

C hecks are a fabulous way to pay your bills, because they give you an indisputable record that the money was sent and accepted. Cancelled checks are useful not only to settle disputes with vendors, but for tax purposes, too.

Unfortunately, every check you write leaves you a bit vulnerable to errors and theft. However, you can protect yourself almost completely if you institute a few simple check-writing policies for your practice. You should take similar precautions whenever you pay bills with credit cards.

13 TIPS FOR STREAMLINING THE CHECK-WRITING PROCESS

1. Limit check-writing to one or two days each month. The 10th and 25th are generally convenient days.

2. Use a book of checks printed three to a page—with a ring-binder type of cover that can be reused.

3. Buy checks that have no-carbon-required (NCR) paper attached to them. That way you'll have an exact copy of every check your office writes.

4. Instruct your assistant always to fill out the stub before the check. In so doing, have her note the reason for every check. If the check is for more than one expense, have her note the breakdown on the stub.

5. Use a check protector to imprint the amount payable on the check.

6. Have your assistant write or type the payee's name in full, or as indicated on the invoice. If you have an account number with a firm, note it on the check.

7. When writing a check to an official of a firm or government agency, include the person's title. That way your check can't be wrongfully deposited into a personal account.

8.   If your assistant makes a mistake on a check, have her write the word *void* in large letters on the stub and across the face of the check. Instruct her never to destroy a voided check. Your accountant or auditor may want to see it.

9.   Does the invoice or statement have a tear-off slip to return with the check? If so, your assistant should attach it to the check, saving the other portion for your records. On it she should note the date of payment, check number, and amount paid.

10.   If a tear-off invoice isn't provided, have your assistant send a photocopy with the payment. Then keep the original, complete with payment information, in your files.

11.   When paying a bill by mail, write "For Deposit Only" on the back of your check. That way, if the check is stolen, the thief can't cash it.

12.   Mail checks in security, non-see-through envelopes, available at office supply stores. Or, wrap checks in folded sheets of paper. Hold the envelope up to the light to be sure you can't read the check through it.

13.   Limit check-writing authority to as few people in your practice as possible.

WHY YOU SHOULD READ EVERY CHECK YOU SIGN

If you're in the habit of signing stacks of checks without looking at them, you're looking for trouble. And it will probably find you.

For one thing, not reading checks allows mistakes to go unnoticed. But more importantly, signing checks without reading them leaves the door wide open for an embezzler. It makes it very easy to ask you to sign an extra check or two made out to the embezzling employee or someone he knows. And how easy—and tempting—it would be to give himself a raise. How would you ever know he increased the amount on his payroll check a little bit, if you don't read the checks you're signing?

Look at each check carefully. Are the dates and amounts on the stub and the check identical? Does the amount seem reasonable? Do you recognize the name of the payee? If anything looks the least bit fishy, ask your assistant for an explanation—and the invoice, payroll record, etc. And even if everything seems in order, spot check every now and then to see that the amounts and payees are correct.

A WORD OF CAUTION ABOUT SIGNATURE STAMPS

Some doctors have facsimile signature stamps made so staff members can process checks and other paperwork quickly, without waiting (and interrupting) for a signature. However, be warned that such stamps are risky. They represent your own signature which could lead to serious problems if applied to unauthorized checks, or to prescriptions, third-party insurance claims, or credit card charge slips.

If you have a signature stamp that's used infrequently, it may be the wisest course to destroy it. The security risks are greater than the benefits of a stamp that's rarely used. However, if you do use a stamp regularly, and you feel it's worth the risk to keep it, prevent problems in these ways:

1. Make only one stamp.

2. Allow only long-term, highly-trusted *bonded* staff members to have access to the stamp.

3. Designate a place with a secure lock for the stamp when not in use. Insist that the stamp be kept there.

4. Do *not* allow your bookkeeper access to the stamp. Of all people, the bookkeeper is the person with the greatest opportunity to write checks, sign them, and make cover-up accounting entries. Access to the stamp is a great temptation.

HOW AND WHEN TO STOP A CHECK

Stopping a check is a serious step. Therefore, you should not do so unless your reasons are compelling. Examples: You may stop a check when you've mailed a check to a company or a person, and after a week or so, it or he still hasn't received it. You may also stop a check if the payee tells you he lost the check before cashing it. (In both cases, notify the person who was to receive the check that you will be stopping payment and sending another check.)

To stop a check, you must usually:

1. Describe it to your bank with "reasonable accuracy." What they'll need: The date, number, exact amount, and payee.

2. Banks vary, but in general, you can phone in your stop-payment instructions. If so, get the name of the person you speak to.

3. As a follow-up, write a letter or drop by the bank to sign a statement. Usually, a written stop-payment order is good for six months, after which it may be renewed in writing. (Most banks won't cash a check more than six months old.) A verbal order may stand only 14 days unless confirmed in writing.

4. You'll have to pay the bank's fee for the stop-payment, typically $10–$20.

If a bank pays a check after you've given *proper* stop-payment instructions, you must show that you suffered a loss because of the bank's negligence. Then and only then will you be reimbursed. When the amount in question is small—less than a few hundred dollars—the bank may accept your assertion of loss at face value. But when the amount is larger, the bank may make you go to court to prove your case.

What if someone quickly cashes your stopped check at his or her own bank, not yours? He isn't really cashing it, but rather, getting instant credit. When your bank refuses to honor the check because of your stop-payment, the other bank will debit the person's account.

Seek legal advice any time you want to stop a check because you're dissatisfied with a product or service. While you may feel justified in stopping payment, your lawyer may advise you that it's not the correct way to proceed. In fact, an "arbitrary" stop-payment may get you into bigger trouble by leaving you open to the charge of breaking a binding contract.

REDUCE THE RISK OF UNAUTHORIZED USE OF YOUR CREDIT CARDS

Every once in awhile, you may come across an opportunity to pay your bills with a credit card. For example, credit cards are commonly used for business travel and meals, and for gasoline for a practice-owned vehicle. But did you know that using an office charge card to buy ordinary supplies for your practice can earn you some extra money? Timed right, the card can give you up to two extra months to invest your money and earn interest on it.

Example: Suppose your card's billing date is the 23rd. If you use a credit card to buy needed supplies on the 22nd or 23rd of the month, the charges will appear on the *next* month's bill. When it arrives, you will have 30 days to pay for it. Pay the bill when it's due, not before, so you can draw interest on your money as long as possible.

Tip: If you use a money market or bond fund check to pay the bill, you may be able to gain up to 7–10 extra days!

When you do use a credit card to pay your bills, be sure you protect yourself against loss and theft in the following ways:

1. Be sure you get your own card back at the end of the transaction.
2. Don't give your card to anyone to use who is not an authorized user.
3. Don't leave cards unattended in public. Keep yours with you in your office, or lock them up.

4.   Check credit-card bills for suspicious charges. Call the company immediately if you spot one, and send a follow-up letter that includes the dollar amount and description of the error, why you think it is an error, etc.

5.   Never give your credit-card number on the phone to anyone who calls and asks for it.

6.   Report stolen or lost cards at once. Do so even if a stranger calls and says he found your card. It may be a ploy to give the thief time to run up charges.

7.   Keep credit card transaction slips filed in a safe place, and destroy those you no longer need to keep. Thieves sometimes get numbers by taking discarded slips out of the trash, so tear or shred them, as well as the carbons.

HOW TO HANDLE A LARGE VOLUME OF CHECKS MANUALLY

If you find yourself writing many checks, and you're not using a computer to print them out, look into a write-it-once system. With this, the check and disbursement ledger sheet are lined up on a pegboard or ring binder with built-in guide pins. The check is written the usual way. However, its carbon backing makes a duplicate on the ledger sheet. The amount of the check is repeated under the appropriate ledger sheet heading, such as taxes, insurance, telephone, supplies, etc.

The ledger sheet then shows all the information that the check stub would show. This prevents transcribing errors and is also a convenient way to add up deductible expenses for income taxes.

Tip: For information about paying incidental office expenses with cash, see, "Keep a Tight Grip on Your Petty Cash Account" on page 147.

C·H·A·P·T·E·R   4-7

40 Ways to Save Money on Office Operations

Keeping a professional practice running well is a costly endeavor. However, there are many simple things you can do to cut expenses, without sacrificing the quality of the services you provide, or your own comfort or efficiency. Below are 40 of the best.

SAVING MONEY ON POSTAGE

1. If you regularly do large mailings (such as statements and patient newsletters), ask for an appointment with a customer-service representative from your local post office. The rep will meet with you free and suggest ways to cut your mailing costs by making effective use of presort, bulk mail, and other services.

About bulk mail: Bulk mail goes third class, requires presorting, and sometimes must be delivered to a specific post office. To qualify for third class bulk mail, items must be identical and "reproduced." (They can't be handwritten or contain personal messages.)

2. Update your patient mailing list regularly. Remove duplicate names, names of people who have moved, and others who for some reason should no longer receive your mail.

3. Observe Postal Service regulations pertaining to the proper size, shape, and thickness of mail. When you don't follow these rules, your mail will be returned and penalty fees charged.

Example: For first class mail, letter-size envelopes can be no smaller than $3\frac{1}{2} \times 5$-inch. All items must be at least 0.007 of an inch thick—about the thickness of an official postcard.

4. When using first-class mail for a piece weighing an ounce or less, try fitting the piece into an envelope no larger than $11\frac{1}{2} \times 6\frac{1}{8}$-inch and $\frac{1}{4}$-inch thick. If your piece exceeds any of these dimensions, a surcharge will be added to the one-ounce rate.

Tip: The standard 9 × 12-inch envelope used by many practices exceeds the maximum dimensions, and is subject to the surcharge. Thus, whenever appropriate, design your mail so it fits into a standard #10 envelope. It will cost much less to mail such a piece (if the total weight is an ounce or less) than one that requires flat mailing in a 9 × 12-inch envelope.

5.   Use a good postage scale, and check it regularly for accuracy. An electronic scale is preferable to an ordinary scale, because it eliminates the need to consult postal rates and regulation charts. (It computes needed information for you.) Thus it reduces errors and saves time.

6.   Use a postage meter. A meter decreases the chances of using excessive postage and discourages office theft of stamps. The cost of leasing a meter is generally offset by increased efficiency in office routine.

Tip: Metered mail moves faster at the post office, since it doesn't have to be cancelled. A meter can also save time, since many seal envelopes as well as print postal markings. The most highly sophisticated meters can be attached to or contain unit-weight scales that automatically compute and print out the postage required.

Bonus: Metered mail conveys a successful image, because it is associated with large, successful organizations.

7.   Investigate ways you can use lightweight mailing materials. *Example:* Lightweight, tough envelopes made of DuPont "Tyvek" (spun-bonded Olefin) weigh less than half of similar-size kraft envelopes.

8.   Collect mail going to one address, and send it in a single envelope or container. If you have frequent correspondents (such as favorite colleagues), create a mailbox for each of them.

9.   Shop for cheaper ways to send packages. Avoid overnight delivery unless it is absolutely necessary.

10.   Use postcards for appropriate messages, since the postal rate for these is significantly less.

Tip: Be aware that postcards can't be used for confidential correspondence (such as collection notices). Before you send a postcard, ask yourself whether the recipient might prefer that others not see the information you're sending.

11.   Look for opportunities to double up your mailings. For example, you may be able to insert practice-building materials (such as letters, newsletters, and brochures) with your statements and recall notices.

Tip: Depending upon the weight and thickness of the paper you use, you can mail up to seven or eight 8½ × 11-inch sheets of paper for the one-ounce rate. That means that as long as your extra pieces don't increase the weight of your mailings to the next highest ounce, they get a "free ride" in the mail you must send anyway.

SAVING MONEY ON THE TELEPHONE

12.   Use toll-free numbers whenever they're offered. To see if a company has one, call 800-555-1212. Or, invest in a toll-free telephone directory.

13.   When placing a long-distance call, announce that fact immediately. For example, "This is Dr. Campbell from Connecticut. May I speak with Edith Hausman please?" This announcement may keep Ms. Hausman's secretary from putting you on hold, or asking you to call back later.

14.   Shorten phone calls by sticking to business matters. When calling people who love to talk, begin your conversation by saying that you must get back to a patient, or be in a staff meeting in five minutes. That way, you won't offend when cutting the conversation short. As well, plan to place all outgoing calls during one particular hour or half-hour of the day. Not only is this good time management, but you'll be less likely to waste expensive phone time chit-chatting if you know you have to speak to five different people in the next 30 minutes.

Tip: You can increase your telephone effectiveness by preparing what you're going to say before calling. Jot down an agenda, if necessary.

15.   Take advantage of minimum rates when placing calls to different time zones.

Example: If you're in your California office by 7:30 a.m. and can call your New York supplier, where it's 10:30, you may pay 60% less than it would have cost if you waited until it was 9:00 a.m. in California.

16.   Use the telephone directory, not Information. Have in your office a set of all the phone books you might want to draw from regularly, especially those from neighboring communities.

17.   Get credit from the operator when you reach a wrong number, or are disconnected.

Tip: Charges for uncompleted calls may appear on your bills from long-distance services. Reason: Billing may begin a set number of seconds after dialing is completed, *not* when the call is answered. Thus, to avoid these charges, don't let the phone you're calling ring more than four times.

Tip: Awareness of this problem is growing, so many people calling *you* long distance may hang up after the fourth ring. That's yet another good reason for your telephone receptionist to pick up incoming calls quickly.

18.   Limit your staff's personal calls. Set a policy and include it in your personnel handbook.

19.   If you haven't already done so, investigate the cost-effectiveness of purchasing your own telephone equipment.

20.   As well, investigate discount telephone networks, and do some careful comparison shopping.

21.　Review your telephone bill critically each month to spot errors and areas for improving telephone usage.

SAVING MONEY ON UTILITY COSTS

22.　Turning off lights in empty rooms can trim your utility bill significantly. However, if you and your staff have trouble remembering to do this, it may pay for you to install automatic light switches that use sensing devices to do this job. What you need to know:

a.　There are three popular kinds of sensors: ultrasonic, microwave, and infrared. Systems using passive infrared sensors and control units are getting the most attention these days.

b.　How these systems work: The sensor detects infrared emissions of the human body, and transmits a signal to a relay that handles the lights. The absence of body heat or motion in the sensor's range causes lights to be switched off.

c.　To prevent frequent on/off switching, some sensors have an adjustable time-delay feature. This is generally set at 12 minutes, but can usually be changed to suit individual needs.

d.　Sensors in an office with 8-foot ceilings will cover a diameter of about 200 square feet. This is adequate for a space about 14×14-foot. Larger spaces may need more than one sensor to cover the entrance and desk area.

e.　Some makers offer inconspicuous sensors that fit flush with the ceiling. Others have sensors in suspended canopy covers or in a bracket cylinders for wall or ceiling mounting.

f.　In addition to reducing energy costs, automatic light switches provide security by detecting the presence of people in the office. Intruders are deterred by lights that suddenly switch on when they enter an empty office.

23.　Save on office lighting costs with fluorescent lights. These, when installed directly into incandescent light sockets, can save as much as 75% of electricity and maintenance expenses. Not only that, but fluorescent lights also last 10 to 20 times longer than the bulbs they replace.

Tip: Look for office areas where fluorescent bulbs are appropriate. Best locations: Storerooms, stairwells, walkways.

Tip: Change your fluorescent light bulbs every three years, not just when they burn out or start flickering. Why: Fluorescent bulbs experience a drop-off in their illumination power after three years. After five years, illumination may be off by as much as 70%! Remember, good lighting is key to high productivity, especially in automated offices.

24. Building lights into work stations or desks is more energy-efficient than having the traditional banks of overhead fluorescent lights. It also delivers more and better task light where the work is done.

25. Incorporating dimmer switches into your lighting plan is cost-efficient and provides flexibility for employees to set the optimal level of light for their needs.

26. During the summer months, do all you can to save on your energy bills:

a. Don't set your thermostat at a colder setting than normal when you start the air conditioner. It won't cool any faster, but it will cool to a lower temperature than you need.

b. Set the fan speed on high, except in very humid weather. A low fan speed will cool less, but will remove more humidity from the air.

c. Clean or replace heavily used air conditioning filters at least once a month.

d. Turn off window or room air conditioners when you leave a room for several hours. Despite popular belief, you'll spend less energy cooling the room again later than if you had left the unit running.

Tip: You may be able to save a great deal of money by arranging an energy audit for your office, and following the advice you are given. Some utility companies will conduct an energy audit for you, or give you a do-it-yourself energy audit kit. If yours doesn't, it may still pay to hire a private consulting firm.

SAVING MONEY ON PRINTING COSTS

27. When printing any materials for your practice, be sure to get competitive bids before proceeding. According to one doctor, "I was going to have 75,000 fliers printed, for a practice building effort. I got bids ranging from $1,600 to $2,540, for the same work, using the same paper, ink, etc."

28. Submit all copy to the typesetter at the same time. Typesetters often charge extra each time you want to change or add material, for setting even the most minimal amounts of copy.

29. For your patient newsletter, have often-used headlines set for the whole year. For example: "Recipe Corner," "A Message From the Doctor," "Book Review."

30. Set copy ragged (unjustified) on the right margin, when possible. Justified columns often force the typesetter to reset a whole paragraph to change a single word or line. You'll be charged more, accordingly.

31.   Design your materials to fit your printer's equipment. Newsletters or brochures that measure 8½ × 11-inch (folded in thirds to fit in a #10 envelope) are standard.

32.   If you're using photos in a printed piece, group several requiring the same percentage reduction. Have the printer shoot litho film for them at the same time.

33.   Investigate whether using one paper stock for several pieces would entitle you to a quantity discount. As well, printers sometimes give you a break if you give them several jobs at once.

34.   When designing brochures, newsletters, stationery, and other formal pieces, tell your artist that you want to use as few ink colors as you can to achieve your desired effect. Encourage him or her to use screens (shades) of one ink color, rather than extra ink colors. Reason: Every extra color you use increases your printing cost, because it requires an additional press run. Screens (shades), however, are cheaper, since they don't.

Example: A brochure printed in black, red, and blue ink requires three separate press runs. It is therefore relatively expensive. However, the same brochure printed in black, gray (a screen of black), red, and pink (a screen of red) requires only two press runs (in black and red), and should cost substantially less.

35.   If you use two colors for a frequently-printed piece, such as a patient newsletter, use one on the unchanged portions that appear in every issue (like the masthead, return address, and editorial box). Pre-print those elements in that color on enough paper for a whole year or longer. Reason: Pre-printing saves you money, since you will pay for the extra color and press run only once (rather than with each issue).

36.   When designing a new form for use in your office, prepare a typed sample of the form, photocopy a small quantity, and test it in actual use to see if it works. Then, make any necessary changes before having the forms typeset and printed into larger quantities.

ADDITIONAL COST-SAVING MEASURES

37.   Buy non-professional items when you can. Profession-specific items may add 20% or more to the cost. For example, an Indiana dentist says he bought clip-on loupes that fasten onto his eyeglasses from a dental supplier. But he found that a non-dental mail-order catalog sold the same loupes for significantly less. As well, he says that he used to buy the paper inserts for his plastic cuspidors from a dental supplier at a cost of $330 a year (for 6,000).

Now, he buys a year's supply of "solo cone sundae dishes" from a retail supplier, for a cost of $56.28. As he explains, "They're exactly the same as the cups from the dental supplier."

38.   Have film processed through a mail-in photo service. According to one doctor, "I use a lot of photos in my goodwill-building efforts with my patients. I used to pay about $7 to have a roll of 24 exposures developed locally. Using mail order, I pay only $3.55 for the same service. Even with the postage, I save about $3 per roll—or about $100 a year. And the quality and service I've received has been outstanding."

39.   If a piece of your equipment suddenly stops working properly, check your cables before calling for service. Make sure all cables are plugged securely into their proper slots in the outlet, and on the equipment.

40.   If your office desks, chairs, and filing cabinets look old and worn, don't automatically assume that they must be replaced. Refinishing is a practical solution that can save you a bundle. For example, repainting a metal desk and installing a new wooden top can cost as little as 20% of the price of a new desk.

Tip: Check your phone directory for local refinishing companies. Look under "office furniture." Many refinishing firms can perform the entire "facelift" in your office overnight, so furniture can stay put and be ready for use the next day.

C · H · A · P · T · E · R   4-8

When and How to Get Advance IRS Approval for Your Tax Tactic

Despite IRS efforts and a deluge of literature the service publishes, some parts of the tax code remain ambiguous. Thus, some business moves you're contemplating may leave you wondering how they'll fare with the IRS.

When only minor amounts of money are at stake, it usually makes the most sense to take your chances on being right. It's certainly easiest, but also cheapest to go through with some transactions, and see if the IRS questions your tax return.

However, this is *not* the best strategy for big issues and amounts. Especially when the tax law changes and there is confusion, any big moves you're considering may have serious tax consequences. Fortunately, you can lessen your risks by taking up the issues *in advance* with the IRS.

PRIVATE LETTER RULINGS: THE NUTS AND BOLTS

A private letter ruling is a formal IRS procedure to let you know whether your tax tactic will work before you try it. To get one, you must write the IRS with all the details of what you propose and what you believe the tax treatment will be.

The IRS will tell you you're right or wrong, and may even bargain with you. If your transaction is approved, you're home free. If you stick to your program, the IRS can't change its mind later, even if approval was an error. And if your tactic isn't acceptable, the IRS may show you how to change it for the results you want.

Relatively few taxpayers ask for private letter rulings. However, of those who do, the vast majority are about business matters. Unfortunately, the IRS rarely responds in under four months, and may take much longer.

Although you can seek a ruling yourself, most people hire legal/accounting help to represent them. Fees for that depend on the complexity of the case.

WHEN TO SEEK A PRIVATE-LETTER RULING—
AND WHEN NOT TO

A private-letter ruling is generally a good strategy when your circumstances pass three tests:

1.   You should have too much money at stake to take a chance. It will pay to go through the ruling process if you can learn whether and how to alter your plans to get huge tax savings.

2.   Your transaction must be months away, or better yet, indefinitely postponable when you mail in your request. If you must move quickly, an IRS ruling after the fact will do you no good.

3.   For best results, your transaction should also be somewhat flexible. If changes are feasible, the IRS will probably suggest them. It's best if you'll be in a position to make them.

In some cases, a ruling may get you into more trouble than you bargained for. It is generally best *not* to ask for a ruling:

1.   If you must proceed with your plan no matter what the IRS says. Once you get a ruling, you *must* attach it to your tax return. If you must go ahead with a questionable move, it's probably wiser to do so quietly and hope your return isn't flagged.

2.   If you know of similar cases where the IRS has issued negative rulings.

3.   If you've already made the move or filed your return. The IRS won't issue rulings after the fact.

4.   If you suggest a vague, hypothetical transaction you are considering for an indefinite date.

5.   If you are seeking advance rulings on such matters as fair market value of an asset.

6.   If legal restraints apply. *Examples:* The IRS won't issue a ruling for returns under audit, cases now in court, or cases under consideration for appeal.

7.   If you have insufficient business reasons for your proposed action. To the IRS, that means tax avoidance is your #1 motive.

HOW TO ASK FOR A RULING

The IRS doesn't supply a form, but has made up a checklist of do's and don'ts for ruling requests. The basics:

1. *Mail your request directly to the IRS in Washington, D.C.* (Your local tax office can advise you of the specific address and individual to whom you should send your request.)

2. *Ask for a ruling on the federal tax consequences of a proposed transaction.*

3. *State the facts:* Names, addresses, taxpayer ID numbers and addresses of the IRS district offices where each one files tax returns.

4. *Explain the move you have in mind in detail,* in simple, concise language. Emphasize your business (not tax avoidance) reasons for it.

5. *Enclose and summarize copies of all documents related to the matter.*

6. *State the ruling you seek and prove your case.* This is the hard part. Comb the tax code regulations, tax court rulings, and other court decisions to support your side. Send copies of all such rulings and related documents.

7. *Emphasize that you know of no IRS field office or Appellate Division branch office that's currently considering the issues you raise.*

8. *Ask for notice and a meeting if an unfavorable decision may be forthcoming.*

9. *Sign the letter.* Or, if your accountant prepares your request, have him sign it and give his qualifications.

10. *List on a separate sheet whatever you don't want mentioned,* even anonymously, when the ruling is announced as the law requires. This is to keep confidential information and documents from being made public.

ABOUT THE RULING ITSELF

Three to six weeks after you mail your letter, an IRS specialist will call for more information or a discussion. If all works out, the result will be a positive ruling you attach to your tax return.

At any time, you can withdraw your requst for a ruling. All it takes is a letter to the same office. Withdrawal means you won't have to attach a negative ruling to your tax return. However, it is no guarantee that your district office won't learn of the proceedings.

Tip: Some experts warn that simply *asking* for a ruling makes you more likely to be audited. Don't let this stop you from going ahead in the right circumstances. When the sums are large, a ruling may be your best course.

For more information on IRS audits, see "Preventing, Preparing for, and Surviving an IRS Audit," pages 231–236.

C·H·A·P·T·E·R   4-9

Preventing, Preparing for, and Surviving an IRS Audit

Even when you have clear documentation for every item on your tax return, there's still a chance you may be audited. The IRS's computers may flag your return for many reasons, including pure chance. However, some returns are more likely to be audited than others. In this chapter, we'll explore practical strategies for reducing your overall audit risk. As well, we'll consider what happens at a typical audit, and what you can do to prepare yourself to meet the challenge.

HOW THE IRS CHOOSES AUDIT TARGETS

While a computer flags questionable returns, the final decision about an IRS audit is usually up to a classifier agent. He/she decides whether to audit, and whether you're to get a full-blown field audit or a smaller-scale review (both described below), based upon guidelines published by the IRS. Obviously, it can be very helpful to know what a classifier agent is looking for. The following are usually considered to be audit red flags:

1. *Sloppiness.* The IRS agent may suspect that missing, illegible or incomplete returns are evidence of intent to mislead the IRS.

2. *Other indicators of intent to mislead.* The agent is warned to look for personal write-offs listed as a business expenses—a common ploy. *Example:* The IRS has learned from experience that many taxpayers try to write off personal life insurance as a business expense. Thus, they might decide to pay extra close attention to insurance deductions.

Tip: Don't list a large deduction for "insurance" with your practice expenses. It's much better to break down this category and list malpractice, overhead, liability, and other business insurance separately.

3. *Relative size of questionable deductions.* Suppose you have a questionable deduction of $5,000. That's more significant to the IRS where total

expenses are $25,000 than it is on a return showing total expenses of $250,000.

4. *Appropriateness of deductions.* The deduction should conform to your situation. For example, it is generally inappropriate for a doctor to claim expenses for operating an airplane. Such a claim will usually raise eyebrows, especially if no explanation is offered.

5. *Inconsistencies.* It's a good idea to offer a brief explanation when any part of your return may lead to questions. *Example:* Suppose you report the sale of stocks, but no dividends. It's smart in such a case to *explain* that the stocks paid no dividends, and to include proof (if you have it).

6. *Income/deduction ratio.* The agent will be examining whether the return shows enough income to justify the deductions claimed.

7. *Appropriate adjustments to income.* If you claim moving expenses, you'd better be sure to account for the sale of a house. If you claim substantial travel or car expenses (such as $25,000 for a $100,000 income), you might offer a brief explanation.

8. *Itemized deductions.* The IRS agent may be paying particularly close attention to:

• Sales tax when more is deducted than the standard amount listed in the IRS tables.

• Interest paid to individuals.

• High medical expenses for small families.

• Charitable contributions if they exceed the usual percentage of adjusted gross income.

• Large donations to miscellaneous charities.

• Claims of large non-cash donations.

9. *Dividends and interest.* If discrepancies show up by computer, you're usually asked to explain, at least by mail.

10. *Practice income.* The agent may search for evidence of fraud by asking:

• Is your profession normally more profitable than reflected on your return? (You might explain if practice net is well below the median.)

• Do you show a high gross business income, low net profit, and claim only the standard deduction?

• Do your address, real estate taxes, and/or mortgage interest indicate a higher mode of living than justified by reported income?

• Does your return reveal large amounts of interest or dividends not in line with current income sources? (If that's the case, you might explain, "Income received from inheritance," or whatever.)

11.   *Capital transactions.* Three types generally raise eyebrows:

• Gain on sale of real property where accelerated depreciation was taken.

• Loss on a sale of rental property recently converted from personal residence.

• Installment sales of property.

12.   *Improvements deducted as repairs.* Claimed repairs are sometimes disallowed, because they are considered capital improvements. Thus, you may wish to include copies of bills for large repairs, itemized to show the work was clearly for repairs, *not* improvements. For more information on this subject, see, "Improvement or Repair? The IRS Definitely Sees a Difference," page 43.

GUIDELINES FOR KEEPING AND HANDLING TAX RECORDS

1.   For meetings and other business travel, you're required to keep a record of the time, place, amount, purpose, and relationship of each expenditure as you make it. Receipts are required for any item over a specified dollar value.

2.   Try to get evidence of *why* you made the trip from the people you dealt with. For example, a seminar brochure is usually considered to be good evidence.

3.   Living expenses while away are somewhat difficult to prove. Do your best to record how much you spend each day for meals, tips, cabs, telephones, and laundry. (A round-figure total for the whole trip won't be acceptable.)

Tip: While traveling, you can simplify record-keeping by bringing along an empty business envelope in which to keep your receipts and a trip expense diary. Bring the envelope with you wherever you go, so you don't miss cash tips and other incidental expenses that generate no receipt. For more information on this subject, see, "How to Get More from Continuing Education Programs," pages 489–495.

4.   For contributions, an appraisal is the best proof of property's value. If you give used clothing, equipment, or furniture to charity, you may claim its value at current retail price—what a dealer in used clothing, equipment, or furniture would *sell* them for, not *pay* for them.

5. When deducting stolen or destroyed property that's appreciated, you can normally deduct its original cost. The best proof of cost is obviously a sales receipt (with cancelled checks, credit card receipts, etc.). The next best proof is insurance records and appraisals made at purchase time. Next: Statements of the seller or other knowledgeable person.

Tip: If you have no records, describe the item as fully as possible. Get expert testimony on what the price would have been at purchase time. For inherited property, deduct the value at the time of the inheritance.

6. If stolen or destroyed property has *depreciated* in value (for example, a car), deduct the lower of the original cost less depreciation or its actual market value. (Unfortunately, you can't deduct the the cost of buying a brand new car.)

A CAREFUL RETURN REDUCES YOUR AUDIT RISK

You can also cut your chances of being audited by taking extra care with your return. In particular:

1. Be sure to fill in all the blanks neatly and carefully, especially lines marked with black darts.

2. Put all deductions into specific categories. A large "miscellaneous" item will pique the IRS's curiosity, and may invite an audit.

3. Don't round off numbers. (They may seem suspiciously like a guess.)

4. File on or near April 15. Despite IRS disclaimers, some experts believe that audit risk is reduced when you file with the crowd.

Tip: Don't use your own postage meter for last-minute filing. A private meter postmark is *not* considered proof of mailing. However, don't automatically rely on a post office postmark, either. Mistakes can happen. Moreover, some post offices forward mail to a central facility for postmarking, resulting in a delay. When facing a tight deadline, use registered or certified mail. (This is also imperative when filing a court appeal from an IRS decision. If you are even one day late, the court will not accept your case.)

5. Anticipate questions, and include explanations and support materials to allay suspicions.

PREPARING FOR AN AUDIT

Audits usually begin with a notification letter from the IRS. Meet the deadline set in your audit notice, or get an extension. (Otherwise, the IRS will probably rule against you automatically.) Preparation for the audit will depend upon the type of examination you must undergo. Generally, these fall into three categories:

1. *For a correspondence audit,* the IRS will want more information to verify an item or two on the return. Mail an explanation of your position along with supporting records. Send *copies,* not the originals, of relevant records (unless you are instructed to do otherwise). If your records are too extensive or bulky to photocopy and mail conveniently (or if you feel it would be difficult to provide a written explanation of your position), you may ask for an in-person appointment.

2. *For an office audit,* the audit notification letter will list the time for a face-to-face meeting at a nearby IRS office. There will be several items checked or listed on back of the notice to indicate the items under question. Gather together all substantiating records. If you have no records for an item in question, prepare an explanation.

Tip: It's also wise to make your own audit to try to uncover deductions you overlooked when you filed. That way if the IRS disallows some deductions, you may be able to counterclaim elsewhere.

3. *For a field audit,* the auditor will come to your office or home. It can involve extensive scrutiny of your entire return. To prepare, organize your records so you know which ones you have and where they are.

SURVIVING AN IRS AUDIT

If you disagree with an agent's findings, you have several ways of appealing his decisions *within* the IRS itself, without going to court:

1. *Informal appeals.* If the agent seems *clearly* wrong about the law or misunderstands the facts, you can ask for an immediate conference with his supervisor. However, it is wise to do this *only* when the issue is absolutely clear cut. If it's a gray area, expect the supervisor to back the agent.

2. *Formal appeals.* Once the auditor's report is reviewed by a senior IRS official, you'll receive a letter explaining the agent's findings and your appeal rights. To appeal, you must file a protest letter within a specified time limit, usually 30 days. State specifically the items you disagree with and the basis for your position. If the dispute is about which *rules* apply, cite cases, rulings, regulations, or code sections you're relying on. If it's a dispute over *facts,* describe your evidence and explain how it supports your claim.

Tip: If the IRS receives no protest letter from you, it will send you a second letter demanding payment within 90 days. Once this happens, the only way to appeal is by going to court.

3. *Before the hearing.* Preparation is the key to winning an appeal. If the issue involves an interpretation of law, research all the relevant cases, rulings, and authorities. If it's a question of proving facts, try to gather more evidence. A quick settlement is sometimes possible before a hearing. But most often the IRS Appeals Bureau will contact you to set a hearing date, usually about a month in advance.

4. *The hearing.* The appeals officer's willingness to settle is usually dependent upon how likely he thinks government victory would be in a court case. Yet, the mere threat of litigation won't force a compromise if the officer thinks you are clearly in the wrong, and have *no* case.

Tip: Have your accountant assess the strength of your case and set a realistic settlement range. If you've got a strong case, you may be able to negotiate an 80–90% reduction in the proposed assessment. A weak case may be worth only 10–20%, if anything.

GETTING AN ADVANCE NOD OF APPROVAL FROM THE IRS

An advance private-letter ruling from the IRS will ensure that an ambiguous tax tactic won't be later disallowed or penalized. For more information on this subject, see, "When and How to Get Advance IRS Approval for Your Tax Tactic," pages 227–230.

P · A · R · T   5

Thinking the Unthinkable: Planning for Your Worst Nightmare

C · H · A · P · T · E · R   5-1

Malpractice Protection:
Management Strategies that Prevent
Malpractice Claims

I n the following three chapters, we will explore various ways the private practice professional can protect himself against charges of malpractice. However, as you read, keep in mind that your best possible course of action will be in *preventing* suits from being brought against you in the first place. Doing so is almost always preferable and less costly than having to defend yourself in front of a judge and jury.

Unfortunately, even when the doctor is completely in the right, and the disgruntled patient doesn't win his suit, the very mention of the word *malpractice* may damage the doctor's reputation. Should the media play up the case and the charge, the damage might be multiplied a hundred-fold. Current and potential patients hearing, reading, or seeing the story are likely to conclude that the doctor is guilty, simply because he has been charged. Or, they may not hear, remember, or even care that he was later cleared of all charges.

THE 12 MOST COMMON CAUSES OF
MALPRACTICE LITIGATION

Let us begin by exploring the top dozen causes of malpractice litigation (in no particular order). Through this, we should be able to see what has been responsible for the ever-growing number of malpractice suits being brought against doctors today:

1. *Lack of proper training of staff.*

2. *Television.* People see many programs in which patients sue their doctors for malpractice, and are consequently more aware of their legal rights.

3. *Larger case loads.* When more patients are treated by the same doctor, there may be more opportunity for something to go wrong or be overlooked. According to a recent state medical association study, there is a correlation between the number/size of malpractice claims and work overload (doctors who spend long hours at the office, who try to solve all their patient's problems, who seldom turn anyone away, etc.)

4. *Poor doctor-patient relationships.* People don't usually sue others they consider to be their friends. Unfortunately, doctors may sometimes have difficulty establishing rapport with their patients, perhaps due to large case loads, or the personality of the patient. As a result, some patients may not feel very close to their doctors, and may not feel comfortable expressing their dissatisfaction directly to them.

5. *Along similar lines, staff members who shield the doctor from patients' complaints.*

6. *The move toward consumerism.* Patients today are more likely to view themselves as consumers of healthcare, and are more willing to complain.

7. *Doctors who criticize the work of other doctors.*

8. *The increase in the number of corporate practices.* Some patients think that the money they will win in a malpractice suit will come out of an anonymous coroporation's pocket (not the doctor's), and do not realize that the suit is going to hurt the doctor. (Some patients try to collect on insurance fraudulently, for the same reason.)

9. *A doctor who doesn't know his or her own limits.* Some malpractice suits develop because the doctor doesn't refer cases to specialists who can better handle the case. Also, in some suits, the doctor falsely raised the expectations of the patient beyond what he could actually perform.

10. *Poor communication with the referring doctor.* As well, when doctors who work in the *same* office fail to communicate effectively with one another, the patients and staff suffer, and malpractice claims increase.

11. *Curbstone consulting.* Informal consultations on the fly create all kinds of malpractice problems, because doctors are rendering opinions without looking at the patient charts—or sometimes, even the patients.

12. *Professional isolation.* According to one study, doctors are more likely to have excessive malpractice claims against them when they lack a day-to-day collegial relationship with peers, and when they don't attend professional meetings to update their skills.

WHO TYPICALLY SUES A DOCTOR?

While there are of course many exceptions, and just about anyone can sue for malpractice, the type of person most likely to file a claim fits into one of four basic categories:

1. *Patients who frequently move from one geographic area to another, without good reason.* Such moving may indicate that the person is a dissatisfied person. It goes to follow that a person who's dissatisfied in one area is likely to be dissatisfed in another.

2. *Patients who don't pay professional fees.* Patients who resist paying your fee may be doing so because they're dissatisfied or confused about the treatment they received.
Tip: If your usual collection techniques have failed to produce a response after 90 days, it is a good idea to talk to the patient yourself to try to uncover problems. For more information on collections, see, "Collecting the Money That's Due You," pages 151–184.

3. *Patients who change doctors frequently.* Beware of the patient who never seems satisfied with the care he received from previous practitioners.
Tip: As a patient rattles off a list of atrocities/complaints about past treatment, avoid showing support for criticisms of another practitioner. Such support could be misinterpreted as confirmation or conclusive evidence he feels he needs (and was waiting for) to file a malpractice claim.

4. *Uncooperative patients.* Beware of patients who consistently ignore your recommendations, miss appointments, or fail to contact you within a specified time. Such a patient may expect you to solve all his problems without cooperation, and try to blame you when things don't work out as he'd hoped.

KNOWING YOUR LEGAL OBLIGATIONS AND RIGHTS

For your patients, you have a duty to possess and exercise the degree of care and competency that your colleagues generally possess and exercise. That means that you have an obligation to use all available and customary diagnostic aids. You have a liability if you fail to do so and it brings harm to the patient, or shortens his life. As well, you have the duty to complete treatment once it has begun.

Realize that you do not have a legal obligation to accept anyone as a new patient. You are free to make inquiry about the credit standing of an individual before taking him on as a patient, even if you and he are not planning to work on a credit basis. Also, you may ask whether the potential patient has switched doctors or geographic areas frequently.

Tip: If you refuse to accept a patient on the basis of his or her race, creed, national origin, etc., you will be in violation of the Civil Rights Act. Your malpractice coverage wouldn't apply in that case. Your records can be used to prove that you have discriminated against the individual, as they may indicate that you never treated or dismissed a patient of that particular race, creed, etc. in the past.

17 STRATEGIES FOR MAXIMUM MALPRACTICE PREVENTION

1.   Be appropriately friendly to patients. Develop good personal relationships with them, so they can bring complaints to you and iron out small problems before they become big ones.

2.   Take a complete medical history of all patients before you begin treatment. Update it before each subsequent treatment.

3.   Maintain exemplary patient records, and document everything you can, especially when there is any chance that a lawsuit might be brewing. For more information on this subject, see, "Managing Patient Records to Reduce Malpractice Risk," pages 249–255.

4.   Don't sue your patients—at least not before weighing all the consequences. Lawsuits increase the chances of being countersued.

5.   Don't guarantee success or specific results to a patient. Once you do this, even orally, you have technically established a "contract" with the patient, and are legally bound to fulfill it. If a suit is brought against you for not fulfilling the guarantee ("breach of contract"), your malpractice insurance is unlikely to cover you.

Tip: Watch your p's and q's. Even saying something as innocent sounding as "You'll look gorgeous (or feel great) when we're done" could be construed as a verbal guarantee.

6.   When you must discharge a patient, give him or her reasonable written notice —several clear warnings—of your intent to terminate the relationship. To determine what reasonable notice is, consider the availability of other doctors and appointments in your area.

Tip: Realize that you do have the legal obligation to follow through with treatment once it is begun—even post-operative treatment. Consult your attorney to be sure your discharge of the patient can't be misconstrued as abandonment.

7.   Examine referred patients yourself, and form your own diagnoses and treatment plans. Do not rely solely on the records or observations of a referring doctor.

8.   Have explicit financial arrangements and make sure each patient is aware of them. Similarly, make sure the patient knows in advance your fee for treatment, and has agreed to pay it. For more information on this subject, see, "Making Firm Financial Arrangements with Patients," pages 113–119, and "Setting, Raising, and Presenting Fees," pages 105–111.

9.   Keep abreast of current developments in your profession/specialty, to avoid claims based on failure to meet the accepted standard of care.

10.   Refer cases definitely and even possibly beyond your skill and experience.

11.   Make it your custom to discuss risks of procedures and drugs with patients, and get their consent before proceeding. For more information on this subject, see, "What You Need to Know about Informed Consent," pages 253–254.

12.   Limit telephone recommendations to patients:

a.   Whose medical histories you're well acquainted with.

b.   Who you're reasonably sure will understand you, and will follow instructions exactly.

c.   Who you're reasonably sure will report symptoms to you accurately.

13.   Don't overestimate a patient's understanding of what you believe to be simple instructions. Write down instructions step-by-step, when appropriate.

Tip: When your instructions are crucial to the patient's well-being, ask him to repeat or summarize what you just said.

14.   Provide adequate written notice when you're going to be absent from your practice for an extended vacation, illness, or move. Be sure patients calling your office are given the name of another doctor who can provide alternate care in your absence. For more information on this subject, see, "Preparing Your Practice for Your Unexpected Absence," pages 267–273.

15.   Recommend the best possible treatment to patients, even if it is not covered by their insurance. In one interesting case, a Los Angeles court ruled that doctors will be held liable if, against their professional judgment, they comply without protest with limits imposed by third-party payors.

16.   Don't admit or suggest your own negligence. If you have a nega-

tive outcome, simply explain it while showing patients and their families that you're doing everything possible to improve the situation.

17.   Conduct and document routine checks of equipment, instruments, and supplies. Prove in writing that you habitually care for your equipment and that you follow proper sterilization and maintenance procedures. Documentation is excellent defense if a patient ever charges that he was injured because you used unclean or improperly maintained equipment or supplies.

HOW YOUR STAFF CAN PREVENT MALPRACTICE CLAIMS

1.   Teach your receptionist (and all staff who handle patients on the phone) to ask questions that will help you determine if the patient's condition is an emergency, or if it in any other way warrants your immediate personal intervention.

2.   Have your staff report *all* patient concerns to you. These include concerns which your staff has screened out as non-emergencies, as well as any other patient complaints or remarks, no matter how minor they seem. For more information on soliciting and handling patient's complaints, see, "How to Respond to Patients Who Complain," pages 371–374.

Tip: Don't be too quick to cancel your bill in an attempt to satisfy a complaining patient. Writing off your fee may be construed by the patient—and by his or her attorney—as evidence that your treatment and services were questionable. Even if a review of your records uncovers a potential problem, don't dismiss the bill without first discussing it with your attorney and/or insurance carrier.

3.   If your business assistant is the one to make follow-up calls after treatment, give her a written list of specific questions to ask. *Example:* "Do you have any fever? Are you experiencing any pain or discomfort? Do you have difficulty swallowing or breathing?

Have your business assistant write the answers next to the questions, noting the date and time of the call. Then have her initial the page. Review these reports *daily* to determine if the patient should be called back. Keep a written record of any further contact with the patient that stems from the post-operative call.

Tip: Print a list of all questions your business assistant might ask during a post-operative call. Then, you can write the patient's name at the top of each sheet, and check those questions you want your business assistant to ask that patient. A standardized form of this kind will simplify the procedure for you and your business assistant.

4.   If you recall patients for periodic examinations, your staff member in charge of recalls should record on the patient's chart that a recall card was sent (or a call made). This can be helpful defense if you are trying to establish the patient's contributory negligence (if he did not return for a recall visit despite your recommendations and efforts, and develops a problem later). Have the assistant who makes the recall attempt initial the entry on the patient's chart, so you'll know which staff member to ask to testify for you. (It may be hard to remember who sent the recall card or who made the call if a patient sues you years later).

For more information on establishing an effective recall system, see, "Setting Up and Maintaining a Recall System that Works," pages 83–89.

5.   Make it policy that your business assistant must inform you before she turns any uncollected account over to a collection agency. Limit the collection tactics she can use by writing out your collection procedure and providing sample letters. Most importantly, be sure you or she (or both of you) have tried to find out *why* the patient hasn't paid your bills. Ask the patient specifically if he was satisfied with the treatment and care he received.

Tip: In some cases, patients don't pay their bills because they are dissatisfied with the treatment/services they received. Dunning letters, especially those from a collection agency, might push these dissatisfied patient into lawsuits.

For more information on effective collection strategies, see, "Collecting the Money That's Due You," pages 151–184.

CHOOSING THE BEST TYPE OF
MALPRACTICE COVERAGE

Watch your step if you're ever attracted to a new malpractice insurance carrier, or a new type of coverage. Switching over may mean you lose some degree of protection.

The two types of malpractice coverage are *occurrence* and *claims-made:*

•   Occurrence policies live forever. Once you pay an occurrence premium, any claim resulting from incidents in that year are covered, no matter when claims are filed.

For example, a 1994 occurrence policy will pay the claim for incidents occurring in 1994, even if the patient didn't file action until 1999.

•   On the other hand, a claims-made (also known as "suit") policy must be renewed yearly to continue protection.

Example: If in 1994, you had claims-made coverage, and performed a procedure that resulted in a liability action in 1999, you'd be protected only if you still had claims-made coverage in 1999 and were insured by the same carrier as in 1994.

Tip: Switching claims-made carriers may result in neither the old nor the new carrier assuming responsibility for the claim, even if there's no lapse in coverage.

Risks: You won't lose protection when you change from an occurrence to a claims-made policy and continue to be insured annually by the same claims-made carrier. Risk is highest when switching from a claims-made policy back to an occurrence policy. Then, neither the current nor the former policy will cover claims filed as a result of an incident that took place in a claims-made year.

Tip: To ensure continuous protection when switching from one claims-made carrier to another, or from claims-made to occurrence coverage, buy a "prior acts" policy or a reporting endorsement (also known as a "tail" policy). Premiums for such coverage are often higher than for a claims-made policy, but most doctors consider it essential.

Tip: Doctors with claims-made coverage also need a "tail" policy if they wish liability protection to continue after retirement, death, or disability. Fortunately, some insurance companies provide this type of policy free if you've maintained claims-made coverage for at least five years prior to retirement, disability, or death.

PROTECTING YOUR PERSONAL WEALTH FROM HUGE MALPRACTICE CLAIMS

Increasing numbers of doctors are being sued for amounts in excess of their malpractice insurance coverage, which means money is taken from their personal resources.

Fortunately, there are several precautionary steps you can take right now to guard your personal wealth from huge malpractice claims:

1. Review the level of your current malpractice coverage. Consider increasing your basic policy, or buying excess malpractice insurance from another carrier.

2. Explore joint tenancy. In many states, property held jointly by husband and wife is protected by claims against one spouse, as long as the non-debtor spouse is alive. In such states, joint tenancy could protect your property from malpractice claims.

Tip: In other states, bankruptcy laws may reduce the protection given to joint property. Moreover, jointly-held property isn't always best (for example, when a divorce occurs, or when joint ownership contradicts your estate planning strategy.) Be sure to consult your attorney and/or financial planner before proceeding.

3. Give gifts. Property given to others, including trusts for your children, is generally exempt from claims, if given before the claims arise.

Tip: To the extent that you retain any control over or interest in the gift or trust, a claim might still be enforced. Balance your concern for liability protection against your desire to maintain control over your wealth.

4. Use retirement plans. Corporate and other retirement plan accounts may still be excellent shelters from liability claims. Check your state legislation, to see if it protects retirement plan accounts from attachment by malpractice and other creditors.

PREVENTING OTHER TYPES OF LITIGATION

Malpractice is the most common type of litigation we hear about against doctors. However, there are other types of legal suits which are worth thinking about—and preventing:

1. You have the legal duty to provide a safe workplace for your staff. Are you careful not to expose your staff to unnecessary radiation, infectious diseases, poisoning, etc? Do you routinely inspect your equipment? Do you exercise caution to protect your staff from improper sexual advances by patients? Do you insist that your staff keep current on their own medical tests and immunizations recommended by your professional association?

Example: Dental office personnel should have their urine checked periodically, to detect signs of mercury poisoning. As well, the dental association recommends immunization with the Hepatitis B vaccine.

For more information on preventing lawsuits from staff, see, "How to Keep Employees from Taking You to Court," pages 349–356.

2. You also have a duty to provide a safe office for your patients. Do you have your staff supervise children so they can't wander at will about your office? Are your reception area and other public areas child-proofed? Are dangerous materials out of the reach of children, and clearly marked? Have you told your staff explicitly that they can't physically discipline a child? Do you keep a well-stocked first-aid kit in your office, and know how to use it?

For more information on office safety procedures, see, "Reducing the Risk of Injuries in Your Office," pages 405–411.

3. Instruct your staff never to accept custody of a patient's purse. As well, don't allow patients to leave their purses or other belongings on the receptionist's desk, or otherwise unattended.

4. Don't go to your office after hours to treat a member of the opposite sex, unless a third person of *your* choice is present. Use common sense when examining or treating any patient. Have a member of your staff present when necessary.

5. Respect the patient's right to privacy. Don't disclose any confidential information about a patient. Have all inquiries about patients referred to you by your staff.

For more information on this subject, see, "The Problems of Guarding Patient Confidentiality," pages 261–265.

FOR MORE INFORMATION

For more information on malpractice prevention, protection, and defense, see:

• "Malpractice Protection: Managing Patient Records to Reduce Malpractice Risk," pages 249–255.

• "Malpractice Protection: What to Do If You're Ever Sued for Malpractice," pages 257–260.

• "What Your Estate Should Know about Selling your Practice," Tip 7, page 278.

C · H · A · P · T · E · R   5-2

Malpractice Protection:
Managing Patient Records to Reduce
Malpractice Risk

C omplete, accurate, and detailed patient records are extremely important to any doctor's malpractice prevention program, as well as to a
sound defense against unfounded charges. Should a suit ever be brought
against you, do you think your current records could be your salvation? Or,
might they possibly be used *against* you in some way?

INITIAL AND DATE EACH CHART ENTRY

All notations in a patient's chart should be initialed and dated by the people who record them. But in some practices, especially large ones, it may be
difficult to tell whose initials were whose. This is often the case when the
notation was made several years ago, when there is substantial turnover in
the practice, or when two or more staff members have identical initials.

To identify initials, maintain a master list of all the doctors and employees who work in your practice. As each new person is hired, type her name on
the master list, the date she was hired, and have her sign and initial to the
right of her name. Make it clear that this is the way she is to initial all documents in your office from that point on. If the employee ever quits, is fired, or
takes an extended leave of absence, note the appropriate dates on this list.

In the case of a lawsuit, this master list will help you and your attorney
identify the correct employee who made each chart entry— former or current.

DON'T ENTRUST RECORDS TO PATIENTS

From time to time, you'll be called upon to send a patient's records to
another practitioner. When this is necessary, there are two important rules to
follow:

1. Never release your only copy.

2. Do *not* allow the patient to transport the record. For one thing, the file could be lost. But perhaps more importantly, the patient is very likely to examine his record, and could misinterpret your notations.

Tip: Make it strict office policy to mail the patient's record directly to the new practitioner's office. Or, if it is a local practitioner, have a member of your staff hand-deliver it.

HOW TO HANDLE SUBPOENA OF RECORDS

A *subpoena duces tecum* commands an individual, or the "custodian of records," to appear at a designated time and place to give testimony and to bring certain documents. You might be served with a subpoena of records in the event of a malpractice suit, but there are also other times your records might be needed in court.

A subpoena is a court order. Those who disregard it could be subject to a contempt citation. Thus, you must take every subpoena very seriously. Here is advice from attorney William P. Isele (Gross & Novak, East Brunswick, NJ):

1. Make sure both the plaintiff and the defendant are named, and that one of them is your patient. If records of someone other than a party to the lawsuit are requested, you may be obliged to assert the physician-patient privilege, and should consult with your attorney about this.

2. Make sure there is a docket number or case number on the subpoena. There have been cases in which unscrupulous individuals have tried to issue "dummy" subpoenas before they filed a suit, in an effort to "fish" for information. This tactic is improper, and your lawyer should deal with it.

3. Check to see that the time and place for you to appear with the records is specified. In many cases, the requesting attorney doesn't really want you—he wants the records. If all else is in order, and your attorney agrees, you might contact him and advise that *copies* will be delivered by the date specified. In most jurisdictions, you can charge a reasonable copying fee.

Tip: Whenever you must provide originals of your records, or when your attorney advises it, you should go with them.

4. The date specified should give you sufficient time to produce the records. Court rules in different jurisdictions vary, but customarily provide that a subpoena be served anywhere from 10 to 20 days before an appearance is required. The courts generally frown upon "forthwith" subpoenae, which require production of records immediately, or within hours.

5. Make sure the request is not overly broad. The requesting attorney should make clear specifically which information is requested, leaving no doubt in your mind.

6. Make sure the subpoena is properly signed. Some jurisdictions allow attorneys to sign on behalf of the court. Others require the court clerk's signature, and a court seal. Learn your jurisdiction's requirements, and point out deficiencies to your attorney.

7. Witness fees and mileage charges (usually a very nominal amount) may accompany the subpoena. Again, amounts vary from one jurisdiction to the next. If the requesting attorney doesn't want you to appear, he should offer to pay the reasonable costs of copying and postage.

Tip: In some areas, local bar associations and medical societies have jointly developed protocols in this regard. Check with those groups in your county to see if a standard has been established.

8. If you have doubts about the legitimacy of a subpoena, don't simply ignore it. A quick call to your attorney should resolve any doubts.

16 RECORDS MANAGEMENT TACTICS FOR MALPRACTICE PREVENTION

1. Keep accurate records of all broken appointments. Note in the appointment book *and* in the patient's file when an appointment is broken or cancelled, and why. As well, note all of your phone and mail efforts to reschedule the patient's appointment. If immediate treatment is needed, confirm the new time and the reasons and urgency for the appointment by letter, referring once again to the broken appointment.

2. Keep records of all patients who leave the practice. When possible, send copies to another practice, not originals. However, if originals of any items must be forwarded, make copies and keep them in your inactive file.

3. Confine your comments to necessary information about the patient's physical condition or treatment. Don't make unnecessary negative comments. You never know when a patient might see the records. And, should records appear in a court case, disparaging remarks could alienate the judge or jury.

4. Take care in making changes in records. Records that look tampered with could wreck a courtroom defense. If changes are needed, *do not erase* any marks. Rather, whoever makes the change should cross out the error neatly (with a single line), initial it, and note when and why the change was made.

5.   Be consistent when noting treatment. If you use abbreviations, try to limit yourself to nomenclature generally recognized within your profession. However, if you feel other abbreviations are necesary, use them universally in all patient records. If need be, keep a master list of these practice-specific abbreviations.

6.   Be precise when recording information provided by patients, and note it as such. For example, if a patient comes to you after being in pain for three weeks, don't just write, "Patient had pain for three weeks." Rather, you might write, "Patient complained of having pain for three weeks, prior to seeking treatment." That way, a disgruntled patient can't claim that *you* delayed treatment for three weeks.

7.   Have the patient sign your informed consent statement. (For more information on this subject, see, "What You Need to Know about Informed Consent," page 253.)

8.   Record a thorough medical history for each new patient, and update it before each subsequent treatment. Date and initial each time you ask the patient whether there has been any change in his medical history, even if his status is unchanged. That way, you can prove that you tried to gather new information on the date noted.

9.   Keep all records permanently. If storage space is limited, you might commit old inactive records to microfilm or fiche.

Tip: To learn why it makes sense to keep records permanently, see, "Understanding Your Statute of Limitations and Long Tail," page 254.)

10.   Realize that your estate can't escape malpractice litigation after your death. Therefore, make your records precise and usable for cases that might occur after your death. Tell your spouse, children, office manager, etc., what to do with your records in case you die suddenly. If necessary, revise your will to make provisions for the care of your records after your death.

(For more information on this subject, see, "Preparing Your Practice for Your Death," pages 275–278.)

11.   Record in your notes when your clinical opinion of a patient's condition differs from another practitioner's.

12.   Document phone conversations you have with patients. Maintain a log for this purpose at home and at the office. Instruct your answering service to keep an accurate, detailed log as well.

13.   Make your records legible. Unreadable records can result in a malpractice action being filed that otherwise wouldn't be. Illegibility may produce suspicion or doubt. If an attorney can't conclude from a set of records whether a claim is defensible, he may file and take depositions to find out.

Tip: If you have illegible handwriting, have your records typed at the end of the day by a staff member, with your assistance. Use a word processor to type them yourself. Or, dictate patient records into a tape recorder and have them typed, checking afterwards to make sure they're accurate and complete.

14.   Be sure to provide a complete written record of diagnosis and to coordinate treatment with referral doctors. Don't give information to your patient to deliver, or just call it in to another doctor's office.

15.   Watch the way you say things. For example, it is risky to call a procedure "simple," if you mean it is "noncomplicated." It is usually unwise to record an act as a "mistake," when you mean to say that the result is "not what was intended."

16.   If a patient refuses to follow your recommendations, be sure to make special note of this in his file. Make certain that at least one member of your staff is also aware of this situation, and could support what you say in a malpractice defense. If possible, get the patient to sign a document stating that he is not following your recommendations. Or, send the patient a letter, return receipt requested, outlining your recommendations, and expressing your concern that he is not following them (and the risks he incurs for not doing so.)

WHAT YOU NEED TO KNOW ABOUT
INFORMED CONSENT

You must inform your patient about the risks of any procedure, drug, etc. before proceeding. You can generally be safe if you tell your patients at least what other doctors would tell them.

The information you provide and the patient's consent need not always be in writing—that usually depends upon the risks involved, how extensive the procedure is, and the usual and customary practice among your colleagues. If the procedure is minor and poses few risks, and the patient has given you verbal consent, date and intial in your record a brief entry that says you did discuss the procedure's few risks, and obtained verbal consent.

Tip: If you are ever in any doubt about what to do, it is always best to get the patient's *written* consent.

All information should be given to the patient in terms that he or she can understand. Be watchful if the patient has difficulty understanding English, or for any other reason does not appear to understand what you are telling him. It is good practice to have the patient repeat what you have told him, to be sure he is understanding everything well. If the patient is a minor, be sure you obtain the informed consent from his parent or *legal* guardian.

Tip: Informed consent is implied only in an emergency. Otherwise, *you* have the responsibility of obtaining consent. You also have the burden of providing informed consent if a suit is ever brought against you.

The following hypothetical examples are offered to illustrate what you might do in two very difficult situations:

1.   First, let's suppose that a patient you treated two years ago sues you on the grounds that you never told him the risks involved in the procedure. If you don't remember discussing the matter with that particular patient (and there's no notation or signed informed consent form in your record), do you have any defense?

Perhaps. You may still be able to show that he gave informed consent by proving that it was and still is your *custom* to discuss risks with patients and get their consent before proceeding with that kind of treatment. Thus, you can protect yourself by establishing standards, and following them. Your staff may even be able to help you prove that it was your custom to get informed consent for various types of treatment, by testifying to this effect on your behalf.

2.   Now, let's suppose that one of your patients says it isn't necessary to spell out the risks of a procedure—or that he doesn't *want* to hear about the risks? Would you have him sign your usual consent form?

If you did, that form would probably not be enough to protect you in court. In such a case, begin by trying your best to convince the patient to let you explain the risks. But if he *insists* that he won't hear them, have him sign and date a statement that reads:

> I've been offered an explanation of the risks involved in this procedure, but I have declined that explanation.

UNDERSTANDING YOUR STATUTE OF LIMITATIONS AND LONG TAIL

Each state's legislature has set a time period beyond which a lawsuit for personal injury can't be commenced. These "statutes of limitations" vary from state to state, and even within states (depending upon the type of injury alleged). The limitation period generally varies from 1–3 years. However, attorney William Isele explains that there are two notable exceptions:

1.   *Minors and incompetents.* Traditionally in common law, a minor has no ability to sue for damages until he or she reaches the age of majority.

Likewise, an incompetent isn't expected to seek judicial relief for injuries during the period of incompetency. The limitation period is suspended until the minor reaches majority, or the incompetent returns to competency.

2. *Discovery rule/long tail.* A series of court decisions in the late 60's and early 70's established a new rule: A person can't be expected to assert a claim of which he or she was *unaware.*

Example: Suppose a surgical patient has a clamp or other instrument left inside which he or she didn't know about for years. Generally speaking, courts will allow the patient to assert a claim 1–3 years (the length of the respective statute) from the time he or she should have *discovered* the injury or negligent act, not from when it occurred. (The courts will carefully examine *when* the patient should have reasonably discovered the injury.)

Bottom line: The long tail rule leaves the doctor's liability exposure somewhat open-ended. Because of this, it makes sense to keep your patient records permanently.

FOR MORE INFORMATION

For more information on malpractice prevention, protection, and defense, see

- "Malpractice Protection: Management Strategies that Prevent Malpractice Claims," pages 239–247.
- "Malpractice Protection: What to Do If You're Ever Sued for Malpractice," pages 257–260, and
- "What Your Estate Should Know about Selling Your Practice," Tip 7, page 278.

C · H · A · P · T · E · R 5-3

Malpractice Protection: What to Do If You're Ever Sued for Malpractice

I n the previous two chapters, we reviewed the many steps you should take to prevent malpractice claims. However, even if you take every precautionary measure suggested, there's still the possibility that you'll be sued. If that ever happens to you, here's what you should know.

HOW TO RESPOND WHEN A PATIENT'S ATTORNEY CONTACTS YOU

Beware of anyone who calls your office and says pleasantly, "Doctor, I'd just like a little information about one of your patients." He or she is very likely to be the plaintiff's attorney, trying to gather ammunition to use against you.

Tip: Even if you feel you have nothing to hide and that there'd be no harm or breach of confidentiality in sharing information, *hold your tongue.* Don't answer even the most seemingly harmless questions, or give any information at all to the inquiring attorney at this point.

For one thing, the small print in your malpractice insurance policy may imply that the policy is void if you try to handle matters yourself. It would be foolish to risk having your policy cancelled because you cooperated with the patient's attorney. But more importantly, remember that your patient's attorney is anything but impartial. He or she will be looking for any shred of evidence—an incomplete sentence, poor choice of words, misnomer, the least bit of confusion, even the slightest hestitation in answering his or her questions—that can be used against you.

Your best bet is to be polite to the inquiring attorney, but to decline to answer any questions. Then, end the conversation immediately. Refer him or her to your own legal counsel for answers to any questions.

Tip: Obviously, you can't afford to have members of your staff answer the attorney's questions without the benefit of your legal counsel, either. Advise them to bring all such inquiries to your attention, and most importantly, *not* to answer any questions from *anyone* until they do so.

MAKE SURE YOU HAVE THE RIGHT COUNSEL

Soon after you notify your insurance carrier that you're being sued, you'll be assigned a defense attorney, and a date for your first meeting. If after that meeting you have any doubts about that attorney, or your ability to get along with him or her, ask your insurer to assign someone else.

Tip: If the subpoena demands damages that exceed your malpractice insurance limit, the defense attorney assigned by your insurer will probably suggest that you engage additional counsel to defend you against the excess. Don't get angry or defensive about this. The attorney is only doing his or her job, and advising you of your rights. It may very well be a good idea to pay the cost of additional legal representation.

Trust your attorney and hold nothing back from him or her. However, do keep tabs on what's happening. Your attorney should be willing to discuss the progress of your case with you at each step. He or she should answer all of your questions, and be responsive to your phone calls.

Remember, too, that your attorney is also required to report regularly on the status of your case to the insurance company that pays him. Ask for copies of these reports, as well as all other relevant correspondence or documentation.

ADDITIONAL STRATEGIES FOR A STRONG MALPRACTICE DEFENSE

How you conduct yourself throughout the malpractice investigation and legal proceedings will have a great deal to do with the outcome. At all times, you must remain highly professional, calm, and in control:

1. Approach your malpractice suit in a businesslike way. Try to channel your emotional reactions elsewhere, so you can keep your mind focused and clear as you handle each part of your defense.

2. In line with this, don't attempt to avoid being served with a subpoena. Accept it, but note the date, time, and place of service, and the name of the server. And, have someone reliable witness these facts.

There's always the possibility that the plaintiff's attorney failed to act before the statute of limitations expired. If you can prove that, the suit will be dismissed automatically.

3. Review all pertinent clinical records thoroughly. The more familiar you are with the facts, the easier it will be for you to explain your actions. Provide all the information you can to your attorney—let him or her screen what won't be needed.

4. Appreciate the importance of your deposition. Giving a deposition is the most important pre-trial event, and may be critical to your case. Pay strict attention to your attorney whenever he or she breaks in. If your attorney tells you not to answer a question, don't. Remember, whatever you say here will be admissible in court. In light of today's crowded court calendars, it may be years before you're on the witness stand. A clear deposition is invaluable.

5. Dress neatly and conservatively for your courtroom appearance. Avoid shows of affluence, such as expensive jewelry, designer suits, or a status attache case. Jurors of lesser means may decide that you can and should pay large damages.

6. Answer all questions clearly, and in a dignified manner. Face the jury squarely, establish eye contact, and answer loudly enough to be heard. Hesitate momentarily before answering. This shows you're considering the question carefully, and it gives your attorney a chance to object.

Do not allow the plaintiff's attorney to anger you. If he or she asks questions in an accusatory or sarcastic fashion, don't get ruffled. Act, rather than react. Keep your voice pitch and volume steady and even, your facial expression and body language relaxed, but attentive. If the attorney shoots a series of questions at you rapid fire, answer evenly, clearly, and calmly. Try your best to slow the pace of such proceedings.

7. Don't try to obscure an obvious fact. Keep cool at all costs. The jury will weigh your composure under pressure as a measure of your credibility and competence.

8. Look for traps. For instance, you should refuse to speculate on what you don't know. Or, if you're confronted with records you've never seen before and are asked to testify about them, refuse to do so, unless you're first given time to study them thoroughly.

FOR MORE INFORMATION

For more information on malpractice prevention, protection, and defense, see:

- "Malpractice Protection: Management Strategies that Prevent Malpractice Claims," pages 239–247.

- "Malpractice Protection: Managing Patient Records to Reduce Malpractice Risk," pages 249–255, and

- "What Your Estate Should Know about Selling Your Practice," Tip 7, page 278.

C·H·A·P·T·E·R   5-4

The Problems of Guarding
Patient Confidentiality

Every doctor knows that personal information about patients is confidential. But what exactly does patient confidentiality mean? How can you and members of your staff prevent breaking a patient's confidence unintentionally? And, how can you keep practice information *other* than that about patients confidential?

Certainly, confidentiality begins with a sensitive doctor and staff who don't gossip or share sensitive information with the wrong people. But guarding a patient's confidentiality is a bit more complex than that.

Every practice needs explicit policies about guarding patient confidentiality. Simply saying, "loose lips sink ships" just won't do. Share the information in this chapter with your partners and staff, both verbally and in your employee handbook.

10 UNDERUSED STRATEGIES FOR
GUARDING CONFIDENTIALITY

1. *The walls have ears.* Don't talk about patients (or other confidential matters about the practice) outside your office. Even if it is appropriate and necessary for you and your staff to discuss a patient, his problems, needs, or circumstances, doing so in a restaurant, on a bus, or in any other public place is dangerous and invites others to listen.

2. *Reduce the risk of a confidence leak.* Don't discuss patients and their circumstances or problems any more than you have to. Say only what you must to get your work done. The less you talk about a patient, the less opportunity there is for confidential information to leak out.

3. *Guard new patient's confidentiality.* Do you help new patients complete their get-acquainted forms? If so, conduct your get-acquainted interviews in a quiet, private room away from the reception area. The information you need to complete such a form is confidential. (Even simple questions about the patient's age, health history, or marital status are personal.)

4. *Guard established patients' confidentiality.* If you have sensitive or confidential questions to ask when established patients come to your office for their appointments (such as to describe their problems), invite them to meet with you in a private room to give you the needed information.

5. *Respect patients' confidentiality on the phone, too.* Take confidential or sensitive phone calls in a quiet, private area away from the reception desk, patients, and other staff members. If the situation warrants it, offer to call back or ask the caller to wait while you transfer the call. He/she will appreciate your discretion if you explain why you're cautious, and usually not object to waiting.

6. *No invisible patients, please.* Never talk in front of a patient as though he isn't there. This is not only rude but one of the best ways to let confidential information leak out.

7. *Label confidential information.* If you tell a colleague or staff member information that you'd like kept confidential, say so. That way you'll avoid misunderstandings. As well, when you mail confidential material, label it as such both on the front of the envelope, and on the back flap. (People opening mail don't always look at the front of the envelope.)

8. *Avoid secrets.* Don't promise a patient or staff member that you'll keep information from someone who should know it. For example, a patient or staff member might say, "I'll tell you but you've got to promise you won't say anything to Dr. Santini." A good response: "I appreciate the sensitive nature of this situation and I do want to know very much. However, I also want to help you. I may have to tell Dr. Santini because he'll want to do what is right for you." Pause and let the person continue. In many instances he will, and you'll avoid the unpleasant situation of holding an awkward or inappropriate confidence.

9. *Be wary of questions.* Don't supply confidential information about patients, partners, or members of your staff to creditors, employers, or other people who ask for it.

Tip: When en employee is fired, tell inquiring patients that the person is "no longer with the practice" and leave it at that. Don't go into the circumstances of events that led up to the dismissal.

10. *Protect confidentiality in print.* If you have a patient newsletter, be sure you don't violate a patient's privacy or confidentiality in any articles you

write. If you wish to publish news or photographs about your practice (birthdays, anniversaries, marriages, births, etc.), check first to get the patient's permission. (The same is true for news about your staff and partners.)

Tip: Also get patients' permission for any other practice building activities that involve them. For example, you may want to publicize information about patients on a reception area bulletin board, write about them in press releases, or talk about them in a speech. If so, get the permission of anyone involved before you proceed.

KEEPING PATIENTS FROM SNOOPING

Confidentiality breeches are most likely to occur with staff. However, it is possible for a patient to get his hands on information he shouldn't have. Therefore, you'll want to take steps to keep patients from overhearing or snooping:

1.   Escort all patients everywhere they have to go in your office. Have a member of your staff take them to and from the treatment/examination rooms, your private office or conference area, the reception area, etc.

2.   If an emergency requires you to leave the patient for a few minutes in your private office, don't leave him there alone. Find a member of your staff to cover for you. That way, patients won't be able to see the things you don't want them to see, such as other patient's records, or personal notes you've made about that patient in his own record.

3.   When you need to discuss confidential information with a staff member or fellow doctor, do so in an appropriate place in your office. The hallway or reception area is generally not a good place. Be sure that the room where you're meeting has a closed door and that sound doesn't travel through the walls to the wrong ears.

GUARDING CONFIDENTIALITY WHEN PATIENTS OWE
YOU MONEY

Even debtors have certain rights to confidentiality. Among your obligations:

1.   Don't share confidential information about patients with collection agencies. Often, agencies ask for a breakdown of a delinquent patient's financial record. When providing this, don't supply too-specific information about the patient's treatment, medical condition, or services.

The best approach is a cautious one. Give a list of financial data and dates. Identify entries loosely as "professional services." Avoid specifics such as "examination" and "surgery." (The fact that a patient had an examination or surgery is confidential.)

2.   Collection letters must be confidential, too. Don't send collection notices on postcards. As well, don't mail notices in envelopes that are printed with the words or symbols denoting "collection." Both actions are considered an invasion of the patient's right to privacy.

3.   Don't discuss a patient's debt or financial arrangement with your practice with the patient's friends, employer, co-worker, or anyone else outside the practice except the patient himself, a collection agency, or a lawyer.

GUARD STAFF COMPUTER ACCESS PASSWORDS

Passwords can be given to staff to restrict their access solely to those areas of the computer system in which they have duties. Some tips about issuing passwords:

1.   Each person should choose a password that's easy to remember so they won't have to write it down. However, make it unusual enough so it's hard to guess. For example, don't use each employee's spouse's name, or middle name, since that will be information known or available to other employees.

2.   Change each person's password periodically. Staff members tend to learn one another's passwords over time, even if unintentionally.

3.   Deactivate the password of any staff member being discharged as soon as he has been given notice.

4.   If any member of your staff has access to computerized personnel records, use employee code numbers in place of names. This can deter employees from learning confidential information about one another.

5.   Restrict access to sensitive files only to staff members who have direct responsibilites in those areas. A good program will allow you to delete sensitive file names from the master menu. This is a desirable feature—the fewer people who know about the sensitive files, the better.

WATCH WHAT YOU "BROADCAST" ON
CELLULAR PHONES

Did you know that transmissions from cellular phones may be picked up on VCRs, TV sets manufactured before 1982, and some radio scanners?

When using a car phone, don't discuss private or delicate matters, especially those that involve a patient, colleague, or staff member. If you *must* discuss confidential matters on cellular phones, invest in a voice security system. Effective ones may cost several hundred dollars.

HOW YOUR STAFF CAN HANDLE
DELICATE QUESTIONS

Every once in a while, someone may ask a member of your staff to supply information about your patients that they can't. Dates of patient visits, services rendered, who handled the treatment, diagnosis, and similar information is confidential, and also might be used against you by a malpractice attorney, family member, or insurance investigator.

Make sure your staff knows that no information of this kind is to be given to anyone but the patient—not even to a spouse. The best response your staff can give to such a request:

I'm not at liberty to say. If you like, I'll be happy to take your name and number and talk to the doctor about your request when he's free.

SECURING PATIENT'S PHYSICAL RECORDS

Keeping patients' files confidential requires a little more than tight lips. To protect the physical file:

1. Have every patient complete a signature card for your records. Check all written requests for the patient's records against his signature. If the signature on the request doesn't match, call the patient.

2. Have staff notify you of all requests for information from patients' records prior to complying—even if they appear to be from the patient.

3. Record all requests for information from patients' files, including the name, address, and title of the person requesting the file, the patient's name, where and to whom the file was mailed, and the date and reason for the request.

4. Check the credentials of anyone who seeks access to your patient records. For example, verify an insurance company representative's employment and the reason for requesting information from your files.

5. Develop an office policy for removing patient's records from your office. For example, many practices keep an out guide and a log of files removed, including the patient's name, the name of the doctor or employee taking the file, the date the file was taken, and the date it was returned.

6. Don't keep files where the public has access to them. If possible, keep your patient files in a locked cabinet.

C·H·A·P·T·E·R   5-5

Preparing Your Practice for Your Unexpected Absence

I s your staff prepared if you are unexpectedly delayed for the first appointment of the day? Do they know what to do if you have a sudden emergency that calls you away from the office for an afternoon or for several days? What will your staff do if you must close your office suddenly for several weeks—or even months?

Most doctors don't think about these difficult situations until they're confronted by them. Unfortunately, all they can do by then is ad lib an explanation to waiting (sometimes irate) patients, and try to muddle through as best they can. However, it is much more sensible to prepare your staff so they know precisely what to do if you are unable to keep scheduled appointments. Preparation will help them handle the situation calmly so patients maintain their good attitudes about the practice—and you maintain your practice's value.

CREATING A CONTINGENCY PLAN

In many cases, you won't be able to talk to your staff when you can't keep an appointment. For example, you may be stuck in traffic, have an accident, become suddenly ill or injured, etc. Therefore, discuss the possibility of these things happening with your staff *now*, so you can set a contingency plan together. Then write your procedure for handling this sort of emergency in your policy and procedure handbook. Some questions you should resolve in your written plan:

1. If you're delayed in the morning and can't get to a phone to notify your staff, how long should they wait before rescheduling waiting patients? (A general rule of thumb—call to reschedule within 20 minutes.)

For example, if your first appointment is at 8:00, what time should your staff tell the patient about the problem? 8:10? 8:15? 8:20? What reason should they give the patient?

Tip: Instruct your staff never to lie, pretending that you're in the office when you're not. A good explanation: "The doctor was unavoidably detained." You can tell the patient a more precise reason later, in a follow-up letter. (More on explaining your absence to patients, below.)

2.   Under the same circumstances, how long should your staff wait before calling patients who have appointments scheduled later that same day? What should they tell them?

3.   If you must cancel all appointments for a half-day, or even several days, who should call the scheduled patients? What should he or she say? Which staff members should remain in the office while you're gone? What should they be doing?

Tip: Your unexpected absence may be a good opportunity for your staff to catch up on collection calls, recall notices, work on marketing projects, do some office housekeeping, etc. Therefore, have each member of your staff prepare a "To Do" list of "rote" work to be done, in case of your unexpected absence.

Example: Your business assistant might include the following activities on her "To Do" list:

Business Assistant: Emergency "To-Do" List

---

1. Rearrange the supply cupboard.
2. Put fresh labels on all patient files.
3. Write articles for the next patient newsletter.
4. Address patient holiday cards.
5. Read specified books, listen to educational tapes, etc.

---

4.   To whom should your staff refer emergencies during your absence? How long an absence is necessary before your staff should refer non-emergency patients?

5.   What steps should you take to inform patients of a prolonged absence?

EXPLAINING YOUR ABSENCE TO PATIENTS

It's essential that patients believe you have a good reason for not seeing them during their scheduled appointments. Without a logical explanation, they're likely to be angry about the inconvenience, especially if they've spent time waiting for you in your reception area. However, it's best to avoid lengthy, complicated excuses and those that are too personal or would reflect badly on you (i.e. you overslept).

Tip: Don't alarm patients by leading them to believe that your reason is more serious than it really is—that you're deathly ill when it's the flu, or that you were in a major highway accident when it was only a fender bender.

Some examples of good reasons the doctor is not there:

1. He was not feeling well.
2. Family illness.
3. Personal emergency. (This is an excellent, all-purpose excuse that can be used in almost any situation.)

If the patient presses your staff for more information, it may be best that they pretend ignorance. For example, they might say:

- "Dr. McBride didn't have time to go into details," or
- "We're not certain. He left the office rather quickly."

SEND FOLLOW-UP LETTERS TO ELIMINATE HARD FEELINGS

Your contingency plan should prevent more patients than necessary from showing up when you're not there. Those who do come only to learn that you aren't able to see them may become angry, unless your staff has made every effort to stop them, and, then, can offer a reasonable explanation.

In any event, it's good form to send a personalized letter to each patient who was rescheduled due to your absence. If you're unable to write the letter yourself, your business assistant or office manager might do it for you.

Example:

Dear _____ ,

We regret any inconvenience caused when Dr. Griffith was unable to keep his appointment with you. We know how valuable your time is, and are very sorry that we were unsuccessful in our attempt to reach you before you arrived at our office.

Dr. Griffith has asked me to thank you personally for your patience and understanding. We're happy to report that his surgery went very well, and he has hopes of being back into full swing in about two weeks. I will call you within the next few days to re-schedule your appointment. Again, thanks for being so understanding.

Tip: If a patient has been inconvenienced greatly, you might follow up yourself with a phone call, when you're able to do so.

WHAT TO DO ABOUT A PROLONGED ABSENCE

Occasionally, a situation may arise in which you may need to be away from your practice for more than a few days. In these cases, telephoning all scheduled patients is best, but may not be practical.

As an alternative, your staff might send a letter to all scheduled patients, to explain what's going on. This letter should be accurate and concise, yet not create undue anxiety.

Example:

Dear _____ ,

I'm writing in regard to your appointment with Dr. Harris that's scheduled for next Wednesday at 10:45. I'm sorry to report that because of illness, Dr. Harris won't be able to keep the appointment. She's asked me to tell all of her patients that she expects to return to the office by mid-January.

During Dr. Harris's absence, patients needing treatment are being referred to Dr. Lisa Barry (address and phone number). Should you require an appointment, please inform that office that you're one of our patients, in order to facilitate communication between offices. (Explain alternative arrangements for coverage here. More on this subject below.)

We regret this inconvenience, and appreciate your understanding. Please call our office within the next few days if we can be of assistance.

If your staff is to be in the office during your absence, have them give a similar explanation to patients who call for appointments. You may want to use a phone answering service or machine to inform patients who call that the office is closed temporarily. If so, give a phone number to call for assistance.

In smaller communities, a brief notice regarding your prolonged absence might be placed in the classified section of the local newspaper. If you decide to place such a notice, don't go into great detail.

Example:

The office of Dr. James Hamlin will be closed from May 15. Patients may call 555-1234 for assistance.

Run a second notice once you return to the office. For example:

> The office of Dr. James Hamlin, which has been closed since May 15, has resumed regular hours. Call 555-1234 for more information.

Tip: Public notices such as these don't serve as a substitute for the other, more personal means of communicating with patients. Use them only in *addition* to letters and phone calls.

ARRANGING COVERAGE FOR YOUR PRACTICE

A common fear, especially among solo practitioners, is that their extended illness or untimely death will result in the total economic ruin of the practice. To assure coverage in such situations, consider entering into a mutual cooperation association with other area solo practitioners.

Under such an arrangement, participating doctors would agree to work to continue the practice of any member during an extended absence due to illness or disability, or after the doctor's death, in order to protect the value of the practice. The disabled doctor, or deceased doctor's estate, would have the financial responsibility of maintaining the practice. However, the doctors participating in the association would provide their services without compensation.

Some tips for establishing such an association:

1.   Include at least five doctors. That will limit each one's obligation to provide services to no more than ten hours per week (provided that the practice maintains a 40-hour work week.)

2.   Be sure that each participant has the professional background and qualifications necesssary to provide services to the absent doctor's patients.

3.   Set up a rotating chairmanship for the association. Outline the chairman's responsibilities to organize a schedule among participating doctors, to communicate with the absent doctor or the family/estate, etc.

4.   Define an extended absence. Determine when the group will commence to provide services for the disabled doctor (i.e., after two weeks of absence?). Establish guidelines for scheduling of hours (not before 7:00 a.m. or after 7:00 p.m., not on Sunday, no more than 10 hours per member per week, etc.).

5.   Agree upon the length of the commitment. For example: Three months of rendering services without compensaton. After that, the obligation is terminated unless the majority rules to continue, pending financial arrangements with the disabled doctor or his/her estate.

6.   Agree how to handle two or more simultaneous disabilities and/or deaths among participating doctors.

7.   Agree how to add new members to the group, expel a member, etc. To resolve disagreements, designate an impartial non-member who will arbitrate disputes.

OVERHEAD INSURANCE OFFERS PEACE OF MIND

Even if *you* can't make it to your office because of a disabling illness, your bills for utilities, telephone, insurance, supplies, and rent will. In addition, you'll still have to pay your staff for running your office in your absence.

Overhead insurance gives you benefits beyond disability insurance that cover the actual expenses of running your office while you're disabled. Policies vary widely, but here's a checklist of benefits worth seeking:

1.   A short waiting period to receive benefits. Generally, policies range from 14–90 days.

2.   Benefits retroactive to the first month of disability (once you get past the waiting period).

3.   Coverage for a long period of time. The usual range: 6–24 months.

4.   A policy that can't be cancelled.

5.   A clause extending benefits beyond the time limit, if not used. Why: Suppose your policy pays a maximum of $1,000 per month for one year, but you use up only $700 per month. After the one year is up, the clause would enable you to use the extra $3,600 ($300 per month) during the rest of the time you're disabled.

6.   A high maximum benefit. Look for policies that have both a high dollar limit and that cover roughly 80% of expenses.

Tip: Overhead insurance premiums aren't usually very expensive. And, part of the cost may come back to you in the form of a tax deduction.

LEAVING INFORMATION FOR YOUR FAMILY
AND STAFF

If you walked outside your office right now, got hit by a car, and couldn't communicate at all for the next 60 days, would your family and staff have all the information they need? Often, people who are in a position to help—a spouse, child, staff member, or friend—are unable to do so because a lack of information and authority restricts them from taking action.

To make sure this never happens to you, write the following information, make copies of it, and be sure staff members and family know where it's kept:

1. Name of your business trustee/power of attorney.

2. Location of your will, as well as its executor.

3. Names, addresses, and telephone numbers of your attorney, accountant, financial planner, practice management consultant, and other service professionals.

4. Bank accounts, retirement plans, stocks, bonds, and other investments. (List account numbers and the name of the banker, broker, or other person who's familiar with your holdings.

5. All insurance policies—disability, life, malpractice, hospital/medical, overhead, etc. (List policy numbers, telephone numbers, and agents, as well as the amount of coverage, effective dates, and beneficiaries.)

6. Practice contingency plan (as outlined in your policy and procedure handbook.) Be sure to include information about coverage by other doctors, who can sign checks to pay staff and bills, procedure for informing patients, etc.

C · H · A · P · T · E · R   5-6

Preparing Your Practice for Your Death

Death is the one subject no one wants to talk about. Very few people like to think about their own wills and estates. Consequently, too many of us never get around to it.

However, in the event of your death, it will be tough enough for your spouse and family to wrestle with the emotional realities of facing life without you. Discussing your personal and business holdings now, while you're alive, and drawing up a carefully constructed will, are good ways to help them cope with the financial realities that will face them. But there's much more you can and should do.

If you're like most doctors, your practice is the most important part of your estate. To help your family go on without you, you must make concrete plans now for liquidating or selling it, quickly and easily, and for a good price. Doing so will the kindest thing you could possibly do for those you leave behind.

Your financial advisor and your attorney will be the people in the best position to counsel you about your own particular estate planning needs and goals. However, this chapter suggests additional practice management strategies for right now, that will prepare your practice for an easy sale in the event of your death.

ESTABLISHING YOUR CONTINGENCY PLAN

You may die without warning. Thus, you will want to be certain that your patients continue to receive excellent professional care after you're gone. To provide for this, you will need to establish a contingency plan for the care of your patients, until your practice is sold.

For more information on creating such a plan, see "Creating a Contingency Plan," pages 267–268, and "Arranging Coverage for Your Practice," pages 271–272.

LEAVING INSTRUCTIONS FOR YOUR ESTATE

The last thing your family would need in the event of your death is to have to wonder what to do, or where to look for your estate planning information. Therefore, to eliminate this problem, make a clear record of all the information and documents your family will need in the event of your death, and tell them specifically what to do, and where this information is kept. A letter of instruction to your family should tell your family where to locate all the records they will need to handle your estate, and any specific wishes or thoughts not expressed in your will.

To begin, review the information provided in "Leaving Information for Your Family and Staff," pages 272–273, for a list of the basic information your family will need. Then, put with this list all of the official documents related to your estate, such as:

- Insurance policies.
- Automobile, boat, and real estate titles.
- Information about credit cards, loans, mortgages, and other debts.
- Funeral/burial/cemetary documentation.
- Prior tax returns.
- Military records and VA claim number.
- Partnership/associateship agreements.
- Incorporation papers.
- Checkbook and check records.
- Birth and marriage certificates.
- Safe deposit box number, location, and key.

Tip: For added protection, photocopy all of your most important records and documents, and store them in two or more safe yet accessible places, such as fire-proof containers at home and in your office, and in your attorney's office.

Important: Do *not* keep this information in a joint bank safe deposit box with your spouse. In many states, when one spouse dies, the joint box is automatically sealed, just when the surviving spouse most needs access to it for documents, insurance records, etc.

Tip: To avoid this problem, you and your spouse might each rent a box in your own names. Then, each box would contain the records the surviving spouse will need in the event of the other's death.

In addition to the information already suggested, also provide in your letter of instruction any information or suggestions you can offer your estate about the selling of your practice. (See below.)

WHAT YOUR ESTATE SHOULD KNOW ABOUT SELLING YOUR PRACTICE

Only six months after a doctor's death, a practice can lose up to half of its goodwill value! Therefore, the faster your estate sells your practice, the better.

To make the selling job easier, faster, and less painful for those in your estate:

1. Don't assume that accounts receivable will cover your office expenses. When debtors learn a business is going out of existence, they tend to defer payment—often permanently. Investigate overhead insurance plans to cover such expenses. (See "Overhead Insurance Offers Peace of Mind," page 272.)

Tip: Many doctors also establish a special savings account in their spouse's name, to provide "ready" cash to cover death and operating expenses, so that their assets won't have to be sold hastily. As well, investigate mortgage insurance, a death rider on your auto financing, "key man" or "key executive" insurance, and any other available insurance so your survivors won't have to make large payments before your practice is sold.

2. If you're in a partnership, try to hammer out a buy-sell agreement with the other doctors. That way, if you die, your estate will have a ready buyer, and life insurance could enable the surviving partners to pay your estate promptly, in accordance with the agreement. The insurance may be a single policy covering the lives of all participants, or separate policies covering each. Either way, the agreement should specify who holds the policies and how the value of each participant's share will be determined.

3. If you're not in a partnership, explore other potential ready buyers for your practice. A colleague or associate might very well be interested. Discuss the possibilities and details now, while you have the chance. Leave for your estate a list of all potential buyers, with their names, addresses, phone numbers, and related information.

4. If you know of a practice broker/appraiser who has a good reputation, note his or her name, address, and phone number in your estate plans. As well, leave the name of your practice management consultant and other individuals who might be helpful to your estate in the selling of your practice.

5.   Instruct your estate on the procedure it should follow for establishing the value of your practice. (For more information on this subject, see "Determining Fair Market Value of Your Practice," pages 279–282.) Be sure your estate has a copy of your most recent practice appraisals, as well as an updated list of all of your practice assets.

6.   Instruct your estate to sell everything in your practice as a package. Breaking up the practice can mean losing up to 75% of its value.

7.   Be sure your estate is prepared to handle claims brought against you after your death. When a practice is sold, the records often are available to it. However, because of the possibility of legal action against your estate after your death, the records must also be available to the estate. Instruct your estate to include a clause in the purchase agreement, giving them access to your records until the estate is closed and the statute of limitations has expired.

8.   If you lease office space, make sure your survivors will not have to count on your landlord's good nature. Get it in writing that your estate has the option to cancel your lease without penalty in the event of your death.

HELPING YOUR ESTATE PREPARE YOUR OBITUARY

On a sheet of paper separate from your letter of instruction, write down all the information you would like your family to have when composing your obituary. (Use an obituary from a local newspaper as a model.) Although your spouse and children may know everything already, they may not be able to recall important details, like the names of organizations you belong to, awards you've won, professional affiliations, etc., especially when they are grief-stricken.

If you have a suitable black and white photograph of yourself, attach it to the information sheet, and place both with your family's copy of the letter of instruction. This is just one more way to simplify matters for your survivors.

C·H·A·P·T·E·R   5-7

Determining Fair Market Value for Your Practice

A professional practice is a unique commodity, incorporating both tangible and intangible assets. Thus, determining an accurate dollar value for a practice is not a simple task. Appraisals require a great deal of experience, day-to-day information on the changing marketplace, and a keen appreciation for what makes a practice valuable to someone else.

WHEN TO HAVE YOUR PRACTICE VALUED

There are several situations in which an independent appraisal of your practice's worth would be necessary or helpful:

1. *Sale of practice.* If you plan to sell your practice, many consultants recommend having it appraised one year in advance. That way, you can structure your last year for the maximum sale price, while beginning to search for a qualified buyer without urgency.

2. *Estate planning.* Intelligent estate planning requires that you plan for an orderly sale of your practice, long before your death. Having an accurate appraisal will help make your plans much more realistic. (For more information on this subject, see, "Preparing Your Practice for Your Death," pages 275–278.)

3. *Partner buy-ins or payouts.* Independent appraisal of your practice's worth can help assure that group arrangements for new and departing partners are fair.

4. *Divorce valuation.* Current laws virtually require appraisals of a divorcing doctor's practice.

5. *Credit worthiness.* An appraisal enables a doctor seeking a loan to present a true financial picture of himself to improve his borrowing power.

6.   *General planning.* An appraisal can be extremely helpful when setting new long-term practice goals, reviewing your insurance coverage, needing self-motivation, or when you're simply curious about your practice's worth.

Tip: Many practice management consultants recommend having an appraisal done periodically, such as every five years, even if no specific occasion calls for it. Just as the value of fine jewelry, antiques, and artwork increases over the years, your practice's value is likely to increase as you mature, become a better communicator, build the right staff, further your education, and generally increase your abilities.

WHO SHOULD CONDUCT YOUR APPRAISAL?

Although you may feel that you already have a good idea of your practice's worth, the most accurate valuation will come from a professional appraiser who has experience, knowledge, and expertise in valuing professional practices. There are many individuals who may offer to appraise your practice for you—practice broker and appraisal companies, practice management consultants, and real estate appraisers, to name a few.

Referral from a trusted colleague or consultant is the best way to choose a worthwhile appraiser. Then, check the individual's experience and credentials. Be sure that the appraiser you engage has hands-on, in-the-field experience, as well as a sincere appreciation for the specific qualities of a professional practice.

Tip: When determining the practice's worth is critical to your planning or actions, you may wish to gather two or more independent appraisals.

Fees vary according to the amount of work, travel, and time involved for the appraisal, as well as the number of qualified appraisers available, and the appraiser's qualifications and experience. As well, you may have a choice of either a verbal or written appraisal from the same appraiser, for two different fees. Therefore, be sure you know precisely what documentation your appraisal fee includes, as well as the appraiser's methodology.

WHAT'S INCLUDED IN A TYPICAL APPRAISAL

To give you an idea of what to expect, here are some of the assets that are accounted for in a typical appraisal:

•   *Practice equipment, furniture, and fixtures.* In general, equipment is depreciated according to IRS or supply house schedules. Or, a formula is used. For example, the appraiser might choose to value old items at 25% of cost, new items at 75% of cost, etc.

 • *Supplies and hand instruments*—again depreciated, or valued according to a set formula.

 • *Leasehold improvements* (depreciated value of remodeling, redecorating, etc.). In general, costs incurred more than seven years ago are considered of no current value.

 • *Accounts receivable.* When appraising a practice that's for sale, the appraiser will usually reduce the accounts receivable by a standard percentage, roughly 5–10%, assuming that amount will be uncollectable. Or, he may evaluate the accounts receivable by age and collectibility.

 Tip: Accounts receivable are usually retained by the selling doctor, and seldom enter into the selling price of the practice. As well, when purchasing a practice, the buyer usually does NOT take over the selling doctor's debts on equipment leases. The selling doctor usually pays off the debt, since equipment leases may contain prepayment penalties, unpredictable final payments, or other surprises.

 • *Goodwill.* It used to be standard to set a figure for goodwill based upon 25% of the previous year's gross. Some appraisers still use this formula. However, most now use alternative, more complex means to determine a practice's goodwill.

 Example: Many appraisers establish a dollar value for each patient record. Active records (patients seen in the last 12–24 months, depending upon the type of practice it is), are given one value, inactive files another.

 However, additional factors beyond patient records might also go into the appraiser's goodwill valuation, including:

 1.   Transferability of the patients to the incoming doctor. This is what the buyer is really counting on. Without it, the practice is worth little beyond the tangible assets.

 Tip: If the selling doctor agrees to continue to work in the practice for a period of time after it is sold, that will significantly increase the transferability factor, and consequently, the practice's goodwill.

 2.   The number of *new* patients per month. A large volume of new patients can override other factors.

 3.   The selling doctor's working hours. For example, if the doctor worked only from 10:00 to 4:00 on Monday, Wednesday, and Friday, a buyer could increase income substantially by extending office hours. This would probably be reflected in the appraisal.

4.   The seller's fees. Increases or decreases might result in more new patients, and could have a bearing on the appraisal.

5.   The office's financial arrangement procedures. If the practice were "cash only," a buyer might liberalize the practice's credit methods, and create big differences in both gross and net incomes. Again, this might be reflected in the practice's valuation.

6.   Quality of the practice's business management.

7.   Percentage of patients with insurance.

8.   Amount of production generated by paraprofessionals.

9.   The practice's referral patterns.

10.   Staff history and longevity.

11.   Area potential and competition, based upon a profile of area professionals.

12.   Overhead percentage/net income.

13.   The office lease (if it has special features).

14.   Practice location (if exceptional).

P·A·R·T 6

Establishing Personnel Policies and Anticipating Problems

C·H·A·P·T·E·R   6-1

Using an Employee Handbook to Head
Off Problems

Being an employer can be a lot like being a parent. You may be frequently called on to make rules and enforce them—and watch out if you're not consistent! If employees believe you showed favoritism to another employee, they can harbor secret resentment that may someday boil over and lead to a legal dispute. Without written policies to back you up, your chances of winning such a dispute are poor.

Thus, the need for an employee handbook. A well-written policy and procedure manual, tailored to your practice, would spell out your office policies and employee benefits in the impartiality of print. It can save time by answering routine questions once and for all. And, it can make personnel decisions more objective, providing the back-up support you need.

A good handbook can speed a new employee's orientation to your practice. And ultimately, it may help you reduce your turnover rate and improve morale. Once everyone knows where they stand with the practice and what benefits they will earn over time, they will be much happier. And, they will be reassured to know that the rules apply to everyone.

Tip: Have your attorney review a draft of your employee handbook. Eliminate ambiguity, potentially discriminatory remarks, and other material that may lead to trouble.

WHAT A HANDBOOK DOESN'T SAY IS AS IMPORTANT AS WHAT IT DOES

A practice-tailored employee handbook can clarify many of your office policies by addressing such concerns as leaves of absence, overtime pay, parental leave, and salary reviews. However, you must be extremely careful about the subjects you cover, and how you cover them. Courts increasingly consider personnel manuals the equivalent of employee-employer contracts, in lawsuits filed by disgruntled former employees.

In light of this, your manual should probably *not* cover the following subjects:

1. *Salary increases.* While you might briefly describe your salary review procedure, do not specify the exact criteria used or list minimum or maximum raise or salary levels.

2. *Termination.* Do not list every possible reason for dismissal. If you do, a former employee might sue on the grounds that you fired him for a reason not listed in the handbook.

3. *Extended disability.* Most employers don't want to commit themselves to a written policy on this subject. Although you would undoubtedly grant a leave of absence to or might even continue the salary of a valued employee who becomes seriously ill, most employers prefer not to lock themselves in by putting such a policy in writing.

4. *Mandatory retirement.* In the past, many employers required retirement at a stated age, often 65 or 70. The Age Discrimination in Employment Act (ADEA) applied only to employers of 20 or more employees. But even in these cases, it prohibited forced retirement before age 70. However, in 1986, Congress amended ADEA, removing the age 70 provision. Now, professional corporations with 20 or more employees can't require retirement at any specific age.

INFORMATION TO INCLUDE IN YOUR HANDBOOK

To have the most complete handbook possible, you'll want to include as much detailed information as you possibly can, and cover a broad range of subjects. On the following pages are many suggestions that draw upon various chapters in this book.

Tip: You might separate personnel policies, such as those in the chart, from personnel procedures, such as how to answer the phone, make appointments, greet patients, etc. Consider having two sections to your handbook, or creating two handbooks, one on policies, the other on office procedures.

INFORMATION TO INCLUDE IN YOUR HANDBOOK

Policy:	What Employees Need to Know:
Introduction	This manual is for the staff's benefit. They should refer to it whenever they have a question. However, state clearly that the handbook does not supplant any legal documents or certificates.
Short history of the practice	Provide a profile of each doctor, and a short description of the kinds of services you provide and the patients you serve.
Practice philosophy	Explain your goals and what you expect from staff in the way of professional conduct, discretion regarding patient records, and dress. However, avoid requirements that are not job-related.
Work hours	Describe the normal work week, including coffee and lunch breaks. However, give yourself the option of changing an employee's hours during any week, at your discretion.
Pay period	Describe when the period begins and ends, and when paychecks are distributed.
Probationary period	State the length of your probationary period and when an employee starts to receive fringe benefits. Avoid a gap between the end of probation and the time an employee is eligible for benefits.
Employee status	Define what a full-time, part-time, flex-time, or job-sharing employee is, and your expectations of each. (See "How to Handle Part-Time, Flex-Time, and Job-Sharing Employees," pages 335–339.)
Overtime	Overtime is to be avoided whenever possible. Describe your overtime payment policy. (See "Reducing and Managing Overtime," pages 321–325.)
Telephone policy	Describe your policies for placing and receiving personal calls at work. State that emergency personal calls will always be put through.

Policy:	What Employees Need to Know:
Tardiness	See "Cracking Down on Absenteeism and Tardiness," pages 297–303.
Time clock or sign-in procedure	Describe the procedure for recording work hours. Some employers consider signing or punching in for an absent or late employee grounds for immediate dismissal.
Group insurance	Describe your plan briefly, and refer employees to the separate booklet provided by the insurance company.
Performance review	Establish a written procedure for reviews at least twice yearly.
Holidays	List practice holidays, and how holidays are to be counted if they fall during a vacation. See "Get-Tough Policies for Staff Vacations and Holidays," pages 291–295.
Vacations	See "Get-Tough Policies for Staff Vacations and Holidays," pages 291–295.
Sick Leave and personal time	See "Setting Trouble-Free Policies for Parental and Sick Leave," pages 305–310.
Extended leaves of absence	See "Setting Trouble-Free Policies for Parental and Sick Leave," pages 305–310.
Taboos	State taboos clearly. For example, you might make it taboo to talk about salaries with co-workers, or to gossip.
Additional topics	Topics worth including: pension and profit-sharing plan, fringe benefits, exit interviews, hiring of relatives, safety, parking, and housekeeping rules, tuition assistance, smoking policy, moonlighting, grievance procedure, gifts, jury duty, funeral leave, personnel records, severance pay, and termination.

GLOSSARY A USEFUL ADDITION TO EMPLOYEE HANDBOOKS

Every practice uses certain words and phrases that are unfamiliar to the layman. As a training tool for new employees, especially those who've never worked in a professional practice before, it is helpful to prepare a glossary of your most commonly used technical or practice-specific words.

Include a glossary in your employee handbook, complete with a definition for each word, and when needed, a phonetic spelling. Require new employees to study the glossary and demonstrate a clear understanding of each word.

Example: Here's a partial list of words and phrases that might be unfamiliar or unclear to new employees in a dental practice:

Sample Glossary for a Dental Practice		
ADA	cosmetic dentistry	PPO
amalgam	courtesy	production
associate	crown	prosthesis
bonding	daysheet	RDH
bridge	DDS	recall
call list	denture	restoration
cancellation	DMD	root canal
case conference	EDDA	specialties:
caries	4-handed dentistry	• endodontics
carrier	hygienist	• periodontics
certified dental assistant	informed consent	• pedodontics
claim	no-show	• orthodontics
collections	operatory	TMJ
co-payment	pegboard	veneer
corporation	post-treatment conference	

THE LANGUAGE AND MECHANICS OF YOUR HANDBOOK

The information in your handbook should be in everyday, easy-to-read language. A recent survey of both users and writers of employee handbooks revealed that both thought the major problem with handbooks was difficult, legalistic language which all but put readers to sleep. Don't intimidate your employees with a litany of "Thou shalt not's." Your handbook won't be effective if it isn't read.

Along the same lines, stress the positive whenever you can. Emphasize employee *benefits* rather than only rules and regulations. Be warm, by using personal prounouns, rather than terms like "the employer" and "the employee."

Example: Instead of writing, "The employer will issue a uniform to each employee," you might write, "We will provide you with a uniform."

An employee handbook need not be fancy, but it should be functional. Some practices distribute typed photocopies, while others spend the time and money to create an attractive, typeset version. However, you do it, plan to give each employee a personal copy.

Don't bind your handbook into a booklet. Rather, use a ring binder with chapter dividers so you can easily add or subtract copy as policy changes occur. Review your handbook at least once a year and budget for changes. Once outdated, a handbook is no longer useful.

DISTRIBUTING YOUR HANDBOOK

When your employee handbook is finished, hold a meeting to explain its purpose to your staff. As well, have your office manager give a copy to each new employee.

Most importantly, be sure to have all employees sign a statement within a week saying that they have read the handbook and understand it. If you must ever dismiss an employee, such a statement serves as concrete proof that you do have office rules and the employee was aware of them. This will protect you from unfair charges by disgruntled former employees.

When distributing changes that are meant to go into the handbook, it is important that everyone receive a copy. Number the pages with a number and letter (i.e., 64-A, 64-B, 64-C), to indicate where it is to go in the book.

You might give handbook changes to each member of your staff with a cover letter that explains all the reasons and background for the policy changes. To be sure everyone is aware of the changes, have each employee sign and date a statement indicating that they have received the changes and added them to their own handbooks.

Get-Tough Policies for Staff Vacations and Holidays

Most employees need time away from their jobs, and want it to be paid time. However, vacations and holidays, if not properly planned for, can wreak havoc in your office and create disputes between employees. In short, these problems defeat the original intent of the time off.

Although you might like to give everyone the time off they'd most like, that is not always possible. You must be firm about your vacation and holiday policies, in order to be fair to everyone in your office.

RULES THAT REDUCE VACATION CONFLICTS

Most practices give full-time employees two weeks (10 working days) of time off for vacation each year. Some offer additional vacation time upon achievement of certain employment anniversaries. *Examples:* Three weeks for five years, four weeks for ten years.

There are several rules you should institute to simplify scheduling and keep peace in your office:

1. Vacation must be taken in minimum increments—typically three to five days. Otherwise, employees will take a day here and there, and won't get needed rest. And you'll have constant work flow disturbance. Bonus: Running the practice without the employee for a straight week is a terrific opportunity to learn a great deal about him.

2. Employees can't receive payment in lieu of vacation.

3. Vacation can't be accumulated from year to year. This leads to scheduling problems later. And, everyone needs a vacation on a regular basis to gain perspective and freshness. Moreover, requiring annual vacations deters embezzlement. (For more information on this subject, see "Preventing Employee Theft," pages 327–333.)

4.   Employees should request their vacation time at least three months in advance.

5.   Vacation scheduling conflicts between staff members will be resolved on the basis of seniority.

"NO WORK, NO VACATION," A STRICT BUT FRUGAL POLICY

One of the most common and expensive problems involving staff vacation time occurs during the first year of employment. Typically, a new employee asks to take one or two weeks of vacation time before he has accrued this time. This seems rather harmless, so most doctors allow it. However, if the employee leaves the practice before the first year of employment is up, you'd have no way to recover the you money paid for unearned vacation, short of small claims court.

Because this happens so frequently, it is wise to establish a policy that says that vacation days cannot be taken until they're earned—period. If an employee insists on taking time off during the first year, allow him to do so. However, pay him for whatever vacation time has actually been accrued, *not* for time that hasn't been accrued. This strict policy is the best and fairest way to ensure that your employees don't leave your practice having taken unearned vacation time.

Tip: Some doctors try to get around this problem by paying salaries two weeks in arrears. They then offset the last pay period against unwarranted vacation time taken, the cost of damage to or replacement of practice property, etc. While such a policy protects the employer, it is generally very unpopular with staff, and should therefore be avoided unless absolutely necessary.

WHAT TO DO WHEN YOU TAKE YOUR OWN VACATION

Most offices try to have the majority of staffers take vacations at the same time as the doctor. However, a skeleton crew can remain in the closed office to bring collections up to date, weed through old patient files, reorganize the filing system, look into new equipment, or take inventory. You might even have remaining staff bring reception area magazine subscriptions up to date or forge ahead on back-burner practice building activities (such as a letter-writing campaign, brochure, open house, or patient newsletter).

Try to keep at least one person in the office when it's closed for vacation, to do these sorts of tasks, and also to:

1. Make or change appointments for patients who call.

2. Handle billing matters in the regular time allotted, and

3. Refer patients needing immediate care.

Tip: Out of fairness, give your staff a minimum of three months notice of when you plan to take a vacation or attend a seminar. Six months notice would be better. If the employee *must* schedule vacations for when the office will be closed, mention this to prospective employees at the job interview.

WHICH HOLIDAYS SHOULD YOU OBSERVE?

Most practices grant at least seven days off with pay each year. The most popular office holidays are:

1. New Year's Day.

2. Memorial Day.

3. Independence Day.

4. Labor Day.

5. Thanksgiving Day.

6. The Friday following Thanksgiving.

7. Christmas Day.

In addition, many practices also provide one or more of the following paid holidays:

1. The day (or half-day) before Christmas.

2. The employee's birthday.

3. A Christmas shopping day or half-day, in early December.

4. Religious days, such as Good Friday and Yom Kippur.

LET STAFFERS HAVE A SAY IN THEIR HOLIDAYS

Many employees would choose different holidays beyond the basics you provide for them. Therefore, why not establish a "master list" of eight or nine holidays, and then let staffers choose two or three more of their own? This approach has many benefits:

1. Staff members will get time off when they most want or need it.

2. Employees of varying religious and ethnic backgrounds may be able to celebrate their holidays without having to use vacation time.

3.   You will probably reduce the number of days your practice will be understaffed unexpectedly.

Tip: In large practices, have staff members make their selections in a written survey. However, be clear that staff requests are subject to your approval.

ESTABLISH ADDITIONAL HOLIDAY POLICIES TO MINIMIZE PROBLEMS

Holidays should be fun and trouble-free, but that's not always the case. There are a few precautions worth taking:

1.   Require staff to work the business day prior to and following holidays, in order to be paid for the holidays. Exception: Pay absent employees who have a doctor's excuse.

2.   Reward employees who work on a holiday. *Example:* Compensate them at time and one-half on those days. Or, grant them comp time-and-a-half off at another time.

3.   Decide how you will handle a holiday that falls during a staff member's vacation. Typically, the holiday is *not* counted as a vacation day. *Example:* If you provide Christmas as a paid holiday, and the staff member takes off the whole five-day week, he'd be using only four vacation days.

4.   Decide how you will handle a holiday that falls on a weekend. Typical: Most practices take off the Friday or Monday adjoining that weekend, usually abiding by the local public school schedule.

ALL ABOUT YOUR STAFF AND CHRISTMAS

The Christmas season is an exciting time, in general. But it is also a time that will require a little bit of extra planning for your office:

1.   It's a good idea to establish some policies about holiday gift-giving among employees. Many offices use a holiday grab bag, and put a strict dollar limit on the gift. That way, each employee needs to buy only one gift, with a restricted price. This puts less stress on your staff, reduces competition, ill-feelings, etc.

2.   Plan one holiday celebration exclusively for your staff. (Don't lump them into an open house for patients or another large party.) Invite their families, if possible.

3.   Do not give a cash Christmas bonus only. This becomes expected, and therefore, is almost always taken for granted. It's much better to give a

more personalized gift, instead of or in addition to money. Some great ideas:

- A year's membership to a health, tennis, or exercise club.

- Season tickets to a local sports team. (This can be divided among your staff. You might buy a block of two or four seats, and then let each staff member go to a few events. Decide who goes when by lottery.)

- A night on the town, for the employee and a guest. *Example:* Dinner for two at a nice restaurant or dinner theater. For sizzle, throw in a limousine rental for the evening.

- Send employees to a conference in a glamorous city they've always wanted to visit.

- A gift certificate to a nice local department store, or for luxury services you know the employee would enjoy. *Examples:* a beauty salon, cleaning service, hot tub rental, etc.

- A discount coupon book good throughout the year for stores and restaurants in your community. (These are available in many cities.)

- A magazine subscription related to the employee's interests. This is a great gift because it keeps on giving with every issue the employee receives.

Tip: Don't give the same gift every year. That's too predictable, and therefore, more easily undervalued. Show your thoughtfulness by varying what you give, even if that only means a gift certificate to a *different* restaurant or store each year.

FOR ADDITIONAL READING

If you're having problems with employee time off that have not been covered in this chapter, read:

1.   "Setting Trouble-Free Policies for Parental and Sick Leave," pages 305–310.

2.   "Cracking Down on Absenteeism and Tardiness," pages 297–303.

C·H·A·P·T·E·R   6-3

Cracking Down on Absenteeism
and Tardiness

There are plenty of employees who seek as much personal time off as possible. And there are plenty of employees who are habitually late. Below are some tips to help you limit unnecessary absenteeism and tardiness in your practice, while at the same time, allowing employees who geniunely need time off for personal business to do so without penalty or guilt.

DO YOUR EMPLOYEES KNOW YOUR
ATTENDANCE EXPECTATIONS?

To begin, you must make certain that employees know for certain what kind of attendance you expect from them. Three simple policies should clarify things:

1. All employees are expected to report ready for work on time each day.

2. Employees should keep their absences and tardiness at an absolute minimum. Employees are expected to miss work only when it is absolutely unavoidable, and then, for as little time as possible.

3. Notify our office immediately when you know you are going to be absent or late.

HOW TO DETER UNNECESSARY TARDINESS

This simple policy will do the trick: "All employees will be docked for any time they miss from work due to traffic, bad weather, or any other outside circumstances that delay their arrival to the office."

Without question, this is an extremely strict policy. It is sometimes impossible to arrive on time for work. In fact, *you yourself* may be held up by traffic or a storm some day. However, there will always be some staffers who make a greater effort to get to work in bad weather or traffic than others. Some live close to your office, some live farther away. Who gets paid—and who doesn't—in such a situation?

The strict policy is, unfortunately, the fairest. It may seem harsh to dock a valued employee who is late because of weather or traffic. But in the long run, it is the best way to keep peace and harmony in your practice.

HOW TO DEAL WITH THE EMPLOYEE WHO'S HABITUALLY LATE

For the employee who is frequently late (or absent), docking his paycheck may not be enough of a deterrent. If you've tried everything else, your next step will be to suspend the employee from work.

Example: Anne is late for the eleventh time in the past two months, because of "problems at home." What you might say: "Anne, take tomorrow and the rest of the week, without pay, to get your affairs in order. We'll see you back on time next Monday." This tells Anne that you're displeased with her tardiness and that you want her to stop.

If it gets to the point where an employee's tardiness is out of hand, you may have to fire him. If so:

1.   Document your case by keeping precise records: The date, what time the employee arrived, his reason, what you said and did about it.

2.   Tell the employee that his job is on the line. Then explain specifically what he has to do to save it.
Example: "Anne, your lateness is hurting the entire staff, and our patients, and I can't allow it. If you're late one more time this month, you will lose your job. And if you begin this pattern of lateness again anytime after this month, you'll lose your job."

3.   Give your last two or three warnings both verbally and in writing.

4.   Follow through and fire the employee if his attendance doesn't improve.

POKER PLAN GETS EMPLOYEES TO WORK ON TIME

So far, we've discussed *negative* incentives for employees to come to work on time. Here's a *positive* one:

1.   Have each employee who arrives on time choose a card from a deck of playing cards.

2.   At the end of the week, those with perfect attendance and punctuality will have five cards.

3.   The best poker hand wins a cash bonus or prize.

HANDLING EMPLOYEE TIME OFF FOR CONTINUING EDUCATION

When a staff member attends a meeting, seminar, or workshop that relates to his job or develops his professional skills, this is usually *not* considered time away from work. Ordinarily, expenses and an 8-hour day are paid for a full-day conference, whether it is 8 hours or not.

Beyond this, make the following decisions to keep staff continuing education expenses reasonable:

1.   Is there a maximum number of days per year that any staff member can be away from the office to attend courses?

2.   What restrictions will you place on hotels? *Examples:* How far away from the employee's home must the meeting be to justify the hotel expense? Must two or more employee's of the same sex double up in a room? Should the employee seek accommodations in an economy, moderate, or first-class hotel?

3.   What restrictions will you place on meals? *Examples:* Will you permit employees to order from room service? Will you put a cap on their daily meal expense? Will you reimburse them for the actual amount spent on meals under that amount? Or, will you simply pay them a *per diem,* from which they can keep whatever they don't spend?

4.   How will staff be reimbursed for travel expenses? *Examples:* Can tuition, airplane, and hotel expenses be charged directly to you? Or must the employee lay out the money and be reimbursed? What kind of expense report must the employee submit? Will copies of receipts be required?

5.   Will you limit transportation? *Examples:* How much per mile will you pay an employee for the use of his own car? If employees fly to a meeting, can they take a cab to their hotel? Or should they they seek less-expensive airport limousine or shuttle service? Are they to take public transportation within a city? Or will you pay for taxis?

6.   For overnight travel, will you reimburse staff for any long-distance telephone calls? Typically: Staff can make calls to the office, and one 5-minute call home per evening.

7.   Will staff be able to buy any additional materials sold at the meeting? (Books and cassette tapes are frequently offered.) What's the maximum they can spend without your approval?

HANDLING EMPLOYEE TIME OFF
FOR CIVIC RESPONSIBILITIES

Employees should arrange to vote on election day before or after working hours. If this is impossible, most practices allow time off to vote—with pay—at the beginning or end of the work day.

If you compensate employees for jury duty time, you may wish to put a cap on this benefit. Typical: 40 hours per year. Furthermore, employees should be required to return to your office for the remainder of the work day whenever they're dismissed or *not* chosen for jury service.

HANDLING EMPLOYEE TIME OFF
FOR PERSONAL BUSINESS

Unavoidable personal business comes up from time to time that requires an employee to miss work. For example, one of your employees may be:

- Summoned to appear in court.
- Giving a a blood transfusion to an ailing friend.
- Taking an important test that's offered only during work hours, such as a driving test or college entrance exam.
- Attending a funeral.

It's essential that the reason for the absence be *compelling* and *unavoidable*. A haircut or matinee tickets don't qualify. Employees should understand that they're to schedule personal business during their own time whenever possible.

Many practices allow staffers one or two days of time off with pay annually for compelling, unavoidable personal business. Doing so makes for a more honest employer-employee relationship, and deters lying and sick leave abuse.

Require a written request for personal time off in advance, as soon as the employee learns of the need for it.

HANDLING EMPLOYEE TIME OFF FOR BEREAVEMENT

Most practices pay for anywhere from one to five days off in the event of the death of an employee's spouse, child, parent, sibling, grandparent, or other very close relative. The employee can then take vacation days for additional needed time off, or elect to take the time without pay.

Dealing tactfully and sensitively with another person's grief can be a challenge. Moreover, you may have conflicting feelings. Although you recognize the necessity for a period of mourning, you may fear the employee's work will suffer. Will he be irritable with patients? Will he need additional time off? Here are some suggestions for your role in the grieving process:

1. Often, bereaved people feel that people they've known for years want to avoid them. Meet with the returning employee right away, appropriately touch his shoulder or arm, pause simply, and say how sorry you are about his loss.

2. People often ask—usually when a parent or older relative has died—how old he or she was. *Don't do this.* You can't assume that the death of an elderly person isn't as upsetting as the death of someone younger.

3. Don't say, "It was a blessing," even if you thought it was. The person in pain doesn't want to hear that.

4. Don't suggest any "shoulds," such as "you should be over this by now." Everyone's clock ticks at a different speed when it comes to recovering from the loss of a loved one. The grief process takes longer than most people think.

5. Let the bereaved share their grief. If you're close to the employee, offer: "If you need to talk, I'm here to listen."

6. Reassure the employee that they did all they could, but avoid moral lessons about death.

7. Don't say, "I know how you feel," unless you've walked in their shoes. Little irritates bereaved people more—especially bereaved parents.

8. Don't avoid mentioning the name of the deceased. Don't look the other way or change the subject if they mention their loved one.

9. Don't tell bereaved parents, "You can always have another child," or "At least you have other children." The child they've lost can't be replaced. Use the same sensitivity when talking to an employee who has had a miscarriage, or has had an adoption fall through.

10. Don't avoid them. The pariah syndrome can turn a very painful experience into a devastating one.

WHAT TO DO WHEN THE ABSENT EMPLOYEE RETURNS TO WORK

When an employee returns to work after an absence, take a few minutes to welcome the person back informally. Then, inquire about the reason for the absence.

If the employee says he was "sick," "didn't feel well," "had personal business," "a civic responsibility," etc., seek a more definitive explanation. Your records should show a specific reason for every absence.

When appropriate, express concern about the employee. If he is bereaved, follow the procedure outlined above. If he was sick, ask, "How are you feeling?" If he took a test, ask, "How did it go?" If he attended a funeral, ask, "Are you all right?"

You have two purposes in asking these questions:

1.   Showing genuine concern for the employee.

2.   Letting him know that you believe him, and that you take these things very seriously.

DOCUMENT EVERY ABSENCE OR TARDINESS

You'll need a simple documentation system to measure each employee's absentee rate. To begin, establish an individual absentee report for each staff member on which you record the days (or hours) absent for vacation and illness, and also days tardy. It might look something like this:

| Attendance Report For: Sandy Kirschenbaum | | |
Date:	Absent/Tardy:	Reason:
1/13/88	1 day	Migraine headache
9/5-9/88	5 days	Vacation
10/18/88	55 minutes late	Traffic
1/26-28/89	3 days	Flu

Next, have your business assistant collect individual absentee reports and prepare a cumulative attendance report every month or quarter. This report should document the rate of absenteeism in your practice and identify when and where absentee problems are occurring. To keep it simple, this report need only include the number of absentee hours and the percentage rate for the practice. If you have a large practice, conduct a cumulative absentee analysis by job category as well (business assistants, clinical assistants, etc.).

When your records indicate that an employee might be abusing your paid time off policies, it's time for a formal interview. In such a meeting, express more concern and note the frequency of absences. Take disciplinary action if necessary. (See "How to Deal with the Employee Who's Habitually Late," earlier in this chapter.)

Tip: Be sure your employees *know* you are keeping these attendance records. The mere fact that you do indicates that you feel reliability is an essential part of each person's job. Thus, employees will know you consider their attendance to be very important, and that you're keeping score.

SAVE ON PAYROLL TAXES DURING EMPLOYEE ABSENCES

Keep careful records of wage payments for periods when employees have paid absences. Payroll taxes are levied only on payments for actual services, *not* payments made when the employee is unable to work.

You may be eligible for refunds of payroll taxes, such as Social Security, paid during an employee's paid extended absence. Check with your accountant.

MONDAY PAYDAY A FINAL TRICK

Practices that distribute payroll on Monday find that absenteeism on that day declines dramatically. This would be most effective in practices with a high Monday absentee rate.

FOR ADDITIONAL READING

If you're having problems with employee time off that have not been covered in this chapter, read:

1. "Setting Trouble-Free Policies For Parental and Sick Leave," pages 305–310, and

2. "Get-Tough Policies for Staff Vacations and Holidays," pages 291–295.

Setting Trouble-Free Policies for Parental and Sick Leave

W ith rare exception, every person in the workforce will be too sick to come to work at one time or another. And chances are, at least one person in your practice will ask for an extended leave of absence because of a new addition to his or her family.

The forward-thinking professional practice needs to have humane parental and sick leave policies. These should enable sick employees and those with new babies to take time off, without worry, guilt, or financial hardship.

Unfortunately, a poorly thought-out or vague parental leave policy can lead to misinterpretation and resentment. And, a too-liberal or overly-simplistic sick leave policy is an open invitation for abuse. Simply paying employees for a given number of sick days without offering an alternative incentive may actually *encourage* them to play hookey.

The smooth operation of your professional practice depends upon the presence of your entire staff. The unplanned absence of just one team member can lower your efficiency and productivity for the entire day. Thus, while you want your sick employees to stay home without penalty, you can't afford to have a staff member fake illness and call in "sick" because he doesn't feel like coming to work on a beautiful Friday or rainy Monday morning.

WHY IT MAKES SENSE TO PAY FOR UNUSED SICK DAYS

Paying for unused sick days creates an incentive for the well employee to come to work, rather than an incentive *not* to. This makes good practice management sense because:

1. Paying for unused sick days leads to fewer unnecessary absences.

2.   Staff members who don't take all of their sick days will feel no resentment towards staff members who do.

3.   Paying for unused sick days boosts morale, especially when it is paid in a fun way, or at year end.

4.   Truly sick employees will still have the benefits of paid sick days.

5.   Paying for unused sick days makes turnover easier. A staff member who gives notice will be likely to work until the last day and help train his replacement, without using up sick days. And if you have to fire an employee, the extra pay may make the parting hurt a little less.

TYPICAL SICK LEAVE POLICIES

Most practices simply allot a given number of paid sick days to employees each year. Typically, they pay for up to six days off, to be used in the event of the employee's own illness. Some additional policies:

1.   Employees are not granted extra pay or time off for illness that falls during a vacation or holiday.

2.   Sick leave exceeding the allotted time is time off without pay. However, staff members can use earned vacation time after sick leave is used up.

3.   Sick leave cannot be accrued beyond one year.

4.   Sick leave is to be used for illness only. All personal business should be conducted on the employee's own time, whenever possible. (See additional time-off policies for personal business and civic responsibilities on page 300.)

5.   Any employee taking more than three days of sick leave in a row must bring a note from the doctor indicating both the cause of the illness and when the employee is fit enough to return to work.

6.   The practice pays employees their regular hourly wage, or a portion of it, for all unused sick days at the end of each year.

WHY YOU SHOULD HAVE A FAMILY SICK LEAVE POLICY

Most practices define sick leave to be used only for the employee's own illness. But as we all know, many employees must take time off from work when their children are ill. As single-parent and two-career households continue to become more commonplace, we can expect this trend to continue— or increase.

Pretending that sick leave is used for personal illness only creates stress for employees. It forces them to lie—they must pretend to be sick when they're not. That's why many professional practices acknowledge the reality of family sick leave and permit sick leave policies to cover the employee's children, spouse, and parents. This type of flexibility:

1. Reduces stress.

2. Increases morale, and

3. Leads to more honest employer-employee relations.

CREATIVE STRATEGY #1: REWARD PERFECT ATTENDANCE ONLY

If you'd like to be somewhat restrictive with your sick leave pay benefits, here's a payback system that rewards perfect attendance only:

1. Divide the calendar year into quarters.

2. For each consecutive quarter of perfect attendance, employees will earn a progressive amount of time off or extra pay as follows:

1st Quarter.........................	$\frac{1}{2}$ day off or 4 hours pay
2nd Quarter......................	1 day off or 8 hours pay
3rd Quarter	$1\frac{1}{2}$ days off or 12 hours pay
4th Quarter.......................	2 days off or 16 hours pay

3. If the employee receives a full year of the perfect attendance benefit, he will start over with a new benefit year.

4. If sick time is taken in any quarter, it will be a zero benefit quarter. The employee then reverts to first quarter benefits with the next perfect attendance quarter.

5. New employees become eligible in the first full payroll quarter worked. Employees must work at least 35 hours per week to be eligible.

6. Employees have the option of taking either the time off *or* the pay. They receive a statement of current status and benefits earned at the end of each quarter in which they have earned benefits. Time off must be arranged the same way as vacation time off, with specified notice and restrictions.

7. Employees may accumulate time off for one year, and take it in conjunction with other vacations or holidays.

8. If an employee elects to take pay, payment can't be accumulated, and will be made in the next payroll check.

CREATIVE STRATEGY #2: THE MONTHLY
ATTENDANCE LOTTERY

Another way to reward perfect attendance is with a monthly lottery. Here's how:

1.   Employees with perfect attendance records qualify for a monthly drawing.

2.   On the last working day of the month, one winner is selected at random from the list of eligible employees.

3.   The winner receives an attractive cash bonus or prize.

4.   The other employees with perfect attendance are rewarded with smaller prizes.

CREATIVE STRATEGY #3: EARN BONUS DAYS OR PAY

Here's a novel sick leave policy from a large Maryland optometric practice. The program works like a "charm," according to the office manager, who says that all five of their offices are fully staffed "99% of the time":

1.   Employees earn one 'bonus' day for every absence-free month— for a potential total earning of 12 days per year.

2.   Employees will not be paid for absences of one or two days as they occur, but will have the opportunity to make up missed days in bonus days in future months.

3.   Bonus days for each employee will accumulate every six months (December until June, June until December), at which time the number of accumulated bonus days will be divided in half. (We) will pay to employees, in June and December, one-half of unused bonus days at the employee's hourly rate and hold the remaining half in reserve time, thus providing employees the opportunity to accumulate a reserve to be used in the event of a future absence. Reserve time may accumulate from year to year to a maximum of 60 days.

4.   A prolonged absence is defined as absences due to illness of three or more consecutive work days, and must be covered by a doctor's written excuse. These absences will be paid and deducted from reserve time and/or bonus days as necessary. It is understood that an employee's work day may consist of more or less than eight hours. However, for fairness' and simplicity's sake, bonus days are charged and credited on the basis of 8-hour days.

CREATIVE STRATEGY #4: SAY IT WITH FLOWERS

If you're looking for the offbeat way to curb sick leave abuse, send a get-well card and flowers or a plant to the staff member's home the day he calls in sick. Similarly, if the employee asks to miss work because his *child* is sick, send someone from the office to his home at lunch time, to deliver a helium balloon bouquet, toy, or a package of coloring books and crayons. Pick out gifts that would help to cheer and amuse an ailing, bedridden child.

If the employee (or his child) truly is sick, he'll appreciate your thoughtfulness and generosity. However, if he (or his child) is *not* sick, he'll realize that you take absences seriously, and that you believed him.

With any conscience at all, the dishonest employee will feel sorry, foolish, and guilty about lying and abusing your sick leave privileges. More importantly, he won't do it again.

TIPS FOR GRANTING PARENTAL LEAVE

Parental leave is a common personnel management problem for the professional practice, As one doctor put it, "I'm starting to think there's something in our drinking water. *Everyone* here is pregnant!"

Most employers provide six or more weeks of unpaid leave after childbirth so parents can stay home and care for their new child. However, there are several things you should know:

1. Some states *require* employers to grant special "parental" leave benefits. See what you *must* do before you decide what you *want* to do.

2. If you offer short-term disability benefits, make them available to pregnant women just as you would to anyone who's temporarily disabled. This is sometimes called the "broken leg" rule. (That means that you will treat the pregnant employee just as you'd treat an employee who has a broken leg.)

3. You can request pregnant employees to submit a statement as to the probable duration of their absence, *if* you require similar information from all others requesting short-term disability leave (such as for elective surgery).

4. It's worthwhile to request the following information in writing for all short-term disability leaves:

- The cause of the disability.
- Starting date and duration of the leave requested.
- The physician's verification of the above information.

• Listing by physician of any temporary or permanent restrictions on the employee's job functions, both before and after his or her leave.

• Written confirmation from the physician that the employee is fit to return to work.

5. If you grant paid or unpaid extended leaves for education, travel, or any other non-work related reason, then generally, you can grant parental leaves on the same basis.

6. Some practices have an explicit unpaid "maternity leave" policy, although requests for other types of unpaid leaves are not routinely granted. To avoid claims of sex discrimination, rename such policies "parental" or "personal" leave and apply them equally to men and women, whether they give birth to or adopt children.

7. Take care that requests for parental leave are not disproportionately denied because you assume the woman will decide not to return to work.

8. One way some practices handle parental leave is to permit a combination of sick, personal, and vacation leaves, resulting in several weeks of paid leave. *Example:* One practice's employees can combine 10 days of accrued sick leave and two weeks of vacation at full pay, plus 20 days of temporary disability leave at ⅔ pay. That equals six weeks of fully paid leave.

FOR ADDITIONAL READING

If you're having problems with employee time off that have not been covered in this chapter, read:

1. "Get-Tough Policies for Staff Vacations and Holidays," pages 291–295, and

2. "Cracking Down on Absenteeism and Tardiness," pages 297–303.

C·H·A·P·T·E·R   6-5

Establishing Guidelines for Employee Dress and Hygiene

Each person on your staff is an important member of a professional team. Patients, colleagues, potential referral sources, and your community at large may meet your staff before they meet you, and form opinions of you and your abilities based upon what they hear and see.

How your staff speaks, acts, and also, how they *look* are all extremely important. Professional, neat clothing, and a fastidiously clean appearance will speak well of you and your staff, and are musts in any professional practice.

Unfortunately, the people who work for you may not share the same ideas about what constitutes a professional appearance. While staff input is helpful and important, and there is room for some individuality, it is nonetheless necessary to establish basic guidelines for dress and hygiene.

Clear rules ensure that your staff knows what is expected of them. As well, they help you treat your staff fairly and consistently on matters of dress and hygiene. And, rules serve as invaluable support if you must confront a staff member because of his appearance.

The trick is in establishing clear and reasonable rules that do not in any way discriminate against any individual because of race, handicap, gender, etc. As always, it is wise to have your attorney review any rules you establish before presenting them to your staff.

TIPS FOR ESTABLISHING A DRESS CODE

A professional practice dress code usually includes descriptions of the uniforms and specific types of shoes that can be worn. For non-clinical staff, it may prohibit certain types of street clothing for reason of safety or appearance.

There are many ways to handle staff uniforms. For example, you might,

1.   Choose one uniform style to be worn by everyone. As well, you might specify the type of shoes, a sweater or jacket, or even the purse and hair accessories that can be worn with it.

Tip: Many practices choose a uniform style and color that is coordinated with the office decor.

2.   Allow staff to choose their own uniforms, in any style they like. Or, you might let them choose the style they like, but designate a color.

3.   Require staff to buy five uniforms in five different colors. Then, you can designate that a different color be worn each day (i.e., pink on Monday, green on Tuesday).

4.   Choose one uniform style, but designate that a different color be worn by each member of your staff, for a rainbow effect.

5.   Require staff to sew a practice emblem/patch onto a plain uniform, on the sleeve or chest pocket. The patch, usually of the practice name and logo, can also be sewn onto lab coats or dispensing jackets worn by the doctor.

Tip: Many practices establish a uniform allowance for the purchase and maintenance of uniforms.

If some employees can wear street clothing to work, it is still important that they look neat, clean and appropriate. They should wear clothing that won't get in the way of their work and that is consistent with your professional atmosphere. Thus, many practices establish dress rules for non-uniformed employees. *Example:* You might:

•   Prohibit the wearing of very high heels, open-backed, or open-toed shoes.

•   Provide a jacket or sweater.

•   Require a tie and jacket.

•   Prohibit backless, low-cut, or see-through dresses and blouses.

ALL ABOUT NAME TAGS

Every member of your staff, including the doctor, should wear a name tag, regardless of who they are and whether they are wearing a uniform. Name tags are the simplest and best way to ensure that patients and co-workers know who they're talking to.

To keep things simple, it is best if *you* provide all the name tags for your staff. That way you have control over what they look like, and can give the tags a consistent, professional look.

Tip: Have a nametag ready for a new staff member's first day. It will help her get acquainted with co-workers and patients more easily, and make her feel immediately part of your team.

Almost any office supply or specialty company can engrave name tags for you inexpensively and quickly. Choose a large, easy-to-read nametag in a color that coordinates with staff uniforms and your decor. When possible, put your practice name and logo on the tag, as well as the staff member's name and title. That way, patients looking at the tag will associate the excellent impression they are getting of your staff with you and the practice—a very subtle form of marketing.

Designate where on the uniform the nametag is to be worn each day. And, whenever your staff appears on your behalf outside your practice, (ie. at a school program or health fair), be certain they're wearing their name tags.

TIPS FOR STAFF COSMETICS, HAIR STYLES, AND JEWELRY

Depending upon the type of practice that you're in or the particular kind of work being done, your practice may have guidelines about cosmetics, hair styles, and jewelry.

Example: The following is often discouraged in professional practices:

- Loose styles for long hair.
- Brightly colored nail polish.
- Very long fingernails.
- Excessive use of cosmetics and perfume.
- Large or noisy jewelry, especially on the hand or arm.

RULES ABOUT CLEANLINESS

A fastidiously clean personal appearance is a must for the staff of a professional office. Patients will notice if a uniform is stained or ripped, hands and nails are dirty, or shoes are soiled and scuffed.

Many practices establish personal hygiene rules, such as:

- Wash hands each time you use the bathroom.

- Wash hands between patients.
- Shoes should be polished and clean—no torn laces.
- Uniforms should be sparkling clean, pressed, and show no signs of wear or stains.
- Scapes and cuts should be covered and dressed with clean bandages.
- Nails should be clean and smooth-edged.

Tip: If you permit colored nail polish, you may insist that the employee have a perfect manicure or remove it. If so, keep a bottle of nail polish remover on hand.

RULES FOR OFFICE NEATNESS

In addition to personal hygiene rules, you may wish to establish rules for the neatness and good order of each employee's work area. A sloppy desk or work station does not reflect positively or project the right image to patients.

Employees should make it a habit to put their work area in good order before they leave the office at the end of each day. That way they'll always return to a clean, organized desk or station in the morning.

RULES FOR STAFF DRINKING AND EATING

Some practices allow employees to eat and drink only in specified areas, such as a break room or kitchen. If employees may eat or drink at their discretion, it should not interfere with a task, or be in front of patients. As well, containers, wrappers, and crumbs should be cleaned up by the employee.

Tip: In addition, most employers prohibit the consumption of alcohol and drugs at the workplace, and make such behavior grounds for immediate dismissal.

RULES ABOUT SMOKING

Most practices don't allow staff to smoke while at work. For information about establishing a smoking policy, see "Establishing a No-Smoking Policy in Your Practice," pages 317–319.

RULES ABOUT GUM CHEWING

Chewing gum is usually prohibited in the professional office. It projects the wrong image and interferes with the staff member's ability to speak clearly.

Along similar lines, most employers prohibit the use of chewing tobacco at the workplace.

KEEPING SUPPLIES ON HAND FOR EMERGENCIES

Sometimes things happen beyond anyone's control. That's why it's a good idea for you and your staff to keep some emergency dress and hygiene supplies in your office, in case you or they have a mishap that spoils their appearance.

For example, many employees keep the following on hand:

- Extra pantyhose.
- Spot remover.
- A nail file.
- Comb or brush.
- Cosmetics.
- Hair clips, barrettes, or bands.
- Shoe laces.
- Safety pins.
- Sewing kit.
- A spare uniform.
- Dental floss, toothbrush, toothpaste, mouthwash.
- Folding umbrella.
- Cardigan sweater.
- Rain bonnet.

These items can be tucked away discreetly in a closet or drawer, and should be replenished when used.

RULES ABOUT STOWING PERSONAL POSSESSIONS

Staff handbags and other personal items should be locked safely out of sight in a desk drawer or cabinet while the staff member is working. Leaving a handbag in plain view in inappropriate—and risky.

As well, you should designate a place in your office for staff coats, umbrellas, boots, and other similar garments. Staff should be told to place their belongings in that place neatly at the start of each day.

WHY TO ENCOURAGE STAFF TO LOOK THEIR BEST EACH DAY

There are two reasons your staff should put some effort into their appearance. First, several studies suggest that the people around us tend to respond best to us when we look our best. Thus we can assume that patients, co-workers, and perhaps even you will respond best to your staff when they look their best.

Second, how you look often affects how you feel. It is psychologically pleasing to look your best. The more positive your staff's self-image, the more positive the image of themselves they will project to patients and co-workers.

MAKING DRESS CODES NON-DISCRIMINATORY

Employee dress codes are unlawful if they can't be applied equally to both sexes. That's the upshot of a federal court case in which the employer had required female employees to wear smocks and male employees to wear shirts and ties. Thus, if you have a dress or hygiene code of any type, make similar requirements for both male and female employees in comparable positions.

In addition, avoid dress and hygiene codes that are targeted to specific racial or ethnic groups. It can be deemed discriminatory in some cases to prohibit hair styles or garments particular to certain groups of people, if these do not interfere with job performance.

Example: An airline was sued by an employee who was fired for wearing a "corn row" hairstyle of traditional braids and beads. She argued that the style was part of her African heritage, and had nothing to do with her job performance or ability.

Establishing a No-Smoking Policy in Your Practice

T oday, many state and local governments restrict smoking in the work-place. At the same time, an increasing number of nonsmokers are suing employers for exposing them to smoke—and winning some support from the courts. Most likely, we can expect more regulations and more litigation brought by nonsmokers in the future.

Because of these trends, your first step in establishing a smoking policy is to be sure that you comply with state and local laws. A number of states have enacted Clear Indoor Acts that restrict or prohibit smoking in work environments if it regularly exposes nonsmokers to a detrimental amount of smoke. (Detrimental levels are determined on a case-by-case basis.) Many cities, counties, and towns in states without comprehensive policies have enacted their own smoking ordinances.

Tip: Check with your attorney to learn about the specific restrictions in your area.

THE HIGH COST OF SMOKING

Cigarette smoking can be hazardous to your balance sheet. According to the Surgeon General's office:

1. Workers who smoke use the health care system up to 50% more than non-smokers, thereby raising health insurance costs.

2. Workers who smoke are absent more and have more work-related accidents leading to higher disability claims.

3. It's costlier to keep an office clean, furniture and carpet in good repair, and the workplace ventilated in offices where employees smoke.

4. Employers spend hundreds of dollars per year extra, on average, for each employee who smokes.

5.   Nationally, smoking accounts for an annual $23 billion in health care costs and $40 billion on lost productivity wages.

According to one university study, lost time due to the act of smoking ranges from eight minutes a day to as much as 15 to 30 minutes per hour. As well, two-pack-a-day smokers are absent twice as much as workers who abstain, the study found.

OTHER REASONS TO INSTITUTE A SMOKING POLICY

On top of the legal and financial issues, there are the personal ones to consider. Most importantly, smoking employees may harm your professional image. Day in and day out, you work to preserve and promote good health. To allow smoking in your office contradicts your efforts. It may offend some of your patients, colleagues, and staff, and lower their opinion of you.

Even if you restrict office areas where employees can smoke, it is difficult if not impossible to contain the smell. In addition, patients may detect smoke on your employee's clothing, breath, and hair, or see that their hands are discolored by nicotine, and find it offensive.

Safety is a factor, too. Smoking cannot be allowed where hazardous and flammable materials such as paper and chemicals are stored. As well, many burns are caused by cigarettes. And obviously, wherever there is smoking, there is the increased chance of an accidental fire.

TO BEGIN, HIRE NON-SMOKERS ONLY

To date, it is perfectly legal to maintain a policy of hiring non-smokers only. The courts have ruled that discrimination charges apply only on the basis of inherent characteristics, such as race, sex, age, or national origin.

According to the Federal Equal Opportunity Commission, who issued a statement on this subject in 1982, discrimination against smokers *does not* violate their civic rights. Again, check with your attorney before proceeding, to learn about any changes or new interpretations of the law.

INSTITUTING A SMOKING BAN

Obviously, the difficulty with instituting a no-smoking policy is with existing staff who already smoke. Individuals who were smoking when hired may be very angry to be told they must now quit. Some may try give up smoking, and not succeed. Some may decide to find another job. However, there are several things you can do to make your ban more palatable:

1. Make clear that your purpose isn't to regulate any individual's personal habits, but to ensure all employees' comfort at work (and patients, too).

2. Structure a strong incentive, such as a cash bonus or attractive gift, that will motivate employees to quit smoking. Be as personally supportive as you can.

3. Discuss your intentions to institute a ban with your attorney before you proceed. Review new court decisions.

4. Consider the potential effects of the ban, good and bad. If a highly valued employee who smokes says she will look for another job if you institute a ban, you may decide to institute permanent smoking restrictions, in lieu of a a ban.

5. Announce the ban to employees ahead of time, perhaps 10 months or so in advance.

6. While waiting for the ban to take effect, restrict smoking to specific areas (see "Instituting Smoking Restrictions," below.)

7. Educate staff on the personal dangers of smoking.

8. Consider paying for stop-smoking clinics, tapes, and other medically sound aids.

INSTITUTING SMOKING RESTRICTIONS

If you decide that you WILL continue to allow smoking in your practice, at least for a limited amount of time, state your intention to accommodate both nonsmoking and smoking employees:

1. Designate separate smoking and non-smoking areas, including break rooms, common hallways, and work areas. Do not allow smoking in front of patients.

2. Explain that employees should try by themselves to resolve problems concerning smoking, using common sense and courtesy. But also advise them that they can bring objections about smoke in their work areas to you, without fear of negative consequences.

3. State that you'll try, within reason, to accommodate the preferences of all concerned or, at your discretion, those of the nonsmokers, and that you expect reasonable willingness on the part of smoking and nonsmoking employees to accommodate one another.

4. Respond quickly and seriously to complaints about smoking in the workplace, just as you would complaints about sexual harassment or other prohibited behavior.

C·H·A·P·T·E·R　　　6-7

Reducing and Managing Overtime

Do you frequently find it necessary to pay your staff overtime? If so, do you know why?

According to one university study, it appears that inefficient offices use the most overtime, and that paying overtime may actually *reinforce* and *reward* office inefficiency. Of the 42 offices studied, the *least* efficient and productive offices almost always used the most overtime. And, even with all the overtime, those offices were less productive than others.

Overtime is undesirable for several reasons. First, your staff deserves to complete their day's work and leave for home on time. Making them work late routinely can erode morale. Second, except for the occasional unforeseen emergency, every office should be able to get all their tasks done by the end of the workday. If you can't, you're either understaffed or managing the work poorly. Finally, overtime is expensive. Money spent on overtime would be better spent on additional staff, incentive bonus programs, and other *positive* staff management projects.

GET AT THE ROOT OF THE PROBLEM

Before getting into the specifics of managing overtime, it is very important to do all you can to eliminate it. To begin, analyze the overtime patterns in your office. Try to find out what created the need for the overtime in every case, and how much overtime was needed. Once you begin to see a pattern emerging, make the changes necessary to correct whatever inefficiencies exist.

For example, suppose you find that your staff works overtime to close out and balance your daysheets whenever you have a particularly long day. Rather than continuing to do things the same inefficient ways, you might adopt a "bank" policy—simply, choose an earlier close-out time roughly one hour before the end of the day, as banks do. The new day, complete with new pegboard sheets or a new daybook page, can then be started for all transactions after that time. That way, the finished sheets can be pulled and totaled earlier, leaving plenty of time for your bookkeeper or business assistant to close the books, check the bank deposit, and have the deposit made, all by your regular closing time, without working any overtime.

THREE COMMON MISCONCEPTIONS ABOUT OVERTIME

For the occasional unavoidable overtime, it is important that you handle payments correctly, according to the law. Unfortunately, many employers don't understand the law, and hold misconceptions about it. The three most common:

Misconception #1: If an employee works a certain number of hours too many one week, she can take "comp time" the next week, and you won't owe her any overtime pay. *The Truth:* Overtime is always calculated by the single workweek. If a staff member works 55 hours one week, you can't cut her hours to 25 the next week so they average out to 40. You owe her 15 hours of overtime pay.

Misconception #2: As long as the employee eats during lunch, she is not working, and can't count that time as overtime. *The Truth:* An employee who eats at her desk can easily accumulate overtime during lunch hours. If she so much as opens the mail or answers the phone, the law says she is working. It doesn't matter that you didn't ask her to.

Misconception #3: If a current or former employee says she is due overtime pay, and it's her word against yours with no records to back her up, the verdict is likely to go with you. *The Truth:* The law requires you to keep complete payroll and time records. Without them, you won't have much chance if a former employee insists she's been underpaid. If it's her word against yours, the verdict usually goes to the *employee*.

WHY YOU MUST INCLUDE BONUSES IN OVERTIME

Many employers don't pay their staffs enough for overtime, and in so doing, invite federal wage-and-hour investigations. Among the primary offenders are those who provide productivity bonuses for employees but don't include these bonuses when calculating overtime.

Bonuses and commissions paid as incentives must be included in the regular rate of pay when computing overtime. For example, if you pay your receptionist a bonus for successful collection calls, this extra money must be included in her regular hourly pay rate when you compute her overtime.

By law, you are required to include *all* compensation for employment in the regular hourly rate of pay, except for these specified payments:

1. Gifts.
2. Special occasion bonuses.
3. Payments to profit-sharing plans.
4. Payments to thrift plans.
5. Payments to savings plans.
6. Irrevocable contributions to *bona fide* trusts.

All other bonuses and commissions must be added to employees' other earnings to determine their regular hourly rate—on which overtime pay is based.

A common error is to assume your bonuses are "discretionary" and therefore needn't be used when computing overtime. The Department of Labor specifically states that for a bonus or commission to qualify for exclusion as discretionary, the employer must offer the discretionary bonus only *after* the exemplary work has been performed. You abandon this discretion once you promise employees extra money to induce them to work more efficiently.

Bonuses that *must* be included in the regular rate of pay are those given for exemplary attendance, individual or group production, quality of work, and bonuses contingent on employment until payment is made.

Tip: Bonuses based on a percentage of *total* earnings—both straight and overtime—do not fit into this category. For example, suppose you give employees a 5% year-end bonus based on their yearly wages. A staff member who works 2,000 straight-time hours at $6 per hour and 190 overtime hours at $9 per hour earns a total of $13,710. His bonus, 5% of that figure is $685.50. Because the bonus itself is already based on overtime earned, you won't need to pay any additional overtime.

NINE MORE RULES ABOUT OVERTIME

There are many more rules governing overtime, in addition to those described above. Your attorney can advise you about the specifics in your state. However, the following rules generally apply everywhere:

1. The federal Fair Labor Standards Act of 1938 (FLSA), as amended, requires that covered employees receive pay equal to time-and-a-half their normal hourly wage for any hours worked above 40 in a workweek. Employers in every state must obey this law.

2.   In addition to FLSA, some states have their own laws regarding overtime pay. These laws frequently cover more employees and are stricter than the federal law. For example, some states require employers to pay overtime compensation for more than eight hours of work in any one day, as well as the usual weekly requirements.

3.   FLSA exempts administrative, executive, and professional workers from its overtime pay provisions. However, title alone won't exempt workers. Exempt status depends upon duties, responsibilities, and sometimes, salary.

4.   The U.S. Labor Department defines an employee's "regular rate" of pay as all pay for employment, with certain exceptions. In general, you can subtract these sums from an employee's compensation to figure his or her regular hourly rate of pay:

• Reimbursements for expenses incurred on the employer's behalf.

• Discretionary bonuses—as described above.

• Payments for occasional periods when no work is performed due to vacation, holidays, or illness.

• Extra pay received for foregoing holidays or vacation.

• Employer payments on behalf of an employee to a *bona fide* savings and profit-sharing plans, as described above.

• Premiums already paid for overtime.

5.   If you've agreed to pay an employee a lump sum for overtime hours—a sum that's independent of how many overtime hours actually worked (for instance, a lump sum to complete a particular job)—this sum *must* be considered part of the employee's regular rate. This is true even if the sum is equal to or greater than the time-and-a-half sum that would be owed on a per-hour basis for the overtime. These lump sum payments can't be credited against overtime compensation due under FLSA.

6.   If an employee performs two or more different tasks at different hourly rates, his regular rate for the workweek is the weighted average of such rates.

Tip: You can make an agreement with the employee to pay overtime for certain work based on the regular rate the employee normally receives for that work only.

7.   Your workweek must be a fixed and regularly recurring period of 168 hours—seven consecutive 24-hour periods. It may begin on any day, but it must remain fixed, except for a permanent change that's not intended to evade FLSA overtime requirements.

8.   Overtime should be paid on the regular payday for the period in which the workweek ends. However, if you can't calculate overtime until later, you may pay overtime compensation as soon as is practical after your regular pay period.

WHERE TO GET MORE INFORMATION

Because laws change, you should have your attorney review and update the guidelines offered in this chapter. As well, contact your attorney if you ever have a specific question or dispute about paying overtime in your practice.

In addition, you may contact your local wage and hour office for more information on federal overtime laws. Look in the phone book under U.S. Government, Department of Labor, Employment Standards Administration, Wage and Hour Division. As well, for information on state regulations, contact your state department of labor.

C·H·A·P·T·E·R   6-8

Preventing Employee Theft

Embezzlement is a particularly unpleasant practice management problem that evokes a strong emotional response. We like to trust people, and believe that they are basically honest. We are surprised, disappointed, and hurt when they are not.

The embezzler is in an excellent position to take advantage of you, because he has inside knowledge of your practice systems. He knows the ins and outs of your bookkeeping, check writing, and petty cash methods. And, he has almost unlimited opportunity to steal. Great sums go into and out of the typical office every day, so it is surprisingly easy for a trusted member of staff to take a little here and there, without being detected or even suspected.

Clearly, the doctor needs to protect his interests. Below, we explore simple techniques that decrease the opportunity and temptation for embezzlement. As well, we learn how to detect employee theft early on, and nip the problem in the bud. And, we explore the different kinds of theft—not only of money, but of other valuable practice resources as well.

KEEPING YOUR EMPLOYEES HONEST

The best way to prevent embezzlement is to hire the right employees, and then, treat them well. Some tips:

1.   Check all references a job applicant gives you. Learn to spot resume fraud, and uncover signs of embezzlement in former employment.

2.   Set a good example. For instance, don't take cash from the petty cash fund to cover your own personal expenses. As well, don't help yourself to practice supplies and products. Doing so sends a signal to your staff. Before long, they'll follow your lead and help themselves.

3.   Offer generous employee discounts. This makes your services and products accessible and affordable to your staff, so they'll be less apt to steal

to get what they want or need. As well, your staff will know you care, which cuts the temptation to steal to "get even" or because "they deserve it."

4.   For similar reasons, pay employees a fair wage. Poorly paid employees may feel justified in cheating you.

5.   Obtain fidelity bond insurance coverage on all employees. The bond can be a relatively inexpensive rider to your general office insurance policy.

There are two basic types of bonds. The first, called a *position-schedule bond,* covers whoever fills a specific position. The second, called a *blanket bond,* covers all employees, whatever the job title or duties performed. Most doctors feel adequately protected by a blanket bond equal to half their annual gross. Those who find this amount requires too high a premium opt instead for a set amount, such as $10,000 or $25,000.

Tip: Insurance companies won't bond individuals who aren't considered trustworthy. However, once an employee is bonded and steals, the insurer must reimburse you.

Tip: Let employees know they're bonded. That tells them they're not above suspicion. And, they'll know that if they're caught embezzling, they'll definitely be prosecuted.

SYMPTOMS OF EMBEZZLEMENT

In many cases of embezzlement, the embezzler's behavior could have tipped off the doctor. It's important to detect the problem early and put an end to it, before the damage becomes severe.

In a nutshell, here are the most common "symptoms" to check for in your office. While none of them *proves* embezzlement, you will want to be on guard if you have an employee who:

- Never wants to take a vacation.
- Refuses to share bookkeeping chores with co-workers.
- Seems to be living far beyond her means.
- Shows an unusual amount of enthusiasm for writing accounts off as bad debts. (She may have already collected—for herself.)
- Repeatedly leaves IOU's in the petty cash drawer.
- Receives phone calls from creditors.
- Shows signs of drinking or gambling problems.

16 TECHNIQUES FOR PREVENTING
BOOKKEEPING EMBEZZLEMENT

It is extremely hard to embezzle from a sound, well-managed bookkeeping system. These tricks make it near impossible to juggle your books:

1. A single-entry bookkeeping system, like a pegboard, is a good way to reduce errors, accidental or intentional.

2. *Daily* bookkeeping is a must. Delays encourage forgetfulness, as well as dishonesty. Record all transactions at the end of the day or the first thing the next morning. Balance cash receipts daily and prepare a duplicate deposit slip with the names listed.

3. Make bank deposits daily, too.

4. Send statements monthly, and be sure that all accounts are billed. When you're ready to give up on an account that hasn't been paid, turn it over to a collection agency. It's a tempting starting point for an embezzler.

5. Bill patients as you provide your services. If treatment occurs over a long time, send periodic statements. Treatment could be delayed and the account could lay idle, giving the embezzler time to tamper.

6. Write all bookkeeping entries and checks in permanent ink. If corrections are necessary, void the check, or draw a line through the incorrect bookkeeping entry and initial the correct one. Don't use erasers, erasable pens, or self-correcting typewriters.

Tip: An embezzler can use a self-correcting typewriter to change the face amount on a check after it's cleared the bank, to cover a previous theft or forgery. Or, he can change the name of the payee to his name, cash the check, and change the name back after it clears the bank.

7. Guard your facsimile signature stamp. (Some offices use these stamps to process paperwork.) An embezzler can use a signature stamps on unauthorized checks, credit card charge slips, or even prescriptions. The best precaution is to have no stamp at all.

8. Review your financial reports monthly. Keep a check on your practice performance, and be critical of changes.

9. Segregate duties. *Example:*
Separating bookkeeping functions as suggested in the following chart means that two or more employees act as a check on one another. It also means that employees could defraud you only by working together—which is far less likely than one embezzler working alone.

Have One Assistant:	Have Another Assistant:
Open mail, list, endorse, and total incoming checks.	Make accounts-receivable entries.
Reconcile bank statements.	Be in charge of receipts and disbursements.
Be responsible for cash receipting.	Be responsible for depositing.
Clear your payables.	Write your checks.

10.   Write pre-numbered receipts for all money received.

11.   Make all disbursements by check except those from petty cash. And, always require that petty cash disbursements be supported by vouchers.

12.   Always sign checks made payable to yourself for any cash you take out for personal needs.

13.   Tell patients to make all payments to your financial secretary, so she is responsible for all incoming funds.

14.   Assure that employees have enough time to balance accounts. Rushing causes errors and lapses in security precautions.

15.   Insist that all employees take a vacation each year.

16.   Insist that all records be kept in the office. Do not allow employees to take bookkeeping chores home to "catch up."

HOW TO CONDUCT A SURPRISE MINI-AUDIT

You can further shield yourself from cash embezzlement with this simple weekly audit that takes only a few minutes:

1.   Pick one day at random to record the name and amount charged to each patient. Be discreet, and jot your notes on an index card as you go through your day. If you don't know the exact charges for a procedure, record it and look it up in your fee schedule later.

2.   At the end of the day, get the day sheets from your front office. Check each entry against your index card.

3.   Total your charges and check them against the day sheet's figures. If you find a discrepancy, pull the ledger card, and find out what went wrong. It may be an honest error.

4. If you can't find the ledger card, have your accountant review your financial records immediately.

Tip: Tell no one you're conducting the audit. Do audits on different days of the week so there's no pattern to them.

PASSWORDS PREVENT COMPUTER EMBEZZLEMENT

If your bookkeeping system is computerized, you will have additional concerns. Computer access passwords given to employees are an excellent safeguard against embezzlement. Passwords restrict staff members' access solely to those areas of the system in which they have responsibilities. For example, an assistant who collects cash from patients can be stopped from changing the charge listed in the computer.

Limited access via passwords also prevents staff members from learning confidential financial data about the practice, such as salaries. (For more information about assigning, using, and safeguarding computer passwords, see, "Guard Staff Computer Access Passwords," page 264.)

PREVENTING THEFT OF SMALL OFFICE SUPPLIES

A roll of tape, a file folder, a pen or scissor here or there— many employees will see nothing wrong with taking these things home with them. But it is wrong, not to mention expensive. Here's the best way to establish a snitchproof inventory system for your office supplies:

1. Set aside one centralized location for inventory receipt, storage, and distribution. Supplies all over the office have a way of walking.

2. Assign your office manager responsibility for maintaining the supply inventory.

3. Store the supplies in a locked cabinet or closet, and give your office manager the key.

4. Track who takes what by having everyone—even yourself—sign for items they take. A "Request for Supplies" form can be circulated regularly, perhaps on a monthly basis.

When employees see that supply requests are kept on record, pilferage and waste will go down.

Tip: If staff members ask you why the new system is being introduced, explain that you're trying to determine patterns of supply usage over time, so you can take advantage of quantity discounts and other special offers.

Tip: Also centralize and track the use of practice postage so employees are not free to take stamps or run personal letters through your postage meter. (For more information, see, "Controlling Waste with a Foolproof, Snitchproof Inventory System," pages 193–197.)

CHECK BILLS CLOSELY FOR TELEPHONE ABUSE

These signs of abuse or unwarranted phone usage can be detected on monthly bills:

• Repeated calls to "time" and "weather" or "900" numbers (such as sports information or dial-a-joke).

• Extra-long calls or frequent calls to the same long-distance number. It's easy to spot calls over nine minutes or more than $9.99.   If you suspect abuse, make a one-minute call to the number to see who answers. This can provide a clue as to who made the call, and tell you whether the call was legitimately related to practice business.

• Excessive evening or night calls. Or, calls on days your office was closed.

Tip: Any of these signs may indicate the honest efforts of a hard-working employee, and not telephone abuse. Don't accuse anyone of foul play unless you have solid evidence.

PREVENTING TIME THEFT

Stealing time on the job is a costly and often overlooked form of employee theft. You have every right to expect that your employees will work for you and only you during the time you pay them to do so.

To begin, check to see that your employees are arriving for work on time and staying until the end of the day. See that they take only the appropriate amount of time off for lunch and breaks. If necessary, install a time clock.

Next, make your expectations clear. Establish rules against personal phone calls, guests, and other personal business during the workday. Tell employees that they are not to use work time to do their taxes, run a side business, entertain a friend, or do anything else of a personal nature that is not directly related to their job duties.

If you catch an employee using work time for personal business, tell her that such behavior cannot be tolerated. Note the incident in the employee's personnel file, and if the situation warrants it, send her a letter of warning. Discuss the event at a performance review, as well as what you will do if the behavior continues. It is reasonable to dock the employee's salary or even to dismiss her if she continues to use work time for personal business. Just be sure you can substantiate your claim and have adequate documentation.

If a pattern develops, check whether the employee is accomplishing all assigned tasks, and assess her attitude about work. A responsible, hard-working assistant will usually not steal time unless she is bored and/or able to get all of her assigned work done first. The best remedy in this case may be to give the assistant more challenging work to do.

C·H·A·P·T·E·R 6-9

How to Handle Part-Time, Flex-Time, and Job-Sharing Employees

S ome people can't work regular full time hours and balance the responsibilities of their work and personal lives. We now have many more single parent homes, and a huge number of mothers of young children—single or married—have entered the workforce. As well, many older people today want or need to continue to work to some extent beyond the usual age of retirement. And, many individuals have school, health problems, and other obligations that limit the number of hours they can work.

Because of the changing nature of today's workforce, there is new demand for good jobs that offer flexible hours and more time off. In short, many workers are looking for alternatives to regular full-time employment, such as:

• *Job-sharing:* A part-time arrangement whereby two or more employees share one full-time position.

• *Flex-time:* The ability to schedule work hours at times other than usual office hours, and

• *Part-time:* A regular staff position requiring fewer hours than full-time.

HOW ALTERNATIVE ARRANGEMENTS CAN BENEFIT YOU

To date, there are very few part-time, flex-time, or job-sharing positions available. Many employers don't want to be bothered with them, or even see any benefits to them. Thus, good jobs are scarce and in high demand.

This can be a great opportunity for you. By offering these alternative employment structures, you can draw from a much broader pool of talented job applicants. As well, you may be able to retain valued full-time members of your staff when their personal circumstances change.

For example, suppose one of your best employees:

- Has a baby and decides to stay home with him or her.
- Becomes ill and requires frequent medical treatments or rest, from now on.
- Has her sick parent move in with her so she can take care of him, or
- Decides to go back to school to earn a degree.

In these cases, a full time employee might have to quit. However, you might be able to retain the employee *if* you allow her to work part-time, flexible hours, or if she can share her job with another person who has similar time constraints.

Employment alternatives may help you find and keep a staff of very loyal, hardworking individuals. People who work part time or who share a job or who have flexible hours generally appreciate that fact, and are highly motivated to keep their bosses happy. Employers who offer alternative structures to the work week report:

- Increased office morale.
- Increased job satisfaction.
- Increased productivity, and
- Decreased absenteeism.

POTENTIAL DRAWBACKS OF
ALTERNATIVE ARRANGEMENTS

Of course, there are some potential problems with non-full-time employment arrangements. The most obvious is that you'll probably have more employees in total than you would if everyone worked full time. Thus, there's more need for performance evaluations, tax records, Social Security payments, benefits, mediating staff conflicts, recruiting, etc.

Another potential drawback is that if employees work different hours or shifts, you may have a tough time scheduling staff meetings so everyone can attend. You may also have a harder time building team spirit. Part-time, flex-time, and job-sharing employees may find it a bit more difficult to be plugged into the practice. You'll need to spend extra time and energy to keep them up to date and included in everything.

Tip: These potential drawbacks *can* be overcome with thoughtful planning and follow-up. Initially, plan to spend a little more time than usual to set up and supervise part-time, flex-time, or job-sharing employees. However, once the honeymoon period is over, they should require no more than the usual amount of time and attention.

TIPS FOR JOB-SHARING ARRANGEMENTS

There are many good reasons to consider job sharing in your practice. For one, it can enable you to find qualified help for difficult-to-staff evening and weekend shifts. For another, having two people trained to do a job will reduce problems with vacations, absenteeism, and turnover. And, two people may bring more talents, experiences, and special abilities to the job than one person could.

Job sharing should be mutually beneficial for the individuals and for your practice. Therefore, before forging ahead, decide:

1.   What are the specific job requirements for this position? What are the day-to-day, week-to-week, and month-to-month activities? Can they be divided? Or must both members of the team master all the tasks?

2.   Will each member of the partnership perform a first-rate job? Are their styles sufficiently similar? Will they respond equally well to tasks, people, and challenges?

3.   Who will be ultimately accountable? Is responsibility shared between the two employees? If so, how? How will you know for sure who has done what?

4.   How will the two partners work through their total responsibility effectively? Specifically, how will you handle promotions and raises? Who will get credit? When? And for what? How will you handle schedules? How many days and hours per week will each employee work? When is extra coverage needed for absenteeism, vacations, or special projects? How is this to be handled?

5.   Will job sharing cost you more or less? What will be your total anticipated costs for salaries, benefits, holidays, vacation and sick days, and overtime? How does this compare with similar costs for a full-time employee? Is the savings or additional expense worthwhile?

6.   How will you handle turnover? On the one hand, if one member of the team leaves, you'll have a hole in your practice until you can fill the position. Thus, you're *twice* as likely to need to recruit for a staff opening than if you had one full-timer. But on the other hand, losing one of the job-sharing employees still leaves you with the other. Downtime needed for training a new employee is greatly reduced because there's someone experienced to do

the training, and to carry the ball until the replacement is up to speed. As well, there's a chance that the remaining employee will assume the position full-time, and you won't have to recruit at all.

7.   Would you be better off with two part-timers? Job sharing is *not* the same thing as hiring two part-time employees. Part-timers generally have separate, limited duties and independent schedules. Employees who share one job work cooperatively and see that the job functions are carried out well and without interruption, as though one person were doing them all. Unlike part-timers, job sharers usually have the flexibility to alter their schedules between themselves, as long as the job is always covered without inconvenience to you, other staff members, or your patients.

Tip: Certain jobs in the professional practice are *not* well-suited to job sharing. For example, one office manager probably should be available all the time. On the other hand, receptionists or clinical assistants might more easily share one job, depending upon the type of practice.

TIPS FOR FLEX-TIME ARRANGEMENTS

Maintaining flexibility in scheduling work hours may not always be practical in a professional office. Except for a very few positions, you'll need your employees to be there for your patients during regular office hours. However, some employees, such as a bookkeeper or marketing coordinator, may find it possible to start working early, or to end a little later. You might allow this as long as it doesn't interfere with the smooth running of your office.

Some practices stagger working hours so some team members start early to prepare for the day's patients, and others arrive later and stay later. However, scheduling in these cases is very important, so the office is covered well when patients *are* there.

Tip: Allowing flex-time in larger practices with many employees means you'll have more to keep track of. To simplify things and keep everyone on schedule, try installing a time clock.

TIPS FOR PART-TIME ARRANGEMENTS

If you feel you need another employee, but aren't sure if the workload will support one, you might hire a part-timer to start with. That way you can control additional salary costs while you learn if the available work warrants the addition of another full-time person.

When hiring a part-timer, there are several things to consider:

1.   It may make sense to hire a part-timer who will be available to work full time in the future. That way, you can save on recruitment and training costs and efforts if you expand the position down the road. However, don't hire a part-timer who prefers full-time work right away. He may take your job reluctantly, keep looking for another, and jump ship as soon as he lands a full-time job.

2.   If the part-timer won't have consistent work hours, make up her work schedule several months in advance. A big disadvantage of having a part-timer is that she may not be available when you need her. This won't be a problem if you both know in advance what her hours will be.

3.   Consider hiring a student for a part-time position. To begin, you might see if your local high school/college has a work experience program. These programs usually test the students' skills and match the best applicant for the position. As well, they often provide ongoing supervision by a teacher or counselor.

Tip: When possible, hire a student in her junior year for a year-round position, with extra hours during summer and school vacations. This prevents rapid turnover, since the student knows she has steady work. And, if things work well, she may continue to work for you through her senior year, or even after graduation.

C · H · A · P · T · E · R   6-10

Working with Your Spouse, Children, and Other Close Relatives

H iring a relative to work in your office *can* work. However, while there are many potential benefits with this arrangement, there are also a great many potential problems. These, and the employment alternatives, must be considered and weighed heavily before making any commitments.

FINANCIAL BENEFITS FOR EMPLOYING YOUR SPOUSE

Having the doctor's spouse help out in the office is nothing new, especially to new practices where keeping overhead to a minimum is essential. But even for more-established practices, there are several good financial incentives for employing your spouse:

1.   Your spouse would be in your practice's pension plan, allowing you to put aside more money from which you'll both benefit when she (or he) retires.

2.   She'll qualify for all other tax-free employee benefits, such as life insurance and disability coverage.

3.   She'll qualify for her own Social Security benefits, which she'll be able to collect, even if you decide to keep working.

4.   You can deduct her expenses while accompanying you on continuing education and other business-related trips, with less chance of being challenged by the IRS.

5.   If you have young children, you can qualify for a tax deduction for child care expenses.

HOW TO LEGITIMATE A SPOUSE'S EMPLOYMENT

Many practitioners don't employ their spouses because they don't accept the strategy's legitimacy. However, it is perfectly legitimate to employ your spouse—or any relative—provided you know and follow the rules. Most of these rules boil down to one common denominator: Treat your spouse exactly as you treat the rest on your employees—on all office records, tax forms, and payroll checks. *Example:*

1.   Establish a personnel file for your spouse.

2.   Have your spouse present his/her Social Security number.

3.   Have your spouse complete your regular application for employment. At a minimum, require your spouse's education, employment history, experience, and references. Keep the completed form in the personnel file.

4.   Have your spouse complete required withholding forms for federal and state income taxes.

Tip: Be sure you and your spouse don't *both* claim your children as exemptions—a common oversight.

5.   Formally agree to employ your spouse. Prepare and sign an "employment letter." Have your spouse sign it, and keep a copy in her personnel file.

6.   Prepare a job title and description for your spouse, listing the specific duties your spouse will perform. Keep a copy in the personnel file.

7.   Establish a *reasonable* wage. Your accountant can help you determine a wage that won't raise eyebrows at the IRS.

8.   Keep accurate records of the hours actually worked by your spouse. The best proof is to use a time clock and have a separate time card for each employee, including your spouse. Or, use a daily or weekly time sheet to record hours and wages.

9.   Pay wages to your spouse exactly as you do the rest of your employees. At the end of the regular pay period, write a standard business payroll check directly to your spouse.

Tip: Don't write these checks quarterly or yearly, or make them payable to a third party to cover personal bills.

10.   Have your spouse deposit paychecks into an interest-bearing account in his/her name. Some experts recommend against depositing the check into a joint checking account or co-mingling the funds in any manner.

11.   Enter all payments into your practice's regular accounting records. Treat them as you would other business expenses on your tax returns and financial statements.

12.   Make sure your state and federal payroll and withholding tax reports reflect the wages you paid to your spouse. Also, pay appropriate FICA taxes and be sure your spouse's FICA is withheld from her paychecks.

Tip: These are guidelines only. In addition, meet with your accountant to discuss *specific* benefits, strategy, and tax consequences of employing your spouse or other family member.

PERSONAL BENEFITS AND DRAWBACKS OF EMPLOYING YOUR SPOUSE

Since your spouse has an existing personal interest in your practice's success, he or she is apt to be a highly motivated and conscientious employee. Honesty, loyalty, and trustworthiness are givens. And, many married couples enjoy working together, and find that such arrangements actually strengthen their relationships.

Of course, there are potential problems, too. The most common is resentment by the rest of the staff, who may feel that the spouse-employee gets special treatment and privileges. Also, an occassional patient may feel it's awkward or even unprofessional to have the spouse work in the office.

The employed spouse may find herself in uncomfortable situations, too. While she's not one of the doctors, she can't always be exactly like other members of the staff. Thus, she may feel that she's neither fish nor fowl in the office social dynamics, which can be isolating.

Finally, many couples find that seeing each other all day—every day—puts a strain on their marriage:

1. It can be very hard to unwind at the end of the day when it is so easy to take the problems of work home with you. Some couples who work together talk about little else.

2. Some marriages do better when the partners spend time apart to develop separate careers and interests. Their happiness depends just as much on the time they spend away from each other as on the time they spend together.

3. Some people are very well suited to one another personally, but find it impossible to work together. (The opposite is also true— some people work very well together, but couldn't be married to one another for five minutes.)

SELF-ASSESSMENT CHECKLIST: DOES EMPLOYING YOUR SPOUSE MAKE SENSE FOR YOU?

Of course, you and your spouse both need to do a lot of thinking before embarking on an employment arrangement, and weigh all the potential pros and cons. As well, if you're in group practice, you'll want to involve your partners in the decision. Some specific questions to answer:

1.   Would you be as compatible as doctor and staff member as you are as husband and wife? Are your working styles and temperaments compatible?

2.   Would you each be able to relax at day's end as well as you do now?

3.   Would you value your private time together as much if you spent all day in the same office?

4.   Is your spouse better suited to another job than the one in your office? Does she lack important skills, training, or other qualities you'd be able to find in another applicant? Or, is she over-qualified?

5.   Would your spouse be happier and more self-fulfilled in another job?

6.   Or earn more in another job?

7.   What would the chain of command be if you hired your spouse? Who would be the boss? Would your spouse have subordinates to supervise? What would be her relationship with the other doctors?

8.   How would the other members of your staff react to your spouse joining their team? Do they know her already? How strong is their current relationship?

9.   How would your patients react to your spouse? Might they find it awkward to discuss financial arrangements or clinical matters with her? (This issue may be important depending upon your spouse's job description.)

10.   How would your children react? Would they be more likely to interrupt normal office procedure than any other staff member's children?

15 GROUND RULES FOR WORKING WITH YOUR SPOUSE

Below are 15 specific tips for working successfully with your spouse, gathered from interviews with numerous working spouses, and doctors whose spouses work with them:

1.   To increase the odds of success, the husband and wife should have an equal commitment to the success of the practice. According to one spouse, "Problems arise when one spouse and the practice are allied against the other spouse."

2.   When at work, the practice must come first. Even the most happily married couples quarrel occasionally. But you can't let private disagreements come into the office. Too many people are involved.

Tip: Decide in advance how you'll handle private disagreements while at work. For instance, can you agree to call a truce until that evening?

3.   Develop independent interests outside of work. Since you work together all day, it's all the more important that you each do *something* on your own—sports, civic activities, take a course, join a club, exercise program, etc.

4.   One of the facts of life for a working spouse is that she must cease to be a spouse when she comes into the office. As one spouse puts it, "I must give up the thought that the doctor is my husband and the office is my office." The spouse must work as part of the team in every way possible. She must not ask for special privileges, be late to work, or expect other staff members to cover for her because she has other commitments.

5.   The doctor has the same responsibility. He must treat his spouse the same way he treats the rest of the staff. He shouldn't just not favor his spouse—he must take extra care not to dump on her simply because she *is* his spouse.

6.   Don't hire your spouse (or any family member) unless you feel you can terminate the working relationship without major consiquences for your marriage. You must feel that you can let her go, and she must feel she can quit. As well, don't hire your spouse if you feel you can't criticize her work performance, or if she feels she can't criticize you or speak openly with you about office matters—as any employee would.

7.   The spouse should refuse to get involved in office secrets or gossip, especially when she's told, "Don't tell your husband this, but . . . ." Holding confidences could put quite a strain on her and on the marriage.

8.   Be on guard for undue pressure on your working spouse. It can be an awful burden for her never to be sure if her position and rewards were earned by what she did, or because of who she is. Be sure to praise her when she does well, as you would any staff member.

9.   Spread the dirty work evenly. One spouse says that her husband used to delegate all the least desirable jobs in the office to her, simply because he knew she would do them and he lacked the managerial strength to delegate unpleasant tasks equally among his staff. (Likewise, don't give everyone else undesirable jobs and not your spouse. This will cause other staff members to resent her.)

10.   Set a policy for how you and your spouse will handle work during non-working hours. One spouse reports that she and her husband have set a 30-minute time limit for discussing office news and events each evening. After that, they must change the subject. If they didn't, she says, they might never

put work behind them at the end of the day—a problem many working couples have. Another spouse adds, "Because of our mutual interest, there's always something to talk about. But it gets tiresome *always* to talk about the same things."

11.   The spouse should refuse to "plead" another staff member's case with the doctor. (That is, she should refuse to ask for raises, shifts in job responsibilities, time off, etc., on behalf of a co-worker.) This is most likely to occur when the staff member is timid or feels the spouse has a better chance of getting the boss's ear and cooperation.

12.   In any marriage, it's normal to discuss concerns and ideas for confidential or difficult work-related matters. But if you confide in your spouse, especially on a personnel matter, it *must* be with the understanding that it will go no farther. Nothing will demoralize your staff more than discovering that your spouse knows and may be disclosing embarrassing details of a private dispute between one of them and you. Once destroyed, the privacy and trust of the employer-employee relationship is very difficult to rebuild.

13.   The working spouse should also avoid difficult situations in which patients tell *her* secrets they don't want the doctor to know. When possible, she should encourage patients to talk directly with the doctor.

14.   Clearly define the spouse's job duties and jurisdiction. Either the spouse is a regular employee, definitely under the management of the head of the office in the same way that the rest of the staff is. Or she is the office manager. There can be no place in the well-run professional office for the in-between spouse.

15.   Be watchful of jealousy. Both you and your spouse will see each other in relationships with members of the opposite sex. If something makes either of you uncomfortable—a touch, a look, a comment—be sure you can talk openly about it. As one spouse put it, "I really do trust my husband, but I can't help but be aware of his physical contact with other women. But because my husband and I have an understanding about this, I can talk with him and share my concern about how this is affecting our relationship."

SEEK HELP WHEN WORKING WITH FAMILY

Several sources of support are available for doctors who employ members of their families:

1.   The National Family Business Association offers counseling and literature to family-owned businesses and practices. For information, write 18246 Rancho St., Tarzana, CA 91356.

2. The Women in Family-Owned Business Association offers a variety of programs. Contact Allyson Sackman, Sackman Enterprises, 165 W 73rd St., New York, NY 10023.

3. Many colleges offer courses specifically designed to help people in family businesses. For example, the Georgia Institute of Technology holds a seminar entitled "Managing the Family Business." To obtain more information, contact Education Extension Services, Georgia Institute of Technology, Atlanta, GA 30332-0385. Or check with your nearby university extention and adult education program.

4. The Small Business Administration offers materials to help family-owned businesses. For example, their brochure, "Problems in Managing a Family-Owned Business" describes what to do when your untalented brother-in-law asks you for a job, or how to handle high turnover among non-family employees. For this (Management Aids publication No. 2.004) and for a free list of SBA's Business Development Pamphlets (Form 115A) and Business Development Booklets (Form 115B), write to the U.S. Small Business Administration, PO Box 30, Denver, CO 80201.

C · H · A · P · T · E · R   6-11

How to Keep Employees from Taking You to Court

W ith the prevalence of high awards in employee rights lawsuits, disgruntled staff members increasingly seek restitution for such offenses as wrongful discharge, sexual harassment, and discrimination. To protect yourself from such lawsuits, you must establish fair personnel policies and apply them evenly to all employees.

AVOIDING LAWSUITS IN RECRUITMENT

To begin, it is very important that you remove bias and unintentional promises from your Help Wanted ads, job application, and interview process. For example, reference in your ads to "recent graduates" may imply age discrimination. Likewise, reference to a position as "permanent" may give prospective employees a false sense of security.

On your application form, it is a good idea to have each candidate read and sign a statement such as the following:

> I understand that this is employment for no fixed term, terminable by the employer at any time, for any reason. This understanding cannot be changed except in writing by the employer.

As well, you should have applicants sign a statement that the information contained on the application form is true, and that he accepts your right to terminate him if any of the information is later found to be false. And, have each candidate sign a release giving you permission to contact references, former employers, schools, etc.

AVOIDING LAWSUITS USING YOUR EMPLOYEE HANDBOOK

It is smart to have your attorney review your employee handbook, to be sure you are not inadvertently discriminating or making promises to employees. Then, have each employee read the handbook, and keep on file a signed statement to that effect.

This policy prevents an employee's claiming you did not properly inform him of office procedures, including legitimate grounds for dismissal.

For more tips on avoiding lawsuits using your employee handbook, see "Using an Employee Handbook to Head Off Problems," pages 285–290.

AVOIDING LAWSUITS FROM JOB DESCRIPTIONS

If you have a written job description for each employee, it is a wise precaution to have them sign and date a statement that accompanies their descriptions, stating that the description is neither all-inclusive nor an implied employment contract. For example:

1. This job description is not intended to be all inclusive. The employee will also perform other reasonably related business duties as assigned by the doctor, office manager, or other office management.

2. The doctor reserves the right to change job duties and hours as need prevails. This document is for better understanding only, and not intended to imply a written or implied contract of employment.

AVOIDING LAWSUITS FROM PROBLEM EMPLOYEES

Unhappy or bitter employees are among the most likely to bring lawsuits against their employers. For this reason, it is smart to standardize your discipline, grievance, and complaint procedures. Then, adhere to them strictly to establish your impartiality.

Be accessible to your employees, too. Your availability to hear complaints and resolve problems may prevent a court confrontation. Often, it's best and easiest to nip personnel problems in the bud.

In addition, install a formal program of frequent employee performance and salary reviews, documenting your findings. In your reviews, don't be too generous with "good" and "excellent" evaluations. Be critical and share your honest observations. Record problems such as unexplained absences, tardiness, and disputes with other employees. Keep copies of all documentation in the employee's personnel file.

Finally, refrain from taking impulsive action with employees. For example, in the event of heated disputes between employees, you might obtain written, signed statements from each participant. Then, review these statements as part of your investigation. Before disciplining a staff member, review his personnel file carefully, giving consideration to former infractions, length of service, and meritorious evaluations.

AVOIDING LAWSUITS WHEN GIVING REFERENCES

If someone contacts you to serve as a reference for a former employee, you must be very careful in what you say. Some employers decide that they will simply verify facts, such as salary and dates of employment, and say nothing further. Others agree to say more, but limit their discussion to the most positive information that will reflect well on the individual.

This is a tricky situation. On the one hand, you don't want to say or write anything that could be deemed slanderous or libelous, or that could hurt a good former employee's chances of getting a job. But on the other hand, you have a moral obligation—and perhaps even a legal obligation—to tell the truth and warn a prospective employer of serious or potentially harmful problems.

It may not be possible to leave out all negative information about an employee. But when you do want to give a reference that includes any sensitive information, it is important that everything you say be indisputably true, and that you can verify what you say. It is always a good precaution to have your attorney review sensitive references. In addition:

1.   Be specific and stick only to the facts when assessing the employee's performance and skills. For example: "Mr. McKenzie typed my letters using our office word processing system. It took him nearly five months to master the system, but once he did, he turned out neat, attractive letters with almost no mistakes."

3.   When appraising the individual's personal qualities, again stick to the facts. "Ms. Chen asked for direction and help more than any other employee. I can recall several instances when she asked me to demonstrate how various pieces of equipment worked, such as our photocopier and telephone system. But because she asked questions, she made fewer mistakes than anyone else in the office."

4.   When you feel you must include damaging or sensitive information about the individual, state the facts plainly and fully. For example, "Ms. Waters had been coming to the office late, averaging three times a week for more than three months. That was the reason for her dismissal." If you wish, you may try to cast a positive light on negative information, but only if you can do so honestly. For example, "Ms. Johnson admitted to me last year that she had a serious drinking problem. She says she spent four months in a clinic and that

she now attends AA meetings faithfully. I believe she has got the problem under control."

5.   If an individual asks you to write a letter of recommendation, or to serve as a reference, be honest if you can't heartily recommend him or her. It's best to tell the candidate that your letter will have to include some negative information. You may even discuss the specific items you're going to include. That way, the candidate can decide whether or not you should proceed with the letter.

6.   If you're asked to write a letter by a prospective employer, you might ask the recipient to call you about the letter, or you can call him yourself. Sometimes it will be easier to put things in perspective on the phone.

7.   Base your letter or phone conversation on solid facts and carefully reasoned opinions that are backed up by concrete example. For example, don't say, "He was lazy," but rather, "I was not satisfied with the way he worked for me," and give specifics.

8.   Do not withhold information that you know to be pertinent. If you only tell half the truth and omit negative information about the candidate that would be critical to the recipient, you may leave yourself open to a lawsuit for failure to warn, and damage your credibility. Provide all the information you'd need if you were on the receiving end, with your attorney's approval.

PREVENTING CHARGES OF SEXUAL HARASSMENT

Sexual harassment was once considered a personal matter between the employee and the employer. More recently, the courts and the Equal Employment Opportunities Commission (EEOC) have stepped in and decided cases.

A doctor accused by an employee of sexual harassment has a great deal to lose. Even unfounded accusations can affect your reputation in the community. A decision against you could mean that you lose your opportunity to practice altogether.

Courts generally require the accuser to show that submission to the harasser's demands were made a "condition of employment." She must prove that she was sexually coerced, that she made an effort to resist, that her refusal resulted in negative consequences involving her job, and in some cases, that members of the opposite sex were not also subject to these consequences.

EEOC guidelines list three criteria for determining whether "unwelcome sexual advances, requests for sexual favors and other verbal or physical conduct of a sexual nature" constitute sexual harassment:

1. Submission is made either an explicit or implied condition of employment.

2. The employee's response influences an employer's decision regarding the employee.

3. The harassment substantially interferes with the employee's work performance or creates an intimidating, hostile, or offensive work environment.

It is a good idea to establish a written policy regarding sexual harassment that outlines step-by-step the grievance procedures. Employees should be informed of their rights. Doctors, office managers, and other employees should be made aware of language, attitude, behaviors, and stereotypes that cause complaints. For example, outward sexual advances can of course be considered harassing. But so, too, can unnecessary touching, suggestive remarks, and even the telling of off-color jokes.

A formal complaint, or a threat of a complaint, may arise out of a dismissal for an unrelated matter. For this reason, it is especially important to document all circumstances surrounding any dismissal, and to consult with your attorney immediately if a sexual harassment complaint is threatened.

Tip: In addition to providing employees with a harassment-free work environment from co-workers, you are also responsible for protecting them against harassment from patients or colleagues. Take immediate action if they complain to you about being harassed by anyone.

PREVENTING LAWSUITS REGARDING PARENTAL LEAVE

There are a number of lawsuits associated with unfair parental leave benefits. Most notably, you have the following obligations:

1. A pregnant employee can't be discharged or forced to resign because she is pregnant. She must be granted a leave of absence if requested. She must be rehired in the same or an equivalent job after the birth of her child, if she chooses to return to work.

2. There can be no loss of seniority or other benefits because of parental leave.

3.   Parental leave and return dates must be set by the employee and her personal physician, not the employer—just as they would be set for any disability leave.

For more information on your obligations regarding parental leave, see, "Setting Trouble-Free Policies for Parental and Sick Leave," pages 305–310.

PREVENTING LAWSUITS FROM MINORS

You may at some time wish to hire a minor to do part-time work in your office. This is a superb idea, since young people work for relatively inexpensive wages, are open to doing just about anything, and are thankful to have a meaningful job opportunity. However, before proceeding, there are several things you should know about child labor laws:

1.   All states have child labor laws and most have compulsory school laws. Local laws apply if they're stricter than the federal laws.

2.   Interestingly, four categories of children aren't covered by federal rules: Your own children under 16 (as long as they aren't employed in jobs declared hazardous by the Secretary of Labor), child performers, children delivering newspapers, and children making evergreen wreaths at home.

3.   The minimum age for employment is 14.   A 14- or 15-year-old, however, may be employed only in certain specified occupations for limited periods of time. Children under 16 may not be employed during school hours, and during the school year they may not work before 7 a.m. or after 7 p.m. During school time, they're also limited to three hours a day and 18 hours a week. During nonschool periods, they may work no more than eight hours a day and 40 hours a week.

4.   You can employ a 16- or 17-year-old in any non-agricultural occupation except those declared hazardous by the Secretary of Labor. There's no limit on the number of hours a 16- or 17-year-old may work.

Tip: Contact your local wage and hour office for a list of the work 14- and 15-year-olds may and may not do.

AVOIDING LAWSUITS RELATED TO YOUR
DRESS CODE

Employee dress codes are unlawful if they can't be applied equally to both sexes. Therefore, if you have a dress code of any type, be certain that you make similar requirements for both male and female employees in comparable positions.

For more information on establishing a fair dress code, see, "Establishing Guidelines for Employee Dress and Hygiene," pages 311–316.

AVOIDING OVERTIME DISPUTES AND VIOLATIONS

Under the Fair Labor Standards Act, there are several things you should know:

1. Any unpaid "lunch break" must be free of all job duties. If a staff member runs errands for you during her lunch hour, she is working, and you must pay her for this time. You must also pay a staff member who stays in at lunch to answer the phone or catch up with paperwork. It does not matter whether the employee volunteered to do the activity.

2. Watch out if the staff member who works lunch hours pushes her hours over 40 per week. By law, if the total work week is more than 40 hours, you must pay for all extra hours at the rate of time and a half. "Comp" time must be given within that same week so that the number of hours actually worked remains under 40.

3. If a staff member asks to cut his unpaid lunch hour to 15 minutes a day to make it a "coffee break," watch out! You could end up paying him for an extra $1\frac{1}{4}$ hours each week. Federal law says that you must pay for any work break from five to 20 minutes.

For more information on overtime restrictions, see "Reducing and Managing Overtime," pages 321–325.

USING BUSINESS FORMS FOR LEGAL PROTECTION

Several business forms, available from your local stationery supplier, can help you protect yourself from potential legal suits and fines:

1. *Employment Application Form:* Subtle interpretation of the law often determines what is discriminatory. Business forms manufacturers have created forms that adhere to EEOC regulations and are still flexible enough so you can ask job-related questions.

2. *Post-Hiring Form:* There is some information you must know about your employees that you can't ask on an employment application. For example, you must know whether an employee is married and has dependents, for tax purposes. You should use a post-hiring form for gathering this information.

3. *Employee Evaluation and Warning Forms:* Good records on each employee's job performance could be effective protection in the event that an employee files a discrimination suit against you. Your performance evaluation forms should document the employee's strengths, weaknesses, development, and progress. When you give an employee a job warning, document it by recording the date, time, and place of violation, and a description of the offense. Also indicate whether the warning was oral or written, what action was taken, and have the employee read and sign what you have written. Provide space for the employee to give her version or answer your charge.

4. *Occupational Illness or Accident Report Form:* A good form covers requirements by the Occupational Safety and Health Administration and helps substantiate insurance claims. It should include factual information (employee's name, place and time of accident or onset of illness, description, tools or equipment involved, and medical attention given). As well, record the cause and cost of the accident (including the injured person's expenses, lost time expenses, make-up time, replacement of materials and equipment, etc.). And, include a follow-up checklist to keep track of insurance reports and claims you should file.

WHERE TO GET ADDITIONAL HELP

Of course, your own attorney can advise you about the legal ramifications of an action, such as demotion, firing, a new employee handbook, a letter of recommendation, etc. In addition, you might contact the legal counsel of your county or state professional society. There, you may be able to learn of specific precedents that have occurred in other practices, that may be relevant to your situation.

Various government agencies can answer questions about fair treatment of employees. Your phone book or local librarian can be able to help you find the right offices to contact. However, you would still need to have an attorney interpret laws as they apply to your practice situation, and to update you on local ordinances and restrictions.

P·A·R·T 7

Managing Problem and Special-Need Patients

C·H·A·P·T·E·R 7-1

Dealing with the Anxious or Fearful Patient

For some people, fear of going to a doctor is akin to fear of jumping out of an airplane without a parachute. No matter how great their need for your services, some patients would rather suffer a thousand painful deaths than set foot in your office.

How can you handle a wide range of fearful patients, from those who are just a little jittery to those who are dragged, sometimes literally, to your office? Begin by understanding what typically frightens patients. Then take aggressive steps to minimize those fears in your office.

Patient fears usually fall into one or more of the seven categories described at length below. As you read, see if you can recognize any of the fearful patients in your practice.

FEAR #1: THE GREAT UNKNOWN

Patients are sometimes afraid because they are in an unfamiliar place and about to experience an examination, treatment, or procedure that is new to them and that they don't understand. Patients who don't know what to expect are apt to anticipate the worst.

How to Handle

Demystify the visit to your office. Help your patients know what to expect before it happens.

Example 1: During the initial phone conversation with a new patient, have your receptionist describe what will happen at the first appointment. "Mrs. Sletson, your appointment is on Monday, June 23 at 1:00. It will take one hour. We will begin with a short tour of our office. Then Dr. Green will meet with you in his private office to get acquainted with you and review your medical history. Next . . . ." When the patient arrives for the appointment, review the agenda.

Example 2: Provide a brief tour of your office so the patient will become familiar with the various rooms and layout. Then, when escorting the patient anywhere in the office, have your assistant tell him what to expect next. Example: "Mrs. Sletson, we're now going to Dr. Green's office. As is his custom with all new patients, Dr. Green will ask you to spend a few minutes with him there so he can get acquainted with you and review your medical history."

Example 3: Describe any clinical procedure before it begins, and especially, how it will feel to the patient. "Mrs. Sletson, I'm going to listen to your heart now. The stethescope may feel a bit cool."

FEAR #2: BEING HUMILIATED

In some cases, patients have neglected their health and know it. These patients are likely to dread your disapproval, or your staff's, and may fear being embarrassed or ridiculed. Fear of humiliation causes these patients to put off needed treatment even longer, until the neglect has caused an unnecessary, sometimes painful emergency.

How to Handle

Never say or do anything in front of the patient that in any way embarrasses him about his condition. Whatever you see, restrict your comments, tone of voice, gestures, and facial experessions to those that convey something positive.

Example: A patient comes to a dentist with a mouth full of decay. *Don't* say: "Your mouth is a disgrace! How could you let it go this far?" *Do* say: "I'm so glad you came to see me today. There's great deal of decay, but fortunately, we can probably save all of your teeth, if we act now."

FEAR #3: LEGENDS AND HORROR STORIES

Some patient's fears are carry-overs from long ago, when we didn't know as much as we do today, and various procedures were more painful. Bad medical and dental experiences have remained in the minds of some patients and trigger current fears. For others, another family member or friend had a bad experience and related a horror story that's had an influence.

How to Handle

As part of your get-acquainted procedure, ask all new patients how they feel about coming to your office, and why. (This is appropriate either in your get-acquainted form, or ask it verbally during your initial consultation with the patient.) If, after some probing, the patient tells you he is afraid of you because of some past experience or horror stories, start by telling him that his fears are not all that uncommon. Knowing that there are other people like him may help him feel better right away. Then discuss advances in your field or the specific steps you take to minimize discomfort.

Example: An ophthalmologist encounters a new patient who is afraid of wearing contact lenses, because his brother had difficult adjustment to hard contact lenses many years ago. (He had red, irritated eyes for a week.) "Mr. Hamlin, your brother's experience is unfortunate, but it need not be yours. Many people do find the adjustment to hard contact lenses difficult. But today, we have many new, wonderful kinds of *soft* contact lenses that are so light and thin that you'd barely feel them in your eye. Your adjustment to such a lens would probably be very easy, nothing like your brother's. Here, let me show you an example of this remarkable lens. You probably won't believe it!"

FEAR #4: BEING VULNERABLE AND HELPLESS

Patients in an examination chair or on a table often feel they can't control the situation. They may be in a position that is unusual and threatening. For some specialties, patients may have to disrobe and don a paper gown. All of this makes them feel very helpless, which heightens their fear.

How to Handle

Give patients more control.

Example: A gynecologist, about to do an examination of a new patient, might do the following:

1. Meet the patient while she's fully clothed, in your private office, not the examination room. It is awkard and perhaps threatening to meet a doctor for the first time while perched on an examination table, barefoot, and clad in an open-backed paper gown.

2. Once in the examination room, talk to the patient, and tell her what you're going to do. *Then* help her lie down in the proper position for the examination.

3. If there's a good chance a procedure will cause some discomfort, warn the patient prior to it, and describe its intensity and duration. That way the patient will feel in control if she experiences discomfort. *Example:* "I'm going to insert the speculum now. Try your best to keep the lower part of your body relaxed, so it won't be uncomfortable. This will take about a minute."

4.   Be sure patients understand their conditions, using visual aids whenever possible.

FEAR #5: MONEY

Some patients avoid needed treatment because they fear a high fee or being embarrassed about their inability to pay for your services. These patients combine their fear of the unknown ("How much will it cost?"), shame ("I'm embarrassed that I don't have enough money to pay for it"), and helplessness ("I can't ever pay for it," *or* "What if they charge more than they say they will?").

How to Handle

Make firm financial arrangements that the patient can be comfortable with, and spell out the dates and amounts of payments for the patient. Look for signs of anxiety about your fees, and address these immediately and honestly.

FEAR #6: THE OUTCOME

Patients sometimes dread the results of their treatment. They may fear that they will look peculiar, be uncomfortable, need more extensive work later, or ultimately, not accomplish what they set out to do. These fears can stand in the way of your care.

How to Handle

Make sure patients understand their treatment and have a realistic expectation of the results they can expect. If the patient is coming to you for a cosmetic reason (plastic surgery, cosmetic dentistry, etc.) pictures and models of actual cases can be extremely helpful. These will draw a vivid picture for patients of the results that have been achieved in other patients with similar problems. Use these kinds of aids whenever possible when making treatment recommendations.

Furthermore, your staff can help the patient gain confidence in your ability by making positive statements about you and complimenting the patient.

Example: When an orthodontist's patient has his braces removed, his assistants might look at the patient's mouth and say to him, "Dr. Shapiro always does such beautiful work. Betty, come here and look at Andrea's new smile. Isn't it beautiful?"

FEAR #7: THE CLINICAL ENVIRONMENT

Many patients fear the doctor's office because it feels clinical and sterile. They associate the sounds, smells, and sights of the office with those they may have experienced in a hospital where they or someone they know went to be treated for a serious or painful ailment. Thus, they link the pain or fright of their hospital experience with their visit to your office.

How to Handle

Humanize your office to make it more comfortable (and less threatening) to patients. *Examples:*

• Avoid highly clinical or frightening words. *Examples:* A "prophylaxis" at a dental office sounds more frightening than a "cleaning." "Pain" is harsher than "discomfort." A "treatment" or "examination" room sounds less threatening than a foreboding "operatory." An "injection" isn't nearly as frightening as a "shot" or "needle."

• Consider having your staff wear uniforms in soft colors, rather than starched white, that remind patients of hospital attire.

• Soundproof treatment rooms. Nothing is quite as jarring to a patient as hearing a shrieking child, the whirring of a dentist's drill, or similar goings on inside your treatment rooms.

• Choose office decor that is attractive, homey, and comfortable. Display objects that make you and your staff seem as human as possible. *Examples:* books and objects relating to your hobbies. Bulletin board displays featuring staff biographies or snapshots of staff.

• Use soothing colors like blue, pink, and rose, and comfortable furnishings. Avoid institutional and military green—it evokes a fearful response from some.

• Install a tropical aquarium in your reception area and/or treatment rooms. Studies show they relax people.

• Play soothing background music in your office.

• Provide distractions for patients to get their minds off of their fears. Best: Strike up a pleasant conversation with patients. Other good distractions: Interesting magazines and books, unusual plants, puzzles, brain teasers.

• Use humor. A recent university study found that laughter can reduce stress as effectively as more complex biofeedback training programs. Look for practical, tasteful opportunities to promote healthy laughter in your office.

Examples: Buy comedy cassette tapes, and offer these with individual tape players and headphones in your reception area. Have humorous tapes and books available for children. Consider installing a video area in your office, not only to show educational tapes, but also humorous cartoons and short movies. Buy humorous books and funny posters for your reception area. Run a "Joke of the Week" contest for your reception area bulletin board. Post funny comic strips.

PREVENTING AND HANDLING FEAR IN CHILDREN

Children tend to have short attention spans, are unusually perceptive of true feelings of adults, and are likely to react to fear with physical resistance. They are impressionable and their imaginations, if not properly handled, can result in adverse reactions to professional services that can last a lifetime.

For this reason, it is essential to be extra sensitive to the fears of children. What you can do:

• Help parents prepare their children for visits to your office. Advise them to: (1) Schedule the child's appointment for early in the day; (2) Avoid telling the child about the appointment until the night before. This way, there will be less chance for the child to build up the experience in his mind, or hear "neighborhood" experiences; (3) Not discuss their own bad experiences within the child's earshot. Avoid words like "hurt," and "shot." (4) Handle routine visits to your office matter-of-factly—it's part of growing up. (5) Let the child know that you'll explain what you're going to do before doing it, so there's nothing to fear.

• When meeting a child patient for the first time, come out to the reception area yourself, smile, stoop down, and shake hands. Escort the child to the examination room yourself.

• Take a photo of you with the new child patient. Send him a copy with a handwritten note after the first appointment.

• Involve children in their treatment as much as possible. Use questions, and give them objects to hold.

• Always, be absolutely honest with children. Telling them a procedure won't hurt when it will can be especially damaging. Telling them it will last only a minute when it lasts several can lead to frustration and mistrust.

• Make your office inviting for children, so they feel welcome. Provide furniture and amusements for them in your reception area. Buy an office mascot, such as a giant stuffed animal. Run contests specifically for children, such as essay contests, poster contests, or "Guess How Many Jellybeans in The Jar."

• Give children a small gift at their departure. Dynamite idea: Give children a "prescription" for an ice cream cone in the flavor of their choice. Have an Rx pad printed with this prescription on it by a local quick-copy shop, redeemable at a local ice cream parlor.

TAKE ADDITIONAL TRAINING IN FEAR CONTROL

Doctors who routinely encounter fearful patients may want to take some additional training in fear control. Helping fearful patients is part of good professional care. But it can also be a drawing card that helps build your practice. Today, it is not unusual to see doctors who promote themselves with slogans like, "We Cater to Cowards."

A great deal of literature exists on the subject of fear, both for the doctor and the patient. As well, there are numerous fear control methods being widely used in the professions, including biofeedback programs, sedation, and even hypnosis.

Consult your professional association for more information and guidance on these and other fear control subjects.

Bringing the Inactive Patient Back to the Fold

D o you let your patients ignore your recall notices? Is your final recall attempt a passive letter or call? If so, you're not alone. Unfortunately, too many practices that depend upon giving periodic or regular care allow their patients to become "inactive" too easily.

MAKE PATIENTS *CHOOSE* INACTIVITY

When a patient ignores all of your recall attempts, or for other reasons "disappears" without explanation, it's up to you to take action. Your best bet is to see if you can make the patient *choose* inactivity. Make each patient decide (and tell you) whether he or she wishes to remain active in your practice.

To begin, have your business assistant *call* every patient who appears to be inactive, and say something like this:

> Mrs. McBride, I've been reviewing our records, and find that you haven't been in to see us in _____ months. We have made numerous attempts to schedule an examination appointment, and you have ignored or refused our efforts. The reason I'm calling is to see if you would like me to remove your files from our active records.

Making the patient *choose* activity or inactivity in this way often pushes the procrastinator to schedule the appointment he's been putting off. More importantly, making patients choose inactivity opens a dialogue, and can help you pinpoint and correct problems. Once a patient tells your assistant that he wants to be inactive, you can try to learn the *reason,* and then do something about it.

Examples:

• If the patient says he'd like to make an appointment, but doesn't have the money right then (lost his job, has financial problems, etc.), you might outline your financial arrangements.

• If he says he's feeling very well and doesn't *need* a check-up, review the reasons and benefits of regular recall, explaining how the patient may not always be able to detect problems.

• If the patient says he's unhappy with you and now going to another doctor, discuss specifically what has made him unhappy, and his reasons for switching.

Through open, personal discussions with your inactive patients, you'll have the best (if not the only) chance you'll ever have to learn about real problems and misconceptions among your patients. Then, you can take the steps necessary to turn them around. This is certainly better than letting inactive patients drift away without ever getting that chance. You cannot afford to be an ostrich about these problems.

Tip: If the patient tells your assistant that he chooses inactivity, it is often most effective if you (the doctor) talk to him personally. You might instruct your assistant to transfer all such calls to you.

ALTERNATIVE: SURVEY INACTIVE PATIENTS

Instead of (or in addition to) the phone conversation described above, you might send your inactive patients a mail survey, along similar lines. Mailed with a cover letter, and a self-addressed, stamped envelope, such a survey would ask the patient to choose his status from four possibilities:

_____ 1. I'd like to remain an active patient and will call for an appointment.

_____ 2. I'd like to remain an active patient. Call me to schedule an appointment.

_____ 3. Please remove my records from your active files.

_____ 4. Forward my records to my new doctor (name, address).

Tip: This sort of mail survey does not allow the same kind of two-way communication that you'll be able to achieve with the phone call. However, it is preferable to no contact at all, and can be especially useful when you're unable to reach the inactive patient by phone.

DIG DEEPER INTO THE REASONS FOR INACTIVITY

When a patient tells you that he chooses to be inactive, and why, and you've been unsuccessful at changing his mind, your next step will be to draw the patient out further, by means of a feedback survey. In this way, you'll be able to get deeper into the patient's true feelings, and in so doing, you may learn some valuable things about yourself and your practice.

Tip: Feedback surveys are usually administered to active patients by mail, or during their office visits. However, active patients are the people *least* likely to tell you what's bad about your practice, since they are still coming to you and are presumably satisfied. Inactive patients may help you get at some hidden problems.

To ensure your best possible response from your survey:

1.   Invite patients to complete your survey anonymously.

2.   Send an explanatory cover letter with the survey, stating that you're genuinely looking for ways to improve your practice, and that you'd appreciate their help. Leave the door open for the patient to return to you.

3.   Enclose a self-addressed, stamped envelope for the response.

4.   Keep the survey short, no more than one page, both sides.

5.   Ask mostly objective questions (multiple choice, true false). If you do ask one or two open-ended questions, do so at the end of the survey. That way, the patient who lacks writing skills or time may still complete the objective portion of the survey.

Tip: Don't proceed with a mail survey of inactive patients unless you're sure you have thick skin. These responses are apt to be more negative than those you receive from active, satisfied patients. Some may be downright offensive.

SAY GOODBYE TO THE INACTIVE PATIENT

When the patient tells you he chooses to be inactive, do *something* beyond the feedback survey to acknowledge that patient's leaving. Action at this critical time will increase your chances of getting the patient back, or at least parting on good terms. Make the patient see that you still care about him, and that you'd be very happy if he'd come back to you.

This sample letter, personalized to the patient, and hand-signed by you, should do the trick:

Dear Mrs. O'Brien:

As you requested, we have sent a summary of your podiatry records to Dr. Ann Schwartz.

I wish to thank you for entrusting your podiatric care to me for the past four years. I regret the circumstances that are responsible for your leaving my care (name them if you know), but wish you the best of health in the coming years.

Please do not hesistate to call on us if we may ever serve you again.

C·H·A·P·T·E·R   7-3

How to Respond to Patients Who Complain

No news may *not* be good news after all. According to one interesting study, 96% of dissatisfied customers never complain to the source about the discourteous service they receive. Yet, 91% of these customers never buy again from the company that they feel offended them.

Even worse: Most dissatisfied customers will relate their bad experience, on the average, to at least *nine* other people. As many as 13% will inform more than 20!

These figures make it quite clear that you simply can't afford to let patient complaints go unresolved. In fact, you may need to do more to *seek* complaints, so you can remedy them.

BEGIN BY ESTABLISHING A COMPLAINT RECORD

These days, professionals can't afford to take lightly even a seemingly minor patient complaint. The risks are nowadays too high, due in part to the move toward patient consumerism, and in part to staggering malpractice awards.

If you find that you're often the last one in your office to hear about a patient's complaint (or worse, if you fear that you don't hear about some complaints at all), you can do yourself a great service by establishing a patient complaint record. How:

1. Make one employee responsible for keeping the complaint record for your practice.

2. Instruct all doctors and staff members that all patient complaints, even those that seem utterly harmless, must be reported to the employee who is in charge of your complaint record. Instruct staff to keep their ears open for all complaints—on clinical or non-clinical matters. Even those about mundane subjects like office air quality or a shortage of coat hangers in your reception area should be reported.

3.   Develop a printed form for recording patient complaints. The form should provide spaces for writing in the patient's name, the complaint, the date and time of the complaint, any special circumstances of the complaint (background about the patient or events that led to the complaint), the name of the person who heard the complaint, and the response the patient was given immediately. Have your complaint record keeper complete a form for each complaint that is reported to her.

4.   Next, your complaint record keeper should insert all completed complaint forms into a loose-leaf notebook. In addition, have her photocopy each form and give a copy to you, to your office manager, and to any staff member directly involved in the complaint. (You might also want to keep a copy of the complaint in the patient's record.)

5.   Update the original complaint form (in the looseleaf binder) to keep track of any later responses or developments that relate to a complaint.

6.   Review your complaint record regularly (perhaps every quarter). Be sure all complaints for the period have been given a satisfactory response.

7.   Through your review, try to identify weak areas in your practice that are the cause of many complaints. Set goals to help you improve in these areas.

DON'T LET COMPLAINTS SLIP THROUGH
YOUR FINGERS

The way you and your staff handle inquiries and complaints reflects upon your practice. Slow or inappropriate responses tell patients (or potential ones) that you don't think they're important. No response may indicate that you simply don't care.

Make complaints a topic for discussion at an upcoming staff meeting. Agree who among your staff is best suited to be your complaint record keeper. Also decide who is best suited to responding to the different types of inquiries and complaints you typically receive (which ones should be referred to the doctor, bookkeeper, business assistant, etc.).

Outline for your business assistant/receptionist the procedure for handling inquiries and complaints. Use the guidelines that follow, adding your own ideas and sample scripts. Keep a copy in your policy and procedure handbook.

GUIDELINES FOR HANDLING WRITTEN INQUIRIES
AND COMPLAINTS

1.   Write or call the patient within 24 hours of receiving the inquiry or complaint. If you can't give a complete reply, explain that you received his or

her letter, and what you are doing about it. Tell the patient when to expect to hear from you next. Then, follow through as promised.

2. If you, personally, are not going to be the one to respond to the patient, arrange for the correct person to do so. However, make a note on your calendar to check and see that the patient is given an appropriate response, as you promised.

3. Bring the patient's letter to your complaint record keeper. She should complete a form for the complaint, and staple the original letter from the patient to it. Then, she should photocopy and distribute copies, as described above.

4. Use personalized versions of standard letters if many inquiries or complaints are received on one specific topic. Use your practice brochure whenever possible to answer general questions about the practice.

GUIDELINES FOR HANDLING VERBAL INQUIRIES AND COMPLAINTS

1. Remain courteous, no matter what.

2. If it is appropriate for you to handle the inquiry or complaint, do so. If not, route the individual to the correct person. If that person is not available, have him or her get back to the patient, preferably that same day. Follow up to be sure a call was returned.

3. If you don't know who is best able to handle the matter, tell the patient that you will find out who that person is and have him or her call him. If that person can't get back to the patient that day, call the patient yourself to tell him or her who will be handling the matter, and when that person will call. Follow up.

4. Avoid putting a complaining phone caller on hold. Above all, don't indiscriminately transfer the call from one person to another, forcing the patient to explain and re-explain the complaint to several people who really can't help him or her. That will only fuel the caller's anger.

SPECIFICS FOR DEALING WITH THE COMPLAINTS

1. Thank the patient for bringing the complaint to your attention. Tell him you're truly glad he did.

2. Let the complainer vent, if he needs to. Rather than becoming defensive or argumentative, you might simply repeat what the patient is saying, until he gets his anger and frustration out. For example, "So you had no place to park today. You must have been very upset by that."

3.   Look for ways to agree with the patient. For example, "You're absolutely right. The parking lot is full sometimes, and that's a real problem."

4.   Apologize. For example, "I'm so sorry you had to deal with this problem."

Tip: If the complaint is unreasonable, say at least that you're sorry the patient feels the way he does.

5.   Try to satisfy the patient. If he's been greatly inconvenienced, take appropriate steps to make it up to him.

Tip: You want to make the patient feel better. However, don't be too quick to cancel your bill in an attempt to satisfy a complaining patient. Writing off your fee may be construed by the patient—and by his or her attorney—as evidence that your treatment and services were questionable. Even if a review of your records uncover a potential problem, don't dismiss your bill without first discussing the matter with your attorney and/or insurance carrier.

6.   Show that you do indeed care and are working toward improvement. *Example:* "I'm quite disturbed about this problem, and am working very hard to find a solution. Already, I've contacted several contractors to see about enlarging our parking lot. I'm even exploring the possibility of moving to an office with more parking space." Ask the patient to bear with you.

7.   When appropriate, follow up with a letter or hand-written note of sincere apology.

8.   If the problem is one that affects many patients, acknowledge it openly in your patient newsletter or a mass mailing. Explain what you're doing to try to solve it.

9.   Contact patients by phone or mail once you've solved the problem they complained about, or at least to update them on your progress.

C · H · A · P · T · E · R   7-4

How to Make a Great First Impression on the New Patient

A phone conversation with your receptionist is usually the first contact a new patient has with your practice. The patient may have been referred by a friend or colleague, and may therefore already have a positive attitude about your practice when he calls. Do you reinforce that attitude with a friendly greeting and proper handling? Or do you make the new patient wonder if his friend was wrong about you?

Here are some concrete suggestions that will help you establish the proper relationship with new patients, by making a superb first impression.

LONG WAITS ARE A TURN-OFF

In one study, a large number of patients cited long waits for appointments as the reason they left a practice. When a new patient calls your office to make his first appointment, he usually wants that appointment right away. If he doesn't get it soon, he may go elsewhere, since he has no relationship with you yet, or loyalty to your practice.

Thus, it is clearly in everyone's interest to schedule the new patient as soon as possible. However, if you can't work him in when he wants, the patient will typically ask, "Is that the earliest the doctor can see me?" When that happens, your receptionist must do her best to be firm but accommodating. For example:

> Yes it is. However, I'll call you earlier if we have a change in our schedule. Could you come in on short notice?

By asking that question, your receptionist will be able to remain in control of the conversation. Then, if the patient indicates that he does want to be called about an earlier appointment, she should confirm the original time and say:

I'll call you if an appointment becomes available. Otherwise, we'll see you as scheduled.

For more information about effective appointment scheduling measures, see, "Taking Control of Your Appointment Book," pages 61–67.

GET IT RIGHT THE FIRST TIME

A person's name is a very important and personal part of him, so it's important that you and every member of your staff learn to pronounce it correctly. The initial telephone conversation you have with the new patient may be the only time you feel comfortable asking him to repeat his name, tell you how it is pronounced, or how to spell it.

Your receptionist should *insist* on getting every patient's name right in the beginning to avoid confusion, mistakes, and embarrassment later. Here's a sample script:

Would you mind repeating your name? (Pause for response.) Thank you, Ms. Fattahi. Did I say that correctly?

Once your receptionist establishes the pronunciation of a difficult name, she should jot it down phonetically. *Example:* (Ef'-fot Feh-taw'-hee). With that out of the way, her next step will be to go on to the spelling:

For my records, Ms. Fattahi, would you please spell your first and last names for me?

Tip: If *you're* still in doubt about a patient's name, you'd better clear it up when you first meet him. A graceful way to do this: "How do you do, Ms. Fattahi. Did I say your name correctly?"

TELL THE NEW PATIENT WHAT TO EXPECT

Once you make an appointment for a new patient, there are many extra things you can do to make him feel welcome and at ease in your practice. Patients appreciate knowing what to expect ahead of time. *Examples:*

1.   Ask the patient if he needs directions to your office. Then explain about parking, public transportation, etc.

2.   Tell the patient approximately how long the first appointment will be.

3.   If you have a practice brochure, tell the patient about it. Let him know that he'll be receiving information about your practice in the mail (or at the time of the first visit, if there is no time to mail it beforehand).

4.   Ask the patient for his daytime telephone number, and explain why you want it.

5.   Tell the patient whether and how you will confirm the appointment.
Example:

Ms. Penman, I'll send a card naming the date and time of your appointment. Many of our patients have requested that I call the day before the appointment, so I should be calling you Monday. Is the morning or afternoon the better time to reach you?

Tip: Don't call if the patient says it won't be necessary of that he prefers you don't.

6.   Ask the patient to bring with him his insurance identification card, social security number, previous medical records, and any other similar information that you intend to ask for at the first appointment.

USE A PRE-PRINTED CHECKLIST TO AID YOUR RECEPTIONIST

To simplify the get-acquainted task for your receptionist, and to make sure she doesn't forget anything, one Briarcliff, NY doctor suggests preparing a checklist. In his practice, the telephone receptionist uses a pre-printed $4 \times 6''$ card to guide her step-by-step through the necessary questions. Later, this card becomes the first document in the patient's file.

To help you create your own checklist, here are the questions listed on this practice's get-acquainted card:

New Patient Get-Acquainted Checklist	
1. What is the patient's name? Preferred title? (Ms., Mrs., Dr., etc.)	Phonetic spelling?
2. Is patient over 18 years old?	
3. If under 18, the age/parent's name?	
4. Address?	
5. Phone? (Day and evening)	
6. Have we seen others in the family?	Who?
7. Give choice of appointments?	Appointment Day/Time:
8. We're glad you called our office. How did you hear about us?	
9. We're in Briarcliff. Do you know how to find us?	
10. Anything special you'd like the doctor to know?	

Tip: At the bottom of your get-acquainted form, leave room for your receptionist to indicate which materials, if any, were sent to the patient in advance of the appointment. Provide a checklist (brochures, directions, doctor's resume, medical history form, etc.) if you are in the habit of sending several specific materials.

END THE FIRST CALL ENTHUSIASTICALLY

The first contact with the new patient is a great opportunity to get the patient "hooked" into the practice, and looking *forward* to meeting you. Therefore, it makes good sense to instruct your receptionist to smile and say something like this at the end of the phone call:

> We'll all be looking forward to meeting you next Tuesday, Mrs. Reed. I can't wait for you to meet Dr. Capone. He graduated from (name of school), is a member of (name of association, academy, etc.), and has taken extensive continuing education courses in the area of (name of area). He's also very personable and caring. I'm sure you'll like him.

CONSIDER REGISTERING THE NEW PATIENT AT HOME

Completing your new-patient questionnaire can be a time-consuming and cumbersome process that many patients find inconvenient. How often patients are greeted in a doctor's office the very first time with a clipboard containing a long questionnaire!

The "Rolls Royce" approach is to have the doctor or a staff member complete the form with the patient within the format of a personal interview. However, if that's not practical in your office, consider home registration as an alternative.

If you know you'll be seeing a new patient in no sooner than three days, you might mail him or her your questionnaire. (First, tell the patient you'll be doing this when he or she calls to make the first appointment.) Include this step in your receptionist's questionnaire (described above). Along with the questionnaire, send instructions to fill it out and bring it to your office on the day of the appointment.

Those patients who do remember to complete and bring your questionnaire have the opportunity to do so at home, at their leisure, where they can use other people and resources to fill in the blanks in their medical histories. This is usually much easier than recalling all of the details on demand in your office.

Tip: Pre-registration usually makes new patients happier. The added plus is that it also encourages them to answer your questions carefully, neatly, and more accurately.

HANDLING THE NEW PATIENT WHO DIAGNOSES HIS OWN PROBLEM

Here's a common problem. A new patient calls to say that he knows exactly what his problem is, and that he wants the doctor to fix it. Or, he may simply ask for an over-the-phone prescription. Handling this situation is difficult, but it can be done well if your receptionist is prepared:

1.   First, determine whether the patient's problem is an emergency. If it isn't, offer him the next available appointment in your book.

2.   Your receptionist should be careful NOT to suggest that the doctor can fix the problem the patient has diagnosed. How she might explain it:

> It would be necessary for Dr. O'Keefe to examine you to determine what the problem is and what services are necessary. Following the first examination, the doctor will want to discuss his recommendations with you. The first available appointment for that exam is _____ .

3.   Use a similar tactic if a new patient calls asking for the doctor to provide just one particular service. (For example, a new optometric patient might call for replacement of a lost or damaged contact lens. A new OB-GYN patients might call for a Pap smear. Or, a new dental patient might want a cleaning only.) It is very important that your receptionist establish firmly that the doctor alone decides how patients will be treated in your practice:

> It is Dr. Burstein's policy that whenever she welcomes a new patient into her practice, she does a complete exam. This helps her determine if the patient has any problems and the extent of them so she can make recommendations for their correction. Which time of day do you prefer to schedule your examination, morning or afternoon?

HOW TO DEVELOP LOYALTY IN
EMERGENCY PATIENTS

There's no guarantee that a new patient, especially one with an emergency, will ever set foot in your office again. However, you may be more likely to lose the emergency patient if you take care of his problem or concern at only one appointment.

Practice management consultants generally recommend that emergency patients are more likely to continue with a practice if they see the doctor at least twice. Through follow-up visits, the patient develops a much deeper relationship with the doctor and the staff. He's made to feel much more a part of the practice.

Therefore, the best way to keep the new emergency patient in your practice may be to plan at least two appointments. The first visit might be very short, and used only to get a handle on the patients' immediate problem. The second and subsequent appointments might be used for more extensive treatment, tests, in-depth examinations, etc.

For more information on this subject, see, "Scheduling Emergencies," pages 62–63.

ROLLING OUT THE RED CARPET AT
THE FIRST APPOINTMENT

So far, we have explored ways to make new patients feel welcome BEFORE the first appointment. While this is obviously very important, it is even more important that each new patient's first few minutes in your office are also wonderful. Do you and your staff make the new patient feel that his arrival at your office was anticipated with pleasure? That's a very hard thing to get across to people if they're greeted at the receptionist's window with "Yes?," or worse, a preoccupied and uncaring receptionist.

A good strategy in smaller practices is for the receptionist to to try to address the new patient by name. For example:

You must be Mr. Trigg. I'm Vicky. We spoke on the phone. We've been expecting you. It's a pleasure to meet you in person.

Then, your receptionist might help the patient get settled in by offering to take his coat and hang it up for him.

If your receptionist wants the patient to sit in your reception area, she should *not* say, "Have a seat." Instead, instruct her to turn this into a gracious invitation, as though the patient is a guest in her home. *Example:*

> Mr. Trigg, Dr. Tucker is looking forward to meeting you. He will be with you in a few minutes. Won't you please make yourself comfortable in our reception area? Please feel free to browse through our magazine selection on the wall to your left.

If your receptionist needs to obtain personal information from the patient for your files, she might invite the patient to a private area for this purpose. She should then try to make the task as pleasant as possible for the patient. For example, she might offer the patient a beverage while he works on your questionnaire. Better yet, she might complete the form with him, through a personal interview. (See "Consider Registering the New Patient at Home," above.)

When the doctor is ready to see the patient, your nurse or chairside assistant should *not* call his name out loud in the reception area. Rather, she should walk up to him and quietly say:

> Mr. Trigg, would you please come with me? I'd like to introduce you to Dr. Tucker now.

As your assistant walks with the patient, she should tell him where they're going and what to expect. For example:

> I'm going to escort you to Dr. Tucker's private office. He'd like to get acquainted before your examination.

When the patient enters your office, your assistant should make a formal introduction. For example:

> Mr. Trigg, this is Dr. Tucker. Doctor, I'd like you to meet Mr. Trigg.

That sets the stage for a warm handshake and a wonderful beginning.

SIX MORE WAYS TO IMPROVE YOUR GET-ACQUAINTED PROCEDURE

1.   Send the new patient a letter after the first appointment, to tell him how glad you are to have met him. A handwritten note from the doctor often makes the best impression.

2.   If the patient tells you she was referred by a friend, respond by saying, "That's nice. Ours is largely a referral practice." This plants the idea in the new patient's mind to refer others.

3.   Make an extra effort to be on time for new patients.

4.   If the new patient is a child, the doctor might come to the reception area personally to escort him or her back. This may alleviate the child's fears.

For more information on working with children, see "Preventing and Handling Fear in Children," pages 364–365, and "Working with Young Children, pages 393–394.

5.   A Phoenix, AZ doctor suggests a simple, effective way to turn one new patient into many. On his get-acquainted form, the patient is asked to list the names and ages of all other family members living in his or her home. Once completed, a member of the staff marks those names of patients seen in the practice, and their last examination date.

Using the form, the doctor then points out to the patient that little Joshua is overdue for an exam or that Tracey has never been in. This prompts him or her to make Joshua's or Tracey's appointment before leaving.

6.   Time is the best investment you can make in a new patient. A few extra minutes will set the tone of your future relationship. He is more likely to return to you, and to refer friends to you if he feels that you care about your patients and are willing to take the extra time with them. Therefore, don't schedule the new patient appointment too tightly. Err on the side of too much time, rather than too little.

Tip: A Fairlawn, NJ doctor does something rather unusual in his get-acquainted procedure. He meets with every new patient in his private office, and gives each a card on which he writes his *home* phone number. Then, he invites the patient to call him at home, if necessary, if there's ever anything she's not able to work out to her satisfaction with a member of his staff. While almost no patients ever call, he says, new patients seem impressed with his level of concern, and his willingness to take responsibility for what happens in his practice.

Post-Operative Patients: Turning "Case Closed" into an Open Door

P ost-operative (or post-treatment) contact with patients is an excellent way to generate goodwill. Through both large and small thoughtful gestures, you can tell your patients, "You are important and we care how you are feeling (adjusting, recovering, etc.)."

Depending upon your area of practice and the particular treatment the patient has undergone, he may be feeling perfectly fine and have no questions. Or, he may be experiencing great discomfort and be very confused. In any case, he will appreciate your concern and and will welcome the chance to straighten out misconceptions or problems.

Because you take time out of your busy routine to contact post-treatment patients, they will feel more at ease calling you in the future if they have problems or questions. They're also more likely to become loyal patients who make referrals.

Don't let the patient who has undergone unpleasant procedures, who is feeling miserable, or who has just completed a long-term treatment feel that you are too busy to bother with little things. Surprise him with unexpected follow-up contact. Show him that your concern about him does not end when he leaves your office.

TEN GREAT WAYS TO SHOW PATIENTS YOU CARE

After you've completed an extensive procedure or a long-term treatment, you may wish to follow up in any number of ways. As long as you don't alarm the patient by making him think he's sicker than he is, sincere follow-up concern is always a plus. Ten great ways to contact patients after treatment:

1.   Call (or visit) the evening after the procedure, to see how the patient is doing.

Tip: When making follow-up calls to patients, identify yourself and say, "I'm calling to see how *well* you're adjusting to your new contact lenses/feeling/doing/etc." This works better than simply asking the patient *how* he is doing, which may worry him or encourage him to think negatively. If you can't reach the patient in the evening, have your assistant call the next day with a similar opener. "Dr. Hirsch and I wanted to know how *well* you're doing."

2.   If a child was your patient, you might call his parents to commend them on the child's good behavior and cooperation.

3.   If you've gotten back favorable test results, call the patient personally to tell him the good news.

4.   Write or rubber stamp the words "Thank You" on the back of the patient's check before you cash it.

5.   Send patients a follow-up survey after treatment. Ask them to evaluate the treatment they received.

6.   Send a letter to the patient to thank him for his cooperation, loyalty, confidence, etc. See "Sample Letter Builds Goodwill," below.

7.   Send flowers or a plant to patients who have undergone major procedures.

8.   Give a flower or other small gift to every patient as he or she leaves your office.

9.   Escort the patient personally to the front desk at the end of a difficult appointment. Offer a firm handshake, smile, and sincere words of thanks.

10.   Send a follow-up letter to the patient to offer information, a brochure, or an article you come across on a topic of particular interest to him.

SAMPLE LETTER BUILDS GOODWILL

Upon receipt of the final payment in long-term treatment, you might send the patient a letter such as the following:

Dear Mrs. Chin:

Thank you very much for your final payment. It has been our pleasure to treat you over the past eight months. We appreciate your promptness and cooperation throughout the treatment, and we want you to know that. You are truly a special patient to us.

We have enclosed several of our business cards, and hope that you'll feel free to recommend us to any of your friends and acquaintances who are in need of quality dental care. If you can think of any ways that we can improve upon our services, we hope that you will share your ideas with us. We do value your opinion.

Concern for your dental health remains our top priority, and we look forward to seeing you again in August for your periodic examination. We also urge you to continue with the home hygiene program that we've begun, and to call us if you have any questions. Preventive dentistry is very important, especially for patients who've had previous problems.

We want you to continue to enjoy the benefits of a healthy mouth. Once again, thank you for your confidence. It has been our pleasure serving you.

DEVELOPING A SYSTEM FOR FOLLOW-UP CONTACT

Post-operative/follow-up contact won't be very effective unless its fairly prompt. You may find it very difficult to do a consistently good job of making the necessary follow-up calls if you try to do them all yourself, squeezing them between appointments.

Therefore, most doctors need to develop a system for keeping track of the follow-up calls they have to make. And if you have a high-volume of calls to make, you may have no choice but to delegate responsibility for some of them to an appropriate assistant. While the call will be automatic, compose a script for your assistant that indicates your concern for the patient without alarming him or her. *Example:*

Hello, Mrs. Russo. This is Beth Hamilton from Dr. Steele's office. As Dr. Steele always does when one of his patients has had an extraction (started a new medication, is discharged from the hospital, etc.), he's asked me to call you to see how well you're feeling today, and if you have any questions.

The doctor should indicate to the assistant which patients to call, and anything special to ask about. A good way to do this is to mark an agreed-upon symbol and comment somewhere on those patient's office visit charge slips.

Tip: This system usually works better than deciding unilaterally that *all* patients who've had an emergency visit, major procedure, etc. should be called. While that kind of system is better than nothing, it leaves the decision of whether or not to call a patient to an assistant, who may not be as familiar with the case as the doctor. The doctor may decide that a patient who has had a simple procedure needs a call because he was terrified of it. Or she may decide that a patient who had an emergency appointment does *not* merit a call. In either case, the *doctor* would be the person in the practice best able to make these decisions.

Adapting Your Practice for Older and Disabled Patients

O f course, some professional practices work largely or exclusively with older and disabled patients. Such practices no doubt are already well-versed in the specific techniques that make working with these patients easier.

The material in this chapter is provided for all the other practices that work with older and disabled patients on an occasional basis. While such patients are much like any other, there are several things you can do to make your older and disabled patients with special needs feel more welcome and at ease when they visit your office.

FIVE BASIC TIPS FOR MANAGING OLDER AND DISABLED PATIENTS

1.   Don't assume that a patient's special needs are more than they really are. For example, don't assume that a blind patient is also hard of hearing, that an aging patient is senile, or that a physically disabled patient is also mentally disabled. These are common mistakes that can understandably offend the older or disabled patient.

2.   When offering physical assistance to a patient who may be or is in need of special care, do so as unobtrusively as possible. *Offer* your help courteously, don't force it.

3.   Let patients with special needs feel that they're a welcome part of your practice by selecting reading material geared for them in the reception area. For example, you might have special materials for older patients (such as *Modern Maturity*), for those who have vision difficulties (such as audio tapes or the large-type edition of *Readers' Digest*), or perhaps some Braille books for blind patients.

Tip: Your magazine selection can also tell *other* types of patients that they're welcome, too. Consider subscribing to at least one magazine for young children (such as *Jack and Jill, Sesame Street* or *Highlights*), one for teenagers (such as *Boys' Life* or *Seventeen*), one for parents (such as *Parents* magazine, *Gifted Children Monthly,* or *Parenting*), one written in Spanish (if you work with Spanish-speaking patients), and one or more for patients with other special interests, such as:

- *Sports Illustrated.*
- *The Walking Magazine.*
- *I Love Cats.*
- *Homeowner* magazine.
- *Vegetarian Times.*
- *Ebony.*

Tip: Do *not* subscribe to any magazines that may offend patients, or give them the wrong idea about you. *Example:* Magazines that focus on hunting, religion, politics, or sex are best avoided, for obvious reasons.

4. Don't talk in front of an older or disabled patient as though he isn't there. Don't whisper or gesture to others in the patient's presence, thinking the patient won't know. Most older and disabled patients you meet in your practice will be aware that you are talking about them. Assume they'll know when they're being talked about, as any patient would.

10 WAYS TO PREPARE YOUR OFFICE PHYSICALLY FOR DISABLED PATIENTS

Below are ten guidelines to help you equip your office physically for patients with special physical needs:

1. Provide ample reserved parking spaces and ramps/curb cuts for disabled office visitors. Be sure these are well-marked.
Tip: For the average-size office, two 12-foot-wide parking spaces close to the building entrance are usually sufficient.

2. Keep your sidewalk grade gentle—8% or less. Avoid widely spaced flagstones or other uneven surfaces. Make curb cuts textured, not smooth.

3. Provide handrails for the entrance ramp to your front door. The ramp itself should be four feet wide, with a nonslip surface. Again, the grade shouldn't exceed 8%.

4. Install an automatic entrance door. Eliminate doorsills and thick doormats.

5.   Make sure all doorways are wide anough to accommodate patients using wheelchairs, walkers, crutches, and canes. Plan on at least 32 inches of clearance.

6.   Provide individual, stable armchairs in your reception area (instead of pillow-back, armless sofas, which can be hard to get in and out of).

7.   Plan your reception area so it is clear of small furniture and other objects that can be tripped over easily. Along similar lines, avoid throw or area rugs, and keep all rooms well-lit.

8.   Design your magazine rack, reception window, public telephones, water fountains, light switches, soap dishes, hand towels, fire extinguishers, coat hooks, and anything else a patient would need to reach so they are less than 4 feet off the floor. (This makes them accessible to patients using wheelchairs.)

9.   Provide handrails wherever patients would have occasion to go in your office.

10.   Allow 5 square feet of floor space in the restrooms. Install:

•   A toilet that's the height of a wheelchair seat.

•   Safety rails on either side that support 250 pounds.

•   A sink that's less than 34 inches high, with enough clearance to accommodate a wheelchair.

COMMUNICATING WITH OLDER AND DISABLED PATIENTS

Although communicating with older or disabled patients is like communicating with any patients, there are a few modifcations you may wish to incorporate in your written and spoken communications:

Don't:	Do:
Write or say "the disabled."	Write or say "disabled people."
Write or say "afflicted with" or "victim of."	Write or say "a person who had polio" or "a person who is blind."
Describe disabled people as "wheelchair bound" or "confined to a wheelchair."	Refer to them as "wheelchair users."
Label groups, such as "the deaf or "the arthritic."	Call them "people who are deaf" or "people with arthritis."
Portray those who succeed as superhuman.	Portray them as real people.

Use the term "old."	Use the terms "aging" or "older."
Say or write "60 years or older."	Say or write "60 years or over."
Print office literature in small type.	Use a minimum of 12- point type.
Print literature in ornate typestyles.	Use clean typefaces. Helvetica and Times Roman are easy to read.
Print literature with little color contrast.	Choose high contrast between ink and paper colors.

ADDITIONAL IDEAS AND CONCERNS

1.   A Campbell River, British Columbia dental practice reports that discounts for older patients are a highly effective practice-building tool. In this practice, older patients are given a wallet-sized discount card, along these lines:

GOLDEN AGE DENTICARE CARD

_____is entitled to a 10% reduction in fees for dental treatment.*

Dr._____

*Excluding laboratory service.

The practice automatically sends a card to each patient 60 years or over, and has reported a very favorable response.

2.   A Greenbelt, MD optometrist reports that his practice was able to attract many new patients who are deaf or hearing impaired, after promoting the availability of sign language in his practice. New patients come from surpringly far away for this service, he says.

3.   As many as one out of every 25 older persons in the United States is the victim of physical abuse. And, according to one study, 70% of the injuries sustained by older abuse victims occur in the face, head, neck, or upper extremities. Most abuse in the older victims studied was inflicted by relatives with whom the victim was living—often children and spouses.

Tip: In some states, professionals are considered "mandatory reporters" and are legally required to report all suspected cases of abuse. Thus, examine your older and disabled patients carefully for signs of a repeated injury or an injury that does not match the patient's case history. If you suspect abuse of an older or disabled patient (or any patient) call your state health department or adult protective services and follow their reporting procedure.

4. A nice thing to do for your older patients is to arrange for birthday or anniversary greetings to be sent to them from the White House. Birthday wishes will be sent to anyone aged 80 or over. Anniversary wishes will be sent to couples married 50 years or longer.

Send information about your patient's upcoming birthday or anniversary at least six weeks in advance to:

Greetings Office
Old Executive Office Building
Washington, DC 20506

Indicate the name and address of the patient to whom the greetings should be sent, and any special information about the event being celebrated that you can offer.

C·H·A·P·T·E·R   7-7

Meeting the Needs of Other Special Patients

*E*very patient we ever meet is special, and has special needs. However, in this chapter, we will limit our discussion to the most common types of special patients, and what you can do to meet (or exceed) their expectations and needs.

WORKING WITH YOUNG CHILDREN

Tell the child what he may honestly expect in advance. However, as with all patients, describe procedures to the child by using the least-stressful synonyms. For example, you might tell a child he'll experience "discomfort" or "pressure," rather than "pain." You might tell him he's going to meet with the doctor in the "Orange Room" or "Room #2," rather than the foreboding "operatory" or "treatment/examination room."

Tip: Working with young children usually means working with his or her parent(s) as well. They may need as much or even more reassurance than the child. And, they can be extremely helpful (or damaging) to the child's preparation and attitude about coming to see you.

For more information on this and related subjects, see "Preventing and Handling Fear in Children," pages 364–365.

WORKING WITH TEENAGERS

Teenagers tend to be self-conscious and are quick to resent being "talked down to" by adults. The key to managing most teenage patients is to treat them like the young adults they are (or would like to be), rather than children. Let them know you have high expectations of their behavior. Then, use praise to motivate and reinforce them. (Praise almost always works better than scolding, threats, or lectures.)

Show an interest in teenager's activities. Discuss the patient's outside interests—school, clubs, sports, etc. However, avoid sounding judgmental about any of these. Teenagers are all too familiar with disapproval from adults, and are quick to tune it out.

WORKING WITH PATIENTS WHO ARE SUDDENLY UNEMPLOYED

Suppose a loyal patient agrees to go ahead with your treatment recommendations, and a rather large fee is involved. He makes his initial payment, as agreed. However, right after that, he loses his job. The patient tells you the truth—that he just can't afford to pay you now—but you feel you should finish what you'd planned to do for him. When you're all done, he has a rather large outstanding debt, and no income. You suggest that he make smaller regular payments, but he says he just can't swing *anything* right now—that he's having trouble just putting food on his table. And you believe him. What should you do?

A Minnesota optometrist suggests a humane but firm solution. Bill the patient as you normally would every month, this doctor suggests, and tell him you'll do so. But, also tell him you'll avoid any more collection efforts as long as *he* stays in regular contact with you. Specifically, ask the patient to handwrite a note on the bottom of his monthly statement, saying that things haven't changed, and to mail it back to you. Also say you'd appreciate even a few dollars when he can send them. As long as the patient sends back the signed statements each month, there's no need to act further. But if he fails to do this, your collection assistant should call him immediately, to see what's going on.

Why this works: This approach is very kind and sensitive to the patient while he is going through a tough time. Yet, it places responsibility on the patient to do something. Also, it *reminds* him monthly that he still owes you a debt, and that you're being very accommodating to him. That may put you at the top of his list when he can spare some money.

WHAT TO DO IF THERE IS A MASSIVE LAY-OFF IN YOUR AREA

Mass lay-offs have raised numerous questions about their affects on professional offices. For example, what happens to the employees' insurance benefits? What should you do about cases in progress? What can you advise patients who no longer have insurance?

Tips:

1.   When an employee is laid off, he usually loses his insurance. Sometimes there is a grace period of up to three months, and sometimes there is none. The existence and length of the grace period may depend upon whether the employer has decided on his own to continue paying the premiums, or whether continued coverage has been negotiated in advance by the union, or by the individual.

2.   Some carriers offer continued coverage for individual employees who wish to pay their own premiums. Others do not.

3.   The situation also varies regarding work in progress. Some carriers will pay as usual on cases that are more than one-half completed. Others will pay nothing on any services provided after the lay-off starts.

4.   Many insurance carriers treat lay-offs of small numbers as though they are terminations. If the group plan allows for a grace period, it will be honored. But if the employee is reinstated at a later date, he is treated as a new employee who often must wait a certain period of time before his policy takes effect, and must meet a deductible all over again.

Tip: If there is a lay-off in your area, contact the personnel department of the employer, to learn whether there is a grace period or the possibility of continued coverage.

Your laid-off patients may be very surprised and angered to learn that their insurance benefits will not be continued. Obviously, their needs for your services will continue, even though their ability to pay you "up front" usually does not. Therefore, if you have laid-off patients who have lost their insurance, or are about to, you will need to make new arrangements with them.

Tips:

•   If they or their families need your services, advise them that they can pay their premiums on their own (if this is an option open to them). Reduced, less-expensive coverage is sometimes better than none, and is often the best option.

• If one worker in the family is laid off, coverage may continue in whole or in part under a policy held by the spouse. The patient should inquire about this.

• If the patient has lost his insurance, remember that this may very well be a temporary situation. Many laid-off workers are called back. Others will find work elsewhere. You may avoid losing a patient by postponing expensive, non-essential services and continuing maintenance and preventive care, at least until he's back on his feet.

• In times of economic stress, doctors are often tempted to insist on payment with each appointment. Such a policy, while eliminating the need for collection tactics, severely restricts growth. Doctors who began offering budget payment plans during the Great Depression retained their patients, continued to provide a full-range of services, and built a cash-flow cushion for themselves. The patient should be given every opportunity to pay at the time of the appointment. But if he feels he absolutely must pay then, he'll cancel if he can't.

• Looking at the brighter side, don't automatically assume that all laid-off patients are in dire financial straits. Some will have substantial savings, additional sources of income, and borrowing power. Also, they will have the time they need but may have previously lacked to have their professional service needs met.

DEALING WITH NON-COMPLIANT PATIENTS

A patient's lack of cooperation with your instructions or recommendations may become a pivotal issue if you are involved in a professional liability lawsuit. Therefore, take these steps to protect yourself when dealing with known or suspected uncooperative patients:

• Learn to recognize when a patient is not or may not be following your instructions, or refuses to cooperate. Patient non-compliance can take the form of broken appointments, refusal of diagnostic tests, rejection of your recommended treatment plan, unwillingness to accept referrals to a specialist, failure to follow your instructions for medications or home care, inconsistent explanations or outright lies by the patient, etc.

• Document all instances of known or suspected non-compliance in your records. Show when and how, specifically, you explained your recommendations or instructions to the patient, that you noticed or suspected in your follow-up appointments that he hadn't followed your instructions, that you confronted the patient about this, that the patient declined verbally to follow your recommendations or instructions and why, and that you discussed with the patient the consequences of disregarding your instructions.

• When possible, have the patient sign a statement admitting his willful non-compliance. For example, if the patient refuses to undergo recommended diagnostic tests, put your recommendations regarding the tests in writing, and have the patient sign and date a statement that he has knowingly and purposefully refused to follow your advice, and that he understands the risks.

• Contact your attorney when the patient's non-compliance puts him in jeopardy. With your attorney's guidance, write a letter to the non-compliant patient to review your recommendations, all instances of his known or suspected non-compliance, the dates of your previous explanations, recommendations, and verbal warnings, as well as the the risks the patient is taking for not following them. Such a letter should be sent so that you can prove to a court that it was received by the patient. Your attorney will advise you about the best method—often that will be "Registered Mail, Return Receipt Requested."

MAKING UNRECOGNIZED PATIENTS FEEL SPECIAL

Your established patients expect you and your staff to remember who they are, and are likely to be insulted if you don't. When your receptionist asks a calling patient, "Have you been a patient here before?" she is admitting that she doesn't remember the patient, and is taking the chance of offending him.

A better way for your receptionist to phrase it: "When was your last visit with the doctor?" With this question, your receptionist will be able to get the needed information without making established patients feel unrecognized.

If an unscheduled patient shows up at your office and your receptionist doesn't recognize him, she will have no choice but to ask him to identify himself. However, if she suspects that the patient has been in to see you before, she should be as tactful as possible. *Example:* She might say:

Please forgive me. I have your name right on the tip of my tongue. You are Mr. . . . (Pause). I'm sorry. Can you help me?

Then, when the patient gives his name, she might say:

Of course, Mr. *Robinson.* (Smile. Sigh of relief.) How silly of me. How are you today? How can we help you?

P·A·R·T   8

Managing Your Physical Plant

.

Keeping Your Office in Ship-Shape Order

A clean, well-maintained professional office is every patient's right, and contributes greatly to staff morale and productivity. Routine office maintenance and cleaning programs should be systematized and then delegated to your staff, to ensure that they are carried out automatically. This chapter offers several important guidelines.

MAINTENANCE RECORD KEEPS OFFICE RUNNING SMOOTHLY

How often have you waited until your copy machine finally "died," or your office carpeting was permanently stained, before you gave them the maintenance they required? Unfortunately, such delayed reactions often lead to costly repairs, down time, and sometimes, unnecessary replacement. In most cases, a simple dose of preventive medicine is all that's needed to keep you a step ahead.

To begin, have your business assistant prepare a maintenance record for all of your existing office equipment and furnishings. Use a large three-ring binder, with pocket dividers for categories such as "Furniture," "Professional Equipment," "Office Equipment," "Building Interior," and "Building Exterior." Then, prepare a separate page for each article, and file it in the appropriate section. For example, under the category of "Office Equipment," you might have separate pages for "Computer System," "Typewriters," "Photocopy Machine," and "Postage Meter."

On each page, describe the item by name, model number, and vendor (including the address, phone number, and name of your sales representative), date purchased, and price. Also describe the recommended maintenance requirements and schedule. Your goal is to build a record that will tell you not only how to clean the carpet, service the typewriter, and replace the filter on your air conditioning system, but also when each of these items was last serviced, by whom, and the cost.

Tip: Remember that traffic and frequency of use will affect the maintenance schedule for each item. Your sales representative or the item's manufacturer can usually offer suggestions. Frequently, directions for cleaning and routine service come with the product. If so, file these special instructions in your binder.

From your maintenance record, your assistant can develop a comprehensive maintenance calendar for the year. You can then use the calendar to calculate routine maintenance into your practice's operating budget. As well, your calendar, once in place, will be invaluable when you evaluate the quality and effectiveness of your maintenance program over time.

Another advantage of this system: A detailed, comprehensive, *written* record will be very valuable to you if your business assistant leaves and someone else must assume responsibility for maintaining your equipment and office furnishings.

HOW TO FIND A GOOD CLEANING SERVICE

1.   Create a complete list of the items you want cleaned, and how often. Include replacing basic supplies like trash-can liners, paper towels, and toilet tissue. Also, include periodic cleanings (such as carpet shampooing, upholstery and drapery cleaning, exterior/interior window cleaning), and other less-frequent but necessary maintenance.

2. Turn to someone you know and trust to recommend a reputable service.

Tip: If you practice in a large office building, and your public areas are well-kept, find out who takes care of them. Or, ask colleagues in neighboring offices which services they use and like.

3.   Invite the firm you're considering to come to your office and review your list. Most firms should be able to tell you how many hours the routine cleaning will take.

Tip: Be sure to ask if the firm provides the less-frequent periodic services on your list (such as carpet shampooing). You can often save time and money by giving your business to one hard-working firm that offers a variety of needed services.

4.   See if you'll have the same individual(s) clean for you each time. (This is usually a plus.) Also, ask whether the service will chart jobs completed during each visit, so you can see whether the company is fulfilling its contract.

Tip: This will also help you evaluate whether any jobs need to be done more or less often.

5.   Ask each bidder for client references. Then, visit one or more of these offices to see how well the work is done, and to chat with the people who work there.

Tip: This step can be delegated to a responsible assistant or office manager.

6.   Make sure the service's employees are bonded and/or insured in case they're injured while working in your office. Find out what the service's responsiblity to you would be if one of its employees damaged or stole any of your property.

7.   Make sure that cash, prescription pads, office supplies, equipment, drugs, and other valuables are locked away after office hours when the cleaning service will be there. Such items are best locked in a sealed storage closet, desk drawer, or cabinet.

CLEANING CHECKLIST: DOES YOUR OFFICE PASS INSPECTION?

Most patients lack the clinical expertise that's needed to evaluate objectively the professional offices they visit. They make judgments, therefore, based on subjective, non-clinical standards. One of their primary "barometers" is cleanliness—how neat and clean the office *appears*.

Does your practice pass the "white glove" test? Take this quiz to find out:

1.   Are reception area magazines old and tattered? How about toys and children's books? Are they dirty, worn, or strewn about the room?

2.   Is office carpeting worn, stained, or dirty? Is wallpaper ripped or coming unglued? Are painted walls dirty with fingerprints or marks?

3.   Are there fingerprints and smudges on or near your light switch plates? Door frames? Glass windows and panels?

4.   Do staff members' uniforms look dingy, worn, or rumpled? Are their shoes old and scuffed? For more information on this subject, see, "Establishing Guidelines for Employee Dress and Hygiene," pages 311–316.

5.   Are treatment/examination room counters cluttered with bottles and other supplies?

6.   Are any of your patient records kept in soiled or tattered folders?

7.   Are there stacks of paperwork in your business area or your private office?

8. Do you have notes, reminders, and cartoons taped informally to walls and equipment that are in view of patients?

9. Are any storage drawers and cabinets left open?

10. Is the chrome trim on your treatment room equipment grimy, scratched, or smudgy?

Your Score: If you said "yes" to even two of the preceding questions, it's time to clean house. If you answered "yes" to five or more questions, you've got a real mess on your hands! Your maintenance problems didn't develop overnight, and won't be solved that quickly, either. A thorough cleaning of the office will help, but attitudes and standards must also be modified, and quickly!

If you don't notice how things look, or if you tolerate sloppiness in your office, the situation will only get worse. Therefore, you must spell out standards in your office procedures manual, stating clearly who is responsible for keeping each area in order and exactly what that responsibility entails.

Tip: Remember that *you* set an example for your staff. If *you* are neat and clean, chances are good that they will be, too.

Reducing the Risk of Injuries in Your Office

E very doctor has a moral and legal obligation to provide a safe office for himself, his staff, and patients. Minimize the hazards in your office by instituting the following safety procedures.

MAKING YOUR OFFICE PHYSICALLY SAFE

Loose carpeting, a broken chair, or burnt-out light bulb can lead to injury. That's why you should conduct regular inspections of your premises and property, and all furnishings. The following questions should help. *Look* at the area in question before you answer:

1. Is your parking lot free of ankle-twisting cracks, patches, and potholes?

2. Are your parking lot and walkways adequately lighted in the evenings? Are they free of ice and snow in the winter?

4. Are there steps up to your front door? If so, are they well-lit? Are the handrails secure?

5. Is your building elevator inspected regularly?

6. Are lobbies, hallways, and other common areas in your building well-lighted? Is the carpeting smooth and well-secured?

7. Does your office have any inconspicuous "step-ups" or "step-downs" that patients might trip over?

8. Is the furniture in your reception area sturdy?

FOUR SAFETY TIPS IF YOU LEASE OFFICE SPACE

The practice that rents its space has four additional safety issues to contend with:

1. When it comes to safety, keep up with the Joneses. If a nearby tenant installs security measures, puts up lights, or removes snow, follow

suit, even if you don't think these measures are needed. In case of an accident on your property, your liability could be established by default. (Your business neighbors will have appeared to know of the potential danger and to have acted to safeguard against harm. Most courts would expect you to have done the same.)

2.   Check your lease, applicable building and safety codes, and other ordinances. They may contain clauses specifying certain kinds of damage you must take care of, such as broken window glass. That makes you liable for injuries caused by such damage.

3.   See if your lease prohibits construction or installation of certain types of equipment, or requires advance permission. Liability may then fall directly on you for injuries caused by your breaking or failing to fulfill stated lease terms.

4.   Don't innocently assume your landlord's responsibilities. Doing so can mean that you take legal responsibility for the outcome. *Example:* If you wipe up a spill in an outer hallway, but someone slips and falls anyway, *you* may be liable for resulting injuries. Had the landlord done the clean-up, *he* would have been liable for the injuries, not you.

MAKING YOUR OFFICE SAFE DURING CONSTRUCTION

When an area of your office is being repaired, rennovated, or constructed, you need to take several extra precautions:

1.   Have construction, maintenance, and repair work done during off-hours, when possible. The fewer people around, the less the risk of injury if hazards are created.

2.   If potentially dangerous repair work must be done during office hours, redirect traffic or activities to other areas. Post warning signs or barriers or have an individual present to warn of and watch for trouble.

3.   Block off and label highly dangerous hazards. Fence in open ditches, excavation sites, and areas where machinery is left or debris is discarded. If visitors must pass through or near an area of known risk, have an employee warn them and escort them through it.

CHILD-PROOFING YOUR OFFICE

Even if you don't have children as patients in your practice, you should be prepared for young visitors:

1.   Make sure that magazine racks and tables are sturdy and not easily tipped over. They should be able to hold up if a toddler leans on them.

2.   Place floor lamps in a protected corner, so a running child doesn't knock them over.

3.   Cover all electrical outlets with safety plugs.

4.   Never allow small children to be left unsupervised in your office, even for a minute.

5.   Keep toxic or dangerous plants out of your office. *Examples:* Dieffenbacchia, sharp cactus.

6.   If you provide toys for children, keep them big and soft. Avoid stuffed animals that have eyes and noses that can be easily pulled off—and swallowed. For the same reason, don't provide small objects, like broken crayons, pieces of chalk, beads, or marbles. Finally, don't provide breakable objects or materials that can be consumed. *Examples:* Glue, paint, glass jars.

DO'S AND DON'TS TO PROTECT YOUR STAFF FROM INJURIES

Although you probably would not consider your office a dangerous working place, there are some general hazards to be aware of and to avoid, by establishing the following do's and don'ts. As well, list specific safety precautions particular to your profession and practice. *Examples:* Infection control procedures, safety guidelines for x-ray equipment or other devices, use of various clinical or cleaning substances, etc.

*   *Don't* tip back in your chair. It is easy to lose your balance and fall over.

*   *Do* close your desk drawer, file cabinet, cupboard doors, etc. when you're done using them. An open door or drawer is unexpected, and easy to run into or trip over.

*   *Do* secure all exposed cords and telephone wires. Keep briefcases, wastebaskets, etc. out of the hallways or aisles in your office. Leave at least four feet of unobstructed aisle space wherever patients or staff have occasion to walk.

*   *Don't* stand on wastebaskets, open drawers, shelves, or chairs with wheels to get at something out of your reach. Use a sturdy step stool.

*   *Do* wipe up spilled coffee or water from the floor at once. On rainy or snowy day, keep a lookout for wet floors, and wipe them up promptly. Provide a place for patients' wet coats and umbrellas, and a mat for wiping feet.

*   *Don't* hurry through the office, around corners, and through doorways. Don't take steps two at a time.

• *Don't* pull out all cabinet or file drawers at once. An unbalanced load can topple any size cabinet if it is not bolted down or back-weighted.

• *Do* take a few precautions with the office photocopy machine. First, avoid spending time in the path of the copier's exhaust. Ozone emissions from copiers (and other high-voltage equipment) can be a special problem to people with asthma or sensitivity to other substances. Second, wear disposable rubber gloves and wash your hands whenever you handle the copier's toner. Toners often contain nitropyrenes—substances that can cause skin irritation. And finally, place soiled gloves in a small plastic bag, seal, and discard.

• *Don't* wear clothing to work that has long, loose sleeves that can easily get stuck in equipment. Avoid backless shoes and those with extremely high-heels or slippery soles.

FIRE SAFETY: A REHEARSED EVACUATION PROCEDURE

Do you hold regular fire drills? Even if you feel foolish going through the motions, a drill is an essential step toward ensuring your own, your staff's, and your patient's safety.

First, determine the fastest way out of the building, as well as alternate routes. Designate a place where everyone will meet outside. Review correct fire procedures. *Examples:* Don't use elevators, check doors to see if they're hot before opening them, cover the nose and mouth with a wet cloth in case of smoke. Also locate fire extinguishers and be sure everyone knows how to operate them.

It may be tempting simply to *discuss* fire procedures, but the physical act of the drill is much more effective. Hold drills at least twice a year, and whenever you add a new member to your staff. Determine how long it takes for everyone to evacuate the office, and where you'll meet. Also, be sure to include fire procedures in your personnel manual.

SIX ADDITIONAL FIRE SAFETY PRECAUTIONS

In addition to a rehearsed evacuation procedure, take the following steps to protect your office from fire:

1.   Use flame-resistant materials when decorating your office. Examples: Draperies, paint, movable partitions.

2.   Post signs both to indicate emergency exits and to warn against using elevators in case of a fire.

3.   If you allow smoking in your office, provide a special metal container for emptying ashtrays. Do not empty ashes into wastebaskets where paper is discarded.

4.   Have your local fire department visit your office to check for fire hazards and make recommendations. In particular, ask them to evaluate your smoke detectors and fire extinguishers. Be sure you have enough of them, that they're in the right places, and that they all work properly.

5.   Check to see that your coffeepot and other hot equipment is turned off before you leave your office at night. Establish and post a routine check-out system and run through it at the end of the day to be sure you don't overlook anything.

6.   Check the condition of your electrical wires to be sure they aren't worn and frayed. Don't run wires underneath your carpeting. (Walking on wires can wear them and create a fire hazard.)

KEEP YOUR OFFICE FIRST-AID KIT FULLY STOCKED

Assign one person in your office to keep your first-aid kit stocked and available at all times. You'll want to have at least the following essentials on hand:

- Adhesive bandages in various sizes.
- Sterile pads, gauze bandages, and adhesive tape.
- First aid cream.
- Boric acid.
- Roller bandage, for wrapping sprain or strain.
- Smelling salts or aromatic spirits, for waking an unconscious person.
- A thermometer.
- Rubbing alcohol.
- Aspirin or equivalent.
- Antiseptic soap.
- Ice pack or bag.
- Hot water bottle.
- Ipecac syrup—to induce vomiting.

You can purchase a complete kit or assemble your own. Either way, observe these guidelines:

1.   Choose your kit's size and contents in proportion to the number of people in your office.

2.   Wrap the unused portion of first-aid materials so they won't be soiled through handling. Discard any item that becomes soiled or is spoiled in any other way.

3.   Restock used items immediately.

4.   Arrange contents so that individual items can be located quickly without unpacking the entire contents.

KEEP EMERGENCY NUMBERS HANDY

If you have the slightest doubt about the seriousness of an injury, call the appropriate physician or first aid squad promptly. Explain what happened, to whom, where the patient is, and what first aid has been given.

Keep emergency numbers in a prominent place on or near the office telephone. Include the following numbers on your list: police, ambulance, fire department, pharmacy, hospital emergency room, physician, first aid squad, poison center.

When it is necessary to call for help, make it policy that your office will be the last one to hang up the phone. In the heat of an emergency, it is easy to forget to tell an ambulance, fire department, or other organization where you are, or other essential information. If *they* hang up first, you know they've gotten all the information they need.

Tip: It's also a good idea to ask on patient registration forms for the name and telephone number of the person to contact for the patient in case of an emergency.

DOCUMENT EVERY ACCIDENT THAT OCCURS
IN YOUR OFFICE

Should an accident occur, it is extremely important that you write down what has happened as soon as you possibly can. Describe the date and time of the accident itself, what lead up to it, exactly what happened, who witnessed it, what injuries were sustained, what you did about them, what you told the injured person, etc. Although lawsuits are relatively rare, they can happen. Your documentation would be extremely important to your legal defense in such a case.

If you have recommended specific treatment or have suggested that the injured person seek medical attention, and he refuses to follow your advice, follow up with a registered letter to review your recommendation. This is important proof that you did indeed try to help the injured person.

Consult your attorney immediately if anyone is seriously injured in your office, or if you have any doubts whatsoever about an accident or the injured person.

HAVE STAFF TAKE FIRST-AID TRAINING

A medical emergency occurs every four seconds in the United States. You may never be faced with a serious emergency in your office—heart attack, stroke, severe bleeding—but you should be prepared at the very least for everyday medical problems and accidents that can occur in your office.

Have your staff learn how to treat common emergencies like a careless burn, cut, choking, a sudden fall, or fainting. Consult your local hospital or Red Cross branch for class listings and recommended literature to keep in your office.

C·H·A·P·T·E·R 8-3

17 Ways to Maximize Limited Office Space

There are very few doctors who feel they have all the office space they would like. If you're feeling cramped, and moving or expanding your office space right now is out of the question, there's still some hope.

In this chapter, we will explore 17 specific, easy-to-implement strategies that will enable you to make better use of limited office space. See if you can find even one or two good ideas along the way that will make your office a more comfortable, pleasant, and efficient place to visit or work.

17 WAYS TO MAXIMIZE LIMITED OFFICE SPACE

1. Look for opportunities to build equipment, furniture, and other space-consuming items into the wall. For example, a reception-area aquarium or a video monitor may be able to be sunk into an existing wall, thereby freeing up precious floor space.

Tip: Reception area seating may also be cleverly built in, in the form of banquettes or window seats.

2. Increase both the neatness and the available work area in smaller examining/treatment rooms by installing wall-hung, fold-away mini-desks that have small writing surfaces and narrow vertical file holders. Many attractive units can be purchased ready-made from office furniture outlets.

3. Install a waist-high, fold-away changing shelf in the patients' restroom, for parents who bring children in diapers to your office.

4. Hang a large bulletin board in your reception area. Use it to post notices neatly and compactly.

5. Purge your files regularly. Move inactive records to an out-of-the-way storage area. As well, use open-shelf rather than pull-out drawer filing. For more information on these and related file management strategies, see "Records Management Problems and How to Avoid Them," pages 423–429.

6. Put away infrequently used items. Remove never-used items altogether.

7. Look up. Could you put a cabinet or shelf higher on your walls? Might you be able to run a row of cabinets up along the ceiling? Or, could you build storage space into existing soffits?

8. Install wall phones, rather than space-consuming desktop models. Also look for wall clocks, wall racks, and other wall-mounted items that will clear counters and desktops.

9. Install space-saver appliances in your staff kitchen area. Coffeepots, microwave ovens, and electric can openers can all be hung under cabinets, thereby freeing scarce counter space.

10. Install a wall-hung magazine rack in your reception area.

11. Shop for innovative, ready-made organizers in your local hardware or discount department store. Some of the best: Lazy Susans (for corner cupboards), under-shelf racks (that clip onto shelves), back-of-door racks.

12. Engage the services of a closet design firm, to design and install custom shelving, hanging rods, and drawers in tight closets. A well-designed closet system can literally double or even triple the amount you can store.

13. Look for interior design tricks that to create the *illusion* of more space. *Examples:* Directional lighting, mirrors, murals, strong vertical or horizontal lines in the wallpaper, lighter colors for paint, wallpaper with very small repeating patterns, more glass and open areas. While these strategies won't solve space and storage problems, they may help everyone feel that there's more space, which can help.

14. Alter your office decoration slightly to make it accommodate seasonal changes. For example, during colder winter months, you might cover chrome and glass tables with warm-looking cloths or mats. As well, you might add reds, browns, and other warm colors to your decor, in the form of throw pillows, draperies, and wall hangings. And, you might scatter pots of winter-blooming plants throughout your office, such as Christmas Cactus, and forced bulbs. On the other hand, during hot summer months, you might make good use of cooler-looking decorative objects, such as straw baskets and rugs, and pastel pillows.

Why? These small, simple decorative changes can make your office much more comfortable to everyone, and do not take up valuable space. The more comfortable your office is, the easier it will be to forget about the limited space.

15. Wet weather can be an especially difficult problem in cramped offices. Therefore, prepare an area out of your way to receive wet coats and

boots. Provide mats for wiping feet both outside and inside your office entrance, and an attractive umbrella stand. If you're in the snowbelt, keep a boot tray in your office during winter months.

Tip: Have a mop and bucket on hand for rainy and snowy days. Appoint someone in your office to make sure your entranceway doesn't become wet, slick, or muddy.

16.   Investigate minor office rennovations that would add extra space, or the illusion of it. Pre-fabricated bay and picture windows, dormers, greenhouses, and skylights all open up limited spaces, without the expense of a major construction effort. As well, you may be able to remove existing walls rather simply, to combine smaller spaces.

17.   In overworked office spaces, it may be more difficult to keep sound from traveling from one area to another. If this is a particular problem in your office, investigate soundproofing materials and technologies, such as acoustic tiles and electronic sound masking systems.

How to Remove the Burglars' Welcome Mat from Your Office

> We've had two burglaries within the past 10 days, so things have been in an uproar at the office. Cash, sunglasses, and plano colored contact lenses were taken. Earlier last summer we had a burglary, too.
>
> —California Optometrist

Many doctors never think about the possibility of being burglarized until it's too late. But from the burglar's point of view, unprotected professional offices are relatively easy and lucrative targets. Most offices are unoccupied at night, possess expensive office equipment, and the possibility of cash and drugs on hand. When the office provides easy access without detection, it becomes a highly desirable target.

Don't lure burglars to your office. Learn from the experiences of others and take the following precautions.

PROFILE OF A BURGLAR

A truly professional burglar is a master of all security systems. He can deactivate any system or device, even those that are the most sophisticated and up to date. While it is impossible to defend your practice against the professional burglar's skill, knowledge, and experience, you are not likely to be his target, since he commits only two percent of the nation's reported burglaries.

More threatening to your practice are the semi-professional and amateur burglars who commit the other 98% of the burglaries. The semi-professional, responsible for 28% of the burglaries, has access to an efficient fencing organization, and can rid himself stolen goods quickly and easily. The amateur burglar's main attribute is his ability to detect an easy target and act fast. He usually won't pursue a difficult target. Nonetheless, he commits 70% of the nation's burglaries.

The burglar wishes to avoid you or anyone else while he's stealing goods from your office. (For the purposes of this discussion, burglars are not to be confused with robbers, who approach their victims and steal from them by using force, violence, or threats.) He usually works in the dark, sometimes with a partner. And while he doesn't plan to hurt anyone, he often carries a weapon. Assume that he'll fight if you take him by surprise.

The burglar is almost always a stranger to his victims, since he doesn't want to be identified. He's an ardent people watcher and pays attention to detail. He's often a young male in his late teens or early twenties, although this isn't always the case. He may be from any social class.

The typical burglar likes an easy mark. He chooses targets that he can get into and escape from quickly, easily, and undetected. He'll take his business elsewhere if you make things too tough for him.

FOIL THE BURGLAR BY PROTECTING YOUR DOORS

All exterior office doors should be solid wood or metal. If yours are hollow or thin, reinforce them on the interior side with 16-gauge sheet metal. Cover the interior side of glass doors or door panels with steel mesh or steel bars, spaced five inches apart. (More on glass doors below.)

Be sure that door hinges are on the inside or that outside ones are not removable. Otherwise, the burglar can take the door from its hinges easily. Also check your door frame—it should be strong, preferably made of metal.

Install a good lock on each door. Avoid all key-in-knob locks, since an adept burglar with a pipe wrench or a pair of slip-lock pliers can twist off this type of lock in a few seconds. Much safer:

1. *Manual dead-bolt lock.* This lock may be activated by a thumb-turn lever on the interior side of the door. However, this is of no use if a burglar can simply break a glass panel next to the door, reach inside, and turn the lever. In such a case, install a lock that is keyed on both the outside and inside. And, don't leave the key in the lock or within reach of the broken glass panel.

Tip: Choose a lock made of sturdy steel or solid brass. Be sure the bolt protrudes at least one inch from the lock.

2. *Electronically powered dead-bolt lock.* This lock is activated by switches rather than keys or levers. It should have a manual override, in case of power failure.

3. *Electromagnetic field lock.* This lock is activated by holding a plastic card containing a microsensor before the door. It can be connected to an alarm which is sounded when a wrong card is used.

4. *Combination or push-button lock.* If you use these, don't keep a copy of the combination in your office.

Tip: Once any of these locks is engaged, the door can't be opened, even from the inside, without being deactivated. It's dangerous to lock an employee inside your office who doesn't know how to disengage the lock.

Example: Suppose you and your staff are in the office before or after hours for a staff meeting, and you dead-bolt the door for your protection. Should a fire or accident occur, employees who don't know how to deactivate the lock might be trapped inside the office. Make sure that everyone in the building when the door is bolted knows how to deactivate the lock.

FOIL THE BURGLAR BY PROTECTING YOUR WINDOWS AND GLASS DOORS

The burglar will break a window or glass door panel in almost 60% of his burglaries. If a window or panel is large enough to allow a person to pass through, have a back-up to a regular lock. Several options are listed below.

Tip: Don't judge the opening by your own ability to squeeze through it. The burglar may be extremely thin and/or agile. Some adult burglars can get through an opening that's only 8 inches across.

1. *Burglar-resistant glazed glass.* The glass is glazed with polycarbonate or acrylic, or is available in laminated construction. If you can afford burglar-resistant glass on some windows only, choose those that are most accessible—ones near ledges or the ground, or that lead to fire escapes.

2. *Glass with embedded wire mesh.* This is not as effective as glazing, but is a less costly deterrent.

3. *Steel bars, narrowly spaced.* Be sure these don't violate local safety codes.

4. *Folding steel window guards.* These should have both bottom and top sliding tracks, burglar-resistant padlocks, and inside hinges for fast and easy emergency removal.

Be sure window frames are strong, so the burglar can't pry them away from the building. Any glass opening can serve as an entry point for the burglar. Don't overlook skylights and exterior transoms.

Tip: Attach window air conditioners to bars placed inside the window, or the burglar may remove the unit to enter.

FOIL THE BURGLAR WITH LIGHTING

A good exterior lighting system is an excellent crime deterrent. Before installing your own lights, check with local authorities to see if you are eligible for a government-subsidized lighting program.

1.   Mount floodlights so they throw light onto your doors, windows, and immediate area—don't point them away from your entry points. *Idea:* Mount lights on the edge of your property and direct them toward your building.

2.   Light your back door and parking area.

3.   Place all permanent outdoor lights where burglars can't reach them and turn them off easily.

4.   Install light-sensors, so your lights go on automatically when it gets dark outside.

5.   Keep landscaping away from your entry points. A camouflage of shrubbery may offset any good you accomplish with your lighting system.

Good interior lighting will further enhance your office security system. Place some lights high on the wall or on the ceiling, so they're difficult to reach. Leave lights on in your office at night, on an automatic timer.

FOIL THE BURGLAR WITH A BURGLAR ALARM

At your request, your local Chamber of Commerce or police department will come to your office, run a security check, and recommend the best security system to meet your needs.

Alarm systems generally fall into two categories. The first includes alarms that are tied to an alarm company or police department. These are usually among the most expensive systems. The less costly systems, known as local or scare alarms, produce a loud noise when a burglar is detected. How various alarms work:

•   *Magnetic contact systems.* Units are placed on doors and windows. The alarm sounds when the burglar breaks the contact.

•   *Microphone system.* Microphones pick up sounds. The burglar's noise sets off the alarm.

•   *Ultrasonic detector.* The alarm sounds when the burglar disturbs a pattern of high-frequency sound waves.

•   *Infrared system.* The alarm sounds when the burglar interrupts the light beams emitted by the system.

- *Microwave system.* The alarm sounds when the burglar disturbs an electromagnetic field.

Often the notification decal of an alarm system, attached to your doors and windows, will deter the amateur burglar. Fake decals are available at some hardware stores.

PROTECT YOUR OFFICE KEYS

Even the most expensive and sophisticated security system won't work without tight control of your office keys:

1. Mark keys with "Do Not Duplicate" to discourage copies from being made without permission.

2. Collect keys from terminated employees. As an added precaution, change the tumblers and make new keys.

3. Keep a record for each key, noting when and to whom it was assigned. Record the key's identification number.

4. Don't give keys to new employees right away. Only assign keys after the probationary period, and then, to as few people as possible.

5. Have staff report missing keys at once. If a key doesn't turn up, change your locks.

6. Avoid skeleton key lock systems.

EIGHT ADDITIONAL WAYS TO DETER BURGLARS

1. Hire a private uniformed guard. To contain costs, join with neighboring practices or business owners to hire one guard to patrol all of your premises.

2. Run a careful reference check of all employees before you hire them. Give them a probationary period, during which you don't assign them keys or give them responsibility for or access to your security system.

3. Bolt down and lock expensive office equipment whenever possible. *Examples:* Computer, typewriter, photocopy machine.

4. It's harder for burglars to fence engraved goods. Therefore, mark all your equipment with an electric engraver, on the frame or some other part that can't be removed or replaced. Use your driver's license number with your two-letter state abbreviation. *Example:* In New Jersey, engrave NJ#3402S76N01.

5.   Don't keep large sums of cash in your office. Make more than one trip to the bank per day, if necessary.

6.   Install your patients' coat rack within view of your receptionist, so he can keep an eye one it. If a patient arrives in a full length mink coat, advise her to keep it with her throughout the appointment.

7.   Lock drugs and small valuables in a cabinet or closet when not in use. Examples: Tape recorders, calculators, credit card imprinter. Store filing cabinet keys in a secure location each evening.

8.   Make sure your office is empty before you leave it at night. Some clever burglars enter offices during the day, hide until they close (in the rest room, for instance), then burglarize them when everybody leaves. Once you're sure the office is empty, turn on your lights, and activate your locks and security system.

Records Management Problems and How to Avoid Them

T here are many strategies for establishing, maintaining, and protecting a professional practice filing system. In this chapter, we will explore some of the basics in file management, and the steps you should take to make your filing system "user friendly."

Tip: For information on proper record-keeping techniques, see "Malpractice Protection: Managing Patient Records to Reduce Malpractice Risk," pages 249–255.

SIX BASIC TECHNIQUES FOR FILE MANAGEMENT

An up-to-date filing system saves money and cuts down on staff filing time and frustration. Some excellent techniques:

1. *Install an open shelf (lateral) filing system.* File folders in an open shelf system are lined up one beside the next, much like books on a shelf. This arrangement eliminates the need for your assistant to pull out a heavy drawer each time she needs access to the files. Without the nuisance of drawers, assistants will be more likely to stay on top of filing chores. Another benefit: Open shelves cut down on floor space. The traditional four-drawer file cabinet requires up to 50% more space than open shelves that house the same number of file folders.

2. *Use checkout markers.* These colorful aides are used to indicate that a folder is missing from the file. They are usually made of bright blue, red, or yellow plastic or cardboard, and are slightly larger than conventional files. Some allow you to place or insert notes on the marker itself, explaining the whereabouts of the file it is replacing.

When your assistant pulls a folder from the file, she should always insert a checkout marker in its place. The marker will make it easy to refile the folder later. And, if it contains a notation, it will enable you to track down a file you are seeking when it is elsewhere in your office.

3. *Establish a file-out log.* An up-to-date log will help you locate every folder that is not in the file, without having to check the marker. It will let you know who pulled the folder, and when, so you can locate the file easily and quickly.

4. *Use plastic file cases.* These wipe-clean pockets, available from stationery suppliers, are to be used on all folders that are out in circulation in the office. They will make files easy to identify, keep them clean, and will prevent loose papers in the folders from falling out or getting separated.

5. *Use file fasteners and pockets.* There are many excellent file accessories on the market that can be adhered to or fastened inside folders to secure papers, x-rays, and other loose items.

6. *Establish a holding area.* Filing all charts each night before leaving the office is time-consuming, yet nonetheless desirable. Patient's clinical records are legal documents, and as such, they must be protected against loss, fire, and prying eyes. However, if nightly filing simply isn't practical, you might set up a secure (and fire-proof) holding area for charts that are in use for insurance claims processing, lab reports, or study. This way, charts that are not ready to be filed immediately can be returned to this secure area at night. Using this system, you'll know where your charts are, thus saving time spent looking for them. Such efforts are important in guarding patient confidentiality.

Tip: For more information on file security, see "The Problems of Guarding Patient Confidentiality," pages 261–265. Additional suggestions for protecting files from fire damage are offered later in this chapter.

ALL ABOUT COLOR-CODING

Color filing systems generally rely on self-sticking paper bands, dots, or stickers in eight, ten, or more colors. Most offices color code each patient's file according to the first two letters in his or her last name. Such a system makes it easy to retrieve files or spot one that's misplaced.

For example, assume that a green color sticker represents the letter *C* and a red dot represents the letter *A*. A file for a patient named *Campbell* would be coded with two colored dots: green and red. Thus, if the *Campbell* file was misplaced in an orange and blue section, it would be easy to spot.

Tip: Other popular options for color coding include colored file folders, and color symbols to indicate important information about a patient (such as allergies or diabetes). However, don't go overboard with color coding. Keep your system simple so you can keep track of it and use it successfully.

Color-coding can also be used to ease the purging of inactive files. While patient records should be kept indefinitely, it's neither necessary nor desirable to allow inactive records to clog up the the active files. The best approach is to establish a "purge cycle," a time frame after which inactive records are moved out of the active file and into long-term storage. To simplify this purging process:

1.   Place a colored tab on the patient's chart the first time he or she is seen in a given year. For example, the first time the patient was seen in 1990, you might have given him a red tab on his chart. Nothing needs to be done with this tab each time the patient returns thereafter in the given year.

2.   The first time the patient is seen in the next year, put a different colored tab on his file, and yet another color for each year thereafter. For example, you might have put a blue tab on the chart the first time the patient was seen in 1991, a green tab the first time in 1992, a yellow tab the first time in 1993, etc.

3.   When it comes time to purge inactive charts, go through the file and spot those patients who've not been in for several years. Following our example above, it would will easy to see that charts with red tabs only indicate patients who were last seen in 1990.

Tip: This system enables you to spot at a glance which patients have not been in to see you in a given year. That will save time if you try to "reactivate" them with a letter or a phone call. For more information on this subject, see "Bringing the Inactive Patient Back to the Fold," pages 367–370.

HOW TO IDENTIFY FILES SENT OUT OF YOUR OFFICE

When you refer patients to other doctors, wouldn't you like them to reciprocate? A good strategy is to put a sticker that identifies your practice on the patient charts you send to other offices. Such a sticker will remind the doctors and staff that this person is also your patient. It will keep you in sight and mind, which may encourage reciprocal referrals.

The sticker should be printed on a peel and stick label, and should leave ample room for typing or handwriting the patient's name, date, and diagnosis. *Example:*

This is the record of:

(Patient's Name)

_____ .

If you or your staff have questions, please do not hesitate to call our office.

Diagnosis: _____

Date: _____

Comments: _____ _____

_____

(Your name, address, phone number.)

HOW TO PROTECT YOUR RECORDS FROM FIRE

If you lose your records in a fire, there's a good chance that your practice will never function well again. There have been a number of court rulings that suggest that a fire is no excuse for failing to produce payroll, personnel, or other mandatory records for government inspection. Obviously, it makes sense to take a number of precautions.

To begin, learn if you have any records protection now, and the extent of your coverage. Then, prepare a list of your practice's essential records. At least include:

a.   Patient records—active and inactive.

b.   Accounts receivable.

c.   Accounts payable. These will help you disclaim unwarranted or already-paid bills, and arrange extended terms with creditors.

d.   Inventory. This is one of the keys to a full and fair insurance settlement.

e.   General accounting—essential to keeping your practice going after a fire.

f.   Contracts, leases, and legal papers.

g.   Personnel, payroll, and tax records.

Now, review these four basic options for protecting your records from fire damage:

1. *Take records home at night.* (Generally a poor choice. There's danger of loss or damage in transit, or of fire in your home.)

Tip: It may make sense to keep some records (such as contracts, leases, and legal papers) off your practice premises entirely, in a fire-proof vault.

2. *Duplicate critical records and store them away from the office.* This is easiest to accomplish with computerized records. For manual systems, duplication may be practical for a limited number of your most important records, such as leases, insurance policies, balance sheets, income tax returns (and supporting data), bank statements, inventory records, and employee pension records.

Photocopying is the most economical method of making duplicates. Microfilming compresses material into tiny space for easier storage, but is more expensive.

Tip: In court, duplicate records don't always carry the value of originals. Therefore, even if you do duplicate records, take additional steps to safeguard the originals.

3. *Install a fire-resistant vault.* This relatively expensive option can make good sense if you own your office. However, keep in mind that about half of all office fires occur during business hours, when a vault is likely to be open. You would need to establish a clear policy about keeping the vault closed, except for immediate access to the files.

4. *Use fire-resistant containers* (file bins, drawers, and safes). Although high-quality file containers can cost three to four times as much as ordinary file systems, good impact-tested containers will last the life of your practice, store your records, and protect them 24 hours a day. Usually, these specially-insulated cabinets protect contents to 170° Fahrenheit.

Tip: Many doctors find it helpful to create a comprehensive photographic file of all practice property and possessions, to substantiate future insurance claims due to fire, flood, or theft. A clear photo record attests to the existence, condition, and value of your property. It can help you remember all of the items you have in the office, so none are left out of your claim. As well, the file can be used to determine the extent of tax-deductible losses over the amount recovered through insurance.

Your photo file should contain clear pictures from several angles of all valuable structures, equipment, and furnishings. Store your photo file off practice premises in a fire-proof container or a safety deposit box. As well, keep your negatives safe, since you may need to send copies to insurance agents and your attorney. In addition, keep originals of relevant sales receipts and appraisals with your photographs. And, be sure to update your photo file immediately as your possessions change. Review it at least once a year to make sure you haven't overlooked recent purchases.

Tip: Many practices now use video equipment to photograph their possessions, claiming it provides a more complete picture than still shots. One benefit is that you can narrate the videotape as you shoot, which is generally easier than taking notes. Many video production firms now specialize in such recordings. Consult your phone book.

WILL YOUR FLOORS SUPPORT HEAVY FILES?

Your floor may not be built to tolerate the weight of your files. At one time, all buildings had 120-pound-per-square-foot tolerance. However, some may have been built in recent years with lower tolerances, sometimes as low as 75-pounds-per-square-foot.

At the same time, office paper in most offices is now heavier and in larger quantity than ever before, thanks to the widespread use of heavy bond papers, the frequent use of copiers (which increases quantity and uses heavier paper instead of lighter carbon paper), and the prevalence of heavy computer manuals and printouts.

All this means that floors may need added reinforcement, especially in heavy storage areas. Here's a formula to decide how much weight can be put where:

1.   Take a stack of typical files that is six inches thick. Include both fat and thin files in this sample. Leave everything in the files—paper clips, photos, x-rays, copies, etc.

2.   Weigh the files and divide by six (for 6 inches) to get the average weight per linear inch of files. *Example:* If the files weigh a total of 12 pounds, divide by 6 and you will get 2 pounds per inch of file, on average.

3.   Take five more samples, 6 inches of files in each. Weigh them and divide the weights by 6, each time establishing an average weight per inch from each of the 6 samples. Then, divide by 6. This should give you a pretty good idea of the average weight for one inch of your files.

4.   Measure in inches all the files you have in your office. Multiply the inches of files by the average pounds per inch, which you've already calculated. You now have the approximate total weight of all your files.

5.   Measure the square feet of floor space where your files are stored.

6. Divide the total weight of your files into the total square feet of floor space where the files are stored. This figure is the pounds per square foot that your files exert on your floors.

Example: Suppose you have 5,000 inches of files, and you've calculated that your files weigh about 2 pounds per inch. Thus, you have 10,000 pounds of files. Say you store them in an area 10 feet by 10 feet, or 100 square feet. Divide the square feet (100) into the number of pounds (10,000), and you get 100 pounds per square foot. On top of that, add in the approximate weight of the file cabinet or shelving unit that holds the files.

7. If you average more than 75 pounds per square foot, or if you have any doubts or concerns at all, alert your building manager or call in a construction engineer to be sure your building can sustain this weight. You may have to rearrange your file furniture or reinforce the floors.

C·H·A·P·T·E·R   8-6

Maintaining Your Sanity While Maintaining Two Offices

A re you experiencing a slowdown because of new competitors? Is your patient load dropping? Is the area where you practice declining? Are growth areas in your community far from your office? Do you have a space problem in your office? Do many current patients have to travel far, or incur significant travel expenses, to receive care in your office? Do you wish to build your practice and a good referral source?

If you can answer *yes* to some of these questions, you may be one of the many, many doctors who is a strong candidate for opening a satellite office. However, keep in mind that while there are many potential advantages of operating two or more offices, with them will undoubtedly come some additional managerial problems and tasks.

CHOOSING THE RIGHT LOCATION FOR YOUR SATELLITE OFFICE

The first thing you must decide about a second office is where it will be. Market research will help you identify population growth areas and trends that could suggest potential second office locations. Good sources of market research information include:

1. *The U.S. Census Bureau:* Check your public library. Or, in larger cities, see if the bureau's local offices employ staff who can ferret out useful information, such as poulation size, age and racial/ethnic distribution, employment and income statistics, and similar information for a potential market.

2. *Chamber of Commerce:* Your local Chamber of Commerce may have gathered and digested worthwhile information from piles of census data and other materials about areas you're contemplating.

3. *Media:* Local newspapers, television and radio stations, and magazines that sell advertising are well aware of the local market. They use data about their readers', viewers' and listeners' ages, incomes, gender, and level of education to sell advertising space. Call the ad departments of local media to see what marketing data they have.

Tip: They'll almost always share their materials if you're considering placing an ad.

4. *Surveys of current patients:* Surveys can reveal which locations would be fruitful. Good questions to ask: Where do you live and work? Which location would be most convenient for a second office (offer four or five choices)? Do you use public transportation to get to the office?

5. *Surveys of potential patients:* In particular, consider surveying individuals in locations you're giving serious thought. Have your business assistant, a temporary employee, or a public relations firm survey potential patients by mail, phone, or in person.

Tip: In-person surveys are usually done door-to-door or in a shopping center or busy downtown location. Get necessary permits to do this.

Ask questions such as: "Would you go to a doctor in _____(the location you're considering)? How would you travel to an office in that location? Do you now see a practitioner regularly?

6. *Telephone directory and newspapers:* The Yellow Pages and ads and articles in local newspapers can be mined for basic information about nearby competitors—an important consideration when choosing a location for a second office. Try to identify all competitors, their locations, areas of specialization, logos, slogans, hours, special facilities, and services offered.

CHOOSING A SECOND OFFICE SITE

The next major decision for your second office is the actual site. What to consider:

1. *Convenience:* Is the site convenient to patients? Is it near bus routes or other transportation? Is ample parking available?

2. *Potential patients:* Who are the people who live and work near the site? (Median income, age, gender, employment.) What are their needs for your services? What professional services do they use presently? Do they need evening and weekend hours? Flexible payment terms? (Use market research sources and the survey techniques described above to answer these questions.)

3.   *Competition:* How close is the site to competitors' offices? How does it compare?

4.   *Growth potential:* Will the site grow with you? If you plan to expand the second office in several years, will more office space be available? If you'll own the office, is there enough land for making an addition to the building and/or parking lot, if you need more space?

ESTABLISHING SECOND OFFICE SERVICES AND HOURS

The services and hours for your second office will be your next important decision. Consider:

1.   The size of your current practice.

2.   How many hours you now have available for the second office.

3.   How many hours your partners and associates have available.

4.   The distance and commuting time between the two offices.

5.   The hours and services potential patients in the second office location are likely to need and want. (Use surveys to determine this.)

6.   The number of current patients who are likely to switch over to the second office. (Again, use a survey.)

STAFFING THE SECOND OFFICE

Once hours and services are chosen, you should be able to project your needs for staff. What to consider:

1.   If you're in a group practice, how will doctor time be scheduled for the second office? Will present doctors be rotated on a scheduled basis? Will one or more doctors work exclusively at the second office? Or, will you need to hire one or more new doctors to help cover the second office?

2.   If you're in solo practice, how will you schedule your own time for the second office? If the offices are far apart, will you have to schedule whole days at the second office? If they're closer together, can you schedule only half days, or evenings, at the second office?

3.   Once doctors are scheduled, what staff will be needed for the second office? Will current staff travel to the new location? Or, will you need to hire additional staff?

4.   Who will coordinate administrative tasks between the two offices?

HANDLING ADMINISTRATIVE DETAILS AT THE
SECOND OFFICE

The administrative details of operating a second office are a bit more complicated than they might seem at first:

1. *Fees:* If possible, use the same fee schedule in both offices. This avoids confusion and resentment from patients.

2. *Billing:* Handle billing and insurance through your main office. Send the charge slips to the main office daily.

3. *Patients' clinical records:* There are different ways to handle patients' records at the second office, each with pros and cons:

• Each record could be duplicated and a copy retained at each location. However, this is expensive, and it's time-consuming to keep records updated. Obviously, there's potential for errors and oversights.

• The patient's records could be retained at the second office. However, this works best when the patient schedules all appointments at the second office, and doesn't use the main facility.

• All patients' records could be retained at the main office. Records of patients who are going to be seen at the second office can then be pulled and transported there the morning they are to be seen. And, they can be returned that afternoon. Of course, difficulties may arise when a patient comes to the second office with an emergency, or on short notice, and his records are at the main office.

Tip: With the availabilty of computer linkage and FAX transmissions between offices, many of these communications problems can be eliminated.

PROJECTING EXPENSES AND REVENUES FOR THE
SECOND OFFICE

A major factor in timing the opening of the new office is the projected expenses and revenues. It normally takes some time before a second office shows a profit—sometimes months, sometimes years.

When projecting expenses, be sure to account for everything, including:

• Rent.

• Salaries.

- New stationery.
- Supplies.
- Building maintenance.
- Insurance.
- Telephone.
- Utilities.
- Remodeling/signs.
- Equipment.
- Furniture.

Tip: Add an extra 10% to your estimated expenses, to be on the safe side.

Projecting revenues accurately is usually a bit harder. Use your past and current productivity levels as a guideline to project patient visits, lab and other expenses, etc.

Tip: Make conservative estimates.

MARKETING THE SECOND OFFICE

Opening a successful second office is much like opening a successful first office. You need to make people aware of you.

Begin marketing the second office before you open it. Some of the best ways to get the word out:

1. Send announcement letters to all referral sources.
2. Send announcement letters to every patient of record.
3. Send press releases to media to publicize the opening.
4. Schedule an open house at the second office.
5. Write about the second office in your practice newsletter.
6. Revise your practice brochure and stationery so they include information about your second office. (More on this below.)
7. Consider placing ads to announce your second office.
8. Give speeches at schools and clubs near your second office.
9. Make a bulletin board display about your second office in your main office reception area.

10.   Write letters to businesses near your second office to introduce yourself and describe your services.

11.   Launch a direct mail campaign targeting potential patients who live or work near your second office.

Tip: It's extremely effective to give current and potential patients a strong *incentive* to try out your new second office. Discounted fees, premium appointment times, and out-of-the-ordinary extra services may tempt patients into giving your new office a try.

DON'T LET TWO ADDRESSES CONFUSE PATIENTS

As a final consideration, if are going to maintain a second office, be sure your stationery doesn't confuse your patients, colleagues, and other referrers. Everyone should know clearly where to send their payments, where to call for an appointment, etc.

One way to eliminate confusion is to indicate in the body of your letter which office you want your reply sent to. For example, if you are sending a recall notice, you might say, "Call Mary in our Springfield office to set up your appointment." Or, if you are sending a collection notice, you might say, "Send your payment to our Falls Church office, to the attention of Mrs. DeKalb."

Tip: Many doctors with satellite offices print on their letterhead which address is their "main office," or where correspondence and inquiries should be sent.

Gearing Up Physically for Office Automation

Most professional practices need to make a number of physical modifications to their offices to accommodate and maximize the effectiveness
of a new computer. Unfortunately, many simply plop the new equipment onto
an existing desk, plug it in, and leave it at that. What results in such a case is
often inefficient computer use, the operator's fatigue and strain, and, sometimes, irreparable damage to expensive equipment.

PLAN ELECTRICAL NEEDS BEFORE PLUGGING IN
YOUR COMPUTER

You may run into problems whenever a computer shares a power source
with other equipment that uses a significant amount of electricity. In particular, x-ray and other large diagnostic and clinical equipment can cause fairly
high power surges, which is anethema to most computers. (Surges can cause
small problems, such as improper writing and storage of data. But sometimes,
major, expensive, and irreparable damage to the unit is possible.)

To protect your computer from surges, and to plan adequately for all of
your electrical needs:

1.   Be sure you use a dedicated electric circuit. Don't share your computer's electric line with any other piece of equipment—not even a seemingly
innocuous coffee pot or desk lamp.

2.   Get extra protection by using devices called spike or surge protectors. These act to minimize current surges caused by outside factors, such as
electrical storms. Protectors vary in price and quality, so you'll want to do
some comparison shopping.

Tip: Be sure the protector you choose is consistent with the voltage in
your area.

3.   Consider using an auxiliary power source that automatically kicks on
when power goes off. An auxiliary source will also function to protect data in

your computer that has not yet been recorded/stored. However, such a device is relatively expensive. Carefully weigh the pros and cons before you buy. *Examples:*

a. Can the auxiliary source be used to power other business or clinical equipment?

b. How likely are you to have a power failure?

c. What would be the potential consequences and damages in case of a power failure?

4. Investigate whether your building has sufficient power to support your computer system. If you don't know, have an electrical contractor do an electrical survey of the building. He may be able to suggest energy-efficient computer units that can eliminate the need for expensive electrical upgrading (even in older buildings).

Tip: The typical computer workstation requires more than one electrical outlet, and as much as 100 watts of power per square foot of floor space. For most offices, this means a major increase in existing electrical capacity.

5. Try to anticipate your future computer and other equipment needs as accurately and far ahead as you can. Then, plan your basic electrical system so it can expand to meet those needs. Otherwise, you'll need to retrace your steps (electrically) again and again each time you expand your system, which will waste time and money.

6. Plan for unit relocation, too. Don't limit your electrical system's physical layout so much that you must redesign the entire system to move one unit two feet.

7. Have your electrical contractor properly identify electrical cables when installing or modifying your system. This may add to the cost of the initial installment. However, it will ultimately save money if you must add, replace, or relocate computer components.

Tip: When designing your electrical system, you may find it difficult to get all the wires where they need to go. Do you have enough risers, ceiling space, and closets to accommodate your wiring needs? Many older buildings don't accommodate modern computer wiring needs, so wires must be superimposed on the existing structures. If that's the case, be sure that all wires are properly secured, and out of harm's way. Do not run wires under carpeting. (This is in violation of most fire codes, and for good reason.) For additional office safety procedures, see, "Reducing the Risk of Injuries in Your Office," pages 405–411.

ANTI-STATIC MATS CAN END SHOCKING PROBLEMS

Static electricity is a constant threat to the health of your computer. Static discharges are a major source of transitory failures, especially for computers located in the snowbelt. As well, it's possible for static electricity to cause permanent harm.

Simply putting an anti-static mat under the chair where users sit when operating the system can eliminate most problems. These mats or carpets can be bought from most computer stores and suppliers.

Tip: When anti-static mats alone don't eliminate the problem, you may need to boost your office humidity. Be sure your office electrical system can power new humidifiers in addition to your computer and other equipment.

AVOIDING VDT DIFFICULTIES: COLOR/LIGHTING TIPS FOR AUTOMATED OFFICES

Did you know that stark white walls are generally not recommended in a computer work area? White walls contribute to overlighting, which leads to glare on the computer screen and the operator's visual fatigue. Another tip: Did you know that bright colors in the computer area are another no-no? They tend to call attention to the environment, and distract computer operators from their tasks.

Medium-light tones are considered to be the ideal color choice for an automated business area. In particular, soft blues and greens have been found to be especially effective in automated areas exposed to sunlight. On the other hand, beiges and rosey pinks are well suited to areas that are artificially lit, since they add warmth while reducing glare.

Employees who work in front of a computer screen for long periods may report discomfort or difficulty with their eyes more often than other workers with visually demanding jobs, according to one medical school report. Thus, it helps to know the minimum requirements for visual work with a VDT:

1. A stable image that does not flicker.
2. Sharp focus with no blurred edges.
3. Contrast between light and dark areas that is at least eight to one.
4. Characters formed in a 5×7 matrix of dots, at the very least.
5. A brightness and darkness control mechanism that the operator can adjust easily.

6.   Proper room and workstation illumination.

Tip: If the operator must look mostly at the screen, room lighting should generally be quite low. On the other hand, if the operator reads a great deal from paper and enters material into the computer, room lighting should be relatively bright.

7.   Glare control. In addition to choosing the proper room color (see above), there are a number of glare control products on the market—filters, terminal hoods, and the like. As well, you may need to redesign room lighting, use color-corrected bulbs, room-darkening window coverings, or move the workstation entirely, to find a glare-free position.

SEVEN WAYS TO CONTROL NOISE
IN AN AUTOMATED OFFICE

Noise from many computer printers makes it hard to carry on a normal phone conversation, and can cause staff productivity to decline. Therefore, you may need to use a variety of noise-control tactics:

1.   Install an acoustical cover/sound enclosure around your printer to reduce its noise level. Noise from some printers is 70–80 decibels. A good cover cuts noise to a more acceptable 45–60 decibels—perhaps less.

2.   Design furniture layout so your printer is as far as is practical from phones and your receptionist's window.

3.   Install sound-absorbent ceiling tiles. Many are now compatible with existing narrow ceiling grid systems.

4.   Install sound-absorbent wall panels. These are available two ways:

a.   Panel systems (relatively costly).

b.   Fabric-wrapped individual panels made to size.

5.   Use more sound absorbers in your office: plants, drapes, pillows, wall art (especially fabric), upholstery.

6.   If sound carries too well in your office, an electronic sound masking sound system may be a good solution.

7.   Hire an acoustical consultant to suggest additional noise control alternatives. Most acoustical consulting firms are members of the National Council of Accoustical Consultants. In addition, most professional acoustical consultants have passed the technical requirements for membership in the Institute of Noise Control Engineering.

Tip: As automation increases, noise increases, but so does heat. Smart office buildings have increased capability to handle the heat, and usually provide separate zone controls, especially in areas with computers.

DESIGNING THE IDEAL COMPUTER WORKSTATION

Unfortunately, you may not be able to use all of your existing office furniture when you automate, at least without some modifications. Imagine each part of your workstation as a separate component, and examine them individually:

1. *Work surface:* How is it used? What's kept on it? How does the spread of papers affect the size and shape of the ideal surface? Is the surface well lighted and glare-free?

2. *Reference area:* How much space is taken up by computer manuals? By other frequently-used reference materials? Where? Is there a better location? How often are the various reference books used? Are those most often used kept within the operator's arm's reach?

3. *Organizers:* What kind (if any) are used/needed? Do they support tasks well? What items need organizing (paper clips, in-file papers, out-file papers, staplers), and where would be the best locations for such organizers?

4. *Shelving units:* Are bookcases needed? Or will strategically-placed shelves support needed materials?

5. *Storage area:* Is this functioning well? For example, is it the right size and in the best configuration? How is the computer covered/secured at night?

6. *Drawer units:* Are these located near the computer, and at the correct height?

7. *Chair:* Ergonomically sound computer chairs are now widely available. The most practical models will have wheels, an easily-adjusted height and back, and arms that can be pushed out of the way (or often, no arms at all). Most chairs that are not specifically designed for computer or secretarial workstations are poor choices, and may lead to fatigue, strain, and ultimately, operator inefficiency.

8. *Text entry:* Text entry ("regular" typing) requires equal use of both hands for keying. Thus, when designing the optimal workstation for word processing/text entry, the keyboard should be directly in front of the operator, at a comfortable height for typing.

9.   *Data entry:* Data entry usually requires one hand for keying, and the other for other activities. For instance, the operator may need to use the free hand to maintain a reference position on a source document. Or, she may need to manipulate several papers. For most data entry tasks, therefore, it is best to place the keyboard directly in front of the operator's keying hand. Leave a large area of the desk free for the activity of the other hand.

Tip: If both text and data entry will be handled at a single workstation, buy a computer with a movable keyboard. Design your worksurface so it can accommodate both functions.

10.   *Copy stand.* A swing-arm stand is a useful addition to workstations where the operator will need to refer to a hard-copy source. Where would be the ideal location of the stand? (Usually, to the right of the computer screen.) Is the swing-arm adjustable? Will an auxiliary light be needed to illuminate the material on the copy stand? (Many stands have built-in lights.)

Tip: Many copy stands are designed to use moveable magnetic arms to secure papers to them. However, be careful *not* to install such a stand at your computer workstation if the magnetic arm is *detachable.* If a computer operator carelessly places the magnetic arm on a diskette, or even drops it accidentally on one, she could permanently scramble and destroy all the material stored on the diskette. For this reason, it's best to keep all free-moving magnets away from your computer workstation.

Housekeeping Tips that Prevent Costly Computer Problems

To get an office computer system up and running requres a substantial investment of both money and time. You can protect your investment by practicing some simple housekeeping and trouble-shooting techniques, and instituting basic computer maintenance policies for your staff.

WHAT TO DO WHEN YOU THINK YOUR COMPUTER NEEDS REPAIR

In a great many cases, you can do your own computer "repairs," and save yourself a lot of time, money, and aggravation. Before you bring your computer in for repair service:

1. See if your computer is plugged in. Reseat all the plugs and cables in their electrical outlet, unit, or peripheral equipment.

2. Check that the electrical outlet is alive. (Perhaps you have circuit breakers or blown fuses.)

3. Check that the computer is the only unit on that electrical line. Remove all other appliances and equipment.

4. Run the diagnostic routines available to you. (They're usually built in, or on disk.) Review and follow the computer manuals' trouble-shooting guides.

5. If you're getting erratic readouts or I/O errors, try cleaning your disk drives.

Tip: Most manufacturers recommend using a cleaner kit to keep your disk drive heads clean. But did you know that these cleaning disks are abrasive? In fact, they can cause more wear on the disk drive heads than months of normal use! For this reason, don't overclean your disk drives. The best course is to follow your manufacturers' cleaning schedule, and avoid more-frequent cleanings unless you experience disk access errors.

7.   Try a back-up disk of your applications program.

8.   If your software won't load, try using an alternate disk drive to boot up your program.

9.   If you have a second computer or extra cords, try swapping them.

KEEP VDT BRIGHTNESS LOW TO AVOID "ETCHING"

Do you find that you leave one image on your VDT screen for prolonged periods during the day? (For example, a basic menu often appears when the program is at "rest.") If so, it's good practice to lower the brightness level when you know you won't be changing the image for awhile. Or, turn off your monitor completely.

Leaving the same image on the screen for a long time can cause it to "burn" into the monitor's inner surface. This damage, called "etching," is irreparable.

Tip: Some computer systems have a feature that automatically turns off the VDT screen when one image remains on it for a prescribed number of minutes. This is generally worthwhile, since the computer "remembers" to turn the screen off for you.

WHY AND HOW TO "BURN IN" YOUR NEW COMPUTER

It is usually recommended practice to leave a new computer on continously for the first two weeks you own it. That way, any electrical problems will show up right away. (Roughly 80% of all electrical circuits that survive this "burn in" test will last an estimated 500 years!)

Tip: When leaving your computer on and not using it during burn in, turn off the VDT screen, to avoid etching (see above).

KEEPING YOUR COMPUTER CLEAN

A computer dustcover is one of the best ways to ensure that a computer remains clean. Make it a practice to cover your computer every night before leaving your office.

Cleaning between and underneath your computer keyboard's keys will prevent costly and annoying problems. This can be accomplished with a cotton swab, soft brush, or a can of compressed air (with a small nozzle). Or, you can use a handheld keyboard "vacuum" (a device made especially for this purpose).

As a final policy, avoid eating, drinking, or smoking near your computer, as these can lead to spills and other obvious problems.

CLEAN HOUSE PERIODICALLY SO YOU CAN OPERATE FASTER

Every one to three years, most professional office computer systems become so full of data that they operate noticeably slower. When this happens, it's time to "clean house," or balance forward. This simply means removing all past concluded financial data from your computer files, leaving only a balance for those patient who owe you money.

Although there is no reason to retain electronic records of payments that have been settled, you should keep a permanent hard record of this data in case it's needed for treatment, malpractice, or financial planning. Thus, you will need to run a printout of all patients in alphabetical order along with their transactions.

Unfortunately, obtaining this printout can take a great deal of time and create havoc in your office. Here are some suggestions for speeding the process along:

1.   Get a faster printer. Consider renting one specifically for this project. If a 100 cpm (characters per minute) printer does the job in 50 hours, a 200 cpm printer can cut the time in half. Also, find out if you can print data while the printer is in its fastest "draft" mode rather than in "letter quality" or "final print" mode.

2.   Temporarily disconnect all but one terminal. The computer checks each terminal before it processes data bits. This is time-consuming and can slow operations.

3.   Use buffers. These store information from the computer and slowly feed it to the printer. Thus, the computer can process data rapidly and be ready for other functions.

4.   If you have a jam-proof printer, run the computer at night, on the weekend, or on a timer.

Tip: Use a heavy-duty timer of 1,500 watts. Look for those made to be used with refrigerators or air conditioners.

5.   Check your printouts for errors. Balance-forward modules are usually used infrequently, and may contain bugs.

HOW TO KEEP YOUR COMPUTER
FROM OVERHEATING

Most computer systems operate at approximately 90° Fahrenheit. However, just a little added heat above proper operating temperature can cause big problems, such as glitches and chip shut-down. To prevent overheating:

1.   Keep your vents clear of books, papers, walls, furniture, and other blockers.

2.   Keep your system low. Heat rises, so systems on high shelves are in the warmest part of the room.

3.   Keep your room temperature below 80° Fahrenheit.

4.   Small flecks of static on your screen usually indicate overheating. If you see them, direct a desk-top fan or a forced air vent onto your computer.

P · A · R · T

9

Personal Skills Development for Better Practice Management

Getting Patients to Accept Your Clinical Recommendations

T hink for a moment about the last time you made a major purchase—say a car or computer or washing machine or television. Why did you buy? Was it the price? The financing available? The guarantee or warranty? The speed and convenience of delivery? The manufacturer's or store's reputation? Was it because you're already using another product by the same manufacturer and are satisfied with it? Were you impressed by the unique features, benefits, or prestige of the item? Did your decision depend upon your trust and relationship with the sales representative? Was it a combination of reasons?

Whatever prompted you to buy, the following was probably true:

1.   The sales environment must have been conducive (or at least not contrary) to buying.

2.   If your sales rep was worth his or her salt, he had a pretty good idea of what would make you buy. He or she probably asked you a number of questions and listened very carefully to what you said. If your rep was particularly good at his job, he or she also listened to what you didn't say, and made note of your appearance, tone of voice, and body language.

3.   The sales rep assessed your needs and wants. If you didn't come to him with specific needs, he or she helped you define them.

4.   Finally, the sales rep tailored his or her message accordingly, to fill those needs.

These four simple steps are the keys to successful selling:

1.   Provide an environment conducive to buying.

2.   Ask questions. Listen and observe.

3.   Define (or create) the customer's needs.

4.   Provide truthful information that fills those needs.

Not surprisingly, these identical four steps are the keys to winning case acceptance from your patients. In most practices, it's usually necessary to convince your patient to proceed with your recommendations, and to pay for that care. In some cases, the patient may resist your recommendations, or look elsewhere for another opinion and treatment. The case conference is your chance to educate these patients about their needs and to motivate them to accept your recommendations.

Tip: Many doctors dislike the idea that they must "sell" the patient on their recommendations. However, selling is pretty much what you must do when you meet with a patient to convince him or her to follow your recommendations. Except for very few procedures, it's a good bet that the patient would rather spend money and time on things other than the services you recommend. Thus, it's usually a selling job to gain case acceptance.

STEP 1: PROVIDE AN ENVIRONMENT THAT'S CONDUCIVE TO CASE ACCEPTANCE

Case acceptance is a very personal, sometimes difficult and emotional decision. It is often stressful for the patient. Thus, the best environment for your conference is one in which the patient feels at ease.

It's very helpful to establish a good relationship with the patient before you offer your diagnosis and recommendations. This personal relationship, built upon trust, must grow from the very first contact the patient has with your practice. That first phone communication sets the pace for the entire relationship between your practice and that patient. If the conversation is rushed and abrupt, the calling patient will sense that care in the office will be the same. If, on the other hand, conversation is caring and comfortable, the patient will perceive the office, staff, and doctor as being part of a caring and comfortable environment. (For more information on this subject, see, "How to Make a Great First Impression on the New Patient," pages 375–382.)

Along similar lines, the patient must feel welcome and comfortable each time he visits your office. Your decor is a factor, of course, and should be designed with colors, textures, and furnishing that make your patients feel comfortable. This will vary from one practice to the next.

Example: Parents and children are likely to feel comfortable in environments that use bright colors and have a children's area, with of toys, games, and books. On the other hand, practices that serve mostly professional and business people might do best with more corporate-looking colors and furnishings.

Staff, too, should do everything possible to make patients feel comfortable when they visit your office. This extends to all dealings with patients, including how they're greeted, escorted, and dismissed at each appointment.

Another essential factor in the patient's comfort level is how familiar he is with you. You'll generally get more acceptance from patients who know you well before you make your recommendations, especially when a high fee, painful, or high-risk procedure is involved. Thus, it's usually good strategy to see all new patients at least once before scheduling a large case conference. That way, you can use the second appointment to follow up, make your recommendations, and answer questions.

Tip: If you do the exam and make your recommendations all at the first and only appointment, the patient will have had little time to get to know you and may not feel comfortable enough to accept your advice. But if you ask the patient to come to the practice at least twice, he'll feel more at home, and often, be more accepting.

Finally, be sure to choose a comfortable environment for the actual conference. Uninterrupted privacy is essential, so be sure you can talk with the patient behind closed doors, without an audience or distractions. If possible, don't hold the conference in the examination room. (Patients generally feel more comfortable in a private office or consultation room that's non-clinical.)

Tip: Overly luxurious offices can work against you, if they make patients question how much of what they pay you is being used to maintain your luxury. Thus, when planning office decor, don't go overboard for your patients, and avoid conspicuous displays of your own personal wealth. For example, unless you serve very wealthy, status-conscious patients, leave pictures of expensive playthings—a yacht, plane, thoroughbred, or antique car—at home. Don't put magazines geared to the rich, jet-setting crowd in your reception area.

In addition, consider these strategies for creating a comfortable case consultation environment:

1.   Sit at the same level as the patient during the meeting, not above or below him. This creates equality between you, and neither threatens the patient nor makes him question whether you know what you're doing.

Tip: If your chair is high, has arms and a high back, and chairs for patients ar lower and smaller, patients may view the case conference as a put down. Use similar chairs to equalize your relationship. If your office is large enough, create a separate area for conferences, with a small table and several identical chairs.

2.   Sit *beside* the patient, not behind a desk, to show again that you're relating to him personally, as an equal, without barriers. Many doctors set up two or more chairs in front of their desks, and sit in one of them for conferences.

Tip: If you have no choice but to sit behind your desk, consider the desk itself. Sitting behind a massive, formal, closed-front desk for a case conference establishes a position of authority and distance from the patient. A ligher, open-fronted desk is more informal, and may make patients feel less threatened.

3.   When appropriate, offer the patient a beverage. (This sometimes takes the edge off a tense meeting.)

4.   Keep the room cool. Set the thermostat two or three degrees lower than elsewhere in the office (but not uncomfortably cold). A cool room will help you keep your patients' attention, and will make them more open to accepting your recommendations.

Tip: Will you be meeting in a very small space? Will the patient's spouse, child, or another individual be present at the meeting? If so, consider setting the temperature even lower, to allow for the warm bodies that will fill the room.

STEP 2: ASK QUESTIONS, LISTEN, AND OBSERVE

The new patient get-acquainted procedure and a thorough examination are your best opportunities to "read" the patient, and plant the seeds for his acceptance. Listen to him as he describes any problems he's having, explains why he hasn't been to a doctor in years, or reveals his fears, concerns, and values. Listen carefully during each meeting, and take notes appropriately. Probe for more information about the way the patient thinks and feels by asking revealing open-ended questions.

Example: a dentist might ask:

1.   How do you feel about your smile?
2.   How do you feel about dentures?
3.   Why did you leave your last dentist?
4.   How do you feel about dental treatment?

As you listen, observe the patient's body language and voice tone. In particular, look for physical signs of uneasiness, embarrassment, or increased interest, such as clenched fists, averted or widened eyes, or fidgeting. Acknowledge these signs and ask the patient about them directly. For example:

"You seem uneasy about that last question. Why?" Or, "You smiled when I said that? Why?" Note the patient's response.

STEP 3: DEFINE OR CREATE THE PATIENT'S NEEDS

To a dentist, a patient may "need" a bridge or a crown. To an optometrist, he may "need" multi-focal lenses. To an orthopedic surgeon, he may "need" surgery.

However, it's a big mistake to assume that the patient feels he "needs" these treatments. Your job before and during the case conference is to define (or create) the needs the *patient* perceives. In so doing, you can show him how the bridge and crown, multi-focal lenses, surgery, or the other treatments you're recommending fill those needs.

Management consultant Rick Pereira (Tucson, AZ) teaches that patients' needs can be classified into four categories:

1. *Aesthetics:* I need to be attractive.

2. *Investment:* I need to save time and money.

3. *Recognition:* I need my friends/colleagues to admire me.

4. *Comfort:* I need to feel good and avoid pain/inconvenience (and live as long as I possibly can).

Pereira suggests that these categories of needs are not mutually exclusive. People are complex, so patients frequently have more than one need.

Tip: Don't assume from a person's appearance that he's motivated by one of these needs and not another. It's usually a good guess that a patient who is well-groomed and dressed in the latest fashion is motivated by aesthetics or recognition. However, don't assume that the poorly-dressed patient feels he needs to make a smart investment (to save money). He may be more intereseted in comfort, aesthetics, or recognition. Thus, try to determine which of these needs strongly motivates the patient on the basis of what he *tells* you, and what you *observe*.

STEP 4: PROVIDE TRUTHFUL INFORMATION THAT FILLS THOSE NEEDS

Instead of presenting a standard, pre-packaged speech to all patients, personalize your remarks, tailoring them to each patient's needs. For example, Rick Pereira suggests that a dentist might tailor a case consultation this way:

Patient's need:	A dentist might suggest:
Aesthetic	If we don't save that tooth, your smile would be much less attractive, and you could end up looking older.
Investment	That tooth may require more extensive treatment if you don't care for it now.
Recognition	A missing tooth may hurt your professional image.
Comfort	The pain in that tooth will get worse if you don't take care of it now.

APPEALING MORE SPECIFICALLY TO THE PATIENT'S WANTS

When providing information to fill any patient's need, stress the specific, concrete *benefits* of following your recommendations. The patient's favorite subject is himself. He wants to know what's in it for him. Be sure to tell him clearly, and perhaps more than once. Stress what the patient stands to gain, especially as that gain relates to his particular needs. Describe in practical, down-to-earth language how accepting your recommendations can make him more attractive, save him time or money, bring him admiration from his friends, or make his life easier, more comfortable, more convenient, or longer.

Remember, it is the rare patient who wants a crown or bridge, multifocal lenses, or surgery. Almost always, your patients will want a pretty, functional, long-lived smile, the ability to see well and comfortably, a long and happy life without pain, etc. Tailor your treatment recommendations to these basic human motivators:

• *People want to gain . . .* health, time, money, popularity, improved appearance, security, praise, comfort, leisure, pride of accomplishment, business/social advancement, self-confidence, prestige/status, happiness, enjoyment, admiration, satisfaction, luxury.

• *People want to be . . .* proud, sociable, up-to-date, influential, first in things, creative, efficient, liked, effective, recognized, powerful, correct/right, accepted, admired, attractive, respected, loved, free.

• *People want to be able to . . .* express their personalities, emulate their heroes and others they admire, acquire things, win affection, improve themselves and their position, look and feel better, live longer and happier.

- *People want to avoid* . . . fear, personal embarrassment, discomfort, pain, worry, doubts, risks, injury, money problems, low social standing, feeling helpless, being limited.

- *People want to save* . . . money, time, possessions, energy, effort.

HOW TO TURN AROUND COMMON OBJECTIONS TO TREATMENT RECOMMENDATIONS

Sometimes, the patient has a clear need for your services, you do an excellent job of tailoring your message to his needs, and he still doesn't accept. Below are some of the most common reasons patients resist recommended treatment, and what you can do to turn things around.

Why Patients Resist Treatment:	What You Can Do:
He sees no need for the treatment.	Have the patient repeat what you've told him (to make sure he understands you.) Review important points, using facts, visual aids, and anecdotes to strengthen your case.
The patient feels he can't afford to follow your advice.	Review the case again. This time, stress payment options and your desire to work out a mutually-satisfactory financial arrangement. For more information on this subject, see, "Making Firm Financial Arrangements with Patients," pages 113–119.
The patient's spouse makes the money decisions for the family.	Schedule another conference when both the patient and spouse can attend.
The patient is a slow decision maker.	Give him some time. However, call within a few days to see if he has any questions (and to prompt a decision). It's usually best if the doctor makes this important call.
The patient is annoyed (and perhaps is denying his situation).	Be humble and politely ask why. Is he upset that he has a problem? With your fee? That he didn't come to you sooner? Meet objections squarely, emphasizing your concern about the patient's health.
The patient is afraid.	Pinpoint the source of his fear. For example, if treatment will hurt, discuss pain control. If he fears that the treatment won't work, discuss the real (not

Why Patients Resist Treatment:	What You Can Do:
	perceived) risks. If he's afraid he'll have to take too much time off from work, discuss scheduling options. For more information on this subject, see, "Dealing with the Anxious or Fearful Patient," pages 359-365.
The patient understands what treatment will do, but doesn't value it.	Explain and demonstrate what may or will happen if the patient doesn't undergo recommended treatment.
The patient thinks he can get another practitioner to do what you propose for less.	Emphasize the quality of your work, your experience, reputation, etc. Review payment options to show that money matters can be worked out.

ADDITIONAL STRATEGIES FOR WINNING CASE ACCEPTANCE

1. Meet patient's objections with the three F's:

a. "It's OK to feel that way."

b. "Other patients have felt that way."

c. "But they found it isn't a problem."

2. Eliminate negative words from your treatment recommendations. Words such as "cost," "down payment," "contract," "sign," and "buy" may be red flags to your patients that put them on the defensive. Whenever possible, stick to words that *don't* arouse negative feelings. *Examples:*

a. "Investment" instead of "cost" or "price."

b. "Agreement" instead of "contract."

c. "Approve" the paperwork instead of "sign."

d. "Own" instead of "buy."

3. Answer questions about fees flatly. Then, outline in simple terms the payment options you offer. However, keep your explanation brief. The detailed financial arrangements should be made by your business assistant. For more information on making financial arrangements, see, "Making Firm but Fair Financial Arrangements with Patients," pages 113–119.

4. Obtain two affirmatives:

a. "Do you feel you are clear on what I've explained to you about x, y, and z?"

b.   "Do you feel clear on what may (or will) happen if these conditions are not corrected/treated?"

If the patient answers "yes" to these two questions, you can ask, "Shall we go ahead with the recommended services?"

C · H · A · P · T · E · R   9-2

How Listening Better Can Reduce Management Errors

L istening is probably the most important, but most often neglected, of the basic communication skills. Consider these facts: The average person spends 9% of his or her time reading, 16% writing, 30% speaking, and 45% listening. However, more than 75% of what we hear is heard incorrectly. And, we forget within a matter of *weeks* 75% of the 25% we got right. With these astonishing statistics in mind, it behooves doctors and their staffs to improve their listening skills.

Listening to what patients say, both verbally and nonverbally, and making sure that they know you understand them, is vital to building a good relationship and providing first-rate care. How many patients tell you that their former doctor didn't seem interested in their problems or concerns, was always busy, or didn't respond to their complaints? Do *you* really listen to your patients' problems? If *you* are distracted or are otherwise a poor listener, you may miss the real meaning behind what a patient tells you, and become the next previous doctor.

As well, many of the problems and unnecessary "busy work" in practice management stem from not practicing the art of effective listening. For instance, many mistakes are due to miscommunications, with poor listening at the root. Moreover, many doctors write unnecessary memos to staff because they're afraid of problems caused by poor listening. As well, staff may feel the doctor is a poor listener, and not say what they want to say. When that happens, morale declines, and the doctor misses out on some potentially great ideas. Furthermore, little is accomplished when everyone talks at a staff meeting, and no one listens. Participants end up being annoyed that they've wasted their time and may avoid future meetings.

As the leader in your practice, it is critical that you call attention to the importance of listening and set an example yourself. Your staff will be less likely to interrupt and override each other, and more likely to listen and learn. Also, staff meetings and other times when you're working together are more likely to remain focused on the problem at hand, rather than detour into side business.

THE 15 DO'S OF BETTER LISTENING

1.   *Tune out "trigger" words.* Certain words may make us see red, so much so, that we can't listen. *Example:*

> You must be even dumber than I thought to make that mistake.
>
> The trigger word, *dumber,* sets off negative feelings toward the speaker, and makes us angry. Therefore, if you want someone to listen, avoid trigger words. If you're a listener, try not to let trigger words upset you so much that you don't hear the speaker's message. (For a comprehensive list of words and phrases to use and avoid in your practice, see, "Checklist of Words to Use and Avoid with Patients," Appendix 1-0, pages 541–542.

2.   *Stop talking.* You can't learn much about the needs of others if you do all the talking. How can you tailor your comments to your listeners unless you stop to listen to their concerns?

3.   *Be sensitive to what may lie between words.* Sometimes, what a person does *not* say is as important as what he or she actually says. Patients may be telling you important things *non*-verbally. For instance, does their body language indicate that they're nervous, angry, or upset (even if they don't say so in words)? Note their posture, facial expressions, movements, gestures, eye contact (or lack or it), and voice. Do they seem eager, reluctant, tired, energetic, closed-in, or open to others?

4.   *Put your listener at ease by showing him or her that you WANT to listen.* Most people have few people—if any—who'll listen to them. A little concern will go a long way. Look at the speaker squarely in the eyes, smile (if appropriate), sit tall with your head bent slightly forward and toward the speaker, and keep alert.

5.   *Minimize distractions.* If you want high-quality interaction, try to get your partner into a comfortable situation—no phones or other interruptions. When you're the listener, especially in a lecture or seminar, don't create or succumb to distractions such as doodling, humming, playing with odds and ends (paper clips, paper, pen), drumming your fingers, or shaking your

leg. (For more information on effective seminar participation, see, "How to Get More from Continuing Education Programs," pages 489–495.)

6. *Empathize.* See the situation from the other person's viewpoint. Try to stand outside your interaction and think about his or her experiences and needs.

7. *Be patient.* It takes some people a long time to get their message out. You may already have organized their thoughts for them and be anxious to jump in and get things rolling. If so, *don't.* Resist the natural temptation to finish the speaker's sentences or thoughts for him or her.

8. *Withhold judgments.* Don't make judgments until the speaker has finished the thought. You may be completely wrong. Look for points of agreement first.

9. *Go easy on criticism.* When a speaker is criticized quickly and harshly, he or she usually learns that it's safer to say nothing. Don't cut off the exchange of information and new ideas, especially from members of your staff.

10. *Resist the one up.* You may have had a more exciting, more interesting, or funnier experience, but by one-upping the speaker, you're really minimizing him or her. The result: He or she won't share any more stories.

11. *Ask better questions.* Not everyone will be totally honest, especially within a patient-doctor or employee-employer relationship. Therefore, you need to sharpen your questioning skills to get at the speaker's true or hidden meanings.

12. *Provide the right environment for listening.* The seating arrangement has a great deal to do with effective listening. Sitting in the round so everyone can see each other seems to be the best arrangement for a staff meeting where ideas are to be exchanged. Sitting side by side, face to face works best for smaller meetings (such as case conferences, performance reviews, or exit interviews with departing staff).

13. *Decide **why** you're listening.* For raw information? To learn what makes a person tick, or what he or she needs? To answer a specific question? To uncover the other person's misconceptions, fears, or concerns?

14. *Listen for signals.* Pay close attention when the speaker says a point is "most important" or "a significant fact" or when he or she says "the major emphasis" or "don't forget this." (Good seminar speakers use these signals liberally.) As well, work on using these sorts of signals when you communicate with others, to help them listen better and sort out what's most important or memorable from what's not.

15. *Help people who are upset by listening to them in a nondirective way.* Repeat to them in your own words what they've just said. Emphasize their feelings. Don't argue, offer excuses, point out that they're illogical, or offer solutions. Talk as little as possible, giving the other person room to open up to you.

16. *Paraphrase.* Simple statements like, "What I hear you saying is . . ." or "Check me if I'm wrong, but this is what I think you are saying . . ." can go a long way in increasing understanding and uncovering misconceptions.

AND NOW THE 15 DON'TS . . .

1. *Don't assume the subject is dull, too complex, or unimportant.* Often a subject has no appeal to us because our interests lie in other areas, or we think we've heard it all before, or it's trivial. In such instances, it's very common to avoid listening, since tuning out is easier. Don't fall into this trap. Almost any subject can become interesting, or at least understandable, if you listen carefully.

2. *Don't react to the speaker.* We may dislike the speaker's accent, style of dress, hairstyle, name, or mode of delivery. Conversely, we may like what we see in the speaker. In either case, we may be hearing only what we expect to hear, based on our reaction to the speaker, not necessarily to what is being said. Try to separate the message from the messenger.

3. *Don't get overly excited.* Excitement, positive or negative, can change what we hear. Our enthusiasm may take a thought far beyond that intended by the speaker. Try to curb your excitement until the speaker has finished and you're sure you've understood correctly.

4. *Don't outline everything.* By sticking to a strict outline when we listen, we may miss the central ideas by paying more attention to the process of outlining than to what is being said. Often, we try to force ideas into our outlines without really listening to them. (This is especially true when attending seminars and staff meetings.)

5. *Don't fake attention.* Many people have become masters at acting as if they were paying attention when, in reality, they have no idea of what is being said. They have developed the ability to nod at appropriate times, or to interject a noncommittal "uh-huh," "hmmmm" or "how interesting," without hearing a word. Ask yourself whether you fly on "automatic pilot" when you conduct a new patient examination or job interview for a staff opening. Even if you really have heard it all before, remember that this is all new to the other person.

Tip: Almost every patient thinks his or her concerns are unique, and that he or she is the only patient that really matters.

6. *Don't try to impress the other person.* Rather, concentrate on *expressing* yourself. Strive to express your concern for others, as well as your thoughts and ideas. Don't try to impress them with your importance, knowledge, wealth, good looks, sophistication, and/or vocabulary.

7. *Don't detour.* Do you find yourself triggered by words or ideas that send you off on tangents? Detouring keeps us off the subject for awhile, exploring some other ideas. We come back to what's being said, but by then we have missed a great deal of the speaker's message. Force yourself to stay with the speaker.

8. *Don't debate.* When we disagree with something the speaker has said, we often get so caught up in our disagreement that we spend time formulating our mental arguments (debating), and completely miss what's being said.

9. *Don't avoid the difficult.* When a subject becomes difficult or uncomfortable for us, we often stop listening. We develop the uncanny knack of tuning out those things we don't want to face. Force yourself to listen, even when you're being criticized by a member of your staff, or a patient.

10. *Don't let prejudice get in the way.* Are you able to listen to advice from someone younger, less educated, and less experienced than you? Don't tune out a good idea because it comes from someone you have preconceived notions about. Rid yourself of preconceptions about what the speaker will say or what point of view he or she may have.

11. *Take notes, but not too many.* Writing one idea may keep you from getting the next one.

Tip: If note-taking gets in the way of your listening at meetings, tape-record the program (with the speaker's permission), for follow-up review and note-taking.

12. *Don't ask questions unless you really want to listen to the answer.* Avoid asking questions like, "How are you?" or "What's new?" or "How was your vacation?," unless you really want to know. Asking may seem polite, but it's actually rude if you don't listen to the answers. People know when you're genuinely interested, and when you're not.

13. *Don't engage in a side conversation or other activity.* This is particularly rude when someone you should be listening to is talking. And, it will interfere with your understanding. Keep focused, no matter what.

14. *Don't assume you know the speaker's true meaning, if it can be interpreted several ways.* If you're not sure, ask, "Oh?" or "What do you mean?" in a non-threatening tone.

Examples of patients' ambiguous comments:

• "Professional services cost so much."

• "I'm a terrible patient."

• "That's so expensive."

15.   *Don't think about what you're going to say while the other person is talking.* Instead, *listen!*

C · H · A · P · T · E · R   9-3

Tricks for Remembering Names, Faces, and Other Information

A well-developed memory is of great value to any doctor. For example, the simple act of remembering a patient's casual request or remark, a new patient's name, or a passing promise to an employee can give you greater piece of mind and more confidence. Your ability to recall data and to bring up important facts at the right time can be extremely important to your efficiency and practice management success.

Fortunately, it isn't necessary to rely on our memory for most pieces of information. We can write things down, and refer to our notes later. (For the how-to's of two excellent note-taking systems, see "How to Keep Track of Hard-to-Keep-Track-Of Information," pages 479–481.) However, when we *must* rely on our memory, most of us can greatly increase the amount and accuracy of what we remember.

THE FIVE BASIC RULES FOR IMPROVING YOUR MEMORY

1. *Concentrate* on what you want to remember. People often don't pay attention when introduced to someone, or when they hear facts they need to recall later. Don't let your attention wander when you're hearing "memorable" material for the first time. (For more information on this subject, see "How Listening Better Can Reduce Management Errors," pages 459–464.)

2. *Picture* what you want to remember. As much as 85% of all you learn and remember in life reaches you through your eyes. Therefore, *visualize* things you want to recall later. For example, if you're trying to remember a date, it's usually easier if you first get a clear picture of the numbers in your mind.

Tip: Actually writing information you want to remember can be a tremendous help. Therefore, instruct your telephone receptionist to *write down* the caller's name as soon as he or she gives it. (Keep a scratch pad near the phone.) With the name in writing, it will be very easy for your receptionist to refer to the patient by name again during the conversation. Plus, your receptionist can forward the call to someone else, without having to ask, "What was your name again?"

3.   *Repeat* what you want to remember. When in school, you were probably taught to memorize by repeating a poem, date, or the alphabet again and again. Repetition improves recall. Think of how many times you see the same ads. After enough exposure to an ad, you're likely to remember it—sometimes word for word.

4.   *Associate* what you want to remember. One of the best associative devices is rhyme. Remember these?

- In fourteen hundred ninety two, Columbus sailed the ocean blue.
- Thirty days hath September, April, June, and November.
- *I* before *E*, except after *C*.

People rarely forget anything they can manage to rhyme. Examples of how you could use rhyme to remember patient's names:

- Eddie Garber is a barber.
- Melodie Kraft is really daft.
- Dominick Quinn has a double chin.
- Jill Malone is thin as a bone.
- Laura Sachs is a battle-ax.

5.   *Verbalize* what you're trying to remember. If you want to remember a patient's name, say it aloud when you meet her. *Example:* "Nice to meet you, *Mrs. O'Toole.*"

Tip: If you're trying to remember all or part of a speech, there is no substitute for reciting it aloud. A friend, mirror, or tape recorder should help.

HOW TO REMEMBER PATIENTS' NAMES AND FACES

You see so many different people in the typical day that it can be quite a job to keep everyone straight. However, one of the best tools for helping you remember patients doesn't rely on memory at all—it's a photograph.

Why not take an instant photograph of every patient, and make it part of his file? That way, you and your staff can review the pictures each morning for the patients you will see that day. By being able to link the face and name, your receptionist can greet patients by name, and your clinical assistant will know who's who in your reception area when she goes to get the next patient.

This is a terrific way to make patients feel you care about them. And, new staff members can use the photos to learn to identify patients before they meet them.

Beyond this, there is more you can do if you're having trouble remembering names:

1.   Pay close attention when you're introduced to a patient or when you greet him for the first time. If you don't hear the patient's name clearly, say so right away, and ask to have it repeated.

2.   Be more observant. Concentrate during the introduction, and don't allow your mind to wander. Observe the person carefully. Get a distinct impression of him. Try to discover outstanding physical or other distinguishing characteristics of the person, especially of his face. For example, note whether the patient is tall, short, overweight, thin, the length and color of his hair, the shape of his face, his complexion, etc.

3.   Repeat the person's name silently to yourself several times. Also say the person's name at least once out loud when you meet him.

4.   If possible, associate the patient's name with a rhyme or some other device.

5.   Write the patient's name within 24 hours of meeting him. Look at the written name, and recall his face.

Tip: If meeting someone at a seminar or other program where nametags are worn, make a conscious effort to say the person's name and read his name tag at the same time. That way, you will both visualize and verbalize the name.

HOW TO REMEMBER A LIST

An acronym is a word made up of the first letters of several other words. For example:

Acronym:	Stands For:
UNESCO	United Nations Educational, Scientific, and Cultural Organization
AWOL	Absent Without Official Leave
RADAR	Radio Detecting and Ranging
SCUBA	Self-Contained Underwater Breathing Apparatus
NATO	North Atlantic Treaty Organization

Use acronyms to help you remember lists. *Example:* the acronym LADDER will help you remember this list of six steps for improving your listening skills:

L—Look at the person.

A—Ask questions.

D—Don't change the subject.

D—Don't interrupt.

E—Emotions—check them.

R—Responsively listen.

Tip: Sometimes you'll have to change an item on a list to make it fit into your acronym. However, if no acronym works, create a *phrase* to remember the first letter of each word in an important list. For example, in music, the notes on the lines of the treble staff are E, G, B, D, and F. Music teachers often coach their students to remember these notes with the phrase: Every Good Boy Deserves Fudge.

HOW TO REMEMBER A JOKE

A well-timed joke can put a nervous patient at ease or break the ice at a tense meeting, *if* you remember it. *Five tips:*

1.   Concentrate when you first hear the joke. Pay attention to the key words, phrases, intonation, gestures, and emphasis used by the joke teller.

2.   Write the joke soon after you hear it, keeping it as short as possible. Read it silently several times.

3.   Practice the joke aloud.

4.   Categorize the joke so you can remember it at the right time. Examples of joke categories: political jokes, cab driver jokes, in-law jokes.

5.   Associate a key word or phrase with the joke so you'll remember it. For example, the following joke might be remembered by associating the phrase *brother-in-law* with the key word *diamond:*

My brother-in-law says he's a diamond cutter. He mows the lawn at Shea Stadium.

HOW TO "REMEMBER" AND USE
PATIENT'S NEWS

You can build tremendous goodwill with patients if you can ask them how a daughter in college is doing or how a recent trip to Europe was. The patient is always so impressed when we care enough to remember these little details they tell us. But with so many people coming and going from a busy practice each day, it's nearly impossible to remember personal information about every person.

Fortunately, you don't have to remember. There's an easy way to record this sort of information.

The most important rule of thumb is to keep personal news of this nature separate from your clinical notes. Develop a form, like the one below, for recording personal notes about patients. Keep one in every patient's file, perhaps right in the front:

PERSONAL INFORMATION FORM

NAME: _____

| Info: | Date: | Heard by: |

_____

_____

_____

Have staff members date and initial any notes they add to the form, so you know who heard the comment, and when. Glance at the form a few moments before you see the patient. That way, you can say, "Dorothy tells me that you were planning to enter Fifi into a dog show last month. How did it go?

Tip: If the patient marvels at your astounding memory, you might simply suggest, "I always remember what my favorite patients tell me."

C · H · A · P · T · E · R   9-4

Composing Effective Letters for Your Practice

I deally, letters you send should be concise, crisp, and professional in appearance. While it's important to avoid misspellings, improper usage, smudges, poorly aligned margins, etc., such beauty is only skin deep. The heart of any letter is its message and the words you use to convey it.

20 LETTER-WRITING TIPS

These 20 tips will help you compose better letters and improve those that you currently use in your practice:

1. Send letters immediately after the event that occasions it. A note of congratulations, welcome to the practice, condolence, or thanks becomes diluted if you don't write it promptly.

2. Make your first sentence work hard. The reader wants to know at once what your letter's about. Tell him. *Examples:*

> The sad news of your father's death reached us this morning.

> When one of our patients recommends us to a friend, we consider it a high compliment.

> You're cordially invited to attend the Family Practice open house next Sunday afternoon, May 12, to be held from 2:30–5:00 p.m.

> Dr. Hubler says he's delighted to be your guest speaker at the Kiwanis Club luncheon next Tuesday, February 7.

3. Choose a salutation and closing that express the same level of formality between the writer and the addressee. *Examples:*

Relationship:	Salutation:	Complimentary Closing:
Very Formal	Dear Sir/Gentlemen/Mesdames	Very truly yours
Formal	Dear Ms. Lowenstein	Sincerely yours
Informal	My dear Jeffrey/Dear Jeff	Cordially/Best wishes

4.   Use the reader's full name in the salutation if you're unsure of his or her gender. For example, "Dear Chris Brown." If you don't know the addressee's name, such as when writing to Editor, Customer Service Manager, etc., use "Dear Sir or Madam" or "To Whom It May Concern."

5.   Use the title *Ms.* when writing to a woman, unless she is a doctor, or has expressed a preference for *Mrs.* or *Miss.*

6.   Avoid adding a postscript (PS). Doing so may suggest that the body of the letter was badly organized.

Tip: There is one notable exception. Postscripts can boost the effectiveness of a sales letter. For example, you might use a well-placed postscript when sending letters to colleagues seeking donations on behalf of a charity.

7.   Be specific so your reader will know what you mean:

Vague:	Specific:
Your recent letter/check	Your letter of July 28 Your July 28 check for $84.50
Your upcoming appointment	Your appointment for July 24 at 1:45
Call if you have questions	Call Kitty Patterson, our office manager

8.   Add the personal touch when you can. Call the reader by name. Use pronouns, such as you, your, we, our, and me, as you would in speaking. *Examples:*

> We heard today that your son, Peter, received an appointment to West Point, and that he'll be heading east this fall.

> Though we'll miss you here, Mr. Allen, we offer to you our sincere best wishes for every success and happiness in Montreal.

9.   End the letter when you've said all you need to say. Avoid trite, unnecessary formalities such as "Please give this matter careful consideration" and "I hope this answers your question."

10.   Be careful with humor, especially sarcasm, or the reader may take you the wrong way. Some examples to avoid:

If you don't pay your son's bill now, he will be a juvenile 'delinquent' in our book.

Dr. Hunter enjoys hurting people—ha-ha!

11.   Use typographic devices for clarity and emphasis:

• Put key ideas into indented paragraphs.

• Underline, but with restraint. Too much underlining is ineffective, and makes reading harder.

• Number or letter your points. Or, use "bullets." Just type the letter *o*, and fill it in with a black felt-tip pen: •.

12.   Avoid legalese and bureacratic language:

Legalese:	Down-To-Earth Language:
The reasons are fourfold.	There are four reasons.
Gratis	Free
Thence	Therefore
Visitation	Visit
Terminate	End
Affirmative, negative	Yes, no
Impact on (as a verb)	Affect

13.   Choose an appropriate tone for the message of the letter. In general, friendliness and informality are most appropriate for a note of thanks or congratulations. *Example:*

We've just learned of the safe arrival on this earth of Holly Tucker. We know how happy you and Catherine must be.

Collection letters, on the other hand, require a very formal tone. *Example:*

Please mail your check for $197.50 today in the enclosed envelope.

14.   Write from the reader's point of view. For example:

Writer-Centered:	Reader-Centered:
We'd like to have you send us 50 copies of your pamphlet, *Welcome to Our Practice.*	Your pamphlet, *Welcome to our Practice,* is one of the finest patient information booklets available. Will you please send us 50 copies for our patients?

15. Keep opening and closing paragraphs short, from one to five lines. Short paragraphs invite reading, add punch, and make a stronger impression.

16. Check the length of your sentences. Those limited to 15–20 words have the highest readability. Use shorter sentences, too, to avoid monotony.

Tip: An interesting study found that as sentence length increases, fewer readers understand what the sentence means. The study's results:

Sentence Length:	Percent of Readers who Understood:
6–8 words	100
15 words	90
20 words	75
25 words	61
30 words	47

Tip: Readability of letters is influenced by much more than simply the number of words in your sentences. For more information on this, see, "How to Measure Readability," below.

17. Avoid negative language. *Example:*

Negative:	Positive:
The office is not open on Sunday.	Our office hours are 8:00–4:30 Monday through Friday. We also offer Saturday hours from 10:00–2:00, for your convenience.

18. It is appropriate and often highly effective to send handwritten informal notes. However, do so only if you can write legibly.

19. Abolish confusing words and jargon from your letters:

Jargon:	Clear:
Optimum	Best
Judgmentally	I think
Interface	Discuss, meet with, work with
Viable	Practical, workable
Implement	Carry out
Utilize	Use

Jargon:	Clear:
Facilitate	Make easy
Transpires	Happens
Endeavor	Try

20.   Be enthusiastic whenever possible. Compare these two letters, written for the same occasion:

Blah:	Upbeat:
Dr. Saperstone is pleased to have the opportunity to speak to your tenth graders as requested in your letter of October 14. He promises to be there promptly at 9:05.	Thank you! With pleasure Dr. Saperstone accepts your invitation to speak to your tenth grade class. He asks that you tell your students he will be there at 9:05 next Friday morning, and that he doesn't plan to put anybody to sleep.

HOW TO MEASURE READABILITY

As already suggested, the number of words in your sentences will strongly affect reader comprehension. However, a well-written sentence of only 15 words can still be challenging for some readers.

To do a simple readability test:

1.   Choose a typical 150-word passage from one of your letters.

2.   Count the number of one-syllable words in the passage.

3.   Divide that number by 10.

4.   Subtract the result from 20.

5.   The number you get should tell you the approximate reading level of your writing. For example, a 3 would mean a third grade reading level, a 7 would mean a seventh grade reading level, a 16 would mean a reading level in the senior year of college.

Example: Suppose that you find 50 one-syllable words in your 150-words passage. Divide that number (50) by 10, getting 5. Then subtract 5 from 20, giving you a reading level of 15. That's college junior level (which is probably too high for most of your letters.)

Tip: This readability formula, called FORCAST, is relatively simple to use. But if you're looking for an easier rule of thumb, keep sentences to an average of no more than 16 words, and word length to an average 1.5 syllables. Avoid sentences that are more than 22 words long. They're difficult to follow and can usually be shortened. And, remember that many U.S. newspapers are written at about a seventh grade reading level. You *can* write simply without insulting your readers.

Tip: Do a readability test on your practice brochures, patient newsletters, and other patient education literature, to be sure your materials are easily comprehended.

ALL ABOUT PRACTICE LETTER BOOKS

If you lack the time or writing ability to develop dazzling letters, there are many good sources of prototype letters that you can buy, adapt, and use. Although the vast majority of materials are written for any type of business, there are some developed especially for use in professional practices. Keep your eye on publishers' catalogs, and even your local bookseller, to see what's available for you.

Tip: As well, there are a number of prototype letters in this book, which can be very helpful in your practice management efforts. Check the index for a directory of these letters.

A Cherry Hill, NJ practice suggests developing your own letter book, keeping copies of your own best letters organized and at your fingertips, for future reference. How? The office manager makes an extra copy of all office correpondence that might be used again. She files these in a looseleaf notebook, with index dividers for sections, such as:

- New patient welcome letters.
- Financial arrangements.
- Insurance claims processing.
- Notes to other doctors.
- Treatment completed letters.
- Employee letters.
- Collection notices.
- Recall letters.

According to the office manager, composing a letter book for the practice in this way can be very helpful, for two reasons. "Often after I've spent the time and mental energy composing a letter, I can adapt it to another similar situation or need, thus saving my time," she says. "And, I can easily track any correspondence through the year, without having to remember a patient's name to look in his file," she adds.

Tip: If you develop your own letter book, be sure to review it at the end of each year. Discard unimportant or unusable letters.

How to Keep Track of Hard-to-Keep-Track-of Information

H ave you ever missed an important deadline, or forgotten an important occasion? Have you wondered where to keep the airline ticket and hotel confirmation for an upcoming continuing education trip, or a birthday card for a special colleague or patient that you're not going to send for two weeks? Have you misplaced someone's business card or the brochure about a seminar you'd like to attend? Did a patient tell you of an upcoming event in his life—such as getting married—but you missed the chance to send a congratulatory note or card because you forgot about it?

Below are two systems to help you keep track of these and similar hard-to-keep-track-of items:

SYSTEM 1: ESTABLISHING A FILE FOLDER SYSTEM FOR DEADLINES AND PAPERS

To put this system into effect, you'll need 31 sturdy file folders, a convenient place to keep them, and about five minutes of your business assistant's time at the start of each day. Mark the tabs on the folders with the days of the month, 1–31.

When you have a due date or an occasion to remember, an airline ticket, or a birthday card, file the item or a written reminder under the appropriate day of the month. Note the month that applies to the message or document in the upper right-hand corner. (Use a Post-It note if you don't want to mar the paper with such a notation.)

Example: If your staff will be attending a seminar on February 16, file all the pertinent details—the seminar brochure, the written confirmation, hotel reservations, airline tickets, etc.—in the file numbered "16." Mark "February" in the right-hand corner of each paper.

Tip: If an assignment is particularly difficult, or requires extra time to complete, file it a few days *ahead* of the deadline, to give yourself ample time. For example, if you need to enroll in the seminar by a certain date, put the registration form in a file several days ahead of that date, to allow for postal delivery.

All your assistant needs to do is to check the file for each date on that morning. For instance, on January 29, she would pull the file marked "29." Then, she would quickly run through it for any notes that apply to January (they will be marked as such in the upper right-hand corner), pull them out, and refile the others.

Tip: On Friday, have your assistant also check the file folders for Saturday and Sunday, since you won't want to miss anything that falls on the weekend. The same is true for days before holidays and vacations.

As your assistant sorts through the notes, have her discard anything already completed. Also instruct her to act quickly upon any project that needs prompt attention, and to refer appropriate items to others.

Tip: Some things must be remembered on a continuous basis—for instance, paying the rent on the first of each month, making the lease payment for equipment on the 15th, etc. Mark these notes on a colored paper, and write "continuous" in the upper right-hand corner. That way, notes that must remain in the folder continuously are easily recognizable.

SYSTEM 2: USE A CARD FILE TO TRACK
IMPORTANT CONTACTS

An alphabetical card file system (or a computerized file) can be a valuable means of keeping in touch with important contacts. *Tips:*

• *Create a cross-indexing system.* That way, you can locate each person both by name or by company, in case you should forget one or the other.

• *Create two cards for each person.* On the first—a white card—type the person's name and title on the top line, followed by the company or practice name, address, phone number, and relevant notes. On the second card—a colored card—type the company name on the top line, followed by that person's name (plus all others who you've had contact with in the company or practice). It is not necessary to repeat all the information which appears on the individual's card, since that can be retrieved if you need it.

• *Within your system, also create "event" cards.* You may come back from a meeting with several new contacts—speakers, colleagues, consultants, sales representatives, vendors, etc. Perhaps you'll associate someone with the meeting, but not remember his or her name or company/practice when you want to contact him later.

An event card could be in a third color, and labeled with the name and date of each event. For example: "New York State Association Meeting—May 199–." Then, list each of the contacts you made at the meeting below, in alphabetical order, cross-referencing to the "individual" and "company" cards you will also create for them (see above).

C · H · A · P · T · E · R   9-6

85 Ways to Save Time and Increase Your Personal Productivity

Do you find yourself frequently running behind schedule? Or, do you feel like you're constantly treading water in your practice, spending all your time and energy just trying to stay afloat? If so, you're having problems managing your time.

Procrastination, poor organization, and other bad habits all play a part in poor time management. Below are 85 specific things you can do to keep on schedule and get more done every day:

1. Admit when you're wasting time.

2. Handle each piece of paper on your desk only once. If you can't, do something to move the project ahead each time you pick it up.

3. Buy a speed-dialer/memory telephone for your desk, that stores frequently called numbers.

4. Identify and abolish unnecessary interruptions from staff, colleagues, and patients. (See "Avoiding Unnecessary Interruptions," pages 69–70.)

5. Improve your dictation. Keep the machine running even if you don't have something to say. That can force you to think faster. For more information, see "Mastering Machine Dictation Saves Time and Money," pages 500–501.

6. Get off mailing lists when information no longer contributes to your objectives. Contact mailers directly. Or, ask the Direct Mail/Marketing Association (New York, NY) for a Mail Preference Service form. Complete and return the form. The association will send your name and address to its members, who will remove your name if it is on their mailing lists.

7. Learn to skim books. Approach them as you would newspapers. Start by reading the "headlines" on the book jacket or in the table of contents.

Then glance through the book quickly. Make good use of the preface and summaries.

8.   Use small bits of spare time more productively:

•   What you can do in *five* minutes: Handwrite thank-you notes to two or three patients who have made referrals. Make a lunch date with a colleague or friend.

•   What you can do in *ten* minutes: Clean up your desk. Read a short article or skim a longer one and mark parts for later study. Give praise to an outstanding employee.

•   What you can do in *30* minutes: Hold a staff meeting. Go through backed-up journals and magazines. Interview a job applicant. Chart out a long-term project you've been putting off (patient newsletter, personnel manual, office re-decoration.)

9.   Write replies to letters on the letters themselves. Keep a photo-copy for your records.

10.   Double up. Many small tasks can be done simultaneously. For ex-ample, sign routine correspondence while waiting for a telephone connection. Or, listen to an informative cassette tape while driving to and from your office.

11.   Have rubber stamps or printed forms made to say things you fre-quently write.

12.   Call. Don't write.

13.   Buy frequently used items in quantity.

14.   Have your most organized and efficient employee be responsible for making your appointment schedule.

15.   Hire an office manager to take over many of your administrative duties.

16.   Have your business assistant prepare daily "To Do" lists for you each day, which outline your goals for the day. Check to see how many items still remain undone at the end of each day. Give yourself a score. Aim for "no miss" days in which every item is crossed off.

17.   Rely on professionals and convenience services when possible. Use an accountant, pick-up and delivery service, travel agent, cleaning per-son, answering service, messenger, carpenter—anyone who can do some-thing you'd otherwise do yourself.

18.   Have your business assistant open, screen, and organize your in-coming mail. See Appendix 1-A, "Checklist for Handling Incoming Mail," page 513.

19.   When traveling to a conference, patronize airlines that offer one-stop check-in for round trip and connecting boarding passes.

20.   Have your business assistant or office manager record a daily report on a cassette tape that you can listen to while commuting to and from your office. Ask her to discuss anything she'd normally bring up at a morning meeting—a recap of the day's events, your next day's schedule, etc. Meet briefly in the morning, only to discuss important matters.

21.   Hold your morning staff meeting standing, rather than sitting.

22.   Organize your storage closets and cabinets. Keep frequently used supplies low and accessible. Store less used items on higher shelves or out of the way. Do not stack more than three pieces that are not a set on top of each other. Immediately assign a place for any new items you buy. Have a place for everything. Keep everything in its place.

23.   Clean off your desk at the end of each day.

24.   If you attend out-of-town conferences frequently, keep a set of basic toiletries in your suitcase.

25.   Organize your office library. Basic categories might include reference, technical, and practice management.

26.   Occasionally come to work 15–20 minutes early.

27.   When making major purchases for your practice, do your comparison shopping by phone.

28.   Establish a "quiet hour" in your office, setting aside some time each day to think and plan.

29.   Use rolling carts or mobile caddies to move supplies and equipment from one room to another.

30.   Keep books, files, and other information you use most often at your fingertips.

31.   Assemble all needed information and materials *before* sitting down to write a letter, make a phone call, etc. Have your business assistant help you get organized.

32.   Anticipate and avoid the "tyranny of urgency." Don't let the immediate situation affect your ability to turn your attention to long-range planning and the accomplishment of long-range goals.

33.   If necessary, physically remove yourself from distraction. The reading rooms and study cubicles in public libraries are conducive to concentration for big projects.

34.   Develop a practice brochure or fact sheet to answer routine questions patients ask you.

35.   Set a time limit on certain activities, such as meetings, reading, and phone calls. Use a kitchen timer if necessary. Or, buy a wrist watch with a built-in timer.

36.   If you wear eyeglasses, keep an extra pair in a convenient place.

37.   Set your watch three minutes fast.

38.   Buy a Swiss Army knife for your office. It will save your searching for the right tool to open packages, pry off tight lids, etc.

39.   Set up "availability hours" for your staff. An open door policy can be abused.

40.   Keep a well-stocked first-aid kit in your office.

41.   Ask married patients if they'd like to bring a spouse to large case presentations. This will save your having to re-explain or answer questions at a later date. It may also improve your rate of case acceptance.

42.   Write form letters for certain occasions, such as a welcome to new practitioners in your area or regrets for not being able to give to a charitable organization. Buy a book of prototype letters to be used for such occasions. Or, develop your own letter book.

43.   Keep a set of clothes and toiletries in your office so you can go right to after-work activities and meetings directly from your office.

44.   Eliminate *things* as well as tasks. Throw away anything you possibly can. The less you have, the less you have to care for.

45.   Get a telephone directory for all cities in your geographic area.

46.   Use a postage meter. Or, buy an accurate postage scale and a large supply of stamps.

47.   Get a big wastebasket.

48.   Carry a small notepad and pen in your pocket to jot down notes and ideas.

49.   Set daily, weekly, monthly, yearly, and lifetime goals.

50.   Establish priorities for paperwork. Divide all tasks into A, B, and C categories. Concentrate on the A's; try to eliminate or delegate the C's.

51.   Say *no*.

52.   Deal with unpleasantness directly. Mentally picture yourself doing things you've been putting off. Then start doing them. If you often procrastinate, ask, "What am I trying to avoid?" Then try to confront it directly.

53.   Don't rely on memory. Write it down.

54.   Know your limits. Stop doing a task if you begin to lose your effectiveness.

55. Don't assume.

56. Mourn your failures, and move on. Don't cloud your thinking with guilt or regrets.

57. Put signs in your office or on your desk to remind you of your goals.

58. Be selective. Ask, "Would anything terrible happen if I didn't do this?" If the answer is *no,* don't do it.

59. Set deadlines for yourself and your staff.

60. Solve recurring problems, once and for all.

61. Reward yourself every time you cut out a time-waster.

62. Observe the "80–20" principle that says that 80% of your results are accomplished in just 20% of your time. Identify your constructive 20%. Use those peak hours to do your most important work.

63. Finish what you're doing.

64. Aim to be early, not on time.

65. Delegate, delegate, delegate.

66. Plan each patient's treatment to accomplish as much as possible during each appointment.

67. Schedule similar kinds of treatment during consecutive appointments during the day so you'll need less time to prepare and switch gears.

68. Train your staff to perform all expanded duties permitted by your professional association.

69. Do much of your thinking on paper. Keep notes in an idea file.

70. Try not to think of work during weekends or family time. Use time off to recharge your battery.

71. Reduce reading time by using summaries and abstracts of longer works.

72. Think before you dial the phone. Ask, "Is calling the most time-effective method of accomplishing this task?" Plan what you'll say, using a written outline.

73. Don't "hold" on the phone for long periods. Either refuse to be put on hold and call back later, or set a limit on how many minutes you'll wait. Keep some paperwork handy so you won't just waste time doodling or staring into space.

74. Confirm your travel itinerary before you leave.

75. If you spend a great deal of time on the phone, buy a headset. That way, your hands will be free to do other tasks while you're talking.

76.   If the party you call is out, leave a *precise* message or question you need answered.

77.   Don't mix business with pleasure calls. If a business associate starts socializing, just say, "I'd love to talk but I'm swamped at the moment. How about lunch next week?"

78.   Log your phone calls to get a handle on your own phone habits and time wasters.

79.   Author and consultant Stephanie Winston suggests sorting every incoming piece of paper by "TRAF": *T*oss, *R*efer, *A*ct, or *F*ile. Here's how:

Toss: The Toss file is your wastebasket. Use it liberally.

Refer: The Refer file is for items you refer to others. Don't let these papers pile up and get in your way. Instruct your business assistant to empty your Refer file daily and see that these papers are delivered or mailed to the appropriate people.

Act: The Act file is for papers that require you to *do* something. Schedule regular time to work on your Act file. Once you've done what's needed, refile the paper in one of the other three files.

File: Establish a box for File items. Instruct your business assistant to file these papers daily.

At the end of each day, your goal should be to have all papers in their proper receptacles. The result will be less confusion, greater efficiency, and a clean desk.

80.   Add more alphabetical breakdowns to your patient files. (Shoot for about 100 for a large practice.) This will speed filing tasks.

81.   Have blank practice postcards printed, with your return address. These cut in half the time needed to write to companies for information/catalogs/samples and can be used in dozens of ways to send short notes to patients and colleagues.

82.   Have your bank automatically pay routine practice bills.

83.   Listen carefully and follow directions.

84.   Establish relationships with supply house sales representatives. Become a regular customer.

85.   Ask, "What is the best use of my time right now?"

C · H · A · P · T · E · R   9-7

How to Get More from Continuing Education Programs

R arely a day will go by that you don't receive some sort of flyer or brochure in the mail announcing a new seminar, conference, or workshop
that claims it will further your education and enhance your professional and
personal success, breadth, happiness, and/or proficiency. Choosing the right
programs for your needs, and then getting the most you can out of them, is
often confusing and difficult. Obviously, because of the great expense and
effort needed for continuing education, and because of the fantastic potential
benefits, it pays to put some extra thought and attention into this area.

DECIDING WHICH PROGRAMS ARE RIGHT FOR YOU

It's very difficult to get a good sense of a program's worth by relying
entirely on the promotional hype. Clearly, reading the literature is a good
place to begin, but there are several additional steps you should take before
mailing in your registration. In particular:

1.   Know what you really want and need. Then, assess whether the
seminar is tailored to *your* particular needs, goals, and practice. For example,
it probably won't make sense to enroll in a practice management seminar
geared to a $750,000+/year practice, if you gross only $90,000 per year.
Similarly, you probably won't want to register for a program that will focus on
aggressive practice marketing strategies, if you don't now and never will feel
comfortable using them.

Tip: If you can't find a seminar that truly fits your needs and situation,
perhaps a practice management consultation or other kind of individualized
instruction can help you best achieve your goals.

2.   Assess the longevity and research behind the program. Check the
credentials of the speaker and the seminar promoter. A good program offers
proven, *field- and practice-tested* ideas, not abstract, unsupported theories.

3.   Check references. Especially when contemplating participation at a multi-day, high-tuition seminar, ask the sponsor to provide you with the names of other practitioners who have completed the program. Call several who have had six months or longer to digest the information, try the ideas, and measure their results.

4.   Estimate the actual cost of the seminar, and what you stand to gain. Actual cost includes more than the registration fee. Also account for travel expenses, materials, time away from the practice (lost production), staff salaries and expenses, and the time, money, and effort you'll need to put forth *afterwards* to share material with staff and put the ideas to use.

PREPARING FOR AND FOLLOWING UP AFTER SEMINARS: A CHECKLIST

You'll get so much more out of the programs you attend if you're well prepared for them, and if you organize your thoughts and notes afterwards.

Before You Go:

• Read up on the subject. Ask yourself, "What do I now know?" and "What would I like to reinforce/learn?"

• Plan questions to raise and bring relevant materials to share. As well, bring helpful study aids—a tape recorder and tapes, pens, file folder, etc.

Tip: Don't assume that the seminar will provide you with good writing paper for notes, or good pens. Many hotel meeting rooms provide no writing materials, or only small pencils and memo pads— which makes note-taking difficult.

• Wear comfortable yet professional clothing to the program. Bring along a jacket or sweater that can be removed. Meeting room temperatures are very often too hot or cold.

• Study advance materials provided by the sponsor. Complete any forms or tests provided.

• Free your mind of current tasks and problems that someone else can handle while you're gone. Rule out phone calls from home, except for emergencies.

At the Program:

• Walk into the seminar room with the attitude of *wanting* to participate. Choose a seat near the front of the room.

• Listen actively and well, to understand and absorb the information, and to evaluate the subjects and speakers. (For specific how-to listening tips, see, "How Listening Better Can Reduce Management Errors," pages 459–464.)

• Speak up with enthusiasm. Be brief, make one point at a time, and relate it to others. Doing this early on encourages active participation throughout the program.

• Discuss seminar topics with other participants during the breaks and meals.

Tip: Eat sensible meals and avoid alcohol during the program. Heavy meals and drinking may make you sluggish.

After the Program:

• Report on the seminar to your staff, partners, and associates who didn't attend.

• Read support materials provided or suggested at the program.

• Review your notes and reorganize them. Keep these, with handouts, in a convenient order and location for future use. Use a ring binder or folder for each seminar you attend, and label by title and date.

Tip: The IRS is continuing its efforts to distinguish between real and "sham" professional seminars conducted at popular resorts. If you're ever audited and have deducted seminar tuition and expenses on your tax return, you may be asked to produce the notes you took at the program. Therefore, to play it safe, keep a copy of the seminar program/agenda with your notes and receipts. As you take your meeting notes, remember that they may be reviewed someday by the IRS. Make them good, and curb the urge to doodle.

• Keep handy the speaker's name and address, if given, so you can ask questions by phone or mail as they occur to you.

BUDDY SYSTEM ENABLES YOU TO DOUBLE YOUR EFFORTS

When attending large conferences, there's usually more going on than you can absorb. Unfortunately, you can't be in two places at once—or can you?

A clever strategy is to team up with another doctor at the conference to share information and cover more ground. That way, when you want to hear two concurrent sessions, you can tape-record the session you attend, and swap tapes with your study partner, who attended and taped the other sessions. You might also photocopy and swap your notes and seminar handouts.

Tip: Be sure the conference sponsors and speakers allow tape-recording of sessions and photocopying of handouts.

Best strategy: Devise a game plan with your study partner as soon as you receive the meeting schedule, so you can decide *in advance* who will cover which sessions.

17 WAYS TO ELIMINATE TRAVEL HASSLES

Travelling to an out-of-town continuing education program can be wearing under the best conditions, but even more so when you're poorly prepared, unorganized, and frenzied. To eliminate "travel hassles" and have a more pleasant trip, follow these 17 tips. You might even find yourself looking forward to your next out-of-town meeting!

1.   Find a sympatico, service-oriented travel agent and stick with him or her. This person should be in tune with your needs and responsive to your calls, and should also have his finger on the pulse of new travel options and deals. Ideally, it is best to work with an agency that offers service beyond the ordinary. For instance, can the agency help you secure passports and visas? Provide information on foreign currency? Deliver tickets to your office? Advise you about ground transportation at out-of-town airports? Custom-design a trip itinerary tailored to your specific needs and desires? Referral is the best way to find such an agent.

Tip: Open a business account with your travel agency, to simplify future travel arrangements. Be sure that they have in your file a record of your airline frequent flyer and hotel frequent guest numbers, as well as your particular travel preferences and needs (such as an aisle or window seat, smoking or no-smoking section, special dietary needs, etc.).

2.   Leave a copy of your written travel itinerary with your staff, listing flight times, airlines, flight numbers, and dates. Add your hotel's phone number and the best times to call, if they need to reach you.

3.   Leave a "to do" list of projects your staff can undertake while you're gone, and the order they should tackle them.

4.   Check a newspaper or the national weather service to make sure your meeting wardrobe will be appropriate. Some travel agencies also provide weather information, upon request.

5.   Make sure your receptionist knows whom to call if patients have emergencies while you're away. Also be sure she knows whom to contact if your furnace dies or plumbing springs a leak.

6.   Label an empty #10 envelope with the dates and occasion of the trip, and carry it with you at all times. Use it to keep your receipts in one

place. List all travel expenses and your notes about them (a travel expense diary) on the back of the envelope or on a piece of paper inside. Be sure you don't overlook small, unreceipted expenses, such as tips to bellhops, parking meters, doormen, etc. After you return home, add up all of your expenses and write the total on the front of the envelope. This should be sufficient documentation of your trip expenses, for tax reporting purposes.

7.   Don't advertise your empty house when you travel. Luggage ID tags will return a lost bag to you, and should be used. However, write your name and *office* (not home) address on the tag.

Tip: Buy a luggage tag with a snap-on leather or vinyl cover that hides your ID information from casual onlookers.

8.   When booking hotels, do all you can to avoid being bumped by over-booking. First, have your travel agent give you your official hotel confirmation number. In the end, that number is the only meaningful proof of a reservation. Second, guarantee payment of your room in advance. Give the hotel your credit card number for billing, even if you aren't sure you'll show up. You can cancel your reservation without penalty at most hotels if you notify them in advance, usually a couple of days ahead. Therefore, ask the hotel clerk to tell you the deadline for cancellations when you book your room, and get his or her name. Third, if you still find that the hotel gave away your room, do whatever you must to get another one. Insist that it find you another comparable room in another hotel. If you arrived by public transportation, have the desk clerk call you a cab, pay for it, carry your bags, etc. If he or she finds you another room that costs more than the one you reserved, insist that the hotel pay the difference.

9.   Ask for late departure checkout when you arrive at your hotel. Your request is more likely to be granted early than in the last-minute rush. Also ask for express checkout to speed your departure. If not available, check out early in the morning. Tell the desk clerk that you'll keep your key until your actual departure later that day.

10.   Play it safe while at the conference. Avoid taking unnecessary valuables with you to the meeting, and make good use of the hotel safe deposit boxes for those you must bring. Use travellers checks instead of cash, and leave a copy of your check numbers with your staff. If travelling to an unfamiliar city, check with the desk clerk or concierge before heading out, to learn about unsavory districts and other potential dangers. Burglar-proof your hotel room while you're away from it by asking the maid service to make up your room early. Check your windows to see that they are secure. Then, when you leave the room, keep the TV or radio on, and put the "Do-Not-Disturb" sign on the door. Know where the hotel emergency exit routes are on your floor. Use the chain or double-bolt lock on your door when in your room.

11.   Rent a car only when it adds convenience to the trip. It's often faster and less stressful to take public transportation. When you do rent a car, get a good map of the area before you leave home, and plan your route. Maps that rental companies give are sometimes limited.

Tip: When arranging a rental car, ask for the smallest one you can tolerate. Chances are it won't be available. If the agency doesn't have it, it will give you a larger one at the smaller car price.

12.   Review your equipment needs before going to trade shows. If you anticipate purchasing a large item, do some homework. Read up on the latest models. Measure the size of the space allocated for the new piece. Make a list of must-have and must-avoid features. (For more information on purchasing equipment, see, "Making Major Equipment Purchases on Your Own Terms," pages 199–204, and tips 13 and 14, below.)

13.   If you have a program listing exhibitors of the type of equipment you're shopping for, drop them a note saying you'll be at the meeting and explaining your interest. You'll be amazed at the attention you'll received by putting booth reps on notice that you're a serious shopper.

14.   Don't wander aimlessly through exhibit halls. Locate the booths of must-see vendors, and go there directly. Leave impulse-shopping for later.

15.   If you plan to eat in a fine restaurant while at the meeting, make reservations in advance. If there's a chance others will join you unexpectedly, make your reservation for two more persons that you expect. Restaurants can always pare down from six to four at the last moment, but obtaining a larger table after reserving a smaller one is often impossible. To be courteous, call the restaurant at least four hours before dinner, if your reservation changes.

16.   Plan a sensible bedtime, and stick to it. If you have an 8:00 a.m. seminar, get to bed early. As a rule of thumb, it usually takes 10 hours of rest in a hotel to equal seven hours in your own bed.

17.   Buy tape recordings, if available, of those programs you enjoyed, and those you missed. Share these later with partners, associates, and appropriate staff members.

ACTION STEPS TO REDUCE AIR TRAVEL PROBLEMS

Air travel is frequently delayed, and therefore can be the cause of many problems and a great deal of stress. While delays are often unavoidable, there are a few things you can do to make your own air travel go more smoothly:

1.   Book your flight as soon as you possibly can. You may need to book or even buy your tickets in advance—often 30 or even 60 days ahead—to take

advantage of some reduced fares. Keep your eye on the ads and instruct your travel agent to advise you of the best possible fares and terms.

2. When possible, tell your travel agent that you want to arrive at your destination at an off-hour, to avoid runway congestion, traffic jams, and hotel delays.

3. Obtain seat assignments and boarding passes when you make your reservation. Also ask for specially-prepared foods if they will be needed, such as diabetic or kosher meals.

4. If you must make connecting flights, try to stay with the same airline. That way, if your first flight is delayed, there's a greater chance that the second flight will be held. It's also more likely that your arrival and departure gates will be near one another, and that airline staff will be present to advise you about connections.

5. Always take with you on the plane those items that you can't afford to be separated from. These would include medications, eyeglasses or contact lens materials, essential notes for your meeting, your hotel location and reservation information, valuables, and money.

6. Confirm flights in advance as your travel agent advises you. Also check flight status before going to the airport.

7. Bring reading material or light work that you can do in the airport and on the plane, in case of delays.

8. Do all you can to avoid being bumped from your flight. Your best protection is to arrive at the airport early, because the last passengers to check in are usually the first to be bumped on overbooked flights. However, if you do end up being bumped, and you are dissatisfied with the airline's offer of compensation, you may be able to pursue matters further. Address your inquiry to: Director, Community and Consumer Affairs, Department of Transportation, 400 Seventh St. S.W., Washington, D.C. 20590.

Tip: It can be very worthwhile to pursue help from this agency. When an American doctor was traveling to a meeting in Mexico, he was bumped from his flight, and ended up having to spend the better part of the day in the airport. Because of this, he also missed his hotel reservation and a good part of the meeting. And of course, he was very tired and stressed from his ordeal. Dissatisfied with the airline's token offer of small compensation, he later contacted this office for help. In the end, he collected more than $800 from the airline, in compensation for the delay.

Communications Skills for Better Practice Management

As we develop proficiency as practice managers, each of us must rely upon a variety of people and personal skills. For some, the tasks of managing a practice will come easily. For others, there may be more of a struggle.

In this chapter, we will explore several very helpful practice management skills, and the specific ways you can develop them to bring out your best effort.

BECOMING A BETTER CONVERSATIONALIST

Many practice management books, articles, seminars, and consultants urge you to *talk* more with your patients. That's fine advice for the people who have a natural gift for gab, and never lack a good question or interesting subject. But what about the rest of us?

Fortunately, almost anyone can become a good conversationalist by working at it. Some suggestions:

1. Prepare specific conversational openers to use when nothing else comes to mind. "How are you?" is a poor excuse for interesting conversation. Better: "Do you know what I saw (did, learned) today?"

2. Identify at least three interesting or exciting things that have happened to you recently which you can talk about, and that others will appreciate hearing. That way, you'll always have interesting answers to the question, "What's new?"

3. Become knowledgeable about new subjects so you have more to talk about. For example, keep up with current events, read current bestsellers, and see popular movies, so you can share your opinions about them.

4.   Use patients' names often in conversation. People like to hear their names, and will respond more when you use them.

5.   Offer compliments that elicit some kind of response beyond "Thank you." For example, instead of "You look very nice today," say, "You look very nice today. Have you planned something special?"

6.   Similarly, when receiving a compliment, try to say more than "Thank you." For example, if a patient says, "I like your watch," tell him about it: "Thank you. It's actually quite old. My wife bought it for me for our anniversary many years ago."

7.   Write notes about each patient so you can remember to ask specific personal questions the next time you see him. For example, if you've noted that a patient's son was planning a visit, ask, "How was your son's visit?" or even better, "What did you do during your son's visit?"

For more information on this kind of note-taking, see "How to 'Remember' and Use Patient's News," pages 468–469.

LEARNING TO PUT PATIENTS AT EASE

Communications researchers identify four major interpersonal spaces: Public, social, personal, and intimate. Using these spaces in office design and dealings with patients is key to establishing trust:

Kind of Space:	Distances Between People:
Public	12 feet or more from one person to another
Social	From four to 12 feet
Personal	From 18 inches to four feet
Intimate	From touch to 18 inches

Except for a handshake, most people in American culture feel at ease sharing intimate space only with very close friends and relatives. That creates a special problem for most doctors, who have to be in intimate space with people they don't know well to provide their services.

Tip: Don't rush the patient from one interpersonal space to the next. Try to move closer to the patient gradually, being aware that the patient may find it uncomfortable to be in intimate space with you right away. Some tips:

1.   Design your reception area so strangers aren't forced to be closer than social space. Use chairs (not all sofas and loveseats) so strangers can maintain a comfortable distance.

2. When the patient arrives, begin the appointment in social space. Have your receptionist greet him first from 7–12 feet away—with a glance, smile, and "hello."

3. Next, let the patient adjust to being in the close phase of social distance, or in personal space. For example, have your receptionist stand and come out from behind her desk to greet the patient at a distance of 2½–4 feet. Or, have her conduct the new patient interview within social distance in a private office.

4. In the treatment room, talk to the patient briefly before positioning him and yourself for the exam. This will give you time to adjust to each other in closer personal space.

Tip: Shake hands with the patient when you meet. This is a comfortable way for most people to initiate communication within personal or intimate distance. (See below.)

HOW TO SHAKE HANDS WITHOUT
FEELING AWKWARD

A warm, friendly handshake is a great way to get started with all patients, especially apprehensive ones. It welcomes the patient, communicates confidence and ease, and initiates physical contact. This helps make later necessary contact with the patient throughout his treatment less awkward.

It is good practice for both the doctor and the staff to extend a hand to all patients—men, women, and children:

1. Be prepared for a handshake by keeping your right hand free when a patient approaches you.

2. Keep your hand warm and dry (a few squeezes or rubbing before shaking hands should help).

3. Avoid wearing large rings on your right hand.

4. Always stand to shake. (Don't reach up from a seated position.) Exception: Squat when you greet and shake hands with a small child. It will seem much more comfortable if you're both at the same level.

5. Try to exert about the same squeeze pressure as your patient. However, if he or she offers a limp hand, exert a bit more pressure, but not enough to be uncomfortable.

6. Give two or three solid shakes.

Tip: There is no substitute for practice if you want your staff to shake hands confidently. Why not practice on one another at your next staff meeting? That way, each of you wil learn to shake hands with ease.

ACCEPTING APOLOGIES WITH GRACE AND CLASS

It takes courage for most of us to apologize. Therefore, when you must accept a sincere apology from staff, patients, or colleagues, do everything you can to put the other person at ease. The last thing you want is for him to end up being embarrassed, or sorry he apologized.

Minimize the awkwardness by smiling, being friendly, extending your hand, and saying something like:

> I accept and appreciate your apology.

> I accept your apology, but I want you to know that I contributed to the problem and apologize for doing so.

> Thank you. As I recall, I've goofed on occasion myself.

MASTERING MACHINE DICTATION SAVES TIME AND MONEY

Here are four excellent reasons to use machine dictation:

1.   Composing longhand averages 10–15 words per minute (wpm).

2.   Dictating to a shorthand writer averages 80 wpm. However, you'll use both your time and your secretary's, and probably spend time on some small talk. As well, interruptions (phone calls, waiting for the secretary to catch up) cause the other person to wait. Thus, the actual effective shorthand dictation rate is more like 35–40 wpm.

3.   Machine dictation can be done anytime, any place, without a secretary who has stenographic skills, without interruption. Thus, the 80 wpm average composition rate is not hampered.

4.   The average rate of transcription from longhand is 10–15 wpm. From shorthand notes, 20–25 wpm. But from machine dictation, the average transcription rate is 30–35 wpm.

To become a more effective machine dictator:

1.   Before dictating, organize your thoughts with an outline or notes. Gather all necessary materials (a patient's file, correspondence, etc.).

2. Start each tape with instructions. Tell what you're dictating—letter, memo, report, etc. Indicate whether it's to be in rough or final form, total length, number of copies, etc.

Tip: If you're not sure, leave the first few minutes of the tape blank, and put your instructions in later.

3. Use different voice tones to distinguish between your dictation and instructions to the typist. Speak conversationally, with special clarity. Avoid idle chatter that could be erroneously included in the dictation. Do not smoke, eat, drink, or chew gum while dictating.

4. Begin each document or project with more details. For example: "Here's a one-page letter to Mrs. Griffith. Put it on letterhead, and leave wide margins all around."

5. Give spellings of unfamiliar names and words when you first say them.

6. Make a correction immediately. Otherwise, wait to make changes on the transcribed copy.

7. Speak your punctuation. Say "comma," "quote," "new paragraph," etc.

8. Label and date the tape. Give it priority when you hand it to the typist: "I need it tommorrow, immediately, etc."

C • H • A • P • T • E • R   9-9

Preventing and Controlling Stress and Career Burnout

An overflowing reception room. Thirty minutes behind schedule. The phone ringing off the hook. An assistant who's ill, so you're short-handed. An employee who quits without notice. An inexperienced new assistant trying her best, but not yet able to pull her weight. Emergency patients. Broken appointments. A desk piled high with things to be done yesterday. An angry patient. A frightened, screaming child. A patient with heartbreaking problems. Too many things to do, and not enough time to do them. Equipment that breaks down. Family problems you tried to leave home, but couldn't . . . .

Clearly, the material offered in this book and many other management guides can help you prevent, eliminate, or at least minimize the most common practice management problems and stressors. However, no matter how effective a practice manager you are, and no matter what type of practice you have or where you live, you will still be dealing with human beings in your work, and therefore, there will inevitably be some problems beyond your control. In many ways, dealing with these problems is the very nature of the "business" you're in.

Certainly, look to the advice in this book, and to other good sources, to learn new and better ways to hone your practice management skills, improve your systems, and prevent as many of these problems as you possibly can. Like most stressors, it is far better to nip a practice management problem in the bud, than to deal with it later in full bloom.

However, additional strategies aimed at reducing stress, as well as those for handling the unavoidable problems in your practice, will be the subject of this chapter.

EVENTS ALONE DON'T CAUSE A STRESS RESPONSE

Events only become stressors as they're perceived—that is, as meaning is assigned to them in our minds. Thus, in all but the most devastating and traumatic of circumstances, it's our unique perceptions that determine whether or not an event is a stressor, and to what degree.

Fortunately, we can change the stressor potential of many common problems. For example, let's consider a stressor that's familiar to all of us— the short-notice cancellation. How you respond to that event will depend largely upon the meaning you assign it. On the one hand, if you're certain the patient has deliberately wasted your time, and focus on your disappointment, you're apt to have a high stress response. On the other hand, if you perceive the short-notice cancellation as an opportunity to call a waiting patient from your call list, or to catch up on back paperwork, you will have a very different physiological response.

Bottom line: The event—a short-notice cancellation—is the same in both of these examples. It is only your response that varies, not the circumstances.

Thus, when we recognize that we are falling prey to stress, our first line of defense will be to step back and see if we can realign our attitudes. Is the situation a hopeless crisis? Or, can we salvage things and use the problem as the opportunity or springboard for accomplishing some good?

WHO IS MOST LIKELY TO SUFFER FROM STRESS?

We all feel stress to a certain extent. However, there are some people who are more likely to be affected by stress than others:

1.   The "one man band," who tries to do fifteen things at once.

2.   The hurry, hurry, hurry person who is constantly trying to meet unrealistic goals and deadlines.

3.   The impatient person who hates to wait for anything.

4.   The continual struggler, with a "volcanic" personality.

5.   The super-competitive person, who always must be #1.

6.   The perfectionist, who must do everything right, no matter how small or unimportant the task might be.

7.   The person who must always do things his or her way.

20 EASY-TO-DO STRATEGIES FOR KEEPING
STRESS AT BAY

Eliminating the causes of stress and reshaping our attitudes about ourselves and problems are the keys to preventing stress. However, since we know that some amount stress is unavoidable, we need a plan for managing it and minimizing its effect. Below are 20 of the very best do-it-yourself stress-reducing strategies:

1. *Take at least one great vacation each year.* As well, plan at least one fun-filled day each month for nothing but pure enjoyment. Look for activities that are a total break from your work routine.
Tip: When you get together with friends, don't talk "shop" during this important enjoyment time. Totally remove yourself mentally from your professional life on a regular basis.

2. *Reward yourself during off-work hours with the pleasures you most enjoy.* Since you spend the majority of your waking hours doing for others—patients, staff, family, friends—set aside some *self* time. Plan what you'll do for yourself—every day if possible—and make sure you go ahead and do it.

3. *Separate your working and personal lives as much as possible.* Try to leave practice-related stress at the office. Get away from the tension at the end of the day, to give your mind and body a chance to rest and recharge their batteries.
Tip: Leaving work at work can be an especially difficult challenge for those who work with their spouses. For more information on this subject, see "Working with Your Spouse, Children, and Other Close Relatives," pages 341–347.

Don't routinely use your evenings and weekends to catch up on paperwork or prepare for treatment conferences. Schedule time in your appointment book during the day to complete this important work before you leave the office, so you can relax when you get home. For more information on this subject, see "Doctor's Study Time and Preferences," page 66.

4. *Talk out your stresses.* Don't keep everything bottled up inside you. Getting some of your problems off your chest can be a tremendous relief. It is especially valuable to talk things over with a person you respect who is in a position to help you solve the problem, or at least to give you sound advice. A *concerned* listener—be it a friend, counselor, psychologist, clergyperson, etc.—can often help us with our problems by asking soul-searching questions.

5. *Know your limits.* If taking on an additional activity will cut stressfully into your valuable personal and family time, don't be pressured into doing

it. Learn to say "no" to people who make demands of you, even when they are persistant.

6. *Use physical activity to relieve stress and build up resistance.* Exercise regularly, not just on weekends or when it is convenient. Make time for exercise.

7. *Get enough sleep.* Avoid getting into the habit of staying awake to watch a particular television program each night. Whatever relaxation this may bring you must be weighed against the constant sleep debt incurred.

Tip: Too little sleep is, itself, a stress on the mind and body. It also reduces your ability to cope with other stressors. Try getting more sleep by establishing regular sleep habits, day after day, week after week. Being well-rested will enable you to handle difficult or challenging situations much more effectively.

8. *Eat well, and keep your alcohol intake at a moderate level (if you drink at all).* Alcohol is a very poor remedy for stress, and as we know, can lead to even greater problems.

9. *Evaluate the priorities in your life.* If you are contemplating a change that will cause you stress, such as taking out a loan to make a major purchase, moving your practice or home to a new location, having another child, etc., first ask yourself if you are truly willing to accept the stress the change will bring to you and your family. Will it make you happier in the long run? Is it really worth it? Would you be better off maintaining the status quo?

Give important life and career decisions careful consideration and weigh the long-range effects. This kind of evaluation can help you realize where your priorities, aspirations, and limitations lie.

10. *Live one day at a time.* Concentrate on today. Your worries about what happened yesterday or what might happen tomorrow (neither of which you can control), added to the stress of today, are more than most of us can take. Don't go through life continually waiting for something to happen in the future, forgetting to live today to the fullest. Concentrate on today's patients, activities, and challenges. Tomorrow comes soon enough.

11. *Keep your desk clear of everything except matters pertaining to what must be done today.* Seeing a desk piled high with papers and notes for things to do today, tomorrow, and next week causes tension. It makes small tasks seem larger, and magnifies the many things you have to do.

Keeping your desk and "to do" lists in a neat and orderly fashion helps reduce stress. It also helps you to find what you're looking for more easily. For more information on this and related subjects, see "How to Keep Track of Hard-to-Keep-Track-of Information," pages 479–481, and "85 Ways to Save Time and Increase Your Personal Productivity," pages 483–488.

12. *Check your office's layout.* Are you making your work harder than it needs to be? For example, do you find yourself retracing your steps and making unnecessary trips? Do you sit for long periods in an uncomfortable position? Are your exam room supplies or study materials right at your fingertips when you need them?

By making even minor changes in your physical working environment, you may be able to eliminate much of the physical stress and fatigue that you feel at the end of the day. See if your work efficiency and enjoyment might be improved by adjusting or changing your chair or stool, installing better lighting, giving yourself a larger desk, rearranging your supplies, equipment and books, taking steps to soundproof your office, improving your office ventilation system, etc. In particular:

• Keep the room temperature moderate. If it's too hot or cold, the body must expend extra energy to maintain body heat at the normal 98.6 degrees Farhenheit. Studies of human fatigue suggest that the optimal working temperature is 68–70° Farhenheit.

• Don't sit or stand in one position for extended periods.

• Adjust lighting to keep the glare out of your eyes, and the light focused on the working area.

• Is the air circulating through your office well? Install an electronic air cleaner and/or ceiling fans, to improve air quality and distribution.

13. *Learn to relax as you work.* Both tension and relaxation are habits. Bad habits can be eliminated, and good habits can be developed.

Consciously learn to relax your muscles. Take a minute between patients to let yourself go "limp." Close your eyes and consciously relax these important muscles.

When you feel yourself tensing up:

• Stop what you're doing for a moment. Dwelling on a problem or a difficult task reinforces tension.

• Take several deep breaths. As you breathe, concentrate on each inhale and exhale.

• Take a short walk to another exam room or the reception area. If you can't walk around, tap your foot, yawn, or stretch. Any change in movement will reduce stress.

• Break away for a few minutes. While you rest, notice nervous signals, like nail biting, squinting, tightened neck muscles, and clenched teeth. Then, picture a mental "stop sign." This technique works much the same way as the old adage to "count to ten." Simply, make yourself aware that you're experiencing stress symptoms, block out other stimuli for a minute or so, and put things back in perspective.

14.   *Learn to make and live with decisions.* Once you have the facts necessary to make a decision, make it. Unresolved problems will keep you from relaxing until the decision is made.

When possible, delegate decision making to one of your employees. Trust that person's judgment and be prepared to stand behind her decision.

15.   *Try to get some breaks during the day.* Even if you take just a few moments to step outside for a minute, or into the restroom to freshen up and comb your hair, this brief time will help you unwind.

16.   *If you know a task will cause you stress, plan it into your schedule judiciously.* For example, if you know that Mondays and the days after holidays are always chaotic, avoid the super-challenging case, performance reviews, and other potentially stressful activities on those days. Rather, schedule these things when you'll have the time and calm you need for them. Try to handle your most difficult or stressful tasks during your peak times, when you'll be at your best.

17.   *Reward yourself when you've done a good job.* Career stress and burnout often results from lack of "closure" or completion of work, and the corresponding relief that goes with it.

18.   *Find ways to network with other people like yourself, to share problems (especially if you're in solo practice).* Loneliness and boredom can exaggerate your stressors, and be a source of new stress. See "How the Solo Doctor Can Combat Isolation," below.

19.   *Once you've identified the stressors in your life, the best course may be to act on the **least** of them first.* By ridding ourselves of minor stressors, we'll have reduced significantly our total stress load. And, we'll have had the very important experience of success. The confidence we gain through controlling minor stressors will help us when we go on to tackle some of the major ones.

20.   *Investigate all additional means for reducing stress:* biofeedback, yoga, breathing exercises, hypnosis, meditation, cassette tapes, isolation tanks, etc. Try to keep an open mind to new and innovative stress reducers.

HOW THE SOLO DOCTOR CAN COMBAT ISOLATION

1.   *Go visiting.* Over the next several months, schedule time out of the office. Visit four or five practices of varied success. To avoid a sense of direct competition, choose practices remote to your area of patient draw—perhaps a half-day drive away.

2. *Choose role models.* Locate three or four highly successful practices—those that combine enjoyable working atmospheres with high productivity and quality care. Ask the doctor why his or her practice has grown. What attracts patients? What stimulates referrals? (Again, these practices need not be close to you. You may meet suitable role models at regional or national meetings.)

3. *Surround yourself with success.* Isolated, you may never see real potential, let alone devise the means to reach it. Foster contacts you've developed with successful colleagues. Spend time with them.

4. *Involve your staff.* Share your discoveries in staff meetings, arrange for staff to visit other offices, and take staff members to seminars. Expose them to other doctors and staff members seeking and achieving growth.

ARE YOU AS HAPPY AS YOU SHOULD BE?
AN EXERCISE

Would you say that you basically enjoy your work? Certainly, no one loves everything about his daily routine. However, you should spend the bulk of your time on activities you like. Not only will this make you happier, but in the long run, it will make you a higher achiever, and less stressed.

Try this exercise to see if your career is all that it should be to you:

1. Write down all the activities that take place in a typical day in your practice—meetings, new patient exams, letter writing, interviewing for a staff opening, treatment planning, treatment (of various types), etc.

2. Place each activity on one of two lists. The first list should be activities you *want* to do, the second activities you *don't* want to do.

3. Tomorrow, check off those activites you *actually* do. Repeat this step for the next several days.

4. Now review your lists. Note which one has more checks. Determine approximately how much time you spent doing the activities on each list each day.

High performers generally find that they spend at least two-thirds of their time doing tasks on the "want to do" list. Thus, if you're in or near this range, great! You probably find your career rewarding, and relatively stress-free.

However, if you find that you're spending the bulk of your time on activities you dislike, chances are your work causes you inordinate stress. People who are unhappy in their work usually experience stress, and can't sustain high performance for very long, at least not without serious personal consequences.

Do you delegate all that you can? Are all of these "dislike" activities really necessary? What specifically do you dislike about them? Can you make them more enjoyable or less time-consuming?

Answering these questions, and acting upon your responses, will make your career more meaningful, productive, and stress-free.

A · P · P · E · N · D · I · X 1

An A–Z Treasury of Quick-Reference Practice Management Checklists

A·P·P·E·N·D·I·X 1-A

Checklist for Handling Incoming Mail

Your business assistant should be making it as easy as possible for you to read and respond to your incoming mail. Thus, when opening and sorting your mail, she should:

1. Double check each letter for the address and signature of the sender, the date, and enclosures.

2. Staple the envelope to the letter, especially when:

a. The address is missing.

b. The signature is hard to read (and the sender's name is not typed or printed on the stationery).

c. The postmark is significant.

3. Write or stamp the receipt date on the letter (especially when the letter is not dated or the date is old.)

4. Note on the letter any enclosures that came with it.

5. Firmly attach all enclosures to the letter with a paper clip. Or, establish a file for the correspondence, in which all enclosures are secured.

Tip: If you frequently receive mail with numerous bulky enclosures (such as brochures, reports, or tapes) buy some large plastic containers for these from your stationery supplier. See-through boxes or sealable pouches are relatively inexpensive, and will enable you to keep all relevant materials together, yet visible.

A·P·P·E·N·D·I·X   1-B

Quick Quiz: Can a Management Consultant Help You?

Are you wondering whether a management consultant can help you with a certain problem, opportunity, or goal? If so, answer *yes* or *no* to each question below:

1. Are you looking for ways to boost your production?

2. Is your net out of line with your gross? Do costs seem out of control, and you can't figure out where to make adjustments?

3. Are you having trouble crystalizing your practice goals to develop solid production plans for the next several years?

4. Is time management a problem in your practice? Do you routinely fall behind or let things slip?

5. Do you have problems recruiting and managing your staff?

6. Do you have a low collection rate? (Ideally, collections should be 95–98%.) Do you have trouble making firm financial arrangements with patients?

7. Do you lack technical expertise to solve a specific problem? For example, do you need help installing a computer or a new appointment system? Do you need help redecorating your office or with new construction plans? Would you like to tackle more practice marketing projects but don't know how?

8. Do you need an objective, informed viewpoint to help you solve a problem or make a major decision? For example, are you undecided about where to relocate your practice or open a satellite office? Are you confused about which partnership or associate agreement is best for you?

9. Are you losing out to the competition in your community, and must you regain your position in the marketplace?

10. Has your recall rate fallen or not improved as you'd have liked?

Your Score: If you answered *yes* to one or more of these questions, management consultation can probably help you. Review the consultant's experience, academic training, positions he or she has held in the business/professional world, and references *before* you enter into any agreement. For more information on this subject, see "How to Evaluate and Get the Most Out of Your Team of Advisors," pages 21–28.

A·P·P·E·N·D·I·X   1-C

Entrepreneurial Character Traits to Avoid: A Checklist

By their natures, business owners (including private practice professionals) tend to have a strong individualist streak. If they didn't, running their own businesses probably wouldn't appeal to them. But sometimes, this streak turns into destructive behavioral problems. Character traits that are most destructive when dealing with patients and staff:

1. *A "me-against-the-world" attitude.* Some business owners see enemies all around them, and act as though everyone is out to get them—employees, suppliers, clients (patients). They don't trust anyone and can never let down their guard. Thus, employees become adversaries who respond with confrontation when you most need their cooperation.

2. *Insecurity.* A domineering attitude (never letting anyone forget who's the boss) can keep employees from exercising their own judgment or creative instincts.

3. *Perfectionism.* Perfectionism may help an individual achieve his fullest potential, but it doesn't play with the rank and file. If you're a perfectionist, and expect that everyone in your employ should always live up to the high standards you set for yourself, you're almost guaranteed to be disappointed with their performance.

4. *The know-it-all.* Once successful, many business owners think they have all the answers. Sometimes, it's difficult to accept that someone with less experience and education can give you good ideas about running your office. But you'll hurt your practice in the long run if you cut yourself off from new ideas, and develop a staff of "yes" men and women. Every practice needs a few people who can tell the boss they think he's all wet if he's about to embark on a potentially harmful course.

A · P · P · E · N · D · I · X   1-D

Resolving Anger without Blowing Up: A Checklist

W hen you're really mad at a staff member, supplier, colleague, laboratory, or patient, do you vent your anger by blowing your stack?

One popular theory suggests that it is healthy to release pent-up frustration and anger, far healthier than bottling it up inside. Yet recent evidence suggests that neither those who bottle up anger nor those who blow up are particularly well off. Among subjects in one university study, "bottlers" showed the highest blood pressure, while exploders were a close second. Who had the lowest average blood pressure? Those who learned to resolve their anger without blowing up.

Here are a few ideas for developing a healthy control of your anger. Try them the next time you see red:

1. *Make a list of things you're angry about.* Next to each cause, list who's at fault and why. Then, in a third column, write down your part in the problem. This process helps you get a handle on the kind of general anger you can feel against someone else, and helps separate legitimiate gripes against others from problems you've helped create.

2. *Stop and try to consider the other person's point of view.* Is he or she under a lot of stress or having a bad day? Sensitivity may dissipate anger and prevent you from lashing back and making a small problem into a bigger one.

3. *Stop and consider your environment.* Are you hot, cold, tired, hungry, sick, just off the crowded freeway, or surrounded by shrieking children or other unpleasantness? If so, you're far more susceptible to explosions of anger and may take your frustration out on innocent others. Here, counting to 10 really does help.

4. *Don't "should" yourself.* Much of our anger is based upon what we think we or others "should" be doing. Try not to apply your value system to others.

5.   *Laugh more—it dissipates anger.* Try to see the humor in the situation.

6.   *Remain courteous.* It's tempting to be rude or sarcastic over anger. However, courtesy helps you feel in control, and prevents provoking greater anger in others.

7.   *If need be, take time out* until you put your anger aside and can act calmly.

A · P · P · E · N · D · I · X   1-E

Protect Yourself When Mail-Ordering Goods: A Checklist

Buying goods by mail can save you money. However, you'll need to take several precautions before placing your order:

1. *Read the catalog/ad carefully.* Look for hidden postage, freight or shipping fees, or other add-ons that will take the edge off your "bargain." Double-check the quantity, make, size, model number, etc., so you know exactly what you're ordering.

2. *Be wary of exaggerated claims.* Is the item you're ordering truly the "newest," the "most complete," the "best?"

3. *Check the conditions of refunds and warrantees.* If you receive damaged or wrong goods, or if you just don't like them, what will you have to do to correct the problem?

Tip: A reputable mail-order company will usually make the return or claim process painless, and give you your money back.

4. *Consider the company's technical support.* For example, can you get free help by phone if you have questions or problems?

5. *Run a check on the company* if you have doubts, especially when substantial sums are at stake. Contact the Better Business Bureau nearest the company to see if anyone has filed a complaint against it, their reasons, and the results to date, if any.

6. *Keep records,* including photocopies of your completed order form, receipts, check stubs, written agreements from the company, and the ads/catalogs that attracted you. (Note the name of the publication and the date of the ad.)

A · P · P · E · N · D · I · X   1-F

Becoming a Better Money Manager:
A Checklist

1. *Have a long-range plan to guide day-to-day decisions.* Your ability to forecast your business situation in one, three, five, and even ten years will affect many decisions you make today. For example, your forecast will help you decide how much office space to rent or build. The wrong projection might mean that you end up with under- or over-used space down the road.

Tip: How well you forecast your future will also affect your tax bill. For example, the doctor who accurately projects that his income will grow in a few years can take steps now to defer expenses to offset higher income. On the other hand, the doctor who anticipates retirement in a few years can accelerated expenses now so he can take every deduction right away.

2. *Be realistic about your prospects.* Don't overestimate income and underestimate expenses. Make conservative guesses.

3. *Know where you stand financially at all times.* Develop a clear picture of both current assets (cash, inventory, accounts receivable) and liabilities. Also project future cash flow—what you expect to receive and pay out in the coming months.

4. *Identify real expenses.* What percentage is spent on housing, salaries, lab fees, supplies, equipment, utilities?

Tip: Most doctors *think* they know their expenses from experience. But an overhead study often proves them wrong.

5. *Base major decisions on logical study.* Few successful business agreements are reached by impulse.

A·P·P·E·N·D·I·X   1-G

Action Checklist for Keeping Tabs on Lab Work

1.   Assign responsibility for maintaining a lab control form to one staff member. (Usually, that assignment is made to the person who packages items to be sent to the lab.)

2.   The lab control form should provide space to write:

a.   A brief description of each item.

b.   The date sent.

c.   The laboratory to which it was sent.

d.   The date by which the item must/should be returned.

e.   The patient's name.

f.   The patient's next appointment date.

g.   A "Received" column where your assistant may place a checkmark when the item/results are returned.

3.   Once an item/result has been returned from the lab, your assistant should open the package, insure that the correct item/results have been returned, and inspect/review it. If the item/results are correct, she should check the "Received" column on the lab control form.

4.   Next, your assistant should review the control form to find the patient's appointment date. She should then go directly to the appointment book and indicate that the item/results have been received from the lab. For example, if you use the symbol "L" in your appointment book to indicate lab work pending, your assistant might circle the "L" to indicate that the item is back from the lab.

Tip: This is the only instance when someone other than your appointment secretary should write in the appointment book.

5.   Once a week, your assistant should check to see which items/ results have been delivered to patients. These items need to be struck off the lab control form with a red line. This procedure allows you to see at a glance how many lab-related cases are pending, how many lab items/results are on order, and how many are in the office awaiting the patient's appointment or consultation.

A · P · P · E · N · D · I · X   1-H

Checklist for Overcoming Staff
Computer Anxiety

C omputerphobia. Cyberphobia. Technophobia. Technostress.

This new jargon describes a very common anxiety about using new automated equipment. Computerizing your office can go smoothly, but only if you face staff fears about their jobs and status. What you can do to overcome computer anxiety:

1. Tell staff your reasons for computerizing. Communicate a positive attitude and your commitment to the technology. Stress ways the computer will help staff get their jobs done.

2. When possible, involve staff in the computerizing process. Get their input at vendor meetings and when assessing needs.

3. Make training accessible to everyone. After intense initial training, make auxiliary programs available for more advanced stages of skill and development.

4. Provide proper facilities for staff using equipment. Consider rest breaks, lighting, ventilation, air conditioning, furniture, and equipment configuration. (For more information, see "Gearing Up Physically for Automation," pages 437–442.)

5. Avoid computer jargon. Translate technical terms when possible.

6. Allow employees to spend time alone with the computer, to work at their own level and pace to develop their understanding of the equipment capabilities.

7. Encourage staff to use the computer by explaining that it let them perform monotonous tasks much more quickly and easily.

A · P · P · E · N · D · I · X   1-I

Insurance Musts for Your Office Computer: A Checklist

W hen selecting an office program, check to see:

1. Which forms are used: Will your insurance company accept these?

2. Will the insurance company optical scanners be able to "read" your printer's printing?

3. Will the program allow you to change items on the form manually? Or are you locked into automatic processing based on your treatment/service transactions?

4. Do you have the option of billing individually or in batch form mode? Can you interrupt/resume should you need to?

5. Does the program leave out any important codes or data?

6. Does insurance form processing depend on executing another function (such as printing of billing statements) before you can print insurance forms?

7. Can you stop or pass over unused sections of the insurance form? Or must you answer every question, relevant or not?

8. Do you have the option of creating a second page of an insurance form if the first page is completely filled?

9. Does the form produced recognize individuals as well as family groups? Or are you locked into one mode?

10. Can you keep track of preauthorization and claims being submitted, paid, etc.? Can you get a periodic report?

A · P · P · E · N · D · I · X   1-J

Property Insurance Options Worth Considering: A Checklist

Y our insurance representative can give you more information about the following types of special coverage:

1. *Replacement costs for equipment:* Most experts recommend an insurance package that pays out on losses, rather than on actual cash value, so you're insured for today's prices. (Often a deductible must be met before payment begins.)

2. *Replacement costs for records:* Does your policy meet the expense of replacing destroyed, lost, or stolen professional records? It take a tremendous amount of time and money to restore patient histories, test and x-ray results, etc.

Tip: To estimate the actual cost of reconstructing patient files, multiply the number of patients by at least the hourly wage of the person who'd do it.

3. *Business interruption coverage:* This option does two things. It helps you set up a new or temporary office. And, it reimburses you for reduced income after property is damaged or destroyed. This coverage can meet the higher rent at a temporary office and even cover the expense of telling patients about your new location.

4. *In-transit coverage:* While this policy is for accidents outside the office, it's usually grouped with office property insurance. Coverage can range from protecting an employee injured in a vehicle accident while running an errand to covering the loss of your property while it's away from the office.

A · P · P · E · N · D · I · X   1-K

What to Ask Before Buying or Leasing a Copy Machine: A Checklist

1. Where in the office will you install the machine?

2. How many employees will have access to it and with what frequency?

3. What range of paper sizes and stock can the machine accommodate?

4. How many sheets are in the average document you need to copy?

5. Do you need a machine that can do dual-sided printing (duplexing)?

6. Do you need to reduce or enlarge your documents?

7. What's an estimate of the total number of sheets you need to reproduce in the average day?

8. Will you want a machine with collating, automatic feeding, or paper stacking capabilities?

9. Do you need a machine that can copy out to paper edges? (Or can you live with one that has border cutoff?)

Tip: Test drive the copier before you buy, with your own documents and paper. When possible, rent the machine for a few weeks first. That way, if you find it difficult to use or you don't like the quality of the reproduction, you haven't made a commitment/mistake.

Tip: Taking proper care of your paper will reduce copier problems. Therefore, take extra care whenever loading paper. (Most packages indicate which side of the paper goes up.) As well, don't open the package of paper until you're ready to use it. Exposure to air will change the paper's moisture content, which can cause it to jam.

A · P · P · E · N · D · I · X   1-L

Guidelines for Answering Zingers:
A Checklist

"**W**hen did you stop beating your wife?"

Your impulse when hit with a zinger (a tough or provoking question) may be to blurt out a short, fast answer so you can put the unpleasant question behind you as quickly as possible. However, you'll rarely convince patients, colleagues, or your staff that you are in control when you do this. The best approach is to listen carefully to make sure you understand the zingers, and to ask questions yourself if you're not sure of the true meaning.

Example: Suppose you tell a patient what his fee will be for a certain procedure, and he shoots you the zinger: "Don't you think that's an awful lot of money?" Your impulse may be to give a short fast response, such as, "No, not really," and get onto another subject as soon as possible. The better response here would be a pause, and a calm and sincere, "What do you mean by a 'lot of money?' " so you can let the patient clarify. He could mean, "I don't have that much money in my checking account" or, "That's more than it was last year," or, "He must be a pretty decent doctor (or I must really be sick) if it costs that much," or, "There goes my trip to Bermuda." Or, it could something entirely different.

Once you know what the patient is really saying, continue to hold back on that impulse to blurt a quick response. Pause two seconds, think, and exhale. Then look the patient squarely in the eyes (or speak directly into the telephone mouthpiece) and use your calmest, most even voice. Think: "I'm in control, you can't ruffle my feathers."

When preparing your answer to zingers, keep these five guidelines in mind:

1. One of the best ways to project an image of control is by using the patient's name frequently in the conversation. For example, "What do you mean by a 'lot of money,' Mrs. Colwell?"

2. Good answers do not belittle patients or make them defensive. Don't become the patient's adversary, either with your words or manner. Don't use sarcasm—it may be misunderstood and make the patient angry.

3. When under the pressure of a zinger, it's easy to become flustered and vague, to leave out important details, and wrongly assume that the patient knows what you're talking about. Be deliberately clear. Don't say "she" if you mean "My assistant, Becky" and don't say "it" if you mean "the examination" or "the appointments." Compare "She will do it" to "My assistant, Becky, will make your appointment for you."

4. Slow down and keep your voice pitch and volume purposely low and even. Don't fidget or let your eyes wander.

5. Good posture will also help you project control. Stand or sit up straight and keep your head erect.

A·P·P·E·N·D·I·X   1-M

Checklist for Determining Whether to Buy or Lease Equipment

In some cases, it can be cheaper in the long run to lease equipment rather than to buy it outright.

To determine if leasing makes sense in a given situation:

1. *Figure the actual cost of purchasing the equipment.*

a. If you must finance the purchase, add in the cost of the interest.

b. Add what your down payment could have earned you if you had invested it. (Use conservative estimates.)

c. Add the cost of installing, servicing and insuring the equipment.

d. Subtract the amount the equipment is likely to bring when it is sold.

e. Subtract tax deductions for depreciation, insurance, etc.

2. *Compute the real cost of leasing:*

a. Add the monthly charges for the period of the lease.

b. Add the cost of installing, servicing, and insuring the equipment (if not included in the regular charge).

c. Subtract the tax savings allowed for deductible business expenses.

3. *If leasing makes financial sense, consider these additional guidelines:*

a. Multi-year leases can act as a hedge to inflation.

b. Leasing provides more flexibility and reduces the problem of obsolescence.

c. If leased equipment turns out to be wrong for your needs, you may be stuck with it until the lease expires. Check your contract.

d. Unless your lease has a renewal clause, you run some risk of having the equipment leased out to someone else when your lease expires.

One Dozen Phrases to Avoid in Friendly Letters: A Checklist

When writing a friendly letter to a patient, be sure to avoid the following formal and judgmental expressions:

1. You state that . . .
2. You should know that . . .
3. You neglected to . . .
4. You misinterpret . . .
5. You are in error . . .
6. We must insist . . .
7. You failed to . . .
8. You claim that . . .
9. You are mistaken . . .
10. You don't understand . . .
11. If you actually did . . .
12. We take issue . . .

A · P · P · E · N · D · I · X   1-O

Checklist of Words to Use and Avoid with Patients

H *ow* you say it can make a huge difference! Below are words and phrases to use and avoid in delicate practice management communications, not only with patients, but with staff and colleagues, too:

Do say:	Instead of:
Our agreement	Contract
Your investment/fee will be . . .	The price/cost will be . . .
Approve the paperwork.	Sign your name here.
Own the appliance/goods.	Buy the appliance/goods.
The account is past due.	You're delinquent. You're in arrears by two months.
My assistant, my nurse	My girl, my gal
Mrs. X, Y, or Z	Honey, sweetie, dear
Reception area	Waiting room
We've had a schedule change.	We've had a cancellation.
Established patient	Old patient
How do you feel about this?	Do you understand?
Interrupted schedule	Running late, falling behind
Follow-up visit	Recall
Conference, education	Convention
Injection	Needle, shot
Discomfort	Pain
He's with a patient.	He's busy.

Do say:	Instead of:
Medication	Drug
Is there anything you'd like me to explain better?	Any questions?

A · P · P · E · N · D · I · X   1-P

Basic Bookkeeping Records of a Professional Practice: A Checklist

The bookkeeping duties of a business assistant include receiving and depositing cash, keeping accounts with patients, preparing and mailing statements (usually monthly), and general record keeping. In addition to providing information on income and expenses, most professional office records must show how much is received from and owed by each patient. Some basic records:

1. *Charges and collection records:* This record is designed so the doctor can determine two things:

   a. How much "business" has been done and whether it was charged or paid for in cash, and

   b. How much cash has been collected from patients. The record of charges provides a daily summary of the doctor's activities. It serves as a source of information for other records.

2. *Patient's card or ledger:* This is a record of charges to and collections from each patient. A card is completed for each patient when he first comes to the office. Entries on the patient's card are made from the information in the charges and collections record. A new balance is determined after each entry is made on the patient's card. Additional charges are added to the previous balance. Credits are subtracted from the old balance.

3. *Monthly statements:* Most offices mail a monthly statement to each patient who has not paid his account in full. The amounts placed on the statements are taken from the patient's card.

4. *Cash payments record:* The doctor must know two things about cash payments:

   a. The amount of cash being paid out, and

   b. What the payments are for.

This information can easily be shown in a cash payments record that has been specially ruled for transactions that will be entered in it. Typical categories of cash payments of a professional practice include:

- Rent.
- Salaries.
- Professional journals.
- Dues to professional societies.
- Reception area reading material.
- Office supplies.
- Telephone.
- Electricity.
- Laundry.
- Uniforms.
- Lab expenses and materials.

5. *Petty cash records:* Most offices need to buy small, unanticipated items such as postage and office supplies. It's inconvenient (and expensive) to write checks for small amounts, and often, cash is needed immediately. To make payments easier, most offices keep a petty cash fund. As cash is taken from the fund, an entry is made in the petty cash record showing the date, explanation, and amount. Accurate petty cash records will enable the office to replenish the fund whenever it begins to get low. For more information on this subject, see, "Keep a Tight Grip on Your Petty Cash Account," pages 147–148.

Checklist of Important Accounting and Bookkeeping Terms

Term:	Meaning:
Assets	Cash and other forms of property owned by the practice or the doctor.
Gross income	The total amount of earnings resulting from operations of the practice.
Expenses	Necessary outlays of income.
Net income	The excess of income over expenses.
Net loss	The excess of expenses over income.
Cash basis of accounting.	The method of accounting frequently used by professionals in which transactions are recorded only when cash has been received or paid out.
Income and expense statement	A financial statement prepared to show in summary form the sources of income and the nature and amounts of expenses connected with earning the income. The statement covers a specific period, such as a month, quarter, or year.
Statement of ownership	A financial statement on which are listed the assets of the doctor or the practice and any claims against the assets. It is also referred to as a "balance sheet" or "statement of financial conditions."
Monthly summary	A cumulative record to which the totals of cash records are transferred monthly.

A · P · P · E · N · D · I · X   1-R

Coordinating Accounting and Bookkeeping Functions: A Checklist

Record keeping is an important part of almost every business assistant's duties. This brief checklist will help you understand the basic purposes of bookkeeping and accounting, and the difference and relationship between them.

1. Accounting is the summarizing and recording of business transactions. Every professional practice must keep records of money received and money spent, of what it owns and what it owes. Periodically every practice must prepare statements that show its profits and losses and its financial condition and outlook.

2. Accounting provides the financial information needed to run the practice. It tells what the practice has done in the past and helps the doctor plan intelligently for the future. Accounting also helps those who are considering lending money or extending credit to the practice decide whether the practice is a good risk. And, accounting supplies figures for the tax returns that must be filed with the local, state and federal governments. In short, accounting provides a history of the practice, not in words, but in dollars and cents.

3. Bookkeeping is the recording phase of the accounting process. An assistant who records the information into the accounting records may be referred to as a "bookkeeper."

4. The term *bookkeeper* dates back to the time when formal accounting records were in the form of books with pages bound together. While this is still occasionally the case, most modern practices prefer to use a computer or pegboard recording system. When the language catches up, the term *record-keeper* will replace *bookkeeper*.

5.   A good bookkeeper generally exhibits common traits and abilities. For example, he or she . . .

• understands and thinks about the transactions being recorded. Thinking logically eliminates careless and senseless mistakes.

• is a detail person. Mistakes or oversights by the bookkeeper can be costly to the practice, not only in financial losses, but also in the loss of patient goodwill.

• is neat and orderly. Good pensmanship is an asset to the bookkeper who keeps books manually. The basic bookkeeping goal: Write small and make the figures small. A messy paper with large figures scawled on it will frustrate anyone trying to use it.

A·P·P·E·N·D·I·X   1-S

Checklist for Getting More from Pegboard Bookkeeping

1. The extension columns on a pegboard billing system's day sheet might be used to record important practice management information. For example:

    a. Production on a per-doctor basis.

    b. Amounts generated by lab work, paraprofessionals, etc.

    c. Total fee reductions for professional courtesy.

    d. In-person collections (as opposed to mail collections).

    e. Work volume for each of several practice offices.

    Tip: If you find that the extra columns are *not* adequate for obtaining all the practice management data you need, you've probably outgrown your pegboard. When that happens, you will have little choice but to automate.

2. Most offices can expand their manual bookkeeping system by using several pegboards simultaneously—an inexpensive yet effective approach. (Since pegboards can handle 100 to 150 patients per day—a general rule of thumb—using several boards at once can accommodate even a busy practice.)

3. An easy way to use a multiple pegboard system is to set up one board with your regular charge/receipt slips for use with non-insured patients, and another with superbills (for use with insured patients). This division will speed things up because two assistants can make entries at the same time. And, it will help you keep your records in order since both sets of charge slips are numbered and all numbers will be accounted for.

A·P·P·E·N·D·I·X   1-T

Making Better Use of Your Bank's Many Services: A Checklist

H ere's a checklist of free services your bank might offer to its most valued customers:

1. *Free checking:* Valued customers can usually get free checking without a minimum balance. (Often, an investment in the bank's CDs or money market fund can substitute for a minimum balance.)

2. *Overdraft privileges:* Your bank may automatically lend you money to cover overdrafts. Or, it may hold off processing them, notify you, and allow you to cover them.

3. *Fast check-clearing:* It's not uncommmon for banks to take two weeks to clear an out-of-town check. But with today's nationwide computerized check-clearing, your bank may be able to clear out-of-town checks more quickly, perhaps in only a few days.

4. *Automatic account reconciliation:* Computerized check reconciliation can save up to a day of your bookkeeper's monthly tasks. This can cut labor costs.

5. *Financial planning and investment advice:* Your personal banker may have valuable information about stocks and municipal or corporate bond offerings. If you're considering a real estate deal, have a talk with the bank's real estate investment expert. (Another bank officer may be able to advise you about other types of investments.)

6. *Estate planning:* Your bank may offer free estate planning services in the hopes that you'll reciprocate by designating it in your will as manager of your estate trust. (The bank may also hope that you'll have it manage your children's trusts, for which it will charge a fee.)

7.   *Other services:* Depending upon your value as a bank customer (and your bargaining ability), your banker might:

a.   Waive the rental fee for your safe deposit box.

b.   Provide free checking for members of your family.

c.   Cancel fees for traveller's checks or for wiring money.

30 Non-Commercial Methods for Marketing a Practice: A Checklist

B elow are 30 outstanding practice marketing projects. Each one is a relatively inexpensive, proven practice builder that doesn't rely on overt commercialism. As you read, note which projects will be the highest priorities for your practice:

1. *Logo:* Have a logo designed especially for you. Use it on all office materials (stationery, brochures, signs, staff name tags, etc.) to establish a unified, professional practice image.

2. *Brochure:* Develop a practice brochure to welcome new patients to your practice. Include: Your name, address, phone number, hours, directions and a map to your office, practice philosophy, the doctor's biography, a brief practice history, and a description of the patient's first office visit. Mail brochures to new patients in advance of their first appointments. As well, use brochures to support other marketing efforts.

3. *Newsletter:* Produce a patient newsletter that includes interesting and educational articles. Also publish news about your office such as changes in hours, courses or seminars you attend, and a biography of one staff member in each issue. Mail the newsletter quarterly to potential referral sources in your community and to all patients of record, especially those you haven't seen in a long time.

4. *Press releases:* Send press releases to area newspapers to announce practice news or to discuss a timely subject. Include good photographs when you can, since they usually help increase your chances of getting your release published.

5. *Letters to the editor:* Write letters to the editor of your newspaper to take a stand on some relevant issue related to your area of practice. The timelier and more controversial the issue, the better your chances of getting published.

6. *Personalized stationery:* Print a personalized business card and memo pad for each member of your staff.

7. *Signs:* Create an eye-catching office sign using your logo. Coordinate it with your other office signs, such as door and exit signs, to achieve a unified look.

8. *Volunteer expertise:* Send a letter to newspapers and radio and TV stations to volunteer to serve as a local expert for your profession. Very often, writers and editors need to interview someone locally for background information, or to give a reaction or interpretation of a news event.

9. *Court media editors:* Clip articles of public concern from your professional journals, and send them to local media editors with a short note. (Explain who you are and why you think the articles would be of interest.) Editors often appreciate this kind of help, and may ask for more information or that you suggest other story ideas.

10. *Staff incentives:* Establish an incentive program for staff members to refer new patients to the practice. Examples: Award $10 to the assistant for each new patient she refers.

11. *Patient incentives:* Provide incentives for patients to make referrals to the practice. *Examples:* Hold an annual appreciation party for patients who make three or more referrals in a year. Or, provide a tasteful gift for each referral.

12. *Surveys:* Conduct patient surveys to get feedback and suggestions Acknowledge all complaints and try to turn them around. Use good suggestions in your practice-building campaign.

13. *Learn from failures:* Always ask a patient who leaves your practice why he's leaving. Happy patients are your best practice builders. Remedy all problems you possibly can.

14. *Thank referral sources:* Ask all new patients how they heard about your practice. Write a letter to thank all the people who make referrals.

15. *Guest courtesies:* Try to think of every one of your patients as a guest in your office. Greet each one by name with a handshake and sincere smile. Have your staff offer to hang the patient's coat and bring him a beverage.

16. *Schedule a special event:* Hold an open house or appreciation party for patients. Or, give an office tour to area school children, clubs, and other interested groups.

17. *Contest:* Sponsor a contest for your patients. Publicize the winners in your newsletter, office bulletin board, and press releases.

18.   *Remember personal information:* Show patients that you listen to them. Make notes of the patient's hobbies, career, and children. Then ask about something he's mentioned at his next appointment.

19.   *Giveaways:* Give patients items to use at home that have your practice's name and address printed on them. Those items will remind patients of you each time they use them.

20.   *Reception area sign:* Install a sign in your reception area that says "New Patients Always Welcome" or something similar. Many of your patients may be under the mistaken impression that you don't want to take on any new patients. The sign will encourage referrals.

21.   *Novel decor:* Seize the opportunity to get people to take notice of and talk about your practice. *Example:* You might sponsor an art show in your reception area, choose an unusual theme or motif, add a greenhouse, or introduce an office mascot.

22.   *Teams:* On behalf of your practice, sponsor a Little League or similar team in your community. Have team uniforms, T-shirts, and/or caps printed with the practice name and logo.

23.   *Be a joiner:* Join clubs and organizations in your community. The more visible you become, the better your chances of attracting new patients and referrals.

24.   *Court personnel managers:* Get to know the personnel managers of companies in your area, especially if those firms provide insurance for employees. Offer to help interpret insurance benefits for their employees, or to do workshops for them. When appropriate, send personnel managers copies of your brochure and newsletter.

25.   *Speaking:* Become a popular public speaker in your community by offering your services to speak to organizations, clubs, and schools.

26.   *Seminar:* Run your own seminar to discuss one or more topics of concern to patients. Choose timely topics that will spark interest, such as the latest advances in your field. Invite patients, and ask them to bring friends. Promote the seminar in letters, on your office bulletin board, and in your patient newsletter. Rent a hotel meeting room or other space for this type of program if you can't accommodate a large group in your office.

27.   *Telephone thank you:* Say "thank you for calling" to every person who calls your office, even to patients who call to cancel or change an appointment, or to complain.

28.   *Court realtors:* Give copies of your practice brochure and newsletter to area realtors. They can be a wonderful source of new patient referrals.

29. *Expanded hours:* Consider ways to offer weekend and evening hours, especially if you're in a community that has a high percentage of two-earner families.

30. *Public service announcements:* Check with local radio and TV stations to learn their requirements for public service announcements. If you're creative about it, you may be able to write an appropriate announcement that benefits the public while publicizing your practice in some way. (For example, many doctors successfully publicize free health screenings.)

A · P · P · E · N · D · I · X   1-V

How to Barter without Getting Burned:
A Checklist

Bartering your services can both save money and attract new patients. However, you'll want to review this checklist of caveats before swapping your care for others' goods and services. If you're going to join a barter club:

1. *Be sure to investigate carefully the club's references and credentials.* Get the club's membership roster and call some doctors who are listed.

Tip: Be wary of clubs that refuse to give you references. Also contact your local Better Business Bureau.

2. *Avoid direct-barter clubs.* If you treat a farmer, you should not have to be paid in eggs. Choose a club that allows you to earn credits that can be used to get he goods and services you want.

3. *Determine the club's coverage area.* Some allow you to use your barter credits only in your immediate geographic area. Others have franchises that let you use your credits in other states.

4. *Ask about the club's accounting system.* Make sure it has an effective way to keep track of your credits.

5. *Know the tax consequences of barter.* According to the IRS, if services are paid for other than in money, the fair market value of the property or service taken in payment must be included as income.

Checklist for Managing Your Summer (or Annual) Vacation

1.   Finish whatever projects you can before taking your vacation. An impending departure date can motivate you to clear your desk and even get ahead.

2.   Give yourself time to relax during your vacation. Avoid break-neck tours unless they invigorate you. You want to be in top form when you return, not in need of another vacation.

3.   Use vacation time to dream and set long-range goals for yourself and your practice. Don't take along any routine paperwork. Instead, read motivational books, take long introspective walks, and do some serious blue sky thinking.

4.   When you return, plunge right away into an important new project—publishing a patient newsletter, automating your office, redecorating your reception area, etc. Undertake these projects now, before getting bogged down again in everyday routines.

5.   While on vacation, you undoubtedly asked a colleague to cover for you. Upon your return, be sure to thank him or her. However, also be sure to call a few of the patients who saw this doctor to see how they fared during your absence. This will give you a good idea about how the covering doctor handled your patients on a personal level. And, it will impress patients with your concern for their well-being.

6.   If you're in solo practice, don't shut down your office completely when you take your vacation. If possible, have at least one person from the practice on hand to make or change appointments, to handle billing matters, and to refer patients needing immediate care.

Tip: Most practices try to have the majority of staff members take vacations at the same time as the doctor. This is certainly efficient. However, a skeleton crew can bring collections up to date, weed through old patient files, reorganize the filing system, look into new equipment, or take inventory. You might even have them bring reception area magazine subscriptions up to date or forge ahead on back-burner marketing activities (such as a letter-writing campaign or your patient newsletter).

A · P · P · E · N · D · I · X   1-X

Quick Quiz: Is Practice Expansion for You?

At some time, nearly every doctor who runs a successful practice is tempted to expand. If one office is profitable, they reason, two might be doubly good. The successful doctor thinks of adding an room or two, buying new equipment, bringing in a new associate, or offering new services.

Yet along with visions of future profits and success come darker images. The expansion could fail and, worse, take your current practice down with it. Why should you jeopardize what you have? Why risk capital, lifestyle, and peace of mind? To cut your risks, answer this quick quiz:

1. Are you temperamentally suited to running a larger practice? Will doing so make you happy?

2. Can you delegate? Some doctors succeed well at running a small practice where they control everything. They make every decision, touch each piece of mail, and remember each staff member's birthday. Sometimes when the practice grows, the old habits persist. Even though the staff might double, the mail triples and the decisions must be made at a hectic pace, would you try to do it all? Would you spread yourself too thin?

3. Is your staff ready for expansion? You're not ready for growth if you're the only one who can make day-to-day decisions, if staff memers regularly turn to you for answers to routine questions, or if all problems, from petty to extraordinary, end up in your lap.

4. Do you lack skill in management, marketing, financial matters, and other vital areas? One key to successful growth is knowing when and where to get help.

5. Is your practice running smoothly? If you plan to turn to banks or other lenders to finance your expansion, the efficiency of your operations will impress them. In addition, a weakness you ignore now could haunt you when you expand.

6. Do you need financing? If so, do you have a strong relationship with a financial institution?

A · P · P · E · N · D · I · X   1-Y

Checklist of Questions to Ask Your Insurance Representative

1.   Does your policy cover employees as named insureds?

2.   Does it protect you from acts of an independent contractor doctor who uses your facility?

3.   If it's claims-made, are you guaranteed that you can buy your same liability limits when you buy tail coverage?

4.   Does it exclude coverage for any act that may be the basis of a disciplinary proceeding by your professional society/board?

5.   Can you add a third-party prepaid plan as an insured on your policy?

6.   Does your company have the highest industry rating (A) available by A.M. Best, which measures financial solvency/management ability of insurance companies?

7.   Does your carrier need your written consent (without any qualifications) to settle a professional liability claim?

8.   Can your carrier issue high liability limits? What are those upper limits?

9.   If your carrier cancels you, can you make an appeal to a review committee?

10.   Is your property package tailored specifically to meet a doctor's office?

11.   Are you covered for your liability when you serve on a peer review committee?

12.   Can you buy insurance from the company if you move to another state?

A · P · P · E · N · D · I · X   1-Z

Identifying and Solving Practice Management Problems: A Checklist

Y ou can't possibly get the right answers to your practice management problems unless you ask the right questions. This checklist, developed along the lines of simple investigative reporting checklists used by journalists, will enable you to analyze your problems objectively and accurately.

Ask:	More Specifically:
What?	1. What, in simple terms, is the problem? Is this the whole problem? Or is it a symptom of a much deeper problem?
	2. In what areas of your practice (case presentation, financial arrangements, personnel, patient relations, collections, etc.) did the problem start?
	3. What will be the consequences if you don't solve this problem? How quickly must you act?
	4. What other problems is this problem related to?
	5. What is your proposed solution?
	6. What risk (operating, financial, personal, other) does the proposed solution entail?
	7. What are the key assumptions on which the solution is based?
	8. What are your alternatives if the solution doesn't work?
Why?	1. Why did this problem occur? (For example, why aren't you getting new patients? Why is your receptionist unfriendly to new patients? Why are your appointments booked ahead so far that new patients have to wait months for an appointment?)
	2. Why didn't you know about the problem sooner? For example, are there communication problems among your staff? Are you keeping incomplete or inaccurate records?
When?	1. When were you informed about the problem?
	2. When can you expect your solution to show significant results?

Ask:	More Specifically:
Where?	1. Where in your practice is it most important that your solution be effective?
	2. Where might you turn for additional support or help?
Who?	1. Who is responsible for the immediate problem? Who is responsible for the underlying problem (if it exists)?
	2. Who should be consulted about the solution? (*Examples:* your attorney, accountant, practice management consultant, supplier, assistant, patient, colleague, etc.)
How?	1. How did the problem first come to your attention?
	2. How have you handled similar problems in the past?
	3. How will you measure the effectiveness of your solution?
	4. How can you prevent this problem from recurring? How can you spot the problem right away if it does recur?

A · P · P · E · N · D · I · X   2

Glossaries of Useful Practice Management Terms and Problems

A · P · P · E · N · D · I · X   2-1

50 Questions Your Receptionist Should Be Able to Answer

A top-notch telephone receptionist has good answers prepared for all the common questions she is asked. In the test below are 50 typical scenarios your receptionist might encounter. See if your receptionist responds to each one as you would like her to. As well, use this list as a training tool for new receptionists you hire.

50 QUESTIONS FOR YOUR RECEPTIONIST

Problem/Question:	Answers/Comments:
1. How would you learn if a caller is a new or established patient?	"When was your last visit with the doctor?" See "Making Unrecognized Patients Feel Special," page 397.
2. How would you handle the patient who says he's experiencing symptoms you're not sure the doctor can help?	First determine whether it is a medical emergency. If it is, advise necessary care (ie. call an ambulance, etc.). If it is not an emergency, take down all the relevant information for review with the doctor. Promise the patient a call back by a specified time.
3. Suppose a new patient has a clinical problem that needs attention the same day, but the appointment book is full and the reserved emergency time has already been used by another patient.	Sometimes, there is no choice but to work through lunch or after regular hours. However, do this as a last resort, after all other good options have been exhausted. When you give the patient an appointment, tell him that you did not have an opening, so he appreciates your situation. Then, explain that you'll be in touch sooner if there is a last-minute cancellation, and that you'd appreciate his coming in on short notice. Look for chances to reschedule patients already appointed

Problem/Question:	Answers/Comments:
	for the day, explaining that you have an emergency. However, don't reschedule an already appointed patient if he objects or seems reluctant.
4. A caller asks, "What are the doctor's qualifications?"	Memorize each doctor's relevant credentials—where he went to school, additional training, years of experience, memberships, licenses, board certifications, honors, awards, etc.
5. A new patient calls to ask how much the first visit (or standard service) costs.	State the fee (or a fee range). However, also explain what that fee includes, in some detail. For example, in an optometric practice, the fee for soft contact lenses might be described in this way: "Standard soft contact lenses are $_____ . That includes the lenses, Dr. Chen's thorough and complete eye examination and lens fitting, instruction on insertion, removal and care of the lenses, all the equipment and a supply of the solutions you'll need to care for your lenses, a complimentary pair of nonprescription sunglasses from our optical dispensary, warranties, trial period, discounts, etc. (Explain all your fee includes.) Different types of contact lenses can be used, depending upon the patient's needs. The fee for these lenses varies."
6. Within what period of time should you be able to schedule a new patient for non-emergency appointments?	Schedule the new patient as soon as possible. Ideally, no new patient should have to wait more than a few days. See "Long Waits Are a Turn-Off," page 375.
7. How would you answer the telephone?	Answer the phone with a smile. A good greeting: "Good morning. Middletown Podiatry Associates. This is Lindsay speaking. May I help you?"
8. On which ring would you answer the telephone—first, second, or third?	Ideally, the second. See "How to Tame the Telephone "Beast"," pages 91–97.

Problem/Question:	Answers/Comments:
9. How and when would you hang up?	Wait for the caller to hang up first, to be sure not to cut him off. Then, return the receiver gently to the cradle or transfer the call.
10. How would you handle an insurance company representative who wants to know about a patient's medical history?	"I'm not at liberty to say. If you like, I'll be happy to take your name and number, and talk to the doctor about your request when he's free." See "The Problems of Guarding Patient Confidentiality," pages 261–265.
11. What would you say to a new patient who says a patient referred him or her?	"That's GREAT! Ours is largely a referral practice. We find that we get some of our nicest and best patients through other patients. We'll be sure to thank (name of referrer)." This plants the seed with the new patient that he, too, can become an appreciated referral source, just like his friend.
12. A physician or another colleague asks to speak with the doctor.	If it is not an emergency, and the doctor's name does not appear on the list of callers to be put through immediately, take a complete message, and promise a call back by a specified time.
13. The doctor asks you to get another doctor or someone else on the phone.	First, be sure the doctor has all of the support materials he will need for the call, such as patient records, test results, etc. Then, when you make the call, identify yourself and the doctor. For example: "Good morning. This is Susan from Dr. Barton's office. Dr. Barton is on the line for Dr. James O'Hara."
14. If the doctor will talk to a patient on the phone, what will be needed?	In most cases, the patient's record, test results, and other relevant materials. If the doctor is returning a patient's call, he will need the time and date of the call, the phone number where the patient can be reached, and specific questions, symptoms, etc. the patient needs to discuss. As well, note who took the call, and what, if anything, the patient was told. If the patient has a

Problem/Question:	Answers/Comments:
	particularly difficult name to pronouce, the doctor will also need a phonetic spelling.
15. How would you explain what will happen at the initial appointment?	Stress the positive. The patient may be very fearful. Do all you can to put him at ease. A good example: "Mrs. Twoomey, your appointment is on Monday, February 7, at 3:00. It will take one hour. We will begin with a short tour of our office. Then, Dr. Penman will meet with you in his private office to get acquainted with you and review your medical history. Next . . . ." Avoid highly clinical or frightening words. See "Dealing with the Anxious or Fearful Patient," pages 359–365.
16. What are the telephone numbers of reliable ambulance and other emergency services (such as poison control, fire, police, etc.)? Where are these numbers posted?	Memorize the most important numbers (including 911). Then, be sure all numbers are clearly posted by or on each telephone in your office, as well as on your office first aid kit.
17. What would you tell a patient who requests a 2 o'clock appointment, when that time is already taken?	"That time is already taken. We can see you at 3 o'clock on that day. Or we have an opening at the 2 o'clock time on the following Tuesday. Which appointment would you prefer?" (By offering this choice, you stay in control of the conversation. And, the patient will see that you're trying to accommodate him.)
18. What would you tell a non-emergency patient who wants to come in for an appointment, when you have no openings available?	"It is not possible to give you an appointment at the present time, Mr. Maxted, because the doctor schedules only three weeks into the future and presently he is completing treatment that has already been started. Might I hold your name and telephone number? I should be able to contact you in a few days to set up a definite appointment time. When do you prefer your appointment, Mr. Maxted, in the morning or afternoon?"

Problem/Question:	Answers/Comments:
19. A sales representative from a supply house wants to talk to the doctor.	See if someone else can help him. If not, take a complete message (unless his name appears on the list of callers to be put through immediately.)
20. What would you do if a patient calls and it is a real emergency, but the doctor is not in the office?	If it is a crisis, advise immediate necessary action (call an ambulance, give life-saving first aid instruction, tell the patient where to go for crisis intervention, etc.) If the problem is not at crisis level, take complete information, and contact the colleague who is covering for the doctor at once. Pull the patient's record in case it is needed.
21. A new patient calls and says he or she is from out of town visiting, and just needs a temporary solution to this problem.	Do not promise any results. See "Handling the New Patient Who Diagnoses His Own Problem," page 379.
22. A patient asks some clinical questions you can't answer regarding his treatment.	"I understand your questions, and have noted them. I would appreciate the opportunity to discuss them with Dr. McBride. May we call you back before noon today?"
23. A new patient calls and asks you to explain one of your standard procedures.	Memorize lay explanations for your most common procedures. (The doctor should provide a list.) Some practices prepare a glossary of standard procedures and explanations, to be used in these circumstances.
24. An area employer wants your opinion of a former employee of your practice, as a job reference.	"I'm not at liberty to say. If you like, I'll be happy to take your name and number, and talk to the doctor about your request when he's free."
25. An attorney calls to ask you about a particular patient.	"I'm not at liberty to say. If you like, I'll be happy to take your name and number, and talk to the doctor about your request when he's free." See "The Problems of Guarding Patient Confidentiality," pages 261–265.
26. A patient asks for directions to your office.	Memorize all standard routes. If you have a map, offer to mail it to the patient in advance of the first appointment. As well, be familiar with public transportation options, costs, and schedules.

Problem/Question:	Answers/Comments:
27. One of your employees calls you to say she's sick and not coming in to work that day.	Determine precisely how long the employee thinks she will be out (half day, whole day, two days, etc.). Ask what specifically you'll need to know about the work she's missing. (For example, did she promise to call a particular patient about something, or to check on an insurance claim?) Notify the office manager of the absence and take the recommended steps. (For example, you might try to engage a temporary worker. Or, you might have to cancel some appointments.) Follow your procedure for sending the sick employee a get well card, flowers, gift, etc.
28. A charitable organization calls to see if the practice can contribute.	Make no promises. Take a complete message and promise a call back.
29. A patient calls to cancel an appointment at the last minute.	Ask the patient to give you his reason for cancelling. Then, respond according to what the patient says, and whether this is a first-time or repeat offense. See "How to Keep Last-Minute Cancellations, No-Shows, and Chronically Late Patients from Crippling Your Practice," pages 75–82.
30. You receive an obscene/crank phone call.	Stop talking as soon as you realize that it is an obscene/crank call. Then, hang up the phone quickly and gently. Do *not* yell at the caller, chastise him or her, or slam down the receiver. He or she is trying to get a rise out of you. If you don't give in, chances are good that he or she will give up, and not call again. Nonetheless, note the time and date of the call, a description of the caller's voice, and the content of his or her message. Then, if the caller does make further attempts, contact the police. Your record will serve as valuable evidence, and will enable them to identify a calling pattern—the first step in tracking down the

Problem/Question:	Answers/Comments:
	offender. *Note:* If you've been threatened by the caller in any way, notify the police at once.
31. A patient says your latest statement is incorrect.	"I'm so glad you called and I'm sorry for any inconvenience. Let me pull out my records so I can go over it with you, and make whatever corrections are needed." Then go through the statement step by step. If it turns out that the statement was correct after all, explain it simply. Don't sound defensive.
32. A patient hangs up on you in anger.	Check your own emotions. Be sure you're not angry, but rather, in control of your own feelings. Then, call the patient back. Say: "Mrs. Stapleton, this is Carolyn from Dr. Gregory's office again. I'm so sorry that I have angered you. That was never my intention. I want to do everything I can to make things right." Then pause, see what the patient says, and respond accordingly. It may be necessary to turn the matter over to the doctor or another member of the staff.
33. Someone you've called asks if he can put you on hold for the second time.	"I'm rather swamped myself. I'd like to talk with you when we'll have fewer interruptions. When would be the best time for me to call back?"
34. A caller tells you he or she couldn't get through because your line was busy for a long time.	Apologize. Then get the details. (How long was he trying?) Unless a one-time extraordinary event tied up your phone lines (which you can explain to the caller), begin to do a busy signal study. See "How to Deal with a Busy Signal Problem," pages 93–94.
35. A minister wants to know whether he or she will receive discounted or free services.	If you have a clear policy, answer the question directly: "Yes, Reverend. Dr. Van Lann is very pleased to provide all members of the clergy with a courtesy reduction of 20% off the total billing." If no clear policy is in place, say: "Our financial secretary, Kathy, takes responsibility for all billing

Problem/Question:	Answers/Comments:
	arrangements. I'll be happy to take down your name and number, and ask Kathy to get back to you today." See "How Not to Let Professional Courtesy Get Out of Hand," pages 121–124.
36. A patient calls to report a problem with the services he or she received recently.	"I'm so glad you called. Dr. Berger will certainly want to address all of your concerns." Take a complete message, and promise a call back by a specified time.
37. A patient wants to apply for an open staff position in your office.	It is generally best *not* to publicize a staff opening broadly to patients, such as on your bulletin board or in a patient newsletter. You must be very careful that you don't lose patients by rejecting them or their family and friends. However, if a patient learns of your opening anyway, and wants to apply, by all means let him. In so doing, be careful not to suggest or imply that he's a good candidate or that he has a good chance of getting the position.
38. A caller asks about your practice because he or she is "shopping" for a new doctor, but is not ready to make an appointment right now.	Doctor shoppers are potential patients for your practice. You must impress them so they believe that yours is the practice they've been searching for. Answer all of the shopper's questions, but also volunteer extra information about you that will tip the scale in your favor. As well, try to get the caller's name and address, and other relevant information, so you can follow up by mail with some brochures, your newsletter, etc. Do your best to coax the caller into making an appointment, but don't push.
39. The doctor's spouse or child says he or she must speak to the doctor.	In most cases, these individuals will be on the list of callers to be put through right away. However, do tell them that the doctor is with a patient, and that he'd have to be interrupted.

Problem/Question:	Answers/Comments:
	They may decide to have him call back later, or to wait to talk to him when he gets home. Or, they may need a simple answer to a question, which you can get for them.
40. A patient calls to ask to speak with the doctor, and only the doctor, and won't say why.	Determine whether it is an emergency. If not, take a complete message, and promise to relay the message, and a call back by a specified time.
41. A patient calls an hour before an appointment to tell you his or her car won't start.	Sympathize. Then suggest other means for him to get to your office, if available. Ask: "Is there any other way you might be able to get here?" If the patient says there isn't, follow outlined procedure. (Depending upon your policy and the location of the patient, you might offer to call him a cab.) See "How to Keep Last-Minute Cancellations, No-Shows, and Chronically Late Patients from Crippling Your Practice," pages 75–82.
42. The Lions club wants the doctor to present a talk for them next Tuesday night.	"That's wonderful. I sure hope the doctor is free that night. Let me take down your name and phone number (and other relevant information), and we'll be sure to get back to you before noon today. Dr. Britton is a fantastic speaker, and his programs always go over very well. I'm sure he'll be very flattered by your invitation."
43. A teenager calls to cancel an appointment and asks you not to tell his or her parents.	Don't promise a patient that you'll keep information from someone who should know it. If something happened to a minor who makes such a request, you could be held responsible. Try your best to find out why the teenager is cancelling, and why he doesn't want his parents to know about it. You may be able to help.
44. The bank calls to tell you that one of your patients stopped payment on a check.	Take down all the relevant information: The check's date, number, exact amount, etc. Then, pull the patient's record to see what

Problem/Question:	Answers/Comments:
	services the check covered, and whether any additional money is owed. Then, call the patient to see why he has stopped the check. Respond accordingly. For example, if the patient says he's had a finanicial crisis, ask him to come in to create a financial arrangement with you. If you sense that the patient stopped the check because he was dissatisfied with the services he received, record what the patient tells you, and notify the doctor at once.
45. A carpet and upholstery cleaning company calls to see if your office wants a free estimate.	Refer the matter to the person in the office in charge of your maintenance schedule. See "Keeping Your Office in Shipshape Order," pages 401–404.
46. A patient asks you to forward his or her records to another doctor.	"I see. Do I understand, then, that you have decided to seek medical/dental/ etc. care at another practice?" If the patient says he has, ask him to explain his decision. Do your best to turn him around, without seeming pushy. Notify the office manager and/or doctor for further follow up. No patient should leave the practice without some attempt to keep him. At the very least, try to identify the reasons for every patient's leaving.
47. A patient's employer or school attendance officer calls your office to see if a patient is there (to verify the patient's excuse for a work or school absence.)	"I'm not at liberty to say. I cannot release such information about any patient without his permission. However, I can supply either a written or verbal excuse for any patient who requests one. I suggest that you have (name of patient) contact me directly to arrange for such an excuse."
48. A caller you don't know gives his or her name quickly, and you're not sure you got it right.	"Would you mind repeating your name? (Pause for response.) Thank you, Mrs. Haupfbrau. Did I say that correctly? (Pause.) For my records, Mrs. Haupfbrau, would you please spell your first and last names for me?" See "Get It Right the First Time," page 376.

Problem/Question:	Answers/Comments:
49. You need a moment to look up some information a caller asks you for.	Ask the caller if he'd prefer to hold or be called back. If he'll hold, tell him what's going to happen: "I'll have that information for you in a few moments" or "I'll transfer your call to Joan. She'll be with you in a few moments." See "When and How to Use the Hold Button," pages 94–95.
50. Someone else in your office is best equipped to answer the caller's detailed question.	"Our bookkeeper, JoAnn Broderick, would be best able to help you. I will bring her up to date on this matter. May we call you before noon with an answer?"

Common Insurance Terms and Their Definitions

I t is very helpful to become familiar with common insurance terminology, so you and the carrier operate on the same wavelength. The following list itemizes the most common insurance terms you and your staff will need to know. For more information on insurance claims processing, see "25 Ways to Improve Insurance Claims Processing," pages 125–130.

COMMON INSURANCE TERMS AND THEIR DEFINITIONS

Allowable benefit: Any necessary, reasonable, and customary service or treatment "allowed," or covered, in whole or part under a plan.

Beneficiary: The person eligible for benefits under an insurance plan. Common synonyms: Eligible individual, enrollee, member, employee.

Benefits: Payments or services provided under an insurance plan.

Capitation fee: A per-person charge made by a carrier for providing health services to individuals or groups for a specified period of time. The average charge may be based on the number of persons actually using the plan or on the total number eligible to use the plan.

Carrier: The insurance company and party to the insurance plan contract who collects premiums and agrees to pay claims and provide administrative service.

Certificate of eligibility: Identification card or similar written document issued to plan members, showing they are entitled to service.

Claim: A demand for payment or benefit by a member under a prepaid health care contract.

Claim form: A statement listing services rendered, the date of services and itemization of costs. A completed claim form must include certification signed by the beneficiary and the practitioner that services have been rendered. The beneficiary's social security number and diagnostic tests and pictures may also be required by some carriers.

Co-coverage: An arrangement under which the carrier and the beneficiary are each liable for a share of the cost of the services provided. For example, a plan may cover 80% of the fee for a service and the beneficiary pays the 20% balance.

Co-payment: The portion of the fee for an insured procedure which the patient must pay.

Contract year: The period of time, usually but not necessarily a 12-month period, for which a plan is written.

Coordination of benefits clause: A provision in an insurance contract that when a patient is covered under more than one group insurance plan, benefits paid by all plans will be limited to 100% of the eligible expenses. The secondary carrier may well cover the deductible charged by the primary carrier in addition to the remaining eligible benefits up to 100%. This clause is designed to eliminate overinsurance, duplication of benefits, and payment of more than 100% of the eligible expenses.

Deductible: Insurance plans rarely extend 100% coverage. Usually an initial amount, called a deductible, is the covered person's responsibility before benefits begin.

Emergency care: Any professional service required when treating unexpected and urgent conditions.

Fee for service plan: Any plan providing for payment to the practitioner for each service performed, rather than on a basis of salary or capititation fee. In a fee for service plan, the benefits paid are based on actual fees either established in the form of a table of allowances or a usual, customary, and reasonable basis.

Indemnity plan: A plan which provides payment to the covered person for the cost of treatment/services, but makes no arrangement for providing care.

Limitations, exclusions, and exceptions: These are variable with each plan. Often there is a waiting period before selected services are allowed.

Maximum allowance: The total dollar amount a plan will pay toward the cost of a particular service as specified in a fee schedule or table of allowances.

Maximum benefits: The total dollar amount a plan usually will pay toward the cost of care incurred by an individual or family in a specified policy year.

The maximum is re-established with the start of each new period of coverage.

Ninetieth percentile: This concept does *not* mean that the practitioner receives 90% of his fee (a common misconception). Rather, it means that if you survey 100 practitioners and rank their fees for a particular service from lowest to highest, the carrier will pay the fees charged by the *lowest* 90 out of 100 practitioners. The carrier will not pay the additional charge for that service of the upper 10%.

Preauthorization, predetermination: Carrier approval of or concurrence with the treatment plan proposed by a doctor before he or she provides that service. Preauthorization is the guarantee of a company that the authorized amount will be paid provided treatment is completed within the period of eligibility marked on the claim form. Predetermination is a calculation of the dollar amount payable if the person is eligible for the benefits when the treatment was performed. (With predeterminations, there is usually no guarantee of payment by the company for any specific period of time. Eligibility must be checked at the time of treatment.) Many carriers assure compensation for routine and emergency services without preauthorization or predetermination.

Procedure codes: Numbers assigned to identify each service.

Service plan: A plan which either provides professional treatment to a covered person or makes some provision for professional care and pays the doctor for services rendered.

Table of allowances: Under this type of plan, the carrier formulates a list of all the services it covers and assigns a payable sum for each one in dollars rather than percentages. The dollar figure allowed for a given service represents what the carrier will pay under the terms of the contract. This compensation for the service in no way relates to the individual practitioner's fees. The beneficiary is responsible for any difference between the allowance and the doctor's actual fee.

Time limits: The periods of time within which a notice of claim must be filed with the insurance carrier.

Usual, customary, and reasonable fees:

Usual means the fee that is generally charged for a given service by an individual practitioner to his private patients.

Customary means the fee is within the range of the usual fee charged by doctors of similar training and experience for the same service within a specific geographic area.

Reasonable means the fee meets the criteria of usual and customary. Or it means that in the opinion of a designated review committee, it is justifiable considering the special circumstances of the particular case in question. In this case, the doctor must usually be able to justify that his level of treatment or his expenses are greater than that customarily provided in the community.

Waiting period: The period of time between enrollment in a plan and the date when a covered person is entitled to a particular benefit.

Glossary of Useful Computer and Office Automation Terms

A s more and more professional practices enter the office automation age and buy and use computers, all office staff will need to become "computer literate." Here are more than fifty of the most important computer terms you and your staff will need to know:

Batch processing (batching): An operation where large amounts of data are processed by a computer at one time, with little or no operator supervision.

Bit: The smallest unit of information that a computer recognizes and stores.

Bug: A term that's widely used to describe the cause of a computer misoperation. Can be in the hardware design or in the software.

Byte: A byte is string of 8 bits. It is the amount of storage space needed to represent one character.

Card: A miniaturized circuit board which often performs specialized functions and may be added to a computer to enhance or enlarge its capabilities.

Character: A letter, number, punctuation mark, or any other single symbol that a computer may read, store, or process.

Computer: A machine capable of accepting information, processing it following a set of instructions, and supplying the results of this process.

CPS (characters per second): A measure used to rate a printer's printing speed.

CRT (cathode ray tube): This term is used interchangeably with "display," "screen," and "video monitor." It refers to the television-like screen in a computer or terminal, and is used for entering data into or retrieving it from the computer.

Cursor: A character, usually a blinking underline or graphics block, used to indicate the position of the next character to be entered on a display screen.

Daisy wheel printer: A device that produces images on paper when a hammer strikes an arm or projection of the print wheel, which looks somewhat like a daisy. The print quality from such printers is usually similar to that of a quality electric typewriter.

Data: The general term used to describe information that can be processed by a computer.

Debug: The process of locating and removing any "bugs" in a computer system, usually as it applies to software.

Delete: To remove or eliminate.

Desktop publishing: The production of high-quality printed materials using word processing, computer-generated page layouts and graphics, and a printer, rather than traditional typesetting, cutting, and pasting.

Disk: A circular metal plate coated with magnetic material and used to store large amounts of data. A disk is installed permanently inside the computer, and is not removed. Also called a "hard disk."

Disk drive: A slot or tray into which a diskette is inserted so that data may be read from or written onto the diskette.

Diskette: A thin magnetic storage device which is inserted and removed from the disk drive.

Display: See CRT.

Dot matrix printer: A printer that works by forming the printed character through the selection of wires which strike the paper. How closely this print resembles the letter of a standard typeface is affected by the number of dots (or "pins") which are available per character.

Down time: The period during which a computer is not operating or is malfunctioning because of a machine fault or failure.

Edit: To change data, a program, or a program line.

Electronic mail: A system of sending and receiving messages using computer networks.

FAX: Electronic facsimile machine. A device which allows one to send or receive copies of any actual document.

File: The collection of related records that is treated as a unit. *Example:* All patient records could comprise the "Patient Master File."

Font: A style of print or type.

Formatting: The process of organizing the surface of a diskette or disk to accept files of data and programs.

Graphics: Computer-generated images, such as charts and graphs, that are not exclusively text or numbers. In "graphics mode," the individual dots or pixels that comprise the image are manipulated.

Hard copy: Printed characters on paper, produced by a printer.

Hardware: The physical computer and all of its component parts, as well as the printer, connecting cables, etc.

Ink jet printer: A printer which shoots ink onto the page, rather than striking the page with an inked key or pin.

Input: Data entered into the computer.

K: Scientific shorthand for the number *1,000,* as in kilogram. In computer science, the symbol is used to equal 1,024. Thus, a computer that has 16K memory would have a memory equal to 16 times 1,024 bytes, that is 16,384 bytes. (*See* Byte and Memory.)

Keyboard: The device used to enter information into a computer. It is often arranged like a typewriter and/or calculator keyboard.

Language: A computer language refers to a set of words and operators and the rules governing their usage. Examples: BASIC, COBOL, FORTRAN, C.

Laptop computer: A small, compact portable computer.

Laser printer: See Ink jet printer.

Megabyte: A unit of one million bytes, usually used in connection with hard disks or memory.

Memory: A portion of the computer that is used to store information (either data or programs). The size of a microcomputer is often determined by the amount of user memory (measured in K—see above) in the system.

Menu: A display, in English, which enables the operator to select the desired function.

Menu driven: Software that is used by selecting items from a sequence of menus.

Microcomputer: A term that applies to smaller (usually) desktop computers.

Modem: A device that couples a computer or terminal to a telephone line. Used to transmit data and connect two systems.

Mouse: A small device used to manipulate and move a cursor without using the keyboard.

Operator: The person who manipulates the computer controls.

Print-out: Output printed on paper by the printer.

Program: A set of computer instructions which, when followed, will result in the solution to a problem or the completion of a task.

Read: The process of obtaining data from some source, such as a diskette or disk.

Screen: See CRT.

Software: A general term that applies to any program (set of instructions) that can be loaded into a computer from any source.

Storage: In contrast to memory, this generally refers to external devices (disks, diskettes, etc.) that store data and software.

Terminal: A device for input and output, usually consisting of a keyboard and a display screen. A terminal also may consist of a printer and a keyboard. (This may be referred to as a "printing terminal.")

User friendly: This indicates that the designer of the system tried to minimze the training efforts and frustrations required to use the system.

Video monitor: See CRT.

Windows: A programming device in which the screen is subdivided into sections so that several tasks may be performed simultaneously.

Word processing: The ability to enter, manipulate, correct, delete, and format text—an application which is used widely in microcomputers. Word processors are used to write letters and prepare documents such as reports and articles.

Chapter-by-Chapter Summary of Practice Management Problems and Solutions

3. What are the advantages of group practice? The disadvantages?

4. What are the advantages of practicing in a same-specialty group? In a multi-specialty group?

5. How can you decide which practice arrangement is best for you?

1. Do you have what it takes to be a successful partner?

2. Why do partnerships commonly fail? Why do they succeed?

3. Why do partners need a written agreement? What kinds of disagreements can occur when no written agreement is in place?

4. What happens to the practice and patients when partners disagree?

5. What topics sould a partnership agreement cover?

6. Do partners have unlimited liability for one anothers' performance?

7. What qualities make partners compatible?

8. How can partners improve communications?

9. How can you know if a practice's existing patient load, potential new patients, and physical plant can sustain a new partnership?

10. How do spouses fit into the partnership agreement?

11. What should you do if partners don't contribute to the practice identically? What happens if they don't contribute equally?

12. What is partnership counseling? How does it typically work? When and how might it be used to settle problems?

1. To what extent should you rely on the advice you receive?

2. What should you do before meeting with an advisor?

3. How much information should you give your advisors?

4. What financial arrangement should you make with advisors?

5. Who within an advisor's firm should handle your work?

6. Who in a group practice should serve as the primary contact for an advisor?

7. When is a second opinion warranted?

8. What should you do if you're dissatisfied with your advisor?

9. How can you evaluate an advisor's performance?

10. What should you look for in an accountant/financial planner? An attorney? A practice management consultant? An insurance agent or broker? A banker?

1. When is it appropriate to negotiate a lease?

2. What should you specify in a lease when renting a new building (or one being remodeled or customized)?

3. Are you entitled to a rent break if you pay for higher quality building materials?

4. How should *square footage* be defined in your lease? What's the difference between gross and net square footage?

5. Which services are included in your rent? Which aren't?

6. How should you handle an escalator clause in your lease?

7. How should you handle a legal fees clause?

8. What kind of sublet agreement is reasonable?

9. How and where should the present condition of the space be documented?

10. What are the limitations on your use of common areas?

11. What should happen to the interest earned on your security deposit?

12. What should happen if you want to open your office when the building is closed?

13. What are the special concerns of leasing space in a shopping center?

14. Must you join a tenant's association? What might this mean to you?

15. How might local zoning ordinances affect you? What do you need to know?

16. What should happen to your lease when you die? How can you protect your estate from paying penalties for lease cancellation?

17. What provisions should you want for cancelling your lease?

18. How can you protect yourself if the landlord cancels the lease or decides to sell the building?

19. What are the five most common methods for calculating rent?

20. How can you protect yourself when subleasing office space? How might such an arrangement work?

1. When might you need a loan?

4. Who in the office is most qualified to do data entry?

5. How can you protect against computer "crash?"

6. Should you use data entry forms? Or might this hurt more than help?

7. Who is the best computer consultant to meet your needs?

8. Should you enter patients as they come in for their appointments? If not, why?

9. Where in the office is the best place to do data entry?

10. What's a data entry "runner," and what should that person's job be?

11. Should you use temporary employees to do data entry? Why or why not?

12. Where should the patient's account number be written?

13. What should you do if you know information about a patient is wrong?

14. What should you tell your staff about your plans for using the data?

15. How soon after data entry should you "go live?"

16. What should you ask other doctors who are using the system?

17. How should you identify red flag patients in the system?

18. How can you check everything you've entered?

19. When should you enter initial data for accounts receivable?

1. What is an umbrella name for a practice? Why might you choose to use an umbrella name instead of your own?

2. What are the six common categories for practice names? What are the pros and cons of each?

3. What are sensible criteria for choosing a name?

4. What are the legal restrictions on practice names?

1. What are the characteristics of a good appointment system?

2. How small should the time increments in your schedule be?

3. Where should the appointment book be stored?

4. Who in the office should control the appointment book?

5. What is a treatment/service plan, and how should it be used?

6. How should emergencies be planned for in the appointment schedule?

7. What kind of training and guidelines should enable the receptionist to screen emergencies?

8. How should the emergency patient be handled on the phone? In person?

9. When might you NOT charge for the emergency visit, and why?

10. How far ahead should you schedule appointments?

11. How can you regain control of an out-of-control schedule?

12. How and why should you use a short notice call list?

13. What are projected appointments, and how might they be used?

14. How should the doctor's study time and preferences be accommodated in the appointment schedule?

15. How can you avoid holes in the appointment schedule?

16. What symbols might simplify appointment book notations?

17. How can you protect your appointment book from fire?

18. How long should you keep a used up appointment book?

1. Why is it poor practice to take calls during appointments?

2. What three lists of callers will enable your receptionist to screen calls properly?

3. How can a call-back period be used to maintain control?

4. How should sales representatives be handled?

5. What information should be included in a telephone message?

6. What should you tell patients when you're unavoidably late?

7. How can you help patients appreciate the fact that they're getting convenient appointments?

8. How should you handle the patient who always throws off your schedule? What should you do when this patient is highly valued?

9. How do bad habits hurt the appointment schedule, and how can they be eliminated?

1. What are the full effects when a patient is late or doesn't show?

2. What exactly are you doing now to control the appointment schedule?

3. Why do patients miss their appointments? What's at the root of the problem? What can you do to help?
4. How should you respond the first time a patient cancels an appointment? Breaks an appointment? Doesn't show? Is late?
5. How should you handle the repeat offender in each category?
6. What are hard but fair tactics for dealing with the chronic offender?
7. How can you dismiss the chronic offender without risking a lawsuit for abandonment?
8. What is the best way to document missed or late appointments?

1. Why is recall so important to a practice?
2. How can you motivate patients to make and keep recall appointments?
3. How might a staff recall incentive be used?
4. How can you make recall notices more effective?
5. What kind of follow-up will improve recall?
6. How can you set up a system for recall if you're not computerized?

1. How can you save time on the phone without seeming rude to callers?
2. How can you avoid telephone "tag"?
3. What should staff do when they place calls on your practice's behalf?
4. What steps do you need to take to guard patient confidentiality when leaving phone messages?
5. How should you identify and handle a busy signal problem?
6. When taking messages, what should your receptionist do to ensure that she doesn't offend callers?
7. What should your receptionist tell callers about your calling back?
8. How can you use and not abuse your hold button?
9. What telephone equipment and accessories will make your job easier?
10. How can you measure how well you're handling your phone?
11. How can you evaluate your telephone receptionist?

1. How can you find a first-rate answering service? What should you look for? What should you ask about a service you're considering?

2. How can you get the best job possible from your service? What can you do to keep them on their toes?

3. When and how should you use an answering machine? What message should you leave? What kind of machine is best?

1. How can you determine a fair fee for any particular service?

2. What can you say when a patient asks about the fee too soon?

3. Should you apologize when the fee seems very high?

4. To what extent should you ask about the patient's personal finances?

5. How should you explain a fee range so the patient won't automatically assume that you'll charge him the higher fee?

6. To what extent should you explain what the fee covers?

7. How should professional fees be listed on monthly statements?

8. With whom, specifically, should you discuss fees? Can you tactfully suggest that the patient's spouse accompany him to his case conference?

9. What should you do when a patient doesn't seem like he'd be able to pay the fee?

10. How involved should the doctor be in the actual financial arrangement?

11. How should the doctor introduce the role of the financial secretary?

12. Which types of professional fees should be the most competitive?

13. How should the doctor's personal productivity influence fee raises?

14. How much should the local economy influence fees?

15. Should rising costs influence fees?

16. How can you explain fee increases to patients without raising eyebrows?

17. How should you respond when the patient says, "That's a lot of money"?

18. How should your fees compare with those of other practitioners?

19. Which is better: few sharp fee increases, or more frequent small ones?

20. How can you remind patients of all you *don't* charge them for?

21. Should you charge for missed appointments? What's fair?

22. Might a fee like $29.99 meet fewer objections?

23. Is a round-figured fee more apt to raise questions than an odd one?

24. Should you lower your fees if a patient asks you to?

1. Who is the person in the practice best able to complete financial arrangements with patients?

2. Why should you offer financial arrangements? Wouldn't it be better to insist on cash on the spot?

3. What are some popular financial arrangements other doctors offer?

4. How detailed should the doctor get with the patient about the fee and financial arrangement? What exactly should he say?

5. How should the doctor introduce the business assistant?

6. Where can you publicize the availability of financial arrangements?

7. What should the doctor tell the assistant before she makes the actual arrangements?

8. What should the assistant bring when she meets with the patient?

9. Where in the office should the financial arrangement be made?

10. How should the assistant begin the conversation?

11. When should the assistant make the first few appointments?

12. What's a tactful way for the assistant to open the sensitive topic of financial arrangements?

13. What visual aids might the assistant use to increase patient comprehension?

14. Where might the assistant suggest that the patient can find outside sources of financing the fee?

15. What should you do if the patient says he needs to discuss the options with his or her spouse? What should you give him?

16. What papers will need to be completed once the patient agrees?

17. When do you need to prepare a Truth-in-Lending form?

18. How should you ask the patient to sign the form, without making him feel like he's signing away his life?

19. Where should the completed financial arrangement be filed?

20. How often should the financial arrangement file be checked?

21. What is a tactful way to conclude the financial arrangement meeting?

22. How can the doctor reinforce the financial arrangement, without seeming overly interested in money?

23. What steps should the doctor take to avoid charges of discrimination in his financial arrangement procedures?

24. How can coupon books be used for financial arrangements?

1. Why shouldn't you abolish professional courtesy altogether?

2. What is a reasonable policy for extending professional courtesy to the doctor's immediate and extended family? Special friends? The doctor's clergyman? Other clergy? Practice personnel? The staff's immediate family? The doctor's personal physicians, chiropractor, optometrist, etc? All other professionals?

3. What are reasonable expectations for professional courtesy?

4. How can you say "no" gracefully, and without alienating anyone?

5. Who should field professonal courtesy questions?

1. How can you streamline insurance claims processing?

2. What should you know about each plan in your area?

3. How can pre-addressing envelopes speed the process?

4. How can you learn tactfully whether a new patient has insurance? When should you collect the information you need?

5. When and how should you photocopy partially completed forms?

6. How can you guard against the patient's poor handwriting?

7. Will your carrier accept "Signature on File"?

8. What should you do when processing a claim for a patient who can't sign his name?

9. When should you mail predetermination forms? When should you schedule the patient's first appointment?

10. What should you do when you received authorization?

11. How can you divide claims and schedule appointments to boost cash flow?

12. When should you submit claims?

13. Where should you store copies of pending insurance claims?

14. How should you track insurance paperwork?
15. With whom at the insurance company should you check on the status of your paperwork?
16. How can you protect yourself when you don't agree with the insurance company.
17. What is an in-house "insurance claims reviewer," and what should his or her role be?
18. What should you tell a patient who is dissatisfied with or confused about her coverage?
19. How should you handle dual insurance coverage?
20. What form can simplify insurance communications with your patients?
21. What's the difference between preauthorization and predetermination?
22. What should you do if an insurer says it never received your claim?
23. Is insurance really a plus?

1. Are most problem checks caused by honest errors?
2. What information do you need to know about the check-paying patient?
3. What iron-clad "nevers" should you enforce about checks?
4. What is the correct procedure for accepting a check?
5. What should you do if you notice an error at the last minute?
6. What can you learn from the paper a check is printed on?
7. What can a check's routing code tell you?
8. Why should you deposit checks promptly?
9. How should you handle an NSF check?
10. What's the correct procedure for accepting a traveller's check?
11. What should you do if you think a check is lost?

1. Are professional practices unlikely targets for fraud?
2. What are the most common types of credit card fraud?
3. What is the correct procedure for processing a credit card transaction?

2. How can you identify the best vendors for your needs?

3. Is it worthwhile to deal with an inexpensive but unreliable supplier?

4. Should you deal with few or many vendors?

5. How can you avoid problems with vendors?

6. Which records can help you make informed purchasing decisions?

7. What is the correct procedure for following up on orders?

8. How should purchasing be handled, step by step?

1. Who should be in charge of your inventory system?

2. What are the duties of the inventory control clerk?

3. How should you inventory items used in your practice?

4. Where should inventory lists be kept?

5. How can color coding help?

6. How should supplies be organized and identified on the shelf?

7. What information should be on the shelf tag?

8. In what order should you use supplies?

9. How can you avoid an excessive inventory?

10. Should all inventory be stored together? Where can you keep bulky supplies?

11. What can you learn from studying your inventory log?

12. When should supply requests be met, and by whom?

13. What should you do if more than one person in the office is allowed access to the supply area?

14. What are reasonable limits for the inventory supply clerk?

15. How do rate of use, shelf life, storage needs, and the cost influence buying decisions?

1. What are the characteristics of the typical sales rep? Why should you control your personal feelings about the rep?

2. Who should define your method of practice, preferences, or equipment needs for you?

3. Who should define your deadline requirements?

4. Who should define your budget and tell you whether you should lease or buy the equipment?

5. Who should teach you about the types of equipment that can satisfy your needs?

6. Who should tell you about the rep's competitors?

7. Who in your practice should take part in the buying decision?

8. Should you trust a rep's verbal promises? Why or why not?

9. What should you do when a rep says, "We never make contract changes"?

10. How can you get through to an elusive Mr. Big?

11. How might playing dumb help in a negotiation?

12. Why and how should you slow down a negotiation?

13. What should be your tactic when you must give up a point?

14. How large an increment should you make when you decide to increase your last bid?

15. What question should you ask when all else fails?

16. How should you respond when you win a negotiation?

17. What contractual changes should you try to make when buying high-priced equipment for your practice?

1. How should you prepare to buy a computer?

2. What are reasonable and unreasonable expectations for a computer?

3. What must you do before looking for software?

4. What are the "hidden" costs of computerizing?

5. What can and can't be delegated in the shopping process?

6. Which should come first, software or hardware?

7. What vendor promises should be red flags to you?

8. How important is price?

1. What are examples of scams against doctors?

2. How real is the threat of being conned?

3. Why are doctors good targets for scams?

4. How can you protect yourself from con artists?

5. How might innocent-seeming refunds be part of a sophisticated scam?

1. How should you streamline the check-writing process?
2. Why should you read every check you sign? What might happen if you don't?
3. Should you have a signature stamp? What are the risks?
4. How and when should you stop a check?
5. How can you reduce the risk of unauthorized use of your credit card?
6. How can you handle a large volume of checks manually?

1. How can you save money on postage?
2. How can you save money on the telephone?
3. How can you save money on utility bills?
4. How can you save money on printing costs?
5. How can you save money by buying non-professional items?
6. How can you save money on film processing?
7. How can you save money on equipment repairs?
8. How can you save money when updating old or worn office furniture?

1. What is a private letter ruling?
2. When should you seek a private letter ruling? When shouldn't you?
3. How do you ask for a ruling?
4. What are your options once you receive a ruling?

1. How does the IRS choose audit targets?
2. What steps can you take in your tax records to reduce audit risk and protect yourself if you are audited?
3. What should you do and not do on your tax return?
4. How should you prepare for an audit?
5. What should you do if you disagree with an audit's findings?

1. What are the 12 most common causes of malpractice litigation?
2. Who typically sues a doctor?
3. What are your legal obligations and rights?
4. What 17 strategies should you adopt to prevent malpractice?
5. How can your staff prevent malpractice claims?
6. What kind of malpractice coverage should you have?
7. How should you protect your personal wealth from huge malpractice claims?
8. How can you prevent other types of litigation?

1. What notations should appear with each chart entry?
2. What should you do to make sure you can identify initials of former employees that appear in your charts?
3. Should you allow patients to transport their own records, if they ask to do so? Why or why not?
4. How should you handle a subpoena of records?
5. What are 16 records management tactics for malpractice protection?
6. What should you know about informed consent?
7. What is the statute of limitations? The long tail?

1. How should you respond when a patient's attorney contacts you?
2. Who is the best counsel for you?
3. How should you handle a malpractice suit?
4. What should you learn from studying your clinical records?
5. How does your deposition come into play?
6. How should you dress for court?
7. How should you answer questions?
8. What should you do if a plaintiff's attorney asks questions in a sarcastic or accusatory fashion? What if he or she shoots a series of questions at you rapid fire?
9. What are common traps you can avoid in court?

1. What exactly does patient confidentiality mean? What are you legal and ethical obligations?

2. Where should and shouldn't you discuss confidential matters? Why?

3. Where should new patient get-acquainted forms be completed? Why?

4. How can you guard patient confidentiality on the telephone?

5. How should confidential information be labeled?

6. What should your staff say when they're asked to reveal potentially confidential information?

7. What should you do if someone asks you to keep an uncomfortable confidence?

8. How can you guard confidentiality in your newsletter and other practice building activities?

9. How can you keep patients from overhearing confidential information or from snooping?

10. What are your obligations to protect confidentiality when a patient owes you money?

11. How can you use computer passwords to guard confidentiality?

12. What do you need to know about cellular phones and confidentiality?

13. What steps do you need to take to secure patient records?

1. Why is it necessary to have a contingency plan for your unexpected absence? What typically happens if no plan is in place?

2. Where should a contingency plan be documented?

3. If you're delayed, how long should your staff wait before rescheduling waiting patients? Who should do this?

4. What should your staff do to keep busy during your absence?

5. To whom should your staff refer emergencies during your absence?

6. How should your absence be explained to patients?

7. What might you say in a follow-up letter to eliminate hard feelings?

8. How should you handle a prolonged absence?

9. What can a solo practitioner do to arrange coverage during an absence?

10. What is overhead insurance and why is it so important?

11. What information should you leave for your staff and family?

1. Who should counsel you about your estate planning needs?

2. What should you tell your family in a letter of instruction? What documents should accompany that letter?

3. Where should this information be kept?

4. What should your estate know about selling your practice?

5. What can you do to ensure that you have a complete and accurate obituary?

1. When is it necessary or helpful to have your practice valued?

2. Who should conduct your appraisal?

3. What valuations are typically included in a practice appraisal?

4. What factors beyond patient records might be included in a goodwill calculation?

1. Why is it a good idea to prepare an employee handbook?

2. What should be your attorney's role in the handbook's development?

3. What subjects should NOT be covered in a handbook, for legal protection?

4. What information SHOULD be included? What do employees need to know about each subject?

5. How can a glossary be used in a handbook?

6. What writing guidelines apply to handbooks?

7. How should the handbook be bound?

8. How, when, and to whom should the handbook be distributed?

1. Why must you be firm about vacations and holidays?

2. What five rules can reduce vacation conflicts?

3. How should vacations be handled during the first year of employment?

4. What should you do when you take your own vacation?

5. Which holidays should you observe?

6. How can you involve staff in the holiday schedule?

7. How should you handle a holiday that falls on a weekend or a staff member's vacation?

8. What should you do to reward a staff member who works on a holiday?

9. How can you ensure that staff members work the day before or after a holiday?

10. What plans should you make for Christmas in your office?

1. What are reasonable attendance expectations for your employees?

2. How can you deter unnecessary tardiness?

3. How should you deal with an employee who is habitually late?

4. How can you encourage punctuality positively?

5. How should you handle employee time off for continuing education? Civic responsibilities? Personal business? Bereavement?

6. What should you do when an absent employee returns to work?

7. How should you document absences and tardiness?

8. How can you save on payroll taxes during employee absences?

9. How might paycheck distribution affect attendance?

1. Why shouldn't you simply pay employees for a given number of sick days?

2. Why does it make sense to pay for unused sick days?

3. What are typical sick leave policies in other practices?

4. Why should you have a family sick leave policy?

5. What are four creative ways to encourage good attendance?

6. What are your legal obligations for providing staff parental leave?

1. Why do you need clear rules for employee dress and hygiene?

2. How do other practices handle staff uniforms?

3. What dress rules are reasonable for non-uniformed employees?

4. What information should be included on a staff name tag? Why?

5. What are reasonable guidelines for staff cosmetics, hair styles, and jewelry?

8. What can your telephone bill tell you about phone abuse?

9. How can you prevent time theft?

1. What's the difference between part-time, flex-time, and job-sharing?

2. How might these alternative employment arrangements benefit you?

3. What are the potential drawbacks for alternative arrangements?

4. How can you make a job-sharing situation work smoothly?

5. How can you make a flex-time situation work smoothly?

6. How can you make a part-time situation work smoothly?

1. What are the financial benefits of employing your spouse?

2. How should you legitimate a spouse's employment?

3. What are the personal benefits and drawbacks of employing your spouse?

4. How can you decide if employing your spouse makes sense for you?

5. What are 15 ground rules for working successfully with your spouse?

6. Where can you get help and support if you work with your family?

1. How can you avoid lawsuits from your recruitment efforts?

2. How can you avoid lawsuits from your employee handbook?

3. How can you avoid lawsuits from job descriptions?

4. How can you avoid lawsuits from problem employees?

5. How can you avoid lawsuits when giving references?

6. How can you prevent charges of sexual harrassment?

7. How can you prevent lawsuits regarding parental leave?

8. How can you prevent lawsuits from minors?

9. How can you prevent lawsuits related to your dress code?

10. How can you avoid overtime disputes and violations?

11. How can you use business forms for legal protection?

12. Where can you get additional help on this subject?

2. How can you make sure you get a new patient's name right the first time?

3. What should you tell the new patient to expect at her first appointment?

4. How can you use a pre-printed checklist to aid your receptionist?

5. Why and how should your receptionist end the first call enthusiastically?

6. Why might you register a new patient at home?

7. How should your receptionist handle a new patient who has diagnosed his own problem?

8. How can you develop loyalty in your new emergency patients?

9. How might you roll out the red carpet at the first appointment?

10. What are six more ways to improve the get-acquainted procedure?

1. Why is post-operative contact with patients so important?

2. What are ten great ways to show post-operative patients you care?

3. How can you build goodwill when you receive the final payment for long-term treatment?

4. What's a good system for follow-up contact?

1. What are five basic tips for managing older and disabled patients?

2. How should you offer physical assistance to a patient who needs it?

3. How can you make special-need patients feel especially welcome?

4. What are 10 ways to prepare the office for visits by physically disabled people?

5. What should you say and not say about disabled people?

6. What have some other practices done to attract older or disabled patients?

7. How can you arrange White House greetings for patients aged 80 or over or married 50 years or longer?

1. What are tips for working with young children?

2. What are tips for working with teenagers?

3. How should you respond when you learn that a patient is suddenly unemployed?
4. What should you do if there is a massive lay-off in your area?
5. How should you handle the non-compliant patient?
6. How can your receptionist make unrecognized patients feel special?

1. What kind of maintenance records are most helpful?
2. How can you find a good cleaning service?
3. Would your office pass the white glove test?

1. How can you tell if your office is physically safe?
2. What are four safety tips if you lease office space?
3. How can you make sure your office is safe during construction?
4. What should you do to child-proof your office?
5. How can you protect your staff from injuries?
6. What should you accomplish at a fire drill?
7. What are six fire safety precautions?
8. What should you keep in your office first-aid kit?
9. Which emergency numbers should be on hand? Where in your office should they be posted?
10. How should you document any accidents that occur in your office?
11. What first-aid training should you have your staff take?

1. How can you free up floor space by moving furniture and equipment?
2. How can wall storage be maximized?
3. How can you provide a baby's changing table in cramp quarters?
4. How and where can papers be posted neatly?
5. How can you free up space in crowded file drawers?
6. How should items be grouped according to frequency of use?
7. How can ceiling space be maximized?
8. How can wall-mounted equipment be used? Space-saver appliances?
9. How can magazines be stored in small space?
10. What kind of ready-made organizers might help?

1. What are five basic rules for improving your memory?
2. How can you remember patients' names and faces?
3. How can you remember a list?
4. How can you remember a joke?
5. How can you "remember" and use patients' news?

1. What is the ideal letter?
2. What are 20 writing tips for better letters?
3. How can you measure the readability of your letters?
4. How might you use a practice letter book? What kind of prototype letters would be most helpful?

1. How can a file folder system enable you to keep track of deadlines and related papers?
2. How can a card file be used to track important contacts?

1. What are the 85 specific things you can do to keep on schedule and get more done everyday?

1. How can you decide which continuing education programs are right for you? How can you identify those that will waste your time?
2. How should you prepare for and follow up after a program?
3. How can you buddy up to get more from a large conference?
4. What are 17 ways to eliminate travel hassles when attending an out-of-town meeting? Specifically, how can you reduce air travel problems?

1. How can you become a better conversationalist?
2. What can you do to put patients at ease?
3. How can you shake hands without feeling awkward?
4. How should you accept apologies?
5. How can you learn or improve machine dictation?

1. What causes a stress response?
2. Who is most likely to suffer from stress?
3. What are 20 easy-to-do strategies for keeping stress at bay?
4. How can a solo doctor combat isolation?

26 checklists for handling such problems as incoming mail, bartering professional services, identifying and solving practice management problems, managing your vacation, deciding whether to lease or buy equipment, overcoming staff computer anxiety, mail-ordering supplies, and resolving anger.

50 typical scenarios your receptionist might encounter, and the right answers. Problems include learning if a caller is a new or established patient; fielding calls from attorneys, insurance reps, colleagues, and others; responding to an obscene or crank call; handling the doctor shopper; using the hold button judiciously, and transferring a call.

Definitions of common insurance terms, including capitation fee, certificate of eligibility, co-payment, fee-for-service plan, ninetieth percentile, preauthorization, predetermination, table of allowances, and usual, customary, and reasonable fees.

Definitions of 56 common office automation terms, including CRT, electronic mail, K, mouse, and windows.

Index

619